THE LOVE OF ENEMY AND
NONRETALIATION IN THE NEW TESTAMENT

Studies in Peace and Scripture
Institute of Mennonite Studies

THE LOVE OF ENEMY
AND NONRETALIATION
IN THE
NEW TESTAMENT

Edited by
Willard M. Swartley

Westminster/John Knox Press
Louisville, Kentucky

Book design by Publishers' WorkGroup

First edition

Published by Westminster/John Knox Press
Louisville, Kentucky

This book is printed on acid-free paper that meets the American National Standards Institute Z39.48 standard.♾

PRINTED IN THE UNITED STATES OF AMERICA

9 8 7 6 5 4 3 2 1

Library of Congress Cataloging-in-Publication Data

The Love of enemy and nonretaliation in the New Testament / Willard M. Swartley, editor. —1st ed.
    p.   cm. — (Studies in peace and scripture)
Includes bibliographical references.
ISBN 0–664–25354–7 (pbk. : alk. paper)

    1. Enemy in the Bible. 2. Love—Biblical teaching. 3. Evil, Non-resistance to—Biblical teaching. 4. Jesus Christ—Teachings. 5. Bible. N.T.—Criticism, interpretation, etc. I. Swartley, Willard M., 1936– . II. Series.
BS2417.L7L68 1992
241'.4—dc20

        92–5219

Contents

Series Preface

Visions of peace abound in the Bible, whose pages are also filled with the language and the reality of war. In this respect, the Bible is thoroughly at home in the modern world, whether as a literary classic or as a unique sacred text. This is, perhaps, a part of the Bible's realism: bridging the distance between its world and our own is a history filled with visions of peace accompanying the reality of war. That alone would justify study of peace and war in the Bible. However, for those communities in which the Bible is sacred scripture, the matter is more urgent. For them, it is crucial to understand what the Bible says about peace—and about war. These issues have often divided Christians from each other, and the way Christians have understood them has had terrible consequences for Jews and, indeed, for the world. A series of scholarly investigations cannot hope to resolve these issues, but it can hope, as this one does, to aid our understanding of them.

Over the past century a substantial body of literature has grown up around the topic of the Bible and war. Studies in great abundance have been devoted to historical questions about ancient Israel's conception and conduct of war and about the position of the early church on participation in the Roman Empire and its military. It is not surprising that many of these studies have been motivated by theological and ethical concerns, which may themselves be attributed to the Bible's own seemingly disjunctive preoccupation with peace and, at the same time, with war. If not within the Bible itself, then at least from Aqiba and Tertullian, the question has been raised whether—and if so, then on what basis—God's people may legitimately participate in war. With the Reformation, the churches divided on this question. The division was unequal, with the majority of Christendom agreeing that, however regrettable war may be, Christians have biblical warrant for participating in it. A minority countered that, however necessary war may appear, Christians have a biblical mandate to avoid it. Modern historical studies have served to bolster one side of this division or the other.

Meanwhile, it has become clear that a narrow focus on participation in war is not the only way—and likely not the best way—to approach the Bible on the topic of peace. War and peace are not simply two sides of the same coin; each is broader than its contrast with the other. In spite of broad agreement on this point, the number of studies devoted to the Bible and peace is still very small, especially in English. Consequently, answers to the most basic questions remain to be settled. Among these questions is that of what the Bible means in speaking of *shalom* or *eirene,* the Hebrew and Greek terms usually translated into English as "peace." By the same token, what the Bible has to say about peace is not limited to its use of these two terms. Questions remain about the relation of peace, in the Bible, to considerations of justice, integrity, and—in the broadest sense— salvation. And of course there still remains the question of the relation between peace and war. In fact, what the Bible says about peace is often framed in the language of war. The Bible very often uses martial imagery to portray God's own action, whether it be in creation, in judgment against or in defense of Israel, or in the cross and resurrection of Jesus Christ—actions aimed at achieving peace.

This close association of peace and war, to which we have already drawn attention, presents serious problems for the contemporary appropriation of the Bible. Are human freedom, justice, and liberation—and the liberation of creation—furthered or hindered by the martial, frequently royal, and pervasively masculine terms in which the Bible speaks of peace? These questions cannot be answered by the rigorous and critical exegesis of the biblical texts alone; they demand serious moral and theological reflection. But that reflection will be substantially aided by exegetical studies of the kind included in this series—even as these studies will be illuminated by including just that kind of reflection within them.

Studies in Peace and Scripture is sponsored by the Institute of Mennonite Studies, the research agency of the Associated Mennonite Biblical Seminaries. The seminaries and the tradition they represent have a particular interest in peace but, even more so, a shared interest in the Bible. We hope that this ecumenical series will contribute to a deeper understanding of both.

Ben C. Ollenburger, Old Testament Editor
Willard M. Swartley, New Testament Editor

Preface

The essays of this volume take up two pervasive New Testament teachings that are foundational to peace: Jesus' commands to love enemies and not to retaliate against those who do evil. While scholars do not agree that these commands originated with Jesus, the scholarly consensus supports two basic observations: While proximate teachings occur in Judaism and Greco-Roman thought, the centrality and prominence of these two related teachings in the New Testament is distinctive to Jesus and his followers; and, except for the Johannine corpus, which scholars view differently on this topic, these teachings function crucially in all major parts of the New Testament canon.

For these reasons this volume, after an article on the history of research (Klassen's essay), includes essays on Jesus and the Synoptic Gospels, the Pauline corpus, and 1 Peter. Further, two essays take up the issue of how we might understand the Johannine writings in relation to Jesus' command to love enemies (Perkins's and Rensberger's). The latter part of Klassen's essay also addresses this issue in an extended exposition of 1 John.

The Bibliography includes the major sources on these topics published in the last seventy years. Since the nonretaliation command is interconnected to God's prerogative of vengeance, the Bibliography includes writings on this topic as well.

Words of appreciation extend in many directions to make this volume possible: to each of the contributors, especially to Walter Wink and Richard Horsley for their willingness to have the exchanges they presented at the 1988 annual meeting of the Society of Biblical Literature appear in this volume (chapters 5 and 6); for the following permissions: from the Journal of the American Academy of Religion to publish Richard Horsley's essay that appeared in volume 54 (1986), pp. 3–31 (here chapter 3); from Scholars Press to publish Walter Wink's essay in the *SBL 1988 Seminar Papers* (pp. 210–224) in revised form (here chapter 4); from Chr. Kaiser Verlag to translate and publish the article by Luise Schottroff printed in *Befreiungserfahrungen* (Munich, 1990), pp. 184–216 (here chapter 10); to Gerhard Reimer, professor of German at Goshen College, for the translation of Luise Schottroff's essay; to Kevin Miller for assistance in typing much of the manuscript; to Jewel Gingerich Longenecker for preparing the Index; and to the editors of Westminster/John Knox Press for their much appreciated editorial skills and administrative efficiency in producing this volume.

Willard M. Swartley

Abbreviations

AB	Anchor Bible
AnBib	Analecta Biblica
ANF	The Ante-Nicene Fathers
ANRW	*Aufstieg und Niedergang der römischen Welt,* ed. H. Temporini and W. Haase (1972–)
BAGD	W. Bauer, W. F. Arndt, F. W. Gingrich, and F. W. Danker, *Greek-English Lexicon of the New Testament* (1979)
BDF	F. Blass, A. Debrunner, and R. W. Funk, *A Greek Grammar of the New Testament* (1961)
BK	*Bibel und Kirche*
BZ	*Biblische Zeitschrift*
CBQ	*Catholic Biblical Quarterly*
CGR	*Conrad Grebel Review*
ChrCent	*Christian Century*
ClassRev.	*Classical Review*
EK	Evangelische Kommentar
EKK	Evangelisch-Katholischer Kommentar zum Neuen Testament
ETL	*Ephemerides theologicae lovanienses*
EvT	*Evangelische Theologie*
ExpTim	*Expository Times*
FS	Festschrift
HBC	*Harper's Bible Commentary,* ed. James L. Mays (1988)
HNT	Handbuch zum Neuen Testament
HNTC	Harper's New Testament Commentaries
HSM	Harvard Semitic Monographs

HTR	*Harvard Theological Review*
HUCA	*Hebrew Union College Annual*
IB	*Interpreter's Bible*, ed. G. A. Buttrick (1952–1957)
ICC	International Critical Commentary
IDB	*Interpreter's Dictionary of the Bible*, ed. G. A. Buttrick (1962)
Int	*Interpretation*
JAAR	*Journal of the American Academy of Religion*
JBL	*Journal of Biblical Literature*
JR	*Journal of Religion*
JSNT	*Journal for the Study of the New Testament*
JSNTS	JSNT Supplement Series
JSOT	*Journal for the Study of the Old Testament*
JThSAfr	*Journal of Theology for South Africa*
LCL	Loeb Classical Library
LSJ	Liddell-Scott-Jones, *Greek-English Lexicon*
MeyerK	H. A. W. Meyer, Kritisch-exegetischer Kommentar über das Neue Testament
MQR	*Mennonite Quarterly Review*
MT	*Modern Theology*
NCB	New Century Bible
Neot	*Neotestamentica*
NICOT	New International Commentary on the Old Testament
NIDNTT	*New International Dictionary of New Testament Theology*, ed. Colin Brown (1986)
NovT	*Novum Testamentum*
NovTSup	Novum Testamentum, Supplements
NPNF	Nicene and Post-Nicene Fathers
NRSV	New Revised Standard Version
NTAbh	Neutestamentliche Abhandlungen
NTD	Das Neue Testament Deutsch
NTS	*New Testament Studies*
OP	Occasional Papers
OTL	Old Testament Library
OTP	*Old Testament Pseudepigrapha*, ed. J. H. Charlesworth
PSI	*Papiri greci e latini (Pubblicazioni della Società italiana per la ricerca dei papiri greci e latini in Egitto)*, Florence, 1912–
QD	Quaestiones Disputatae
RB	*Revue Biblique*
RGG	*Die Religion in Geschichte und Gegenwart*
RQ	*Römische Quartalschrift für christliche Altertumskunde und Kirchengeschichte*
RSV	Revised Standard Version
SBL	Society of Biblical Literature
SBLDS	SBL Dissertation Series
SBLMS	SBL Monograph Series

SeC   *Second Century*
SNTS   Society for New Testament Studies
SNTSMS   SNTS Monograph Series
SPS   Studies in Peace and Scripture
ST   *Studia Theologica*
SUNT   Studien zur Umwelt des Neuen Testaments
TBC   Torch Bible Commentary
TBl   *Theologische Blätter*
TDNT   *Theological Dictionary of the New Testament*, ed. G. Kittel
         and G. Friedrich (ET 1964–1976)
ThEv   *Theologia Evangelica*
THKNT   Theologischer Handkommentar zum Neuen Testament
TLZ   *Theologische Literaturzeitung*
TNTC   Tyndale New Testament Commentaries
TOTC   Tyndale Old Testament Commentaries
TP   *Theologie und Philosophie*
TPINTC   Trinity Press International New Testament Commentary
TQ   *Theologische Quartalschrift*
TSK   *Theologische Studien und Kritiken*
TTZ   *Trierer theologische Zeitschrift*
TWNT   *Theologisches Wörterbuch zum Neuen Testament*, ed. G.
         Kittel and G. Friedrich (1933–1973)
TZ   *Theologische Zeitschrift*
WMANT   Wissenschaftliche Monographien zum Alten und Neuen
         Testament
WUNT   Wissenschaftliche Untersuchungen zum Neuen Testament
ZEE   *Zeitschrift für evangelische Ethik*
ZNW   *Zeitschrift für die neutestamentliche Wissenschaft*
ZST   *Zeitschrift für systematische Theologie*
ZTK   *Zeitschrift für Theologie und Kirche*

1

"Love Your Enemies": Some Reflections on the Current Status of Research

William Klassen

> The question of the relation of the Christian to enemies or how the Christians' enemies are to be overcome becomes repeatedly of highest importance for the individual and for the Christian community. Precisely here we are so completely without understanding, and, left to ourselves, our ideas are so totally perverted that our text [Rom. 12:17–21] begins: "Don't consider yourselves clever." . . . When you confront your enemy think first of all about your own enmity with God and about God's compassion towards you.
>
> —Dietrich Bonhoeffer[1]

What Bonhoeffer describes as "of highest importance" has never been considered a basic part of Christian theology and never seen as belonging to the kernel of the New Testament kerygma.[2]

Nearly thirty years ago I began a serious study of peace and its relation to dealing with enemies by reviewing the most significant literature on the origin and meaning of Jesus' command, "Love your enemies."[3] It was singularly intriguing that the commandment, while generally recognized as originating with Jesus, had never been dealt with in the form of an English monograph. Above all, it seemed not to be of scholarly interest to many. This important and somewhat neglected topic I later dealt with in a book of modest size directed to a lay audience, which for the most part received a kind response from my academic colleagues.[4] It was written in an international climate of threatening war between the superpowers. The major part of the research was begun in Jerusalem during and in the immediate aftermath of the Arab-Israeli war of 1973–1974. By the time it was published, in 1984 I had again returned to Jerusalem and was able to deal with its contents in advanced interfaith seminars.

In this last decade of my active teaching career it is a welcome opportunity to review the literature from this perspective. In few areas of academic research has the situation changed so radically as in "Love Your Enemies" research. At the same time, much still remains to be done.

A Brief History of Research

I shall attempt first to outline briefly what was noted in my first essay: the sudden emergence of a flurry of publications on the theme of enemy love during the first decade of this century. Scholars more familiar with intellectual trends of that decade will need to place it in context; all that can be attempted here is to evaluate the treatments from an exegetical point of view. Those studies were clearly influenced by the comparative religions method and to some extent by a romantic notion that love of enemies is to be found in the natural realm as well as among humans. Moreover, we will survey the treatments on this topic which emerged during the first and second world wars, demonstrating that, objective as scholars may try to be, they are nevertheless not impervious to major events around them and they attempt to allow the religious sources they work with to speak to the immediate situation.[5] C. H. Dodd[6] did seek to formulate a theology of pacifism in the beginning of the Second World War. It was a fine piece of work, seldom cited by either friend or foe. Today his six central characteristics of the kingdom of God as set forth in the New Testament are generally accepted even if his conclusion that war and the kingdom of God are irreconcilable is not. He viewed the kingdom as follows:

1. The kingdom aims to make all one, for it transcends all human divisions which are in fact brought into unity in Christ.

2. The method of bringing about this unity is through reconciliation, not coercion, for the latter violates human freedom.

3. The creation of a new humanity takes place through the working of divine agape, an "energy of sheer goodness, going out towards its objects without regard to their deserts." Its characteristic form of expression is the forgiveness of sinners (which is, strictly speaking, unjust), and divine forgiveness is itself the power of its life.

4. The divine charity is directed toward human individuals. In

accepting this charity, the individual rises to full personhood, accepting individuality, freedom, and responsibility.

5. In the whole action of God in Christ this divine charity suffers even to death. Through Christ's resurrection God reigns from the tree. The manner of the kingdom is not power added to love but love manifesting itself as power to create.

6. Under the kingdom of God we are children of our Father in heaven and siblings one to another.

Dodd concludes: "It is not necessary to spend words in proving that war, by its very nature, contradicts these principles, point by point" (Dodd, "The Theology of Christian Pacifism," 11–12). War is "fundamentally antagonistic" to the kingdom and at this moment "represents a concentration of all those things in human life which are most irreconcilably opposed to the will of God as shown in Christ" (p. 13). "War itself is evil. . . . We cannot christianise war by taking part in it."[7]

Other scholars of first rank allowed their passionate patriotism to get the better of them and were used by the forces of destruction to justify their actions.[8] One of the most painful examples of this is the case of Heinrich Rendtorff, a distinguished church leader and academic. Popular as an expositor of the Bible, he published in 1937 a booklet, apparently to be used by German soldiers, in which he quotes with approval the words of Ernst Arndt that the "Christian is friendly towards his friends and courageous against his enemies."[9]

Still others tried seriously to come to grips with the issue, among whom Reinhold Niebuhr[10] and his student Dietrich Bonhoeffer[11] stand out as worthy of note. The latter has brought the issue of enemy love into the center of the discussion not only through his writings but also through his life and the difficulty the issue caused for him.[12]

We review, moreover, the monograph and periodical literature that has been published in the decade of the 1980s in an effort to find where we are at present. The reader must be warned that the "Love your enemy" command covers a very large area in which biblical studies and ethics converge. We have to come to terms here not only with literary and redactional questions; there are also questions of authenticity, of the social context in which this commandment was heard, the relationship not only between Gospel writers and their communities but also between Paul and the Gospel tradition. Since Jesus himself clearly grounded this command in the nature of God—that is, in theology—we miss something vital if we do not draw in both theology and Christology. These considerations require our attention before we can speak with any authority about the relevance of loving one's enemies for contemporary Christian application. It is also clear that here, as in few other areas, the question of interreligious interdependence of Judaism and Christianity, at least, must be addressed.

During the first three decades of this century, four major books were written on the theme "Love your enemies."[13] Major articles appeared on its meaning in Christianity,[14] on its relationship to Judaism,[15] on its distinctiveness in Christianity,[16] and on how consistently it was practiced by the early Christian martyrs.[17] In the several decades following the Second World War, articles appeared by Otto Seitz,[18] W. C. van Unnik (on motivation),[19] Dieter Lührmann on the question of genuineness,[20] and Paul Hoffmann on the political context of this teaching.[21] One of the major issues has been to test the originality or genuineness of the command; does it in fact go back to Jesus?

The Origin of the Double Love
and Love of Enemies Commands

Jürgen Becker considers it beyond dispute that the love command came into Christianity through Jesus. The key witnesses are the command to love enemies, the double command of love, and the parable of the Good Samaritan.[22] Nevertheless others conclude that the double command has no claim to be genuine to Jesus himself.[23] It is argued, for example, that Jesus speaks very seldom about the neighbor and that apart from the command to love the enemies, he seldom commanded love or even used the word "love." Rather, the neighbor is described concretely: tax collector, prostitute, victim of a robbery, debtor, woman threatened with divorce. Likewise the deed of love is concretely viewed and described: table fellowship, emergency aid, release of debt, healing. As certainly as Jesus researchers rightly are united in seeing the "love your enemy" command as a normative summary of the attitude and action of Jesus, so the words "neighbor" and "love" are not terms of Jesus. He thinks in terms of concreteness. Nevertheless the double commandment and the command to love the enemy are variations on the theme of going beyond the boundaries enunciated by Jesus.[24]

Simon Legasse distinguishes love of neighbor from love of enemies and notes that except for Luke 10:29–37 they are always kept separate in the gospel tradition. He refutes Jürgen Sauer's critical view and attributes the saying to Jesus. Availing himself of all the recent literature, Legasse devotes five of his eight chapters to the topic of enemy love, and, although he sees the antecedents for the teaching in both Hellenistic moral teachers and Jewish sources, he follows the consensus in regarding Jesus' teaching as original in the clarity of its expression, the way it grounds its ultimate motivation in the nature of God, and the bold centrality it has in his teaching.[25]

Becker sees these commands rooted in the help of the Creator, an emphasis embedded in three dominant teachings of Jesus:

1. Jesus' proclamation of the kingdom makes clear that qualifications or determinations of the love object are meaningless. The goodness of God promised in this message on the human side presupposes a universal place under the judgment of God as seen in John the Baptist (Luke 13:1–5). If all are universally under judgment, then it is not their innate goodness which calls forth God's or our love. The radicality of this starting point is clear when it is placed alongside the Stoics, who based their philanthropy on their belief that all people carry the same divine nobility. This demands reciprocal human noble relations—thus love. Love, as Jesus defines it, aims first of all at unconditionally overcoming lostness; it does not begin with nobility but with human misery.[26] Or as Wolfgang Huber puts it, "The radical nature of enemy love lies in that precisely the enemy is defined as the one to love and that thereby the ethos of reciprocity is exploded" (Huber, "Feindschaft und Feindesliebe," 139).

2. Love is a consequence of the rule of God, a by-product of the experience of salvation.

3. Jesus tended toward a worldwide human horizon. The Samaritan did not ask whether the one he was helping was an Israelite (Luke 10:29–37; cf. Mark 2:27; 7:15).

It is important to observe how the New Testament views love. Love is not fundamentally an emotional response; rather, it is seen as an act of will, thus the audacity to command it. Second, it involves simply an act for the good of the other, perceived as such. In a state of enmity one expects but one thing from the other: actions meant to hurt, sometimes to kill physically or emotionally. To love the enemy is to take the other by surprise and act as if the life of the other is so important to you that you seek to enrich it, to further it, and to improve it.

Ethelbert Stauffer, in his *TDNT* article on *agapē*, observes love's central role in Judaism:

> But the thinking of the rabbis constantly returns to the love of God. This stands supreme. It is perhaps concealed in this age of stress, but it will the more gloriously manifest itself in its own time. It is strong

as death. Only the victorious words of the Song of Solomon are adequate to convey the elementary force of this love.[27]

Great difficulties are created by this close relation to Judaism for scholars who are determined to treat Jesus as a Christian rather than as a Jew. For, the argument goes, the coupling of these two commandments is an un-Jewish act; indeed, that broadening of the concept of neighbor to include the enemy is inimical to Judaism. Little wonder that Andreas Nissen concludes with a question: "If indeed Jesus' double command of love was the sum and measure of God's will, what does it then mean when it is said: "Jesus was a Jew?"[28] John Piper focuses the issues sharply: "The perceptive Jew must have viewed Jesus' love command as an attack on the Torah. . . . Jesus' command to love the enemy as well as the friend contained the seed for the dissolution of the Jewish distinctive."[29] The problem is one of Piper's own creation: to see Christianity as unique he must posit a Jesus who attacked the Torah. How can this be, since there is no evidence of such an attack in the New Testament sources themselves? The problem does not exist when the sources are read carefully.[30]

Apparently the early church found convenient and useful the summary of covenant obligations in the double love commandment left by Jesus. Jesus and his followers in this respect built solidly on Jewish foundations and in continuity with Jewish teaching. To Simon the Just is attributed the statement that the fundamentals of life are summed up in Torah, worship, and brotherly love, thus bringing together divine as well as human relations.[31] There is abundant evidence that Judaism had over many years sought to isolate central affirmations and distil formulae that can be described as the summary of Torah.[32] That they did not seek to distil the law into "principles" is obvious; equally obvious is the fact that Jesus refused to treat love as a principle.

There is no evidence that Jesus sought to do away with Torah when he summarized it in the double love command; rather, Jesus expressed his concern with people and relationships. While his common ground with Judaism may well reside, then, in the love command, and while it seems evident that virtually all the illustrations he uses can be traced back to Jewish and Greek sources, the novel element in Jesus is the way he focuses everything on the precise formula "Love your enemies" as a mandate. So far no one has found such use prior to his time. With Jesus' extensive use of the Hebrew Bible it is striking that the themes of vengeance so prominent in the psalms are missing in his speech. One thinks in particular of such striking contrasts between the foot-washing incident of John 13 and Ps. 58:10: "The righteous shall rejoice when he sees the vengeance; he shall wash his feet [LXX, "hands"] in the blood of the wicked." H.-J. Kraus[33] describes the images as "drastic and impressive." He also insists that "of vengeance and desire for retribution *there is no mention here (kann hier keine Rede sein).*" Rather, the speaker is one of those who hungers and thirsts for righteousness.

Given the use of *naqam* here, I am tempted to follow Kraus's intriguing parallels to the book of Revelation. Still, the language is so much more vivid here that I cannot. I would certainly see parallels to Rom. 12:17–31.[34] In any case, no such desires for retribution are found in the sayings of Jesus.[35] At most, he expresses his deep-felt pain for the suffering coming to others and his passionate concern through the use of a prophetic woe and also a prophetic action in the Temple. But the uniqueness lies at a deeper level. Even if the identical words were to appear in earlier sources, the manner in which Jesus laid down his life for his enemies in order to enable them also to partake of the love of God, and the way in which the words were used by the early Christian community, make them unique.[36]

"Love Your Enemies" in Theological Historical Context

The command to love enemies is grounded ultimately in the nature of God and God's actions toward humans (Sir. 18:8–14). Hebrew thought also affirmed that God had created both good and bad, but derived from that mainly skepticism (Eccl. 9:2–3), "for the same fate befalls every man," good man and sinner alike (v. 2). Jesus takes this typical experience and exalts it to an insight at a productive level: "God is indiscriminately good." God guarantees to everyone without exception the constant provision of elementary essentials for life prior to their human self-actualization into good or evil. People are to imitate this. If they do so, they become children of God, a salvation predicated of the just (Wisd. Sol. 2:18; Sir. 4:10).

The enemy is not the most distant neighbor—rather, the enemy defines the basis for the love. The extreme case becomes the occasion for every social relationship, which is basically always determined by love. "Consequently," Becker concludes, "a division into personal, social, vocational or political enmity is rejected, for love imitates God who, everywhere, constantly creates new possibilities for life." Love never asks, "Who is the other?" but only what the present possibilities might allow that one to become. Then it is also clear: "The imperative is no legal exaggeration, but rather an opening of a perspective, without exception, to meet everyone in a life promoting or enhancing way, just as God the Creator does."[37]

Although the command to love enemies is found only twice in the Gospels, seldom has its authenticity been questioned.[38] Furthermore, it is recognized that the idea is found in the epistles without the precise commandment. It was the most frequently cited saying of Jesus in the second century[39] especially by the Apologists as evidence that the early Christians were not haters of humankind.[40] From as early as the second century, however, to modern times the idea has been either relegated to the personal realm or more frequently totally confined to a select group of Christians in religious communities, either in monastic orders or, since the Reformation, to people generally dismissed as "enthusiasts."

This century, however, has experienced a wave of interest in the teaching. Through the work of Hans Haas[41] and Michael Waldmann[42] it was demonstrated to be far from unique in Jesus. What had begun in this century as an attempt to show that enemy love was even found in the natural realm (Randlinger and Bach) soon became a deadly earnest pursuit during the First World War when scholars began seriously to study the idea of enemy love within Judaism and to explore its uniquely Christian aspect. Moreover, the history of the idea and the extent to which it was practiced by the early martyrs was analyzed.[43]

It was not, however, until the coming of the Second World War and the threat that international enmity now posed to human civilization that scholars were drawn more deeply into the discussion and devoted much research to the theme. Nevertheless the subject has so far brought forth only two book-length English contributions by biblical scholars: William Klassen and John Piper. Klassen proposes that the ultimate source of the commandment can be traced to ancient Greek wisdom, but above all to Judaism also, from which Jesus took it, and that it has fundamental relevance for guidance on how to live today.[44] Piper regards the command to have derived directly from Jesus and sees it as a radical departure from Judaism.[45] As with Nissen,[46] Piper's understanding of Judaism makes it impossible to see enemy love as mandatory within that religious framework.[47]

The argument for its genuineness, based by Rudolf Bultmann and others on its discontinuity with Judaism, must now be reopened. Indeed, it has been challenged recently in a brilliant essay on this topic by Jürgen Sauer. After a careful analysis of the Lukan and

Matthean versions he arrives at a Q text and compares it with the Pauline materials in detail. He concludes that the tradition on which the Pauline materials on enemy love are based antedates the materials in the Gospels.[48] Instead of attributing the origin of the command to love enemies to Jesus, he believes it originated in Christian literature around the middle 50s. Paul, however, did not have access to it, otherwise he would have used it.

In my judgment, however, it makes better historical sense to give full credit to Jesus himself for having first formed the idea of enemy love into a bold command for his community. The early Christian communities then developed their traditions in response to what they remembered Jesus as saying, but they also did a selective recall and no doubt added their own illustrations of what this meant in their context.

Luke and Matthew appear to be drawing from a common source that included at least the words: [*agapate tous echthrous hymōn*] "Love your enemies." Luke repeats the command after giving some illustrations:

Do good to those who hate you
Bless those who curse you
Pray for those who treat you spitefully

These three imperatives spell out further what it means to love enemies, but they also spell out more fully the category of an enemy:

Love	Enemy
do good	Those who hate you
bless	Those who curse you
pray for	Those who treat you spitefully

The first of these instructions is rooted in Greek thought and especially the maxim enunciated in many places that the goal of education to maturity (= *paideia*) is to learn to treat your friend right and to take revenge on those who do evil to you. That same idea appears in the Hebrew Bible when Joab is astonished that King David does not follow that pattern but instead: "You love those who hate you and hate those who love you" (2 Sam. 19:6).

Luke's second, third, and fourth instructions—the ability to return a soft answer for wrath, to return a blessing for a curse, and to pray for the one who treats you spitefully—are found often in Jewish ethics. Only in Judaism, which believed in the power of a blessing and in a sovereign God who answers prayer, could such an attitude emerge. But the power of prayer is here used not to curse but to bring good things, and with this statement Jesus declared decisively that the curse no longer has a place. The kingdom in which God rules has no room for curses.

Luke then offers four concrete examples on what the disciple is to do:

If hit on the cheek	offer the other one also
If your coat is taken	offer the shirt as well
To everyone who asks	give
From one robbing you	do not demand it back

In sharp disjunction to this, Luke then introduces the so-called Golden Rule based on reciprocity. "Treating others as you would like them to treat you" is, however, to be understood here as putting yourself in the place of the other.[49] This idea emerges first in Greek literature in Isocrates, but most likely it originated in the Greek theater.[50] It is found in Jewish literature also, and both invite the actor to consider the impact of the action if roles are reversed between giver and receiver. It is one of the wisest and most useful rules for human relations, even though it appears to contradict the nonreciprocal teaching on loving the enemy.[51]

Luke follows the example with three queries, each one ending with the same question: "What credit is that to you?" If you love only those who love you, do good only to those who do good to you, lend only if you are fully repaid? What in Matthew becomes the intensified righteousness is here the *poia hymin charis?* And the adversative *plēn* in Luke 6:35 introduces the standard to which Jesus invites:

> But you must love your enemies
> and do good
> and lend without expecting any return.
> Then you will have a rich reward: you will be children of the Most
>   High, because that one is kind to the ungrateful and wicked. Be
>   compassionate as your Father is compassionate.

What is most important is that for Luke the disciple can become a child of God. The attribute of God that is most important is compassion toward the ungrateful and the wicked. Any utilitarian motive is lacking. This ethical guidance is fully and exclusively rooted in the nature and behavior of God. The only reward in sight is a relationship to God.

Can the enemy mentioned here be more closely defined? Some have argued that the illustrations point to personal life and therefore one should not think of international or civic enemies. Richard

Horsley has recently concluded that it refers to "village squabbles." Rejecting "foreign enemies" or even outsiders as referents, he sees here a call to "take economic responsibility for one another."[52] Others are persuaded that the term *echthros* is the standard New Testament term for enemy in its broadest sense and that the occurrence of the plural may indeed stress an inclusive usage.[53] An increasing number of scholars take *echthros* in its broadest sense, even as they seek to find the sociological background of the original Q source as well as of the Matthean and Lukan sources.[54] Out of this broader meaning has come an intense search for the way this command can be applied in international and national politics.[55]

In a major study reviewing recent literature, Heinz-Wolfgang Kuhn has convincingly argued for this wider application:

> Inasmuch as the oldest context of the love for enemies command, namely being considered a child of God and the replication (*Erwiederung*) of God's pattern, certainly goes back to Jesus, precisely this context shows that the word concerning love of enemies applies not only to the small circle of Jesus' followers but applies to all who open themselves to the message of the rule of God. Certainly the promise to be called a child of God could not for Jesus be restricted to this small circle. Nor did the love for enemies command apply only to an immediate situation of hostility towards the disciples, sent as they were as lambs among the wolves (Luke 10:3) but to all who were being offered the status of children of God. . . . The directive is without boundaries. The religious, the political, and the personal enemy are all meant. Every enemy is meant. One cannot conceive of the love of enemies command without Tora, without the Bible of Jesus, and without the early Jewish tradition. Nevertheless, originally it apparently did not stand in any direct relationship to the Tora.[56]

Kuhn also stresses that the question about the possibility of keeping the commandment is falsely put. For that possibility is always linked with whether we can in the presence of God's rule act as God does; the actualizing of this "utopian" potential is joined to the coming and presence of Jesus.[57]

For Matthew, the "love your enemies" teaching contains an edge against the Jewish tradition, for it is found in the series of antitheses in which Jesus' teaching is set against "what has been said" (Matt. 5:21–48). The first problem that presents itself is the introduction: "You have heard . . . , Love your neighbor, hate your enemy" (Matt. 5:43). Much effort has been spent trying to understand why Matthew added, "and hate your enemy." The answer seems to be quite simple. The formula "Be good to (or love) your friends and hate your enemies" was very widespread in the ancient world and occurs in many layers of documentation. Rather than look in vain throughout Jewish sources, including Qumran, for these exact words, we should simply treat them as a part of general folk wisdom which Jesus' listeners had heard and which were well known to Matthew's audience as well.

The motivation for the command in Matthew is the same as it is in Luke: to become a child of God—"only so can you be children of your heavenly Father." Instead of stressing the gentleness and compassion of God, Matthew stresses God's impartiality. The sun rises on good and bad alike; the rain is sent on the just and the unjust alike. An insight that appears in Jewish wisdom literature and there drives to cynicism—[So who cares?]—is used here to strike forth into a new ethical sphere. Both Luke and Matthew ask, "If you love only those who love you, what credit is that?"

Matthew adds only one further point, the matter of "greeting" not mentioned by Luke. Johanan ben Zakkai, who escaped from Jerusalem when it was under siege to found the Academy at Yavneh, had the reputation of greeting Gentiles and others before they would greet him. In this way there could never be any doubt about his prayerful desire that the one he met should have God's shalom. Along the same lines Matthew invites his readers to exceed the friendliness of the heathen and to greet all whom they meet. It is a striking illustration, too often overlooked, bringing the entire discussion about enemy love into the concreteness of daily life.

Matthew's concluding statement, "Be you therefore mature even as your Father in heaven is mature (*teleios*)" (Matt. 5:48), refers to the way in which enemies are treated. Don't play favorites. The term "perfect," as it is sometimes translated, creates difficulties not contained in the original text and suggests an impossible standard, which is hardly the intention of Jesus for his followers. Rather, he provided them with permission and the empowering freedom to live as a child of God who loves even enemies.

Both Matthew and Luke appeal to God's mercy, although they use different examples to demonstrate that mercy. In both, God's action is to be followed, which becomes in Paul an *imitatio Christi*.[58]

Luke's parable of the Good Samaritan (Luke 10:25–37) expands the lawyer's question, "Who is my neighbor?" to include the enemy. W. Monselewski has listed a series of distinguished interpreters who see the parable as an illustration of how someone viewed traditionally as an enemy, the Samaritan, can love his enemy, the

Jew, and help him in his distress.[59] Thus, to be a neighbor you love your enemy. The Samaritans were well liked by Luke, to be sure, for he almost always portrays them in a favorable light. From Josephus we learn that the Samaritans occasionally terrorized the Jews (*Ant.* 20.6.1–3) and little love was lost between these two groups. Yet in the parable, it is the Samaritan who proves neighbor to his "enemy" and shows that categories, like enemies and friends, can change to the assaulted and the neighbor who assists the one assaulted.

The similarities between this parable and the "love your enemies" pericopes in Matthew and Luke have often been noted; they are traced in detail by Monselewski. He sees four elements as determinative: (1) the authority of Jesus, (2) the reference to God's covenant with the people, (3) reward, and (4) the reference to the authority of God and a personal relationship to him. He also believes these motifs may have been at the basis of the parable and with Günther Bornkamm wonders whether the parable may not have been the oldest form of the "love your enemies" command.[60]

Did Jesus himself love his enemies? Matthew 23 seems to suggest that he did not, and other events of his life are often cited. If, however, he saw the injustices around him as being capable of being righted only through the death of those who truly cared for their people, then his teaching and self-sacrifice do harmonize.

The question whether the text legitimates self-love when the commandment reads to "love the neighbor as yourself" has been much debated. In our narcissistic culture, inundated as we are with psychology, most have taken this as a command for self-love. The issues are complicated and will not be pursued here, since this essay focuses on enemy love. The text, however, does not command self-love; possibly it recognizes its existence, at the very most it legitimates it.

Since this is a quotation from Lev. 19:18b we need to see how the two parts of this command were understood in Judaism, where they were seen as two independent commandments and treated separately. In the second part the underlying Hebrew means "as yourself"; it means to care for the neighbor, to let the neighbor have what is the neighbor's own and to obtain it for the neighbor, accordingly to provide the neighbor rights in accordance with the neighbor's position, "just as you would do for yourself."

The measuring rod is not "self-love."[61] Certainly "as yourself" does not include the command to love oneself or state that one should love oneself. The comparison was not intended to recognize the legitimacy of self-love but to point to the power of self-assertion.[62] In Anders Nygren's scheme, "Agape . . . excludes all self-love . . . [and] recognizes no kind of self-love as legitimate."[63]

The comparison appears quite frequently in Jewish sources beyond the Bible itself, especially in the context of enemy love, for example, *T. Sim.* 4:6: "In all his days [Joseph] did not reproach us for this deed, but he loved us as his own life."

Again it appears in the context of enemy love in *T. Benj.* 4:3:

> For a good person does not have a blind eye, but is merciful to all even though they may be sinners. And even if people plot against such a one for evil ends, by doing good this one conquers evil, being watched over by God. He loves those who wrong him as he loves his own life. (Cf. *Jub.* 36:4; CD 6:20; *Ahikar Arm.* B 2:71; Sir. 7:21; 31:14.)[64]

Could it be that what is meant in these texts is the same as Epictetus refers to in his repeated references to "self-interest"? If so, then self-interest is here expanded to include the enemy.

Johannine Sources

Two sources in the New Testament have been charged with letting go the love of enemies command: John's Gospel and epistles by ignoring the idea, and Revelation by violating it and promoting hatred instead.

Bultmann, while admitting that "John 13:34–36 refers not to love for humans in general, not to love for neighbor or enemy, but rather love within the circle of the believers,"[65] has not been able to persuade his colleagues that "it is obvious that" this love commandment does not render invalid but rather includes love of neighbor and enemy. What Bultmann described as obvious has been rejected by a consensus. But the evidence, in my judgment, supports Bultmann against the consensus. To demonstrate this, I examine John's epistles in three sections which present an expanding circle of issues.

In the first section, the matter of "newness" and "oldness" is taken up. The author would have it both ways: it is old (1 John 2:7)—you had the word from the beginning—and it is also a "new" command—"it is true in him *and in you.*" Evidence for this truth is that "the darkness is passing away and the true light is already shining." There are three possible responses to this:

1. One says he is in the light and hates his brother—he is in the darkness still.

2. Another loves his brother and remains in the light, and there is no cause for stumbling in him (or it, i.e., the light).

3. A third hates his brother, he is in darkness, walks in darkness and has no idea where he is going, for the darkness has blinded his eyes.

The author's major concern is with those who hate the brother. While there may have been conflicts among the disciples when Jesus lived with them, a problem as serious as this is not reported. "God is light," and when we walk in that light "we have *koinōnia* with each other" (1 John 1:7). The one who lives with integrity and keeps his word, truly in that one the "love of God has been fully realized" (1 John 2:5). To be sure, the commandment to love the enemy is not found, but the proscription against hating the brother is strong. The writer regards the problem as extremely urgent within the community. The topic is not the outside enemy, but love and not hatred within the fellowship.

The second section (1 John 3:10–18, 23) is, on the one hand, more condemning but, on the other, also much more tender. The tenderness comes to expression in the form of address: "brothers" in 3:13, "children" in 3:18, and "beloved" in 3:21. The tenderness is also manifest in the repeated use of the personal plural pronoun; thus the author identifies with his audience (1 John 3:11, 14b, 18, 23) when he refers to the love command. It is also more condemning because the lines are more sharply drawn: Cain killed his brother, signifying that he was of the evil one. He hated Abel because his works were righteous. The one who does not love remains in death (3:14). So hatred and manslaughter are closely joined together; in this respect he had not only the story of Cain but Jesus' own words of warning against anyone who is angry with the brother, consigning to the fires of Gehenna anyone who called the brother a fool (Matt. 5:22). So with all the discussion of hatred the author wants to contrast Jesus, the positive model of love of enemies, with the model of Cain who in hatred did not love his brother.

In 1 John 3:16ff. Christ's love manifest in the "laying down of his life" is appropriated directly to the believer's response to the brother or sister in material need. The one who has this world's goods and yet refuses to help cannot say that God's love abides within. This concrete illustration strips love of all noble sentiment and puts it in the service of the needy in the community. The author then elaborates how the practice of love relates to confidence or security. In a short penetrating creedal statement he states how a guilty conscience can be stilled before God: "And this is his commandment, that we should believe in the name of his Son Jesus Christ and love one another, just as he commanded us" (3:23).

This section (1 John 3:10ff.) began with an affirmation that love and doing justice reveal whether we have our origin in God or in the

devil. Since our *angelia,* our reason for existence, is "that we should
love one another," one can only say that one who does not love one's
brother or sister is not of God. This is not an eternal decree. One
can change one's base of origin by doing justice and loving one's
fellow Christian. To be transferred from death into life can be a state
of certainty—"we know"—and can be tested simply by the question: "Do you love others, and specifically your brothers and sisters?" (3:14). The author then connects this love in deed to boldness
of expression, freedom of speech (*parrēsia*) before God, and loss
of the condemning heart. Ultimately our case, the author affirms,
rests in the God who is greater than our hearts, knows all things,
and is indeed a God of love. The appeal is to *remain* (abide) in this
authentic love. The stress on *remaining* is original with this author[66]
(occurring 23 times in 1 John and 43 times in the Gospel). "And by
this we know that he abides in us, by the Spirit that he has given us"
(3:24b). The ultimate mark that they are remaining in love comes
from beyond them but resides within. While "Greek philosophy
contemplated that which is eternal (remains) the OT confesses the
One who remains."[67]

The third section (1 John 4:7–21) begins with the call, "Beloved,
let us love one another." The reason is that *agapē* has its origin in
God and therefore anyone who continues to love signifies birth from
God and knowledge of God. On the other hand, the person who
remains in a state of not loving (so the present participle) does not
know God, because God's very nature is *agapē.* This famous and
pithy definition of God has to do with ethics, not with essence. It is
not to be turned on its head as if, wherever there is love, God is
also. Again, as the personal plural pronouns indicate, the author
identifies deeply with his readers, and he enters into the depths of
the incarnation. The readers (or listeners) are reminded that God's
love was manifested among us (*en hēmin*) by this means: "He sent
his only begotten Son into the world in order that we might live
through him" (1 John 4:9). The obligation to love springs directly
out of that divine initiative.

The introduction of the formula "In this we know" (1 John 4:13)
signals the matter uppermost in the author's mind: How can one be
certain? He returns to the presence of the Spirit: God's gift to the
believers, first brought into the discussion in 3:24. We are eyewit-
nesses and continue to bear witness to the Son as savior of the
world. Whatever may have been the content of the creed for this
community, the essence of their faith is: "So we have known and
have believed [both verbs in the perfect tense] the love which God
has for [*en* stresses internalized and personalized love] us" (4:16).

Here, then, is a second affirmation that God is love. God remains in love, and love is made complete by its abiding presence in the community. Love banishes fear; for this author, the two cannot exist side by side (4:18). Love then marks the abiding nature of God and the unchanging nature of God's way of dealing with the community and indeed with the whole world (5:2).

Two specific appeals are then made to test one's union with God in love. The first is to expose the lie: to claim love for God and harbor hatred for the brother or sister (4:20–21). The second appeals to the parent-child identity in character. If God the parent is loving, why should not the children be the same, unless they want to deny their parentage. "When we love God and obey his commands, we love his children too" (5:2).

This survey has shown that John's agenda is to restore love as the central reality of his community. Most modern writers accuse John of lacking the very love he espouses in his dealings with those who hate their sisters and brothers.[68] But is this really true? He does not condemn them irrevocably to damnation or to separation from God. Those who have left are not told they cannot return. At the same time, the community is to be one of love, not of hate. To hate the brother is a serious offense which, if left unchecked, will destroy the community, as it may well destroy those who through hatred have lost their way and are wandering around in the dark. Hatred can lead to murder. Above all, the community of Christ must begin within its own midst to nurture the tender plant of love. In his appeal to the Galatians, Paul likewise urges that while working for the good of all, the "members of the household of faith" (Gal. 6:10) are to receive priority. Jesus, when a woman brought an expensive gift of love and some criticized this as a waste that could have been used to help the poor, allowed the gift to stand; Mark adds, "Wherever in all the world the gospel is proclaimed, what she has done will be told as her memorial" (Mark 14:3–9). In this way Mark and his community affirmed their belief that love begins with those closest to you. Love for enemies and love for fellow Christians are not in conflict with each other—they nurture and nourish each other. Both are empowered by the divine initiative of love. Both have their pattern in the life of Jesus, for if we are in him, "we bind ourselves to live as Christ lived" (1 John 2:5).[69]

It has been stated that "where the command of brotherly love is understood as it is in 1 John, the command to love the neighbor is at least restricted, if not repealed."[70] Surely this does not stand. The author's writing addresses the topic that is most pressing at the moment. It is incorrect to argue that because he does not mention that husbands should love their wives, therefore he does not believe it! Nor is it clear that he has "a shrunken point of view in which there is room only for a conventicle of brothers who love each other and keep the world at a distance."[71] He affirms that the whole world is redeemable (1 John 2:2) and indeed that God who is love sent his Son *into the world* that we might live (4:9). There is clearly a sense of mission in this epistle; at the same time, it is written to restore the community to a correct sense of priorities. It is doubtful that we dishonor him by taking seriously his view of the world. Certainly his message that love within the brotherhood is essential is in harmony with Peter's admonition to his people, "Love the brotherhood" (1 Peter 2:17).

Love of Enemies in the Revelation to John

The writer of Revelation has been described as "living from a high pitch of hatred,"[72] as missing the "glow of love for enemies" and displaying instead a "virtuosity of hatred"[73] and a "glowing hatred against all enemies."[74] In Revelation, W. D. Davies saw an "abortive hatred" toward the powers,[75] but the strongest indictments against the book have come from D. H. Lawrence[76] and C. G. Jung, both of whom failed to see its rich symbolism as a carrier of truth. The latter saw the book as the hateful explosion of an old man at the end of his life who had spoken about love so much that he repressed all feelings of hatred.[77]

An examination of the text reveals that *agapaō* as verb appears only four times and as noun only twice, and that *phileō* appears only three times. Of these usages, Rev. 1:6 joins with other New Testament witnesses in placing Christ's redemptive love as the cornerstone of the Christian community. Love (*phileō*) is related to discipline leading to repentance (Rev. 3:18) in citing Prov. 3:12 (cf. Heb. 12:5, which follows the LXX in using *agapaō* as well). The church at Ephesus is rebuked for having lost her first love (Rev. 2:4), the warm affirmation of affection for each other and the translation of emotion into responsible moral action. Thyatira is praised for her "love and faith, service and fortitude" (Rev. 2:19).

At the core of our understanding of Revelation, however, is the symbol of the Lamb. Introduced in Revelation 5 in a critical stage of the drama, it stands without modifier and from that point on is the main actor. Clearly the description of this Lamb epitomizes love as self-giving, for the reason the Lamb is celebrated in song as worthy is: "he was slain and by his blood persons of every tribe and language, people and nation" were purchased for God and made into a royal house (Rev. 5:9). There is no direct love command in the book. Nevertheless, since the church is tested by its love, and above all since the call to steadfastness revolves around remaining faithful in following the Lamb, and at no place are readers urged to use violence or commanded to hate their persecutors, we may see the book as an example of leaving the execution of wrath in the hands of God and of the Lamb. There is, according to George B. Caird,[78] no need to see the book as a deviation from the New Testament ethic of love, which in any case is not incompatible with a deep commitment to the sovereignty of God. Indeed, Caird states that the author had "learned from Christ that the omnipotence of God is not the power of unlimited coercion but the power of invincible love."[79] Especially in Revelation 22 he finds the image of Paradise restored to the nations "still bearing the wounds of those battles by which their hostility to the Lamb has been beaten down, smashed by the iron bar of his inexorable love."[80] The message of the book would seem to be that those who follow the power of love rather than the love of power will conquer. But only those who follow the Lamb in serving others unto death will share in that victory. It may well be that in the Revelation to John the symbol of sacrifice is taken over by a small beleaguered community and is transformed into a victory symbol.

The book, where not vilified, has usually been neglected among writers on peace and enemy love. Although my earlier attempt to deal with the theme of vengeance received favorable review and limited acceptance, it is clear that much needs to be done to bring together two very active areas of New Testament research: apocalyptic and peace/love your enemies.[81] It is still possible that, given the apocalyptic world of symbolism, we are here in the presence of the profoundest effort of the early Christian community to use the suffering Lamb Christology to defuse all desires of participating in vengeance against the strongest enemy the church had seen. By stressing the continuity of what the Lamb had done with what followers of the Lamb should do, this community was able to resist the demonic powers that sought to vanquish them.

Paul's Understanding
of Love of Enemies

From every aspect it is Paul who makes the profoundest contribution to the Christian understanding of love. Paul sees himself deeply loved by God/Christ and his life depends upon that love.

Indeed, the life which he now lives is not his, but the life which Christ himself lives in Paul, "I live by faith in the Son of God, who loved me and sacrificed himself for me" (Gal. 2:20). Personal faith in divine personal love sustained Paul and had called him into service. This is so basic that God becomes for Paul "the God of love" (2 Cor. 13:11), likely his way of saying that God is love. The hymn to love in 1 Corinthians 13 is a succinct and attractive statement of how love behaves and at each point it is the exact opposite of the way in which enemies behave toward each other.

The question has often been debated why Paul did not cite the commandment to love enemies. Did he in fact know about it and teach it? The evidence when correctly read confirms that he did, even though the precise words of the dominical command do not appear. The love of God is central to Paul's view of life. In the midst of the imponderables of history there is hope, and such "hope is no mockery, because God's love has flooded our inmost heart through the Holy Spirit he has given" (Rom. 5:5). The proof of that love is that while we were still sinners, indeed God's enemies (Rom. 5:10), Christ died for us (Rom. 5:8). Consistent with Pauline theology, the pre-Christian state is described as under the dreadful judgment of God. But God, rich in mercy, out of the great love he bore for us, brought us to life (Eph. 2:4).

Because the precise command "Love your enemies" does not appear in Pauline letters, it is argued that Paul does not know this command.[82] A closer study of his writings makes it evident that the substance of the teaching is there. The center of Pauline teaching on this matter is found in his grounding all of the Christian commands in the affirmation that "God loved us while we were his enemies" (Rom. 5:10). In addition, Paul prescribes behavior toward those who persecute and those who curse along the same lines as Jesus does (Rom. 12:9–21; 1 Cor. 4:12–13). All vengeance is to be avoided and all retaliation in kind rejected. In line with the Jewish wisdom tradition he cites Prov. 25:21 and urges that Christians feed a hungry enemy and give him something to drink. The victory he foresees of good over evil through this course of action may be related to the coals of fire following the usage of the proverb derived ultimately from Egypt[83] and thus has no direct connection with a desire to increase the vengeance upon the enemies.[84] For Paul here uses Jewish and perhaps some Hellenistic wisdom concepts of battle and victory,[85] and his concept of vengeance is related more to divine sovereignty than to personal satisfaction.

Paul did not himself consistently live up to this teaching if we take as historical (and I do) Luke's account of his encounter with the high priest Ananias (Acts 23:1–5). The pressures to omit this incident, given the Stoic age in which Luke wrote and the frequency with which his contemporaries discussed what a wise man does when hit in the face, inclines one to treat the incident as genuine. Furthermore, there is, in my opinion, a clear case of Paul's departure from the teaching of Jesus when he expresses the wish (in Gal. 5:12) that his enemies would accidentally castrate themselves. This is a sin Paul committed here. It can be understood and forgiven. Under no circumstances should it be made a model for Christian behavior.

Conclusion

Our survey has shown that, as a whole, the early Christian writings unite in affirming the love of enemies commandment found in Jesus, who in turn was indebted to Judaism, especially the wisdom tradition, and later Jewish literature, for example, the *T. 12 Patr.* and Qumran. We know of no Greek or Roman community in which love of enemies played such an important role. For the early Christians, although there is little mention of love in the Synoptic Gospels, the coming of the kingdom in the person of Jesus was a sure sign of God's love for all people, indeed for the world. At the same time, Paul's own strong sense of call was grounded in the love of God, and the church's constitution rested on that love. In turn, a fruit of the Spirit was love (Gal. 5:22), and for Paul it was the greatest gift of all. Love was therefore freely commanded to Christians, first toward each other, then to all people, including the enemy. The documents show considerable tension between insider and outsider, stemming no doubt from an awareness that the boundaries of a community have to be established and maintained. The emergence of formulae like "the God of love" (2 Cor. 13:11), and the "God of peace," and the "love of Jesus Christ" (Rom. 8:35) in early communities shows that they were able to develop both a theology and a Christology of love. This theology, built in the first instance on the Jewish experience, was given strong impetus first by Jesus, who spoke little about love but practiced it in an exemplary fashion, and by Paul who, alongside the Johannine community and the Petrine group, placed love in a central place. Anyone who wishes to understand them must give serious attention to the liberating and empowering view of love they brought to the world.

There are three aspects, at least, of the commandment to love our enemies that deserve further work.

1. Just as we may point fingers at scholars who in days past dis-

torted this commandment, so those who follow us will point to our blind spots. One of mine is the androcentric way in which I treated the topic until recently. There is a very distinct need to allow a feminist hermeneutic to inform this discussion. Even as I worked on *Love of Enemies* during the 1970s it became increasingly clear that the issues of violence against women were on the increase, and it became more and more urgent to address whether, for women, there is any meaning at all in this command. Can it be applied to conflict in the home—conflicts that arise sometimes from serious abuse and that can lead to such profound alienation that divorce or worse sins are committed? In this area I have done a lot of soul-searching but am convinced that there are answers that can serve us.

Above all, we can learn much from Luise Schottroff, and others like her, whose courageous dealing with the "love your enemies" theme, even long before it was popular, set a standard for the rest to follow. Wedded deeply to a commitment to doing something about the violence in the world, she had the courage to join with protesters and preach at an Easter service at a large American rocket base in Germany in 1985. That base is no more!

More recently Schottroff has analyzed the three illustrations of "love the enemy" found in the Sermon on the Mount and concluded that they are thoroughly androcentric.[86] Any woman of that time who would have followed them literally would have invited rape. Could Jesus have had this in mind? Without questioning the basic theme, "Love your enemies," we may have to conclude that even today literally following those examples would be to "send the wrong message" to the enemy. There is much work here for further research and it would be a pity if only half of the human race would be interested in pursuing this.

2. The relation of "Love your enemies" to justice also needs further work. It is remarkable that large church bodies have donated money to groups dedicated to killing the enemy and they have done so in the name of justice. By now we should be able to see the fruits that have come from that. Related is the sophomoric way in which violence is still viewed and the romantic tone in which it is portrayed. Above all, this issue will force us to explore in greater depth the relation of the apocalyptic literature to "love your enemies." It is not clear that justice is "a higher value than love" in the Revelation to John.[87] Peter Lampe is certainly correct when he observes that this author does not project peace into the far distant future and that "the thesis of 'inner peace' would have been energetically resisted by John."[88] The liturgy clearly installs God as king, and by the end

of the book the Lamb which has achieved its credentials by loving its enemies to its death is sharing the throne with God.

> Recollection of the liturgy therefore becomes a subversive recollection. So the reading of the book of Revelation leads not least to celebrating the liturgy as training in resistance. Should that not be a specifically Christian contribution to a peace which includes justice?[89]

3. Finally, and closely related to the last point, is the inherent energy in the "Love your enemies" command. Throughout the centuries many people have noted it but followed with the lament, "Too bad it doesn't work." For this reason the love your enemies idea is well served by some distance from pacifism. But in my opinion it always leads to pacifism, cannot lead to anything else, but pacifism may not lead to loving your enemies. In any case, Christians are children of God, and their values come from that relationship; their behavior is patterned upon God and upon Jesus the Lord, whose command to love the enemy and the neighbor—and the pattern he gave us—is to be followed.

Too often such a view of love is robbed of its power, for it is taken out of history and romanticized. Accordingly, those who advocate love of enemies are seen as irrelevant and uninterested in the course of history. It should rather be seen as a rebellion against history. As Albert Camus put it, those who rebel against history at the appropriate moment are the only ones who truly advance history. But this rebellion "cannot exist without a strange form of love." It involves living for others, for the humiliated.

> This insane generosity is the generosity of rebellion, which unhesitatingly gives the strength of its love and without a moment's delay refuses injustice . . . and is prodigal in its gifts.

For Camus, this strange form of love which prodigally spends itself for the humiliated must never be "contaminated by resentment." If it does, it denies life and dashes toward destruction. If it does not, then is born that strange joy which helps one live and die.[90]

Once again Camus, an unbeliever, has something to teach us. Resentment, just another word for hate, can be overcome through an active energy of goodwill toward the one alienated. Loving the enemy, as Victor Furnish observed, "sets [Jesus'] ethic of love apart from other 'love ethics' of antiquity and best shows what kind of love is commanded by him." That love he further defines as affirming the enemy, and this means "to be constructively and compassionately extended to [the enemy].[91]

While there continue to be people who think that only hatred is ruled out, and not violence and killing,[92] it is increasingly recognized that in this command we have a clear mandate on how to deal with enmity, personal, social, and ethnic as well as national. As with so much of what Jesus taught, the prescription has not so much been tried and found wanting. It is still wanting to be tried.

Notes

1. From a sermon preached in 1938, printed in Eberhard Bethge, *Dietrich Bonhoeffer: Gesammelte Schriften* (Munich: Chr. Kaiser Verlag, 1965), 4:427–434, here 430.

2. So Wolfgang Huber concludes after surveying theological handbooks and encyclopedias, in "Feindschaft und Feindesliebe: Notizen zum Problem des 'Feindes' in der Theologie," *ZEE* 26 (1982): 128–131.

3. William Klassen, "Love Your Enemy: A Study of New Testament Teaching on Coping with an Enemy," *MQR* 37 (1963): 147–171. It appeared also in *Biblical Realism Confronts the Nation* (ed. Paul Peachey; Nyack, N.Y.: Fellowship Publications, 1963), 153–183. See also William Klassen, "Coals of Fire: Sign of Repentance or Revenge?" *NTS* 9 (1963): 337–350.

4. The book, *Love of Enemies: The Way to Peace* (Philadelphia: Fortress Press, 1984), was reviewed by many scholars of diverse backgrounds and taken seriously in the discussion. Even in such cases where critical comments were made they furthered the discussion, and I am profoundly grateful for those who subjected it to rigorous scrutiny, in particular, to my now colleague Tom Yoder Neufeld's review in the *CGR* 3 (1985): 319–324 from which I have learned a lot. See my response in *CGR* 4 (1986): 69–74. My unusual connection between enemy love and peace signifies my agreement with Huber's statement, "Love of enemies is considered as the way to make peace in the Sermon on the Mount" (Huber, "Feindschaft und Feindesliebe," 140).

5. In addition to the examples cited in the literature noted below, there is a curious deviation from the historical-critical approach in R. H. Charles, *The Revelation of St. John* (2 vols.; Edinburgh: T. & T. Clark, 1920), 1:75. Commenting on Rev. 2:27, which he takes to refer to an actual destruction of the heathen nations with the members of the heavenly hosts as actual agents of destruction, he says, "At this moment that I am writing we can witness at least a partial fulfilment of this dread forecast, in which England and her allies are engaged in mortal strife with the powers of godless force and materialism. . . . The present heathen system of international relations will sooner or later be destroyed and replaced by international relations of a Christian character."

6. See C. H. Dodd, "The Theology of Christian Pacifism," in the volume, apparently edited by Charles Raven, *The Bases of Christian Pacifism* (London: Council of Christian Pacifist Groups, 1938), 5–15.

7. Ibid. See also C. H. Dodd, *The Epistle of Paul to the Romans* (London: Hodder & Stoughton, 1932), where Rom. 12:21 is described as "an admirable summary of the teaching of the Sermon on the Mount about what is called 'non-resistance,' and it expresses the most creative element in Christian ethics" (p. 201). What he wrote about Rom. 12:17–21 would, in my estimation, call for a simple substitution of the words "love of enemies" for "non-resistance," for this is what Dodd, and Paul, are talking about.

8. In Germany, some New Testament scholars courageously opposed Hitler. There were unfortunately others who did not; see Max Weinrich, *Hitler's Professors: The Part of Scholarship in Germany's Crimes Against the Jewish People* (New York: Yiddish Scientific Institute, 1946), 40–45, 65–67. For the way in which the Christian clergy supported the war efforts, see Ray H. Abrams, *Preachers Present Arms* (New York: Round Table Press, 1933; rev. ed., Scottdale, Pa.: Herald Press, 1969).

9. Heinrich Rendtorff, *Soldatentum und Gottesglaube* (Berlin: Furche-Verlag, 1937), 6. He also states that it is no joke that the words "God with Us" appear on the buckles of the soldiers (p. 6). The most serious error Rendtorff makes is to suggest, as he appeals to both Martin Luther and Martin Niemoeller, that the best soldier is the one who is at peace with God and with himself. He can be truly courageous and do his work well and be a "whole" man (p. 26). No reference to this book is made in the article on him in *RGG,* nor indeed in the Festschrift that honored him in 1950, nor in the obituary published in *TLZ* 86 (1961): 313–314.

10. Reinhold Niebuhr's position is clearly and unequivocally stated in his essay "Love Your Enemies," first published in *Christianity and Society* (Autumn 1942). The text I cite is found in *Love and Justice: Selections from the Shorter Writings of Reinhold Niebuhr* (ed. D. B. Robertson; Meridian Books, 1967; Gloucester, Mass.: Peter Smith, 1976). Niebuhr is at great pains to convince his reader that love of enemies is no "psychological absurdity." It does demand "that we should desire the good of the enemy." If this is achieved, we will be purged of hatred. The whole discussion takes place from the standpoint of the policeman, and so the soldier can be "forced to harm in the immediate instance." Bomber pilots are not to hesitate to partake of Communion before going on bombing raids, for the Eucharist is, after all, meant for sinners (p. 223)! One has to carry orders out without "rancor or self-righteousness." By a clever exegetical trick, Niebuhr can validate killing and bombing and ask only that it be done without hatred! Since Aristotle, the question has been debated whether the soldier is more effective if hate is an element. For the current debate, see John Ballard and Aliecia J. McDowell, "Hate and Combat Behavior," *Armed Forces and Society* 17 (1991): 229–241.

11. Most brilliantly in his book *Nachfolge,* first published in 1937 (Munich: Chr. Kaiser Verlag), and then (not very well) translated by Reginald

Fuller as *The Cost of Discipleship,* abridged 1948 and complete in October 1959 (London: SCM Press) and often reprinted. Bonhoeffer's words on "Blessed are the peacemakers" (p. 102) are some of the best ever written on that topic, and the sections on "Revenge" (pp. 126–130) and "The Enemy—The 'Extraordinary' " (pp. 131–138) are absolutely classic. Equally clearly he stated the Christian position in his sermon of January 23, 1938, based on Rom. 12:17–21; see *Gesammelte Schriften,* 4: 427–434. Again it has been poorly translated, by Evan Drake Howard, under the title "Loving Our Enemies," in *The Reformed Journal* (April 1985): 18–21. For an excellent study of Bonhoeffer's position on this topic and the Sermon on the Mount in general, see Clarence Bauman, *The Sermon on the Mount: The Modern Quest for Its Meaning* (Macon, Ga.: Mercer University Press, 1985), 249–274. He is deeply indebted to the best such study: Larry L. Rasmussen, *Dietrich Bonhoeffer: Reality and Resistance* (Nashville: Abingdon Press, 1972), 94–126.

12. Huber ("Feindschaft und Feindesliebe," 151–156) rightly credits Bonhoeffer with comprehending the meaning of the commandment to love the enemy much more sharply than his predecessors by uncovering the basis and thereby the radical nature of the command in a new way. Reuter, also using Bonhoeffer as a starting point, goes even farther in trying to assess the political nature of this command. Both treat it as a genuine child of theological ethics and succeed to a very large extent in doing justice to it. See Hans-Richard Reuter, "Liebet eure Feinde! Zur Aufgabe einer politischen Ethik im Licht der Bergpredigt," *ZEE* 26 (1982): 159–187. I owe a great deal to both of them.

13. Michael Waldmann, *Die Feindesliebe in der antiken Welt und im Christenthum* (Vienna: Mayer & Co., 1902); F. Steinmüller, *Die Feindesliebe* (Regensburg, 1903); Stephan Randlinger, *Die Feindesliebe nach dem natürlichen und positiven Sittengesetz: Eine historisch-ethische Studie* (Paderborn: F. Schöningh, 1906); and Eugen Bach, *Die Feindesliebe nach dem natürlichen und dem übernatürlichen Sittengesetz: Eine historisch-ethische Untersuchung* (Kempten: J. Kösel, 1914).

14. F. Kattenbusch, "Über die Feindesliebe im Sinne des Christentums," *TSK* 89 (1916): 1–70.

15. Paul Fiebig, "Jesu Worte über die Feindesliebe im Zusammenhang mit den wichtigsten rabbinischen Parallelen erläutert," *TSK* 91 (1918): 30–64.

16. Tertullian wrote: "Our individual, extraordinary, and perfect goodness consists in loving our enemies. To love one's friends is common practice, to love one's enemies only among Christians" (*Ad Scapulam* I) cited in Hans Haas, *Idee und Ideal der Feindesliebe in der ausserchristlichen Welt . . .* (Leipzig: University of Leipzig, 1927), 3. In the variant reading that Justin Martyr supplies for Matt. 5:46 and Luke 6:32, the conviction is expressed that Christians are following a new way: "If you love the ones loving you, what new thing are you doing?" (*ti kainon poieite, First Apol.* 15). Because of the popular idea that love for enemies is a uniquely Christina teaching, one does not expect to find it among non-Christians, but our

integrity demands that we admit that we encounter it as frequently there as in the Christian world (Haas, *Idee und Ideal,* 3). In the current scene it is Gorbachev, the publicly confessed confirmed atheist, who practices it, while Reagan and Bush and indeed most Western leaders follow his moral leadership because they really have no other option.

17. See Walter Bauer, "Das Gebot der Feindesliebe und die alten Christen," *ZTK* (1917): 37–54.

18. O. J. F. Seitz, "Love Your Enemies: The Historical Setting of Matthew V.43f.; Luke VI.27f.," *NTS* 16 (1969/1970): 39–54.

19. W. C. van Unnik, "Die Motivierung der Feindesliebe in Lukas 6:32–35," *NovT* 8 (1966): 284–300.

20. Dieter Lührmann, "Liebet eure Feinde (Lk 6,27–36/Mt 5,39–48)" *ZTK* 69 (1972): 412–438.

21. Paul Hoffmann, *Studien zur Theologie der Logienquelle* (NTAbh n.F. 8; Münster: Verlag Aschendorff, 1972).

22. Jürgen Becker, "Feindesliebe-Nächstenliebe-Bruderliebe: Exegetische Beobachtungen als Anfrage an ein ethisches Problemfeld," *ZEE* 25 (1981): 5–18, citation from p. 6.

23. J. Sauer, "Traditionsgeschichtliche Erwägungen zu den synoptischen und paulinischen Aussagen über Feindesliebe und Wiedervergeltungsverzicht," *ZNW* 76 (1985): 21–26; Christoph Burchard, "Das doppelte Liebesgebot in der frühen christlichen Überlieferung," in *Der Ruf Jesu und die Antwort der Gemeinde* (ed. E. Lohse; FS J. Jeremias zum 70. Geburtstag; Göttingen: Vandenhoeck & Ruprecht, 1970), 39–62.

24. Becker, "Feindesliebe-Nächstenliebe-Bruderliebe," 16.

25. Simon Legasse, *"Et qui est mon prochain?" Etude sur l'objet de l'agapè dans le Nouveau Testament* (Lectio Divina 136; Paris: Editions du Cerf, 1989), 100.

26. Becker, "Feindesliebe-Nächstenliebe-Bruderliebe," 8.

27. Ethelbert Stauffer, *"agapaō," TDNT,* 1:35–55, citation from p. 42.

28. Andreas Nissen, *Gott und der Nächste im antiken Judentum* (WUNT 15; Tübingen: J. C. B. Mohr [Paul Siebeck], 1974), 416.

29. John Piper, *"Love Your Enemies": Jesus' Love Command in the Synoptic Gospels and in the Early Christian Paraenesis* (SNTSMS 38; Cambridge: Cambridge University Press, 1979), 91–92, 204 n. 83.

30. Already in 1934 in his article on love in Kittel, Quell observed that the Hebrew Bible allows for the possibility that "enemy love" is included in love for the neighbor. He concludes that what is in view are concrete acts of love, but not an attitude *(Gesinnung)* of love toward the enemy: "only a specific relation to the enemy is obligated which brings about the practical training leading to enemy love" *(TWNT,* 1:26 [Klassen trans.]).

31. R. Travers Herford, *Pirke Aboth: The Ethics of the Talmud; Sayings of the Fathers* (New York: Schocken Books, 1971), 37–38.

32. Nissen, *Gott und der Nächste,* 389–415.

33. H.-J. Kraus, *Psalmen* (2 vols.; Neukirchen: Neukirchener Verlag, 1960), 1:415–419.

34. See Klassen, *Love of Enemies,* 119–121.

35. Here I follow the general thrust of Joachim Jeremias, *Jesus' Promise to the Nations* (London: SCM Press, 1956), 41–46, although I suspect the wrath of the synagogue that Jesus experienced in Nazareth was based more on his illustrations than on the absence of the theme of vengeance.

36. I am of course aware that the Fourth Gospel has Jesus laying down his life for his friends (John 15:13).

37. Becker, "Feindesliebe-Nächstenliebe-Bruderliebe," 7.

38. See Lührmann ("Liebet eure Feinde") who describes as foolhardy anyone who would doubt the genuineness; but see Sauer, "Traditionsgeschichtliche Erwägungen," 23.

39. Helmut Koester, *Synoptische Überlieferung bei den apostolischen Vätern* (Berlin: Akademie-Verlag, 1957), 44, 76.

40. Eric Osborn, "The Love Commandment in Second Century Christian Writings," *SeC* 1 (1981), 223–243.

41. Haas, *Idee und Ideal.*

42. Waldmann, *Die Feindesliebe.*

43. Bauer, "Das Gebot."

44. Klassen, *Love of Enemies.* With respect to the origin of the saying, Sauer ("Traditionsgeschichtliche Erwägungen") concludes essentially the same thing but does not stress as much the creativity of Jesus and Paul.

45. Piper, *"Love Your Enemies,"* 56–65.

46. "A love for the enemy, even for the personal, not religious-moral enemy, consequently does not exist in Judaism; not only is it not present in our preserved sources but is ruled out from the outset and must be ruled out, if not, beginning with the starting point, the whole structure (*Gesamtgefüge*) of the Jewish ethos and consequently revelation itself is jeopardized (*ins Wanken geraten soll*)" (Nissen, *Gott und der Nächste,* 316).

47. Piper, however, is able to follow his teacher, Leonhard Goppelt, and find in the text support for resisting wrong for the sake of his neighbor. As long as this is done without hatred, from which faith frees, this accords with the Sermon on the Mount. How this is derived from the text itself is not clear; but the shades of Luther's two kingdoms view, now largely discredited, are obvious.

48. Sauer, "Traditionsgeschichtliche Erwägungen," 21, 23, 26, and n. 160.

49. See van Unnik, "Die Motivierung."

50. Klassen, *Love of Enemies,* 14.

51. Van Unnik; and Albrecht Dihle, *Die goldene Regel: Eine Einführung in die Geschichte der antiken und frühchristlichen Vulgärethik* (Göttingen: Vandenhoeck & Ruprecht, 1962).

52. Richard A. Horsley, "Ethics and Exegesis: 'Love Your Enemies' and the Doctrine of Non-Violence," *JAAR* 54 (1986): 3–31, esp. 23. See also idem, *Jesus and the Spiral of Violence: Jewish Resistance in Roman Palestine* (San Francisco: Harper & Row, 1987), 272–273. I have no quarrel with Horsley's attempt to find the social context of this saying. I simply see no reason to restrict it to the immediate social context.

53. So Wolfgang Schrage, *The Ethics of the New Testament* (Philadelphia: Fortress Press, 1988): "Personal, religious enemies, the enemies of God and of God's people . . . but political and social enemies are also included" (p. 76). Surely few things so clearly indicate the shift in scholarship as the prominent place given in Schrage's book to the command to love one's enemies.

54. Of course, between the time Jesus spoke those words and when the Gospel editors recorded them the definition of enemy changed; few definitions change as quickly.

55. See, e.g., Carl Friedrich von Weizsäcker, "Die intelligente Feindesliebe," in idem, *Der bedrohte Friede: Politische Aufsätze 1945–1983* (Stuttgart: Carl Hanser Verlag, 1981), 535–537. The most thorough contributions in this area are by Wolfgang Huber and Hans-Richard Reuter.

56. Heinz-Wolfgang Kuhn, "Das Liebesgebot Jesus als Tora und als Evangelium: Zur Feindesliebe und zur christlichen und jüdischen Auslegung der Bergpredigt," in *Vom Urchristentum zu Jesus* (ed. H. Frankemölle and K. Kertelge; FS Joachim Gnilka; Freiburg: Herder, 1989), 194–230.

57. Ibid., 228.

58. Birger Gerhardsson, "Agape and Imitation of Christ," in *Jesus, the Gospels and the Church* (ed. E. P. Sanders; FS W. R. Farmer; Macon, Ga.: Mercer University Press, 1987), 163–176.

59. W. Monselewski, *Der barmherzige Samaritaner* (Tübingen: J. C. B. Mohr [Paul Siebeck], 1967).

60. Ibid., 166–174.

61. Contra F. Maass, "Die Selbstliebe nach Leviticus" (FS F. Baumgaertel; Erlanger Forschungen; *Geisteswissenschaften* 10 [1959], 109–113.

62. Otto Michel, "Das Gebot der Nächstenliebe in der Verkündigung Jesu," in *Zur sozialen Entscheidung* (Tübingen: J. C. B. Mohr [Paul Siebeck], 1947).

63. Anders Nygren, *Agape and Eros: A Study of the Christian Idea of Love* (London: SPCK; Philadelphia: Westminster Press, 1953), 217.

64. Nissen, *Gott und der Nächste*, 287–288.

65. Rudolf Bultmann, *Das Evangelium des Johannes* (Göttingen: Vandenhoeck & Ruprecht, 1959), 405–406.

66. Jürgen Heise, *Menein in den johanneischen Schriften* (Tübingen: J. C. B. Mohr [Paul Siebeck], 1967), 171.

67. Ibid., 28.

68. See Raymond E. Brown, *The Community of the Beloved Disciple* (New York: Paulist Press, 1979), 131–135.

69. As C. H. Dodd puts it, "The test for the reality of the experience of union with God in Christ is the imitation of Christ" (*The Johannine Epistles* [London: Hodder & Stoughton, 1946], 32).

70. Martin Rese, "Das Gebot der Bruderliebe in den Johannesbriefen," *TZ* 14 (1985): 54.

71. Ibid.

72. W. Bousset, *Die Offenbarung Johannis* (Göttingen: Vandenhoeck & Ruprecht, 1966), 271.

73. Herbert Preisker, *Das Ethos des Urchristentum* (Gütersloh: C. Bertelsmann, 1949), 205 [1st ed., p. 185]. Friedrich Nietzsche described it as "the most obscene of all the written outbursts which has revenge on its conscience" and would have us "appraise at its full value the profound logic of the Christian instinct, when over this very book of hate it wrote the name of the disciple of love" (*The Genealogy of Morals*, vol. 13 of *The Complete Works of Friedrich Nietzsche*).

74. Bauer, *Das Gebot,* 40.

75. W. D. Davies, "Ethics in the NT," *IDB*, 2:176.

76. D. H. Lawrence, *Apocalypse* (London, Penguin Books, 1931), who does recognize the difference between Greek and Hebrew images (p. 54) but in the end has only contempt for the book and makes no effort to enter into its imagery. The tone of the Revelation is a "grandiose scheme for wiping out and annihilating everybody who wasn't of the elect . . . in short, of climbing up himself right on to the throne of God" (p. 9).

77. C. G. Jung, *Answer to Job* (New York: Meridian Books, 1960), 133–203.

78. George B. Caird, *The Revelation of St. John the Divine* (New York: Harper & Row, 1966).

79. Ibid., 19.

80. Ibid., 280.

81. William Klassen, "Vengeance in the Apocalypse of John," *CBQ* 28 (1966): 300–311. See also Adela Yarbro Collins, *Crisis and Catharsis: The Power of the Apocalypse* (Philadelphia: Westminster Press, 1984), especially the last chapter.

82. Sauer ("Traditionsgeschichtliche Erwägungen," 26) suggests that the command and the words "Do good to those who hate you" became part of the tradition about the middle of the 50s of the first century.

83. Klassen, "Coals of Fire"; and Ernst Käsemann, *Commentary on Romans* (Grand Rapids: Wm. B. Eerdmans Publishing Co., 1980), ad loc.

84. Krister Stendahl, "Hate, Non-Retaliation and Love. 1QS x, 17–20 and Romans 12:19–21," *HTR* 55 (1962): 343–355.

85. Abraham Malherbe, "Antisthenes and Odysseus and Paul at War," *HTR* 76 (1985): 143–173.

86. In a paper read at the conference, "The Pacifist Impulse in Historical Perspective," held in honor of Peter Brock, May 9–12, 1991. Paper forthcoming in the proceedings.

87. So Collins, *Crisis,* 170.

88. Peter Lampe, "Die Apokalyptiker—ihre Situation und ihr Handeln," in *Eschatologie und Friedenshandeln* (Ulrich Luz et al.; Stuttgart: Verlag Katholisches Bibelwerk, 1981), 104–106, 112.

89. Klaus Wengst, *Pax Romana* (Philadelphia: Fortress Press, 1987), 135. I have explored the topic "Peace in the Apocalyptic Communities" at greater length in a paper read at the annual SNTS meeting in 1991.

90. Albert Camus, *The Rebel* (New York: Vintage Books, 1957), 302–306.

91. Victor Paul Furnish, *The Love Command in the New Testament* (Nashville: Abingdon Press, 1972), 66–67.

92. Irving Singer's three-volume opus on love (*The Nature of Love*) touches on enemy love and indeed compares Aquinas's view of love of enemies with that of Freud and judges the latter never to have attained the wholesome vision of what humans can attain through love (1:350–351). Yet he surprisingly pontificates: "When Jesus exhorts us to love our enemies, he does not expect us to stop annihilating them. If they are enemies of God, they must be dispatched to the safekeeping of hell, and as rapidly as possible" (1:262). Fortunately such nonsense is not often heard among theologians anymore. See Irving Singer, *The Nature of Love,* vol. 1: *Plato to Luther* (Chicago: University of Chicago Press, 1966).

2

Transforming Nonresistance: From *Lex Talionis* to "Do Not Resist the Evil One"

Dorothy Jean Weaver

Strewn across the landscape of the New Testament Gospels are numerous sayings that have over time gained notoriety as "the hard sayings of Jesus." These are the sayings that not only create controversy for the exegetes but also provide embarrassment for the expositors. They are the words that—if truth be told—we might wish Jesus had never spoken[1] or the Gospel writers had never preserved.

A prime case in point is the saying in Matt. 5:38–42.[2] There can be little question that, word for word and phrase for phrase, this text has stirred up as much controversy and embarrassment as any of the so-called "hard sayings of Jesus":

Matthew

5:38   You have heard that it was said,
        Eye in place of eye
        and tooth in place of tooth.

5:39   But I say to you,
        Do not resist (*mē antistēnai*) the one who is evil (*tō ponērō*).
            But if someone strikes you on the right cheek,
                turn to them the other cheek as well.

5:40   And if someone wishes to sue you and take your tunic,
        let them take your cloak as well.

5:41   And if someone compels you to go one mile,
        go with them for two.

5:42   Give to the one who asks of you;
       and do not reject the one who wishes to borrow from you.*

Matthew 5:39a alone presents a whole spectrum of difficulties for
the exegetes. The questions raised by this text range from the most
specific exegetical issues to the most fundamental hermeneutical
concerns. At virtually no point is there consensus on how to resolve
the difficulties or answer the questions.

The difficulties begin with the translation of the text. The command of Matt. 5:39a, *mē antistēnai tō ponērō*, contains only two
key words, *antistēnai* and *ponērō*. The contextual force of both of
these words is disputed.

The command *mē antistēnai* has traditionally been understood as
a general call "not to resist [evil]."[3] As J. C. Fenton puts it, "The
Law allowed a person who had been wronged to take an equivalent
from the person who had wronged him. Jesus will not allow retaliation of this kind: evil actions are not to be resisted."[4] A variation
on this interpretation views *mē antistēnai* as the call not to engage
in *stasis*, namely, "violent rebellion," "armed revolt," or "sharp dissension" (cf. Mark 15:7; Luke 23:19, 25; Acts 19:40).[5] An alternative assessment of Matt. 5:39a, however, views this command as the
specific charge "not to testify against an evildoer in a court of law."[6]
In Stuart Currie's words:

> Matthew wants it understood that Jesus quoted Deut. 19:21: "You
> have heard it was said, 'An eye for an eye and a tooth for a tooth,' "
> and then went on to add, "But I tell you, 'Do not protest against the
> wrongdoer. Don't file a complaint; don't make a court case of it,
> don't seek damages.' "[7]

The substantive *tō ponērō* fares little better than the verbal form
mē antistēnai. Here the translation hinges on interpretation of the
grammatically ambiguous dative singular form of *tō ponērō*. If *mē
antistēnai* is interpreted in juridical terms ("Do not testify against
. . . in a court of law"), then *tō ponērō* is most naturally construed
as a masculine form and thus in personal terms ("the one who is
evil").[8] But those who interpret *mē antistēnai* in the more general
sense of "do not resist" diverge in their understandings of the "evil"
not to be resisted. *Tō ponērō* is variously construed as a masculine
form with a human referent ("the one who is evil"),[9] as a masculine
form with reference to Satan ("the Evil One"),[10] as a neuter form

---

*All translations of the Greek NT and LXX are by the author.

("that which is evil"),[11] and as a fundamentally ambiguous term carrying both personal and impersonal force.[12]

A second question with regard to Matt. 5:39a and the related sayings concerns the social context of these words of Jesus and the subsequent social settings within which they were handed down in the early church. Gerd Theissen cites first-century Jewish precedents for the effective use of nonviolent tactics as a means of social protest against the Romans.[13] He concludes from this evidence that Jesus formulated his sayings on nonviolence and love of the enemy in a setting in which such concepts would not have been rejected out of hand by those to whom Jesus spoke.[14]

Richard Horsley, however, rejects that notion. As he views it, "the focus of 'love your enemies' and the related sayings . . . is not on the Romans or even on domestic political enemies."[15] Instead, these words "depict circumstances of severe economic hardship among those addressed,"[16] circumstances in which "people are at each other's throats, hating, cursing, and abusing."[17] As a result, "these sayings of Jesus . . . call people in local village communities to take economic responsibility for each other in their desperate circumstances."[18]

The differences are not resolved when one moves from the level of oral tradition (the words of Jesus) to the level of sayings source (Q). Theissen attributes the transmission of the sayings in question to "wandering charismatics," Christian prophets who were often driven from town to town by the persecution they encountered and for whom Jesus' words about nonviolence and love of the enemy would have had immediate relevance.[19] Here as well, Horsley objects, maintaining that for Q "the context indicated by the content of the individual sayings is that of social-economic relations in a village or town."[20]

Nor is there consensus on the social setting of the Matthean text. Theissen assesses the Matthean context as that of the Jewish Revolt and the succeeding postwar era, a time in which Jesus' words about love of enemy would have contrasted noticeably with prevailing Jewish sentiment concerning the Romans.[21] Here Horsley acknowledges that "Matthew evidently reinterpreted the thematic saying he found in Q, 'love your enemies,' to refer to persecutors of Jesus' followers."[22] But he once again concludes that "most of the other sayings . . . refer to the internal relations of the local community."[23]

A third question, integrally linked to that of social context, relates to the focus of the sayings in question. Here viewpoints span the spectrum. On the one end Martin Hengel, citing Luke 6:27–36∥Matt. 5:38–48 as his evidence, finds there both "the conscious rejection of violence" and "the heart of the proclamation of Jesus."[24] Hengel's view concerning the focus of these texts attracts wide scholarly support.[25] On the other end of the spectrum, however, Horsley draws the opposite conclusion from his study of the same texts:

> Perhaps Jesus advocated non-violence. Yet there is little or no evidence that he ever directly or explicitly addressed this issue of violence vs. non-violence. Surely non-violence was not the primary focus or purpose of his praxis and preaching. . . . Since the sayings grouped with "love your enemies" do not refer to foreign or political enemies and do not focus on the question of violence, the lesser components of the usual picture of Jesus as advocate of non-violence will not hold together.[26]

But beyond the questions concerning the translation, social context, and focus of Matt. 5:38–42 lies an even more difficult question, one that concerns the ethical force of the text and the scope of its applicability. It is this question above all others which haunts the exegetes, embarrasses the expositors, and classifies Matt. 5:38–42 among "the hard sayings of Jesus."

Viewpoints on this issue divide into two major camps. A large majority of scholars view the sayings of Matt. 5:38–42 as words of Jesus addressed to individual disciples. As such, these words are applicable strictly on the personal level, between individuals, a sphere either explicitly or implicitly distinguished from that of social structures and state institutions.[27] The comments of W. D. Davies and Dale C. Allison exemplify this approach:

> While in the Pentateuch the *lex talionis* belongs to the judiciary process, this is not the sphere of application in Matthew. Jesus . . . does not overthrow the principle of equivalent compensation on an institutional level—that question is just not addressed—but declares it illegitimate for his followers to apply it to their private disputes.[28]

Other scholars, by contrast, view the words of Jesus as addressed not solely, nor even most importantly, to individual disciples but rather to the church itself as the community of disciples.[29] Viewed in this light, the words of Jesus are seen to have "political" implications that move well beyond the "private sphere." As Luise Schottroff puts it,

> Non-resistance must be applied concretely in the area of politics. In this way Matt. 5:39–41 par. would have been understood in two different ways, the one within the community and the other toward

outsiders. Within the community it would mean refusing to plan an insurrection or to put up a show of violent resistance. Toward those outside it would mean assuring everyone of peaceable intentions, making a political apology: We Christians are not revolutionaries.[30]

Without any question, however, the most fundamental controversy surrounding Matt. 5:38–42 concerns the relationship between these words of Jesus and the Jewish law to which they respond, the *lex talionis* (Ex. 21:22–25; Lev. 24:19–20; Deut. 19:15–21). Here, as elsewhere, viewpoints span the spectrum.

John Piper represents one end of the discussion. In his words,

> Jesus' command not to resist evil (Mt 5:39–42) demands the opposite of the Old Testament legal principle, "an eye for an eye and a tooth for a tooth." . . . If and when Jesus' word is binding, then the other is not. . . . The antithesis between this Old Testament legal principle and Jesus' command is real. Taken absolutely they exclude each other; they are contradictory. Jesus was in some sense abolishing the *lex talionis*.[31]

On the other end of the discussion Horsley rejects this "antithetical" approach. In its place he proposes an approach based on the concept of "fulfillment":

> These sayings do not constitute new Law in the broad sense, certainly not to the point of abolishing the old, Mosaic Law. . . . Like many other assumptions and conclusions about these sayings, this misconception is rooted in the acceptance of the Matthean framing of the material into "antitheses." Since the early redaction criticism on Matthew and the Sermon on the Mount, it has been clear that Matthew implies no abolition of the old Law in favor of the new. Jesus has come to fulfill the Law, to restore the proper functioning of the Law to the true righteousness originally intended by God in giving the Torah.[32]

As the evidence indicates, Matt. 5:38–42 has over time been the object of intense scrutiny. Study of this text has led to significant controversy and virtually no consensus. The passage has clearly earned its reputation as one of "the hard sayings of Jesus." Nor is that reputation likely to be dislodged in the future. Yet it is precisely for this reason that Matt. 5:38–42 continues to lure scholars back for yet one more examination of an elusive text. Such is the nature of the task at hand.

Matthew 5:38–42 in Canonical Context:
The *Lex Talionis*

If Matt. 5:38–42 has aroused controversy on almost all fronts, there are nevertheless two points on which scholarship is unanimous: (1) Matthew 5:38 presents a citation, in the words of Jesus,[33] of the *lex talionis,* the "law of retaliation," as found in the Jewish scriptures (Ex. 21:22–25; Lev. 24:19–20; Deut. 19:15–21);[34] and (2) Matt. 5:39–42 presents Jesus' words in response to that "law of retaliation." It is these two points of consensus which create the point of departure for the following study and provide its basic structure. If Matt. 5:38–42 is a response to the Jewish *lex talionis,* then analysis of this "law of retaliation" is prerequisite to analysis of the Matthean text.

The first matter for consideration, then, is the Jewish *lex talionis.* This law was neither unique to the Jewish people nor original with them.[35] The origins of the *lex talionis* reach far back—to "extreme antiquity"[36]—within ancient Near Eastern society, apparently to legal formulations governing the intertribal relationships of nomadic peoples.[37] Widespread literary evidence—from the Code of Hammurabi and the Middle Assyrian Laws to Greek, Roman, and Jewish formulations, both scriptural and rabbinic[38]—points to the virtual universality of such a "law of retaliation" in the ancient world.

The force of this law in its original formulation was unambiguous: The person who has injured another shall receive back in punishment the same injury that he or she has inflicted upon the victim.[39] The *lex talionis,* however, was not license for personal acts of vengeance against the evildoer. Instead, this law was invoked and carried out by the court of law as an act of public justice.[40] Accordingly, the intent of the law was to prohibit personal acts of vengeance by relegating justice to the courts and strictly delimiting the punishment to be meted out.[41]

It was this ancient and universal law which found its way into the Jewish scriptures and stands as the backdrop for the words of Jesus in Matt. 5:38–42. But before comparisons can be drawn between the Jewish *lex talionis* and the Matthean text, there is a prior question to be resolved. Since there are three versions of the *lex talionis* within the Jewish scriptures (Ex. 21:22–25; Lev. 24:19–20; Deut. 19:15–21), it will be essential to establish which one of these formulations lies most directly behind the Matthean text.

A comparison of Matt. 5:38–39a and the three LXX versions of the *lex talionis* indicates that Deut. 19:15–21 has the strongest verbal and contextual links to Matt. 5:38–39a. All three LXX passages mirror the Matthean text word for word in the language of the talionic formula, "eye in place of eye, tooth in place of tooth" (*ophthalmon anti ophthalmou, odonta anti odontos*).[42] But only in the Deuteronomic text does the verbal linkage move beyond the talionic formula to the description of the situation calling forth such punishment. In Deuteronomy, as in Matthew, the text focuses on matters of "opposition"/"resistance" (*anthistēmi*) and "evil" (*ponēros*).[43] In the light of the fact that these two terms constitute the key vocabulary of Matt. 5:39a, this linkage is of major significance. Accordingly, both the verbal evidence and the contextual evidence identify Deut. 19:15–21 as the literary backdrop to Matt. 5:38–42.[44]

This linkage is crucial to the understanding of the Matthean text. If the Deuteronomic version of the *lex talionis* provides the literary backdrop to Matt. 5:38–42, then by the same token it provides the theological backdrop to the Matthean text as well. This raises a second question: What is the significance of Deut. 19:15–21? Or in other words, what meaning does the *lex talionis* derive from its specifically Deuteronomic context?[45]

The answer to this question begins with an examination of the overall literary-theological context in which the talionic formula is found, the legal corpus of Deuteronomy. This body of laws is effectively framed by parallel formulations in Deut. 6:1–3 (the words of Moses) and Deut. 27:9–10 (the words of Moses and the Levitical priests) which characterize their substance:

Deuteronomy

6:1   And these are the commandments
          and the regulations
          and the decrees
              which the Lord our God commanded me
              to teach you
              that you should do thus
              in the land which you are entering, to inherit it,
                  in order that you fear
                      the Lord your God
6:2   and keep
              all his regulations
              and his commandments
              which I am commanding you today—
                  you
                  and your children
                  and your children's children—

all the days of your life,
in order that you have a long life.
6:3   And you shall hear, Israel,
and you shall be careful to do
these commandments and regulations and decrees,
in order that it be well with you
and that you be greatly multiplied,
just as the Lord, the God of your ancestors,
promised to give you
a land flowing with milk and honey.

27:9   And Moses and the Levitical priests spoke to all Israel,
saying,
Be silent and hear, Israel:
On this day you have become
a people belonging to the Lord your God.
27:10   And you shall obey
the voice of the Lord your God,
and you shall do
all his commandments
and his regulations
which I am commanding you today.

As this framework makes clear, the legal corpus of Deuteronomy is addressed to the people of Israel as a unified body ("all Israel": 27:9a; "Israel": 6:3; 27:9b)[46] whose corporate identity lies in the fact that they are "a people who belong to the Lord [their] God" (*eis laon kyriō tō theō sou:* 27:9). The Deuteronomic legal corpus itself consists of "the commandments, the regulations, and the decrees" (6:1; 27:10) which, as Moses indicates to the people, "the Lord our God commanded me to teach you" (6:1).

Prominently bracketing this legal corpus is the charge to the Israelite community to "hear and do" all those "commandments, regulations, and decrees" which Moses has received from the Lord and now passes on to them.[47] The urgency of this imperative relates to the two factors that have primary impact on the life of the Israelite community, the "land which they are entering" (6:1) and the "God to whom they belong" (27:9).

The "land which they are entering," on the one hand, is no empty territory. Rather, it is filled with nations that are not only "great" (*mega:* 1:28; 4:38; 7:1; 9:1) and "many" (*poly:* 1:28; 7:1, 17) but also "stronger" (*ischyroteron:* 4:38; 7:1; 9:1) and "more powerful" (*dynamoteron:* 1:28) than the Israelites. These nations have their own gods (*theoi heteroi:* 6:14; 13:6 [LXX 13:7]; *theoi tōn ethnōn:* 6:14; 13:7 [LXX 13:8]; 29:18 [LXX 29:17]; cf. 12:30), who lead them in turn into "abominable deeds" (*bdelygmata:* 18:9) and "impious acts" (*asebeian:* 9:4, 5). It is these nations, their gods, and their evil practices which will physically surround the Israelite community in "the land which they are entering" and thus exert a powerful influence upon them.

The other factor that enters the picture, however, is the character of the God to whom the Israelites belong. "The Lord [their] God" is described on the one hand as "a faithful God" (*theos pistos:* 7:9) who "keeps covenant . . . with those who keep [my] commandments" (*ho phylassōn diathēkēn . . . tois phylassousin tas entolas autou:* 7:9) and "does mercy . . . to those who love me" (*poiōn eleos . . . tois agapōsin me:* 5:10). On the other hand, however, this God is described as "a jealous God (*theos zēlōtēs:* 4:24; 5:9; 6:15) who "repays the sins . . . of those who hate me" (*apodidous hamartias . . . tois misousin me:* 5:9; cf. 7:10) and will "utterly destroy [the Israelites] from the face of the earth" (*exolethreusē se apo prosōpou tēs gēs:* 6:15; cf. 7:10) if they worship the gods of the nations round about them.[48]

It is because the Israelites live in the midst of "the nations" and yet belong to a "faithful"/"jealous" God that Moses impresses upon them the urgency of "hearing" and "doing" the "commandments, regulations, and decrees" of the Lord. This, then, is the overall literary-theological context of the *lex talionis* of Deuteronomy.

The fundamental task at hand, however, is the analysis of the talionic formula within its immediate context, Deut. 19:15–21:

Deuteronomy

19:15   No single witness shall prevail against a person
              with respect to any wrongdoing
              or any transgression
              or any sin which he might commit.
         Instead, every charge shall be established
              by the mouth of two witnesses or three.
19:16   But if an unjust witness sets himself against a person
         and accuses him of impious actions,
19:17   then the two people who have the dispute shall stand
                 before the Lord,
                 and before the priests,
                 and before the judges,
                     whoever they may be in those days,

19:18   And the judges shall examine the matter carefully.
        And if the unjust witness has in fact brought unjust witness
        and has opposed (*anestē*) his brother,
19:19   then you shall do to him in the same manner
            as he planned to do evil (*eponēreusato*) to his brother.
        And in this way you shall remove
            the evil one (*ton ponēron*) from your midst.
19:20   And when the rest of the people hear this,
            they will be afraid.
        And they will no longer carry out
            such evil (*to rhēma to ponēron touto*) in your midst.
19:21   Your eye shall not spare him:
            life in place of life,
            eye in place of eye (*ophthalmon anti ophthalmou*),
            tooth in place of tooth (*odonta anti odontos*),
            hand in place of hand,
            foot in place of foot.

This law concerns the bearing of witness in court. It is an apodictic law ("You shall/shall not . . .") which leads into a casuistic
ruling ("If . . . , then . . ."). The overall formulation identifies the
parties involved, the crime committed, the legal procedure to be
followed in dealing with the crime, the punishment to be meted out
to the offender, and the purposes to be achieved by carrying out this
punishment. Accordingly, the following analysis of Deut. 19:15–21
will focus on these issues.

The court case described here is one that, in one way or another,
implicates the entire Israelite community as involved parties. The
perpetrator of the crime is described as "the single witness" (*martys
heis:* 19:15), "the unjust witness" (*martys adikos:* 19:16, 18), and
ultimately "the evil one" (*ton ponēron:* 19:19). The victim of the
crime is alternately described simply as a "person" (*anthrōpou:*
19:15, 16) or more specifically as "his brother" (*tou adelphou autou:* 19:18, 19). Beyond these "two people who have the dispute"
(*hoi dyo anthrōpoi, hois estin autois hē antilogia:* 19:17) are "the
Lord" (*kyriou:* 19:17), the priests (*tōn hiereōn:* 19:17), and the
judges (*tōn kritōn:* 19:17), before whom the disputants are to stand
as they await a decision on their case. Beyond the legal framework
of the court lies the entire Israelite community, designated by the
corporate second-person singular form "you shall remove" (*exareis:*
19:19),[49] the second-person plural references to "from your midst"
(*ex hymōn autōn:* 19:19) and "in your midst" (*en hymin:* 19:20), and
the third-person plural reference to "the rest of the people" (*hoi epi-*

loipoi: 19:20). Accordingly, no sector of the Israelite community lies beyond the impact of this law.

The crime in question relates to the words and the actions of the "unjust witness." He is variously charged with "setting himself against a person" (*katastē . . . kata anthrōpou:* 19:16), "accusing him of impiety" (*katalegōn autou asebeian:* 19:16), "bringing unjust witness" (*emartyrēsen adika:* 19:18), "opposing his brother" (*anestē kata tou adelphou autou:* 19:18), and "planning to do evil to his brother" (*eponēreusato poiēsai kata tou adelphou autou:* 19:19). His crime is then summarized—as is his identity itself (*ton ponēron:* 19:19)—as "this evil deed" or simply "such evil" (*to rhēma to ponēron touto:* 19:20).

As a result, the actions of "setting oneself against," "accusing," "bringing unjust witness," and "opposing" not only correspond to each other but likewise give specific and communitarian definition to the "evil thing" that has been planned by the "evil one." Here "evil" is no abstract moral reality, to be defined in absolute terms detached from all reference to specific context. Rather, "evil" is defined as the concrete act of "opposing the brother," an act that both presupposes the context of the community and at the same time destroys the reality that it presupposes. The crime in question is above all else a crime against the entire community.

The description of the judicial process by which the "evil" is to be brought to light and the "evil one" brought to justice reinforces this communitarian concept. Here, however, the language points away from the disputants and toward the leadership of the community. The "two people who have the dispute" are instructed to stand "before the Lord" (*enanti kyriou:* 19:17), "before the priests" (*enanti tōn hiereōn:* 19:17), and "before the judges" (*enanti tōn kritōn:* 19:17) to present their case for adjudication.

Since "evil" is viewed as a crime against the community, it is the community itself, in the persons of its leadership, which is to take the initiative for responding to this crime. There is no question here of personal acts of vengeance carried out by the one who has been wronged. Both the authority and the responsibility for responding to "evil" belong to the community *as community.*

This is no insignificant task. The judges are pointedly instructed to "examine the matter carefully" (*exetasōsin . . . akribōs:* 19:18). Nor is the authority granted to the community a matter of insignificance. When the disputants bring their case for adjudication, they stand not merely before the priests and the judges but ultimately before the Lord. By the same token, when the judges decide the case, they are acting not finally on their own authority nor on that of the priests but rather on the authority of the Lord. Accordingly, justice within the community of Israel is seen to be not only public justice, as opposed to private revenge, but also divine justice initiated through human agents, the justice of God set in motion by the community in the persons of its leadership.

If the judicial process involves the entire community in the person of its leadership, the punishment for the crime involves the entire community in the persons of its membership. To begin with, the punishment itself is defined in communitarian terms: "And you shall do to him *in the same manner as he planned to do evil to his brother* (*hon tropon eponēreusato poiēsai kata tou adelphou autou*). It is precisely that "evil" which was intended to harm the brother *and thus, in effect, destroy the community* which now becomes the standard for the community's punishment of the evildoer.

Further, it is the community itself which is charged with the execution of this punishment: "*And you shall do to him* (*kai poiēsete autō:* 19:19a).[50] The divine justice authorized by the Lord of the community, initiated by the judges of the community, and defined by that crime which has destroyed the community is to be enacted by the community as a corporate body.

It is significant that it is precisely within this communitarian context that the talionic formula itself appears: "Your eye shall not spare him: life in place of life, eye in place of eye, tooth in place of tooth, hand in place of hand, foot in place of foot" (19:21b). This ancient formula, which in the light of its history certainly predates its present connection to the legal ruling concerning the "unjust witness,"[51] has now been impressed into service by the Deuteronomist as the explanatory gloss giving specific substance not only to the intended actions of the offender but, by the same token, to the nature of his punishment.

Accordingly, *hon tropon,* that is, the "same manner" by which the evildoer is to be punished, ranges from capital punishment ("life in place of life") to the exaction of member for member and limb for limb ("eye in place of eye, tooth in place of tooth, hand in place of hand, foot in place of foot"). It is this *hon tropon,* now linked by the Deuteronomist to the ancient talionic formula and defined by that same formula, which constitutes the fundamental response of the community to "the evil one [in their] midst." The evil deed intended against the "brother," and thus in reality against the community itself, determines *point for point* the punishment to be meted out to the evildoer by the community.

This linkage between the *lex talionis* and the law concerning the "unjust witness" has major hermeneutical implications. While question has been raised about the extent to which the *lex talionis* was literally enacted in the ancient world in general,[52] and about the centrality of the talionic principle within Israelite law in specific,[53] there can be little question about the role of the *lex talionis* within its Deuteronomic setting. By attaching the talionic formula to a law whose enforcement, contrary to that of the *lex talionis* itself, can scarcely be called into question, the Deuteronomist establishes the force of the talionic formula as that of viable legislation. The addition of the warning clause, "your eye shall not spare him,"[54] confirms this conclusion. For the Deuteronomist the *lex talionis* is an active and enforceable piece of legislation that defines in specific terms the punishment to be meted out to the "unjust witness."

This is confirmed by the presence of motive clauses, statements that indicate the purposes to be achieved through enactment of a law and in this way motivate the listeners to obey the law in question.[55] There are two such motive clauses attached to the ruling concerning the "unjust witness." The first of these points backward to the crime that has already been committed within the community: "And in this way you shall remove the evil one from your midst" (19:19b). The second one points forward, away from the crime, to the future life of the community: "And when the rest of the people hear this, they will be afraid. And they will no longer carry out such evil in your midst" (19:20). Both of these clauses, however, serve the common function of linking the law of the "unjust witness" to a broader pattern of laws within Deuteronomy.

Most important in this respect is the first of the motive clauses: "And in this way you shall remove the evil one from your midst" (*kai exareis ton poneron ex hymon auton*). This formula—either verbatim[56] or in a variant formulation[57]—is found throughout Deuteronomy in a prominent series of legal rulings,[58] each of which deals with a capital crime[59] and each of which legislates capital punishment as the means for dealing with the offender.[60]

Accordingly, the series as a whole concerns itself with capital punishment. This means that the primary emphasis of the law concerning the "unjust witness" lies on the first directive of the *lex talionis,* the call to exact "life in place of life."[61] While the talionic formula goes on from there to speak about "eye," "tooth," "hand," and "foot" as well, it is precisely the initial call—that is, to exact "life in place of life"—which establishes the link between this legal ruling and the remainder of the series.

The implications of this linkage are significant. What this means in the broadest terms is that for the Deuteronomist the fundamental hermeneutical key to interpretation of the *lex talionis* lies precisely in its association with the "removal formula," an unambiguous reference to the enforcement of capital punishment against an offender.

What this linkage means in more specific terms can be seen from closer examination of the "removal formula" of 19:19b. The grammatical form of the text (*ton ponēron* = accusative singular masculine[62]) determines that the object of the verb "remove" is personal rather than impersonal in its force and must therefore be translated as "the evil one."[63] Accordingly, the Israelites are charged to remove from their midst not simply "evil in general" but rather "the evil person in specific."[64]

Nor is there ambiguity about what this "removal" implies. As the talionic formula itself ("life in place of life") indicates and the linkage of this text to its broader context (laws mandating capital punishment) confirms, there is for the Deuteronomist one fundamental means for "removing the evil one from your midst," namely, *the execution of the offender by the community.*[65] This action alone will suffice to deal with "the evil one" and to "remove from the midst" of the community the "evil" that he has carried out.

Here the Deuteronomist's communitarian understanding of "crime and punishment" becomes most visible. The reference to "the midst" confirms that for the Deuteronomist "the evil one" is guilty not merely of "opposing his brother" by the "evil" that he has done but in fact of threatening the very existence of the Israelite community.[66] Viewed within the Deuteronomic context, it is apparent why the community is obligated to "remove the evil one *from their midst.*"[67] The Israelites are "a people holy to the Lord [their] God" (*laos hagios . . . tō theō sou:* 7:6; 14:2, 21; 26:19; cf. 27:9; 28:9). And the God to whom they are "holy" is a "jealous God" (*theos zēlōtēs:* 4:24; 5:19; 6:15), a God prepared to "utterly destroy [them] from the face of the earth" (*exolethreusē se apo prosōpou tēs gēs:* 6:15; cf. 7:10) if they worship the gods of the nations round about them. Accordingly, as "a people holy . . . to a jealous God" the Israelites cannot, by very definition, allow either "the evil one" or "the evil" that he has done to remain within their community.[68] Rather, the "evil" that has taken place *"in [their] midst,"* and that has in this way threatened the life of the community, must be removed *"from [their] midst"* through the execution of "the evil one."

Further, this execution must be carried out *by the community itself:* "And in this way *you* shall remove the evil one *from your midst.*"[69] If "evil" is by definition an offense *against the community,* then it must be *the community as community* that takes action to rid itself of this offense by "removing the evil one from [their] midst."[70]

The first motive clause (19:19b), then, points backward, to the crime that has already been committed, and instructs the community how to "remove" the "evil" that threatens both its identity and its existence. The second motive clause (19:20) looks forward, away from the crime, to the ongoing life of the community: "And when the rest of the people hear this, they will be afraid. And they will no longer carry out such evil in your midst" (*Kai hoi epiloipoi akousantes phobēthēsontai kai ou prosthēsousin eti poiēsai kata to rhēma to ponēron touto en hymin*). This "fear formula"[71] shows the ultimate concern of the Deuteronomist to be ethical in nature and not merely sacral.[72] While the "evil one" and the "evil" that he has committed must be removed from the midst of the community which is "holy to the Lord," that is not the end of the matter but rather only the beginning.

The ultimate concern here is the ethical impact of this act of "removal" upon the community that hears of it. The ruling concerning the "unjust witness" will achieve its intended purpose only if the Israelite community "hears" of the incident, "fears" God,[73] and "no longer carries out such evil in [its] midst." The "fear formula" serves, in the first instance, to deter the remainder of the Israelite community (*hoi epiloipoi*) from following in the footsteps of "the evil one" and continuing on in his "evil" practices.[74]

But within the Deuteronomic conception, "deterrence" is only the first half of the ethical concern. If the Israelites are called to the task of "removing the evil one from their midst" so that they will "no longer carry out such evil in their midst," this negative task merely highlights by contrast the positive task that lies beyond, namely, "doing what is good and right" (*poieō* + *to kalon kai to areston*: 6:18; 12:25, 28; 13:18 [LXX 13:19]; 21:9), a formulation directly parallel to "doing the commandments, etc." (*poieō* + *entolas,* etc.: 1:14, 18; 4:1, 5, 6, 14; 5:1, 27, 31, 32; 6:1, 3, 24, 25; and throughout). It is this positive imperative which defines the ethical import of the central command of Deuteronomy, "to love the Lord your God with your whole heart and your whole soul and your whole strength" (Deut. 6:5).[75] Thus it is this positive imperative which constitutes the ultimate ethical concern of the Deuteronomist.

Accordingly, the positive concern for "doing what is right and good" gives rise to the negative concern expressed in the "fear formula": The community cannot "do what is right and good" until they "fear [the Lord their God] and refrain from doing what is evil." As a result, the call to "hear, fear, and not do evil" is a *negative* command necessitated precisely by the *positive* ethical concern of the Deuteronomist.

Here lies, finally, the answer to the question concerning the role of the *lex talionis* within the larger context of Deuteronomy. What can be said about the "fear formula" can be said as well about the *lex talionis* as a whole. The command to exact "life for life" and in this way to "remove the evil one from your midst" is, for the Deuteronomist, the fundamental means of eradicating "evil" from the community *and in so doing* of empowering the community to "do what is good and right." This is the ultimate force of the *lex talionis* as found in Deut. 19:15–21.

Matthew 5:38–42 in Matthean Context: The Response of Jesus

The task that remains is to examine the text of Matt. 5:38–42 in the light of its canonical context, the *lex talionis* of Deut. 19:15–21. In order to highlight comparisons and contrasts between these texts, the analysis of the Matthean text will follow the same outline as that of the Deuteronomic text.

The initial question thus concerns the literary-theological context of this saying of Jesus within Matthew's Gospel. The immediate context of Matt. 5:38–42 is the first major discourse of Jesus within the framework of Matthew's narrative, the so-called Sermon on the Mount (Matt. 5:1–7:29).[76] Directly prior to this discourse Jesus has initiated his public ministry in Galilee and announced its fundamental concern, the kingdom of heaven (Matt. 4:17, 23; cf. 9:35; 11:1). Now in the Sermon on the Mount, Jesus' "inaugural address" to his listeners, he exposits his announcement of the kingdom of heaven by describing the characteristics and setting forth the imperatives of life within that kingdom. It is significant that Jesus frames this discussion in thoroughly Deuteronomic language and concepts. The passages that bracket this address (Matt. 5:17–20; 7:24–27) are strongly reminiscent, in both vocabulary and tone, of the passages that frame the Deuteronomic legal corpus (Deut. 6:1–3; 27:9–10):

Matthew

5:17   Do not think that I have come to repeal the law and the
      prophets.
      I have not come to repeal them but to fulfill them.
5:18   For I say to you, until heaven and earth pass away,
      neither the smallest letter
      nor the least stroke of the pen
         will pass away from the law until all things come to pass.
5:19   So whoever relaxes one of the least of these commandments
      and teaches people to do the same
      will be called "least" in the kingdom of heaven.

But whoever keeps the commandments
and teaches people to do the same
will be called "great" in the kingdom of heaven.
5:20   For I tell you, unless you exhibit surpassing righteousness,
greater than that of the scribes and Pharisees,
you will by no means enter into the kingdom of heaven.

7:24   So each one who hears these sayings of mine
and does them
can be compared to a wise man. . . .
7:26   And each one who hears these sayings of mine
and does not do them
can be compared to a foolish man.

The correspondences between the Matthean text and its Deuteronomic counterpart are evident. The Matthean framework passages, as do those of Deuteronomy, focus on "doing the commandments/words" (*poieō* + *tas entolas/tous logous:* 5:19a; 5:19b; 7:24; 7:26) and emphasize the language of "hearing and doing" (*akouō* + *poieō:* 7:24; 7:26).[77]

But the differences between the two texts are equally striking. While the Deuteronomic text concerns itself with "doing the commandments," the Matthean text heightens the language to that of "fulfilling the law and the prophets" (Matt. 5:17) and "exhibiting surpassing righteousness, greater than that of the scribes and Pharisees" (Matt. 5:20). As a result, more is at stake in the Matthean challenge to "do the commandments" than mere repetition of Deuteronomic language or the simple restatement of an ancient biblical command.

This conclusion is confirmed by the "antitheses" that follow in Matt. 5:21–48 and create the immediate context of 5:38–42. Here Jesus illustrates the character of "surpassing righteousness" through a series of six pronouncements (5:21–26, 27–30, 31–33, 34–37, 38–42, 43–48), each of which is structured in similar fashion: (1) "You have heard that it was said" + citation of a Jewish law; (2) "But I say to you" + saying of Jesus. Both the structure and the substance of these "antitheses" confirm that within the Matthean context "fulfilling the law and the prophets" and "exhibiting surpassing righteousness" move beyond the Deuteronomic conception of "doing the commandments."

Matthew identifies the addressees of the Sermon on the Mount as the disciples of Jesus, in distinction to the Jewish crowds: "And when [Jesus] saw the crowds, he went up onto the mountain. And when he had sat down, his disciples (*hoi mathētai autou*) came to him. And he taught them (*autous*)" (5:1–2).[78] The contents of the teachings point toward the same audience: "You are the light of the world" (5:13); "You are the salt of the earth" (5:14); "Blessed are you when they revile you and persecute you and say every evil thing against you, telling lies about you on my account" (5:11). The Sermon on the Mount is thus directed to the community of those who have left everything behind to become disciples of Jesus (cf. 4:18–22; 9:9; 19:27), children of the "Father who is in heaven" (5:16, 45, 48; 6:1, 4, 6, 8, 9, 14, 15, 18, 26, 32; 7:11, 21), and family to each other (5:22, 23, 24, 47; 7:3, 4, 5; cf. 12:46–50).[79]

As with the Israelite community, the disciples live in the midst of a wider community, with whom they come into close and frequent contact. This community is, for the most part, Jewish in makeup: "scribes" (*hoi grammateis:* 5:20; 7:29); "Pharisees" (*hoi Pharisaioi:* 5:20); "the council" (*to synedrion:* 5:22); "tax collectors" (*hoi telōnai:* 5:46); and "people" in general (*hoi anthrōpoi:* 5:16, 19; 6:1, 2, 5, 14, 15, 16, 18; 7:12). But this community includes as well those who are not Jewish, namely, the "Gentiles" (*ta ethnē:* 6:32; *hoi ethnikoi:* 5:47; 6:7).

With few exceptions, however, this community of Jews and Gentiles is described as hostile to the disciples of Jesus who live in their midst. They are depicted as engaging in a variety of activities that display this antagonism. They are the ones who "revile" (*oneidisōsin:* 5:11), "persecute" (*diōxōsin:* 5:11; *diōkontōn:* 5:44), "say evil things" (*eipōsin pan ponēron:* 5:11), and "tell lies" (*pseudomenoi:* 5:11) about the disciples. They are the "adversary" (*tō antidikō:* 5:25) who initiates court proceedings; the "council" (*tō synedriō:* 5:22) before whom people are brought to trial; the "judge" (*ho kritēs:* 5:25) who pronounces sentence; the "court assistant" (*tō hypēretē:* 5:25) who throws people into prison. In simple terms, they are "the evil one" (*tō ponērō:* 5:39a) and "the enemies" (*tous echthrous:* 5:44).

The God to whom Jesus' disciples belong as they live in the midst of a hostile community is, above all, their "Father who is in heaven" (5:16, 45, 48; 6:1, 4, 6, 8, 9, 14, 15, 18, 26, 32; 7:11, 21). This God is, as the title suggests, "King" of the "kingdom of heaven" (*basileia tōn ouranōn:* 5:3, 10, 19, 20; 6:10, 33; 7:21), the one who has heaven as "throne" (*thronos . . . tou theou:* 5:34) and earth as "footstool" (*hypopodion . . . tōn podōn autou:* 5:35). This one has ultimate power over the destiny of humans, granting "reward in heaven" (*ho misthos en tois ouranois:* 5:12; cf. 5:46; 6:1, 2, 5, 16) and "casting into Gehenna" (*ballō eis geennan:* 5:29; cf. v. 30).

At the same time, however, this God is not only "King" but also "Father," the one who "comforts" (*paraklēthēsontai:* 5:4), "grants inheritance" (cf. *klēronomēsousin:* 5:5), "satisfies" (*chortasthēsontai:* 5:6), "shows mercy" (*eleēthēsontai:* 5:7), grants "sight" of God (cf. *opsontai:* 5:8), "provides [food and clothing]" (*prostethēsetai:* 6:33), and "names his children" (*huioi theou klēthēsontai:* 5:9). Above all else, this Father in heaven is one who is "perfect" (*teleios:* 5:48), one who "lets the sun shine on both the evil and the good and sends rain on the just and the unjust" (*ton hēlion autou anatellei epi ponērous kai agathous kai brechei epi dikaious kai adikous:* 5:45).

This is the setting of the Sermon on the Mount. It is this community of disciples—"followers" of Jesus and "children" of their "Father in heaven" who at the same time live in the midst of hostile neighbors—to whom Jesus addresses the words of Matt. 5:38–42. As is now evident, these words both parallel Deut. 19:15–21 and move beyond it.

Moses' address to the people of Israel lays down the "commandments, regulations, and decrees" that are to govern the life of the Israelite community "in the land which they are entering, to inherit it" (Deut. 6:1). The urgency of these "commandments, regulations, and decrees" stems from the fact that the Israelites live in the midst of nations with "other gods," while they themselves are "a people holy . . . to a jealous God."

Jesus' address to his disciples describes the "surpassing righteousness" which "fulfills the law and the prophets" and thus governs the life of the kingdom of heaven, that "kingdom" which the disciples are "entering" (Matt. 5:20; cf. 5:3, 10) to "inherit" it (Matt. 25:34). The urgency of this "surpassing righteousness" emerges from the fact that they who live in the midst of "evil ones" and "enemies" are nevertheless "children" of a "perfect Father in heaven."

The saying of Matt. 5:38–42 itself, as each of the other antitheses, consists of two sections: (1) the formulaic statement "You have heard that it was said" (5:38a) followed by the substance of the law in question (5:38b); and (2) the formulaic statement "But I say to you" (5:39a) followed by Jesus' response to the law in question (5:39a–42). The substance of Jesus' response, in turn, consists of the command (5:39a) followed by two double sayings (5:39b/40; 5:41/42) which illustrate this command.[80]

Matthew

    5:38   You have heard that it was said,
           (*ēkousate hoti errethē*)

Eye in place of eye
(*ophthalmon anti ophthalmou*)
and tooth in place of tooth.
(*kai odonta anti odontos*)

5:39 But I say to you,
(*Egō de legō hymin*)
Do not resist the one who is evil.
(*mē antistēnai tō ponērō*)
But if someone strikes you on the right cheek,
(*all' hostis se rhapizei eis tēn dexian siagona sou*)
turn to them the other cheek as well.
(*strepson auto kai tēn allēn*)

5:40 And if someone wishes to sue you and take your tunic,
(*kai to thelonti soi krithēnai kai ton chitōna sou labein*)
let them take your cloak as well.
(*aphes auto kai to himation*)

5:41 And if someone compels you to go one mile,
(*kai hostis se angareusei milion hen*)
go with them for two.
(*hypage met autou dyo*)

5:42 Give to the one who asks of you;
(*to aitounti se dos*)
and do not reject the one who wishes to borrow from you.
(*kai ton thelonta apo sou danisasthai mē apostraphēs*)

Two primary parties are in focus in this text, a protagonist and an antagonist. The saying itself is addressed to a collective protagonist, a plural "you" (*ēkousate:* 5:38a; *hymin:* 5:39a) which must within this context be a reference to the disciples of Jesus (*hoi mathētai autou:* 5:1; *autous:* 5:2), the designated addressees of the discourse as a whole.[81] Accordingly, this text, like its Deuteronomic counterpart, is communitarian in its thrust. While the "community" in question has shifted its identity from "Israel" to "the disciples of Jesus," there can be little question about the fact that this text is addressed to a community *as community.*[82]

At the same time, the saying concerns itself with an individual antagonist, whom Jesus characterizes in 5:39 as "the one who is evil" (*tō ponērō*).[83] In distinction to the Deuteronomic text, however, the Matthean saying distinguishes the corporate "you" being addressed from the "evil one" in question. This suggests that the "evil one" is not a disciple but rather a member of the larger community of Jews and Gentiles which surrounds the disciple commu-

nity and is hostile to them.[84] Accordingly, this word of Jesus
instructs the community of disciples how to deal with the "evil one"
whom they encounter in the larger community of Jews and Gentiles
within which they live.[85]

The substance of the saying appears to confirm this conclusion.
In 5:39c–42 Jesus identifies the "one who is evil" by means of an
illustrative list of offenses ranging, in descending order,[86] from
physical assault (5:39c) to financial importunity (5:42a/b). "The one
who is evil" is that one who "strikes you on the right cheek" (5:39c),
"wishes to sue you and take your tunic" (5:40), "compels you to go
one mile" (5:41), "asks of you" (5:42a), and "wishes to borrow
from you" (5:42b).

At the top of the list (5:39c) and gravest of the offenses is that of
"striking [another] on the right cheek." This action could take place
in any Jewish setting where one person grows angry with another;
and it might well take place in those settings where the disciples of
Jesus and the message they bring are unwelcome.[87] It is undeniably
a physical assault upon the one thus struck.[88] But within such a
context the slap "on the right cheek"—by very definition a "backhanded" slap—represents not so much an act of physical brutality
that injures the victim as it does the supreme form of insult to the
one who receives the blow, a much more serious insult than a slap
with the open palm.[89]

Second on the list of offenses (5:40) is that of "wishing to sue
[another] and take [his] tunic." Here is a clear allusion to the apparently common Jewish practice of seizing a person's garment in
pledge for an unpaid debt. What is striking about this offense, however, is the type of garment that is seized, namely, the tunic (*chitōn*)
or undergarment. Jewish law (Ex. 22:25–27; Deut. 24:10–13, 17;
Amos 2:7–8) specifically prohibits extended seizure of the cloak
(*himation*) or outer garment, since that is the garment that serves its
owner at night as a blanket. No such restriction, however, applies to
the tunic (*chitōn*) or undergarment; and it is therefore this garment
which is requisitioned by "the one who is evil."[90]

The third offense (5:41), contrary to the first two, moves beyond
a strictly Jewish setting to identify a Gentile, specifically a Roman,
as "the one who is evil." Jesus' reference to "the one who compels
you to go one mile" points to the Roman military practice according
to which soldiers may "compel" (*angareuō*) individual civilians to
carry military gear or other burdens for the distance of a thousand
paces or one "mile."[91]

The final offenses on the list (5:42a/42b) fall under the common
rubric of financial importunity. Here "the one who is evil" is one

who "asks [money] of you" (5:42a) on the one hand or "wishes to borrow [money] from you" (5:42b) on the other. While neither of these actions is in and of itself "evil," their presence in the illustrative list of offenses committed by "the one who is evil" clearly implies that "asking" for money and "wishing to borrow" money are both viewed as importunate requests on the part of the one who asks.[92]

The illustrative list of offenses committed by "the one who is evil" thus ranges broadly over the spectrum of "evil" circumstances that the community of Jesus' disciples might face as they live in the midst of hostile neighbors both Jewish and Gentile. They are subject to physical abuse and verbal insult, lawsuits and corresponding loss of property, forced labor at the behest of occupying forces, and financial importunity. While the offenses that Jesus cites are specific in character (a slap on the *right* cheek; a lawsuit over a *tunic*), the form of the saying ("the one who . . . and the one who . . . and the one who . . . .") implies that this list of "offenses" is merely illustrative in nature and could go on indefinitely, limited only by the real-life experiences and the imagination of the disciples.[93]

Accordingly, the "evil" and the "evil one" to which Jesus refers do not differ in essence from the "evil" and the "evil one" of Deut. 19:15–21. But there is a striking difference in the procedure to be followed in response to such "evil." In distinction from Deut. 19:15–21 the setting of the Matthean text is not that of a court case. Not only is there no mention of an appearance "before the Lord, the priests, and the judges" (Deut. 19:17); but there is also, significantly, no mention of any "careful examination" by the judges (Deut. 19:18) to establish the guilt of the antagonist. By contrast, the character of the antagonist as "the one who is evil" is portrayed as a self-evident "given" of the situation. Further, the form of the saying encourages the community itself to define the character of "the one who is evil" by making its own additions to the open-ended list started by Jesus.[94] Within this context, "evil" is neither that which requires definition by means of legal process nor that which demands recourse by the courts on behalf of the community.

This conclusion is confirmed by the "antithetical" form of the saying, even apart from its substance. Jesus opens with "You have heard that it was said, 'Eye in place of eye and tooth in place of tooth,' " an unambiguous reference to the well-established legal procedure for dealing with cases of personal injury.[95] He goes on to add, "But I say to you . . . ," an indication that he is about to challenge the legal procedure to which he has just made reference. While the community is enjoined to take action, as becomes evident from the imperative that follows "But I say to you," this action lies beyond established courtroom procedures.

If procedures differ from those outlined in the Deuteronomic text, so does the response of the community to "the one who is evil." The ancient biblical principle of "punishment in kind" (*hon tropon*) and the corresponding command to exact "injury in place of injury" and "life in place of life"[96] give way to a startling new command: "But I say to you, *Do not resist the one who is evil.*" The "startle effect" (or, as Robert Tannehill describes it, the "imaginative shock"[97]) of this command derives from the form of the saying as well as from its substance.

The formulation of the saying as a *negative* command ("*do not resist the one who is evil*") indicates first of all that what Jesus is here challenging is a *normal* human response or a *conventional* practice of society, that which people, individually or collectively, are most likely to do under ordinary circumstances. Accordingly, "resisting the one who is evil" is just such an action, not only the instinctive reflex of the individual who has been wronged but even more significantly the corporate response of the community in accordance with established legal codes. It is just such a deep-rooted human/societal response that Jesus counters with the command "Do not resist. . . ."

The impact of this negative command can hardly be overestimated. With the words "do not resist," Jesus disallows both the principle of *hon tropon,* "punishment in kind," and the *lex talionis,* the "law of retaliation" which embodies that principle. In so doing, he invalidates the most ancient and fundamental standard that individuals and societies have for dealing with "the one who is evil."[98]

Nor is this the only difficulty with these words of Jesus. There is an even greater obstacle here which arises not merely from the negative formulation of the command but from the specific substance of the imperative as well: *"Do not resist . . . the one who is evil."* This command appears to be nothing less than a counsel of capitulation, the command to adopt a passive and powerless response in the face of aggressive and overpowering "evil."[99] Here Jesus instructs his disciples to concede *in advance* the superior power of "evil" and to submit themselves *without resistance* to all the brutalities and injustices perpetrated by "the one who is evil." This is not merely a "hard saying" of Jesus; this is nothing short of scandalous.[100]

But this is neither the end of the saying nor the end of the matter. This word of Jesus does not stop with the command "Do not resist the one who is evil." Rather, the primary command (5:39a) opens out immediately into a series of secondary imperatives (5:39b–42), each of them highly specific in nature:

Matthew

5:39b But if someone strikes you on the right cheek,
       turn to them the other cheek as well.
5:40   And if someone wishes to sue you and take your tunic,
       let them take your cloak as well.
5:41   And if someone compels you to go one mile,
       go with them for two.
5:42   *Give* to the one who asks of you;
       and *do not reject* the one who wishes to borrow from you.

Here the true force of Jesus' call "not to resist the one who is evil" finally comes to light. In the form and the substance of these secondary imperatives lies the key to the interpretation of the primary command. With one exception these imperatives are positive in their formulation: "turn," "let," "go," "give," and "do not reject."[101] It is precisely these positive imperatives which exegete the negative command of 5:39a ("Do not resist"). As a result, the command "Do not resist" is neither a call to passivity nor a counsel of capitulation.[102] Even while it constitutes in grammatical terms a negative command and in semantic terms a call to inaction, Jesus' command "not to resist the one who is evil" is, paradoxically, a positive command and a call to action.

The substance of the secondary imperatives confirms this conclusion. The most striking feature of these imperatives as a group is the radically, even absurdly, unanticipated character of the responses to which they challenge the listeners.[103] Those who have been insulted and physically abused by a backhanded slap are to turn the other cheek as well to the one who has assaulted them. Those who have been taken to court and sued over their *chitōn* or undergarment are to offer up their *himation* or outer garment as well to the adversary. Those who have been coerced into service carrying baggage for the occupying forces are to extend their services without coercion and carry the load for two miles instead of one. Those who have been importuned financially are to give without hesitation to those who ask money of them. The single observable principle that governs these responses is that they run directly counter to all human instinct, individual or societal.[104] As a result, the command "not to resist," far from being a call to passivity or a counsel of capitulation, constitutes a challenge to the most radical of human responses.

Nor is there any question about the ethical character of these re-

sponses. By placing the imperatives of 5:39b–42 in deliberate juxtaposition to the *lex talionis* ("eye in place of eye and tooth in place
of tooth"), a law that is not merely violent but ultimately death-
dealing, Jesus repudiates the essential violence of the talionic principle and establishes the character of his own call to action, by
contrast, as fundamentally life-affirming.

This is not the end of the matter. While the imperatives of 5:39b–
42 are without question "real life" commands calling for "real life"
responses,[105] these imperatives in no way exhaust the meaning of
Jesus' command "not to resist the one who is evil." Nor do they
function as so many "legal rules" to be observed. Rather, they serve
above all an "illuminating" function with respect to the command of
5:39a.[106] On the one hand, these imperatives create an illustrative
list of potential interpretations of the command "not to resist the one
who is evil." On the other hand, this list, because of its extreme
specificity and vividness, calls for its own extension to all those
other specific circumstances not here enumerated in which the community of Jesus' disciples likewise encounters "the one who is evil."
In this way the illustrative imperatives that Jesus sets forth not only
suggest specific ethical alternatives for the community of disciples
but ultimately reshape the entire ethical landscape. Such is the force
of the paradoxically "positive" command "not to resist."

But an even greater paradox comes to light here. Not only do the
illustrative imperatives of 5:39b–42 show Jesus' call "not to resist
the one who is evil" to be a positive command despite its negative
formulation. They also demonstrate that this command is one that
empowers the community of disciples, even while it appears to enjoin a stance of *powerlessness.* The fact that Jesus does not merely
invalidate the principle of *hon tropon* and the corresponding *lex talionis* but also illustrates a new mode of response to "the one who is
evil" means that *for the first time ever initiative has been placed in
the hands of the community.*

As long as the *lex talionis* was in force, the only option open to
the community for responding to the evildoer was to repay the evil
deed, in essentially mechanistic fashion, with "punishment in kind."
As a result, all prerogative for "action" remained with the evildoer;
while the community, bound by its own legal code, could do nothing
more than "react."

Now all this has changed. Precisely through the scandalous command "not to resist the one who is evil" (5:39a) and the absurdly
unanticipated imperatives that give it substance (5:39b–42) Jesus
paradoxically holds out to the community of disciples a power they
have never before experienced, *the power to act in the face of evil.*[107]

Initiative no longer belongs solely to "the one who is evil." Now through the word of Jesus the community of disciples finds itself empowered and impelled to respond to the evildoer with initiatives of its own which are as daring and unexpected as they are positive and life-affirming.

This is Jesus' answer to the (Deuteronomic) "law of retaliation." At this point the saying ends. There are no motive clauses and no further words of explanation.[108] After his listing of illustrative imperatives (5:39b–42) Jesus simply moves on to the sixth and final "antithesis" (5:43–48). But here in this final "antithesis" Jesus puts into words that which until now has remained unspoken. The motive clause that is missing from the command "not to resist the one who is evil" finds clear expression in the saying that follows:

Matthew

5:43   You have heard that it was said,
          You shall love your neighbor and hate your enemy.
5:44   But I say to you,
          Love your enemies and pray for those who are persecuting
          you,
                in order that you might be the children
                of your Father who is in heaven.
                For he makes his sun to rise
                    on the evil and the good [epi ponērous kai aga-
                    thous].
                and he sends rain
                    on the just and the unjust [epi dikaious kai adikous].

          . . . .
5:48   *You shall therefore be perfect,*
          as your Father in heaven is perfect.

The command to "love your enemies and pray for those who are persecuting you" states the obverse of the preceding command "not to resist the one who is evil." Accordingly, the motive clauses attached to the latter command apply as well to the former. As a result the command of 5:39a reads as follows in its "completed" form: "Do not resist the one who is evil . . . in order that you may be the children of your Father who is in heaven; for he makes his sun to rise on the evil and the good and he sends rain on the just and the unjust. You shall therefore be perfect, as your Father in heaven is perfect."

With this connection the picture is now complete and the comparison clear. It is because the Israelite community "belongs to a jeal-

ous God"—a God who "will utterly destroy [them] from the face of
the earth" if they follow the gods of the nations around them—that
they are commanded to "remove the evil one from [their] midst" by
exacting "life in place of life and member in place of member." It
is, by the same token, because the community of disciples are the
"children of a perfect Father"—who "makes his sun to rise on the
evil and the good and sends rain on the just and the unjust"—that
Jesus now commands them "not to resist the one who is evil."

For Matthew, as for Deuteronomy, the ethics of the community
of faith emerge directly from the community's theology, or, in other
words, from the community's understanding of the character of
God. It is this shared reality which confirms that Jesus *is indeed
"fulfilling the law and the prophets"* (5:17), *even as he proclaims
"But I say to you"* (5:21–48). It is, accordingly, in the light of this
same reality that the Deuteronomic command to "remove the evil
one from your midst" finds its ultimate "fulfillment" in the command of Jesus "not to resist the one who is evil."

Notes

1. Here I refer to the claims of the Gospel writers concerning what Jesus
said. I make no claims of my own concerning the *ipsissima vox* of Jesus;
nor will the following essay engage in the search for that *ipsissima vox*.
Rather, this study will focus its attention on the canonical form of Matt.
5:38–42 and the significance of this canonical text within its Matthean
context.

2. See Matt. 5:38–48‖Luke 6:27–36.

3. Cf. Robert Banks, *Jesus and the Law in the Synoptic Tradition* (Cambridge: Cambridge University Press, 1975), 196. On this interpretation of
antistēnai, see Gerald Friedlander, *The Jewish Sources of the Sermon on
the Mount* (1911; New York: KTAV, 1969, 66; Willoughby C. Allen, *A
Critical and Exegetical Commentary on the Gospel According to S.*[*sic*]
Matthew (ICC; 3rd ed.; Edinburgh: T. & T. Clark, 1912), 54; Erich Klos-
termann, *Das Matthäus-Evangelium* (HNT; 2nd rev. ed.; Tübingen:
J. C. B. Mohr [Paul Siebeck], 1927), 48; M.-J. Lagrange, *Evangile selon
Saint Matthieu* (7th ed.; Paris: Librarie Lecoffre, 1948), 112; Julius
Schniewind, *Das Evangelium nach Matthäus* (NTD 2; Göttingen: Vanden-
hoeck & Ruprecht, 1956), 67; H. Clavier, "Matthieu 5:39 et la non-
résistance," *Revue d'Histoire et de Philosophie Religieuses* 37 (1957): 44;
Floyd V. Filson, *A Commentary on the Gospel According to St. Matthew*
(London: Adam & Charles Black, 1960), 89; Krister Stendahl, "Hate,
Non-Retaliation and Love: 1QS x, 17–20 and Romans 12:19–21," *HTR* 55

(1962): 355; J. C. Fenton, *Saint Matthew* (London: Penguin Books, 1963), 92; Paul Gaechter, *Das Matthäus Evangelium* (Innsbruck: Tyrolia, 1963), 189; W. F. Albright and C. S. Mann, *Matthew* (AB; Garden City, N.Y.: Doubleday & Co., 1971), 68; Banks, 197–198; John Piper, *"Love Your Enemies": Jesus' Love Command in the Synoptic Gospels and in the Early Christian Paraenesis* (SNTSMS 38; Cambridge: Cambridge University Press, 1979), 53; Georg Strecker, *The Sermon on the Mount: An Exegetical Commentary* (Nashville: Abingdon Press, 1988), 82; and Ulrich Luz, *Matthew 1–7: A Commentary* (Minneapolis: Fortress Press, 1989), 329.

4. Fenton, 92. In a similar vein, see Strecker, 83.

5. Thus Walter Wink, *Violence and Nonviolence in South Africa: Jesus' Third Way* (Philadelphia: New Society Publishers, 1987), 13.

6. Stuart D. Currie is a major proponent of this interpretation in "Matthew 5:39a—Resistance or Protest?" *HTR* 57 (1964): 140–145. See also Adolf Schlatter, *Der Evangelist Matthäus: Seine Sprache, sein Ziel, seine Selbständigkeit* (5th ed.; Stuttgart: Calwer Verlag, 1959), 186; Walter Grundmann, *Das Evangelium nach Matthäus* (THKNT 1; Berlin: Evangelische Verlagsanstalt, 1968), 171; David Hill, *The Gospel of Matthew* (NCB; London: Oliphants, 1972), 127; Eduard Schweizer, *The Good News According to Matthew* (trans. David E. Green; London: SPCK, 1976), 129; Robert A. Guelich, *The Sermon on the Mount: A Foundation for Understanding* (Waco, Tex.: Word Books, 1982), 219–220; Robert H. Gundry, *Matthew: A Commentary on His Literary and Theological Art* (Grand Rapids: Wm. B. Eerdmans Publishing Co., 1982), 94; Richard A. Horsley, "Ethics and Exegesis: 'Love Your Enemies' and the Doctrine of Non-Violence," *JAAR* 54 (1986): 14; and W. D. Davies and Dale C. Allison, *A Critical and Exegetical Commentary on the Gospel According to Saint Matthew*, vol. 1: *Introduction and Commentary on Matthew I–VIII* (Edinburgh: T. & T. Clark, 1988), 543.

7. Currie, 145.

8. Thus Hill, 127; and Guelich, 219–220.

9. Thus Klostermann, 48; Schniewind, 67–68; Filson, 82; Stendahl, 355; Albright and Mann, 68; and Strecker, 82.

10. Thus Banks (pp. 197–198), who determines that "*ponēros*, as in 5.37; 6.13; 13.19, 38, must refer to Satan." Cf. Friedlander (pp. 66–67), who translates *ponērō* as "the Evil One, i.e., the world." But while this interpretation reaches back to Origen and Chrysostom (Davies and Allison, 543), it is widely disavowed in more recent scholarship. See the comments of Klostermann, 48; Lagrange, 112; Schniewind, 68; Gaechter, 189; and Strecker, 82–83.

11. Thus Lagrange, 112; Gaechter, 189; and Luz, 329.

12. Thus Allen, 54: "We need not ask as to the gender of *tō ponerō*. Just as in v. 37 it meant the evil and sinful element in life regarded from the abstract point of view, so here it is the same element contemplated as in action through an individual." See also Clavier, 50–52; and Fenton, 91.

Cf. Piper (pp. 52–53), who translates the phrase as "Do not resist evil" but cites James 5:6 ("the righteous person does not resist [the rich person]") as "an essential parallel" to Matt. 5:39a.

13. Gerd Theissen, "Gewaltverzicht und Feindesliebe (Mt 5, 38–48/Lk 6, 27–38) und deren sozialgeschichtlicher Hintergrund," 160–197 in *Studien zur Soziologie des Urchristentums* (WUNT 19; Tübingen: J. C. B. Mohr [Paul Siebeck], 1979), 192–194. The first of these incidents took place in 26/27 C.E. under Pontius Pilate, the second in 39 C.E. under Gaius Caligula.

14. Ibid., 192–196. Theissen makes clear, however, that this in no way establishes a direct causal link between specific events in first-century Palestine and the words of Jesus. Cf. the comments of Wink (p. 14), who in similar fashion locates the words of Jesus within the context of Roman oppression of the Jews.

15. Horsley, "Ethics and Exegesis," 23. Horsley in fact denies the existence of any established group of "Zealots" prior to 67–68 C.E., the time of the Jewish Revolt (p. 10).

16. Ibid., 21–22.

17. Ibid., 22.

18. Ibid.

19. Theissen, 185–191.

20. Horsley, 20.

21. Theissen, 178–180.

22. Horsley, 20. He does not, however, specify who these "persecutors" might be.

23. Ibid.

24. Martin Hengel, *Was Jesus a Revolutionist?* (Philadelphia: Fortress Press, 1971), 26–27.

25. See, e.g., Friedlander, 66; Clavier, 44; Dieter Lührmann, "Liebet eure Feinde (Lk 6,27–36/Mt 5,39–48," *ZTK* 69 (1972): 412–438; Luise Schottroff, "Non-Violence and the Love of One's Enemies," pp. 9–39 in *Essays on the Love Commandment* (Luise Schottroff et al.; Philadelphia: Fortress Press, 1978); A. Strobel, "Macht und Gewalt in der Botschaft des Neuen Testaments," pp. 71–112 in *Macht und Gewalt: Leitlinien lutherischer Theologie zur politischen Ethik heute* (ed. Hermann Greifenstein; Hamburg: Lutherisches Verlagshaus, 1978); Theissen, 160; W. Lienemann, *Gewalt und Gewaltlosigkeit: Studien zur abendländischen Vorgeschichte der gegenwärtigen Wahrnehmung von Gewalt* (Munich: Chr. Kaiser Verlag, 1982); Gerhard Lohfink, "Der ekklesiale Sitz im Leben der Aufforderung Jesu zum Gewaltverzicht (Mt 5,39b–42/Lk 6,29f)," *TQ* 162 (1982): 236–253.

26. Horsley, 24. It must be noted, however, that Horsley is able to arrive at these conclusions only by excluding Matt. 5:38–39a ("Matthew's redactional framing") from consideration (pp. 13–14).

27. Thus Friedlander, xxiii; Allen, 54; Klostermann, 48; Lagrange, 112; H. Cunliffe-Jones, *Deuteronomy: Introduction and Commentary* (TBC; London: SCM Press, 1951), 118–119; Schniewind, 67; Filson, 90;

Fenton, 92; Gaechter, 190; Grundmann, 172; Albright and Mann, 68–69; Hengel, 27; Hill, 127–128; J. A. Thompson, *Deuteronomy: An Introduction and Commentary* (TOTC; London: Inter-Varsity Press, 1974), 218; Peter C. Craigie, *The Book of Deuteronomy* (NICOT; Grand Rapids: Wm. B. Eerdmans Publishing Co., 1976), 270 n. 21; Gundry, 94; and Davies and Allison, 542.

28. Davies and Allison, 542.

29. Thus Schweizer, 204–209; Schottroff, 26–27; Strobel, 98; Lohfink, 248–250; Strecker, 82–83; and Luz, 330–331.

30. Schottroff, 26. Cf. the distinctly less irenic tone of Lienemann, who points out

> dass der hier geforderte "Weg der Friedfertigkeit" eine implizite Absage an die politische Theologie der zelotischen Bewegung darstellt, aber unverkennbar ist auch, dass Jesu Tod wie seine Verkündigung "Analogien zur Botschaft der Zeloten" enthalten, denn der von Jesus gebotene Gewaltverzicht fördert nicht Quietismus, sondern eine Aktivität, deren Stärke gerade durch ihre Gewaltlosigkeit gesteigert und damit durchaus als bedrohlich wahrgenommen werden muss. Die verkündete Nähe des Reiches Gottes ist ihrer Gestalt nach gewaltlos; ihrer Wirkung nach ist sie politisch brisant. (Lienemann, 62)

31. Piper, 89. See also Piper's further discussion, pp. 89–91. Cf. Theissen, 164–165; Guelich, 224; Lienemann, 61; and Luz, 278–279, 330. But note the significant difference in the approach of Davies and Allison (p. 540): "What Jesus rejects is vengeance executed on a personal level. He still assumes that God, the only wise and capable judge, will, in the end, inflict fitting punishment on sinners. . . . So the law of reciprocity is not utterly repudiated but only taken out of human hands to be placed in divine hands."

32. Horsley, 15. Cf. Hill, 127–128.

33. Here I make reference to "the words of Jesus" as represented by the Matthean text. See n. 1 above.

34. Thus Friedlander, 65; Allen, 54; Klostermann, 48; Lagrange, 111; Schniewind, 68; Schlatter, 185; Filson, 89; Fenton, 92; Gaechter, 189; Grundmann, 170; Albright and Mann, 68; Hill, 127; Banks, 196; Schweizer, 129; Piper, 51; Guelich, 219; Gundry, 94; Davies and Allison, 540; Strecker, 82; and Luz, 323.

35. Cf. the discussion of Anthony Phillips (*Ancient Israel's Criminal Law: A New Approach to the Decalogue* [Oxford: Basil Blackwell, 1970], 96–97), who notes that the law cannot be Jewish in origin, since there is no evidence of the practice of physical mutilation within Jewish society.

36. Martin Noth, *Exodus* (OTL; Philadelphia: Westminster Press, 1962), 182.

37. Thus Hans Jochen Boecker, *Law and the Administration of Justice in the Old Testament and Ancient East* (Minneapolis: Augsburg Publishing House, 1980), 174. Cf. A. D. H. Mayes, *Deuteronomy* (NCB; Greenwood, S.C.: Attic Press, 1979), 291.

38. See, e.g., Hermann L. Strack and Paul Billerbeck, *Kommentar zum Neuen Testament aus Talmud und Midrasch*, vol. 1: *Das Evangelium nach Matthäus* (Munich: C. H. Beck, 1922), 337–341; David Daube, *The New Testament and Rabbinic Judaism* (London: Athlone Press, 1956), 255–256; Mayes, 291; and Strecker, 82.

39. Cf. Noth, 182. The extent to which this law was practiced in literal fashion within ancient Near East society remains open to question. See, e.g., Noth, 182; Gerhard von Rad, *Deuteronomy* (OTL; Philadelphia: Westminster Press, 1966), 129; Anthony Phillips, *Deuteronomy* (Cambridge: Cambridge University Press, 1973), 132–133; Craigie, 270; and Dale Patrick, *Old Testament Law* (Atlanta: John Knox Press, 1985), 76–77.

40. Thus Friedlander, 65–66; Boecker, 175.

41. Cf. Meredith G. Kline, *Treaty of the Great King: The Covenant Structure of Deuteronomy—Studies and Commentary* (Grand Rapids: Wm. B. Eerdmans Publishing Co., 1963), 104; Gundry, 94; David F. Payne, *Deuteronomy* (Philadelphia: Westminster Press, 1985), 116–117.

42. Here it is evident, syntactically speaking, that the entire phrase *ophthalmon anti ophthalmou kai odonta anti odontos*, as it appears in Lev. 24:20; Deut. 19:21; and Matt. 5:38, has been extracted verbatim from the syntactical setting of Ex. 21:23, where the nouns *ophthalmon* and *odonta* serve as the direct objects of the preceding verb and thus stand in the accusative case. See Gundry, 94; and Davies and Allison, 540.

43. Thus Deut. 19:18–20: "And the judges shall examine the matter carefully. And if the unjust witness has in fact brought unjust witness and has opposed (*anestē*) his brother, then you shall do to him in the same manner as he planned to do evil (*eponēreusato*) to his brother. And in this way you shall remove the evil one (*ton ponēron*) from your midst. And when the rest of the people hear this, they will be afraid. And they will no longer carry out such evil (*to rhēma to ponēron touto*) in your midst." Cf. Matt. 5:39a: "Do not resist (*antistēnai*) the one who is evil (*tō ponērō*)."

44. Thus Guelich (p. 220), who likewise identifies the immediate proximity of the fourth antithesis (Matt. 5:33–37 on "truth-telling") to the fifth (Matt. 5:38–42) as a significant point of linkage between the Matthean and the Deuteronomic texts: "Of the three Old Testament parallels, Deut 19:21, LXX, fits 5:38–39a as though tailormade. First, the setting of Deut 19:16 involved the hypothetical trial of a false witness, a most appropriate and hardly coincidental sequel to the previous Antithesis. Second, the false witness had accused (*anestē*) his brother in court (19:18). Third, the penalty was based on the *lex talionis* principle by assigning to the false accuser the same penalty that would have been incurred by the accused. And fourth, the reason given for such action was to remove the evil one (*ton ponēron*) from the community. All four elements found in Deut 19:16–21 constitute the premise and antithesis of 5:38, 39a." See also Currie, 141. It is important to note in this context that since the verbal linkage between Matt. 5:38–42 and Deut. 19:15–21 lies in the respective

Greek texts, the following discussion will base itself on an examination of the LXX version of Deuteronomy and not the Masoretic text.

45. While this question is crucial to the understanding of Matt. 5:38–42, it has not, to date, exerted influence on the discussion of the Matthean text. By contrast, commentary on Matt. 5:38–42 has long paid significant attention to the basic concept of retaliation expressed by the *lex talionis* in its various ancient Near Eastern versions. See, e.g., Strack and Billerbeck, 337–341.

46. The corporate nature of the reference to Israel also becomes visible, not only in the evident abandon with which the Deuteronomist switches between second plural (*hymeis/hymas*) and second singular forms (*sy/sou/soi*) in addressing the Israelites as a people, but even more in his apparent preference for second singular forms over the second plural alternatives. Cf. the comments of Paul-Eugène Dion ("Tu feras disparaître le mal du milieu de toi," *RB* 87 [1980]: 349) concerning the use of the second person singular form of address throughout Deuteronomy and the comments of Patrick (p. 102) concerning the text of Deut. 24:7.

47. The centrality, for the Deuteronomist, of the language of "hearing" (*akouō*) and "doing" (*poieō*) in conjunction with the language of "commandments/regulations/decrees" and other similar terms is immediately evident when one consults a concordance.

48. That these two divine characteristics correspond to each other as "the two sides of the coin" becomes clear from the juxtaposition of descriptions in Deut. 5:9–10 (where God is identified as "a jealous God") and Deut. 7:9–10 (where God is identified as "a faithful God").

49. That this is a corporate reference becomes evident not merely from the Deuteronomist's frequent use of second-person singular forms in addressing the Israelite community (see n. 46 above) but from the immediate context of the verb as well: the preceding second-person plural formulation "and you shall do" (*kai poiēsete*) and the immediately following phrase "from your [pl.] midst" (*ex hymōn autōn*).

50. See n. 49 above.

51. Thus implicitly Phillips (*Ancient Israel's Criminal Law,* 96), and Mayes (p. 289), who identify the talionic formula as a secondary addition to the ruling concerning the "unjust witness."

52. See n. 39 above. Cf. Phillips' discussion (*Ancient Israel's Criminal Law,* 97–99) concerning the *lex talionis* and the prohibition of murder.

53. Thus Boecker, 171–172; Millard Lind, "Law in the Old Testament," pp. 9–41 in *The Bible and Law* (ed. Willard M. Swartley; OP 3; Elkhart, Ind.: Institute of Mennonite Studies, 1982), 21–24.

54. Cf. Deut. 13:8b (LXX 13:9b); 19:13a.

55. See the discussion of Calum M. Carmichael (*The Laws of Deuteronomy* [Ithaca, N.Y.: Cornell University Press, 1974], 37–40) on the motive clauses in Deuteronomy.

56. Thus Deut. 17:7; 19:19; 21:21; 22:21, 24; 24:7.

57. "And you shall obliterate the evil one from your midst" (*kai aphan-*

ieis ton poneron ex hymon auton: Deut. 13:5 [LXX 13:6]); "And you shall remove the evil one from Israel" (*kai exareis ton poneron ex Israel:* 17:12; 22:22); "And you shall wash away the innocent blood from Israel" (*kai katharieis to haima to anaition ex Israel:* 19:13); "And you shall remove the innocent blood from your midst" (*sy de exareis to haima to anaition ex hymon auton:* 21:9).

58. Deut. 13:1–5 (LXX 13:2–6); 17:2–7; 17:8–13; 19:11–13; 19:15–21; 21:1–9; 21:18–21; 22:13–21; 22:22; 22:23–27; 24:7; cf. 13:6–11 (LXX 13:7–12); 18:15–22. For a detailed study of this series of texts and the "removal formula" which creates the series, see Dion. See also Moshe Weinfeld, *Deuteronomy and the Deuteronomic School* (Oxford: Clarendon Press, 1972), 355–356; and Mayes, 233–34.

59. The crimes include false prophesying (Deut. 13:1–5 [LXX 13:2–6]; cf. 18:15–22, where the crime of the prophet is speaking in the name of other gods, but where the "removal formula" is absent); serving and worshiping other gods (17:2–7; cf. 13:6–11 [LXX 13:7–12], where the crime is that of inciting others to the worship of other gods, but where the "removal formula" is absent); disobeying the legal rulings of the priest in a court case (17:8–13); murder (19:11–13; cf. 21:1–9, where the case involves an unresolved murder case); false witness in court (19:15–21); rebellion against parents (21:18–21); loss of virginity prior to marriage (22:13–21); adultery (22:22); rape of an engaged woman (22:23–27); and kidnapping and enslavement or selling of an Israelite (24:7). That the crimes in question are in fact "capital crimes" becomes evident precisely from the "capital punishment" which is legislated as the punishment.

60. The punishment is variously designated: The offender shall be "stoned with stones" (*lithoboleo en lithois:* 17:6; 21:21; 22:21; 22:24; cf. 13:10 [LXX 13:11]); you shall "kill" the offender (*thanatosai:* 17:7; *apokteneite:* 22:22; 22:25); the offender shall "die" (*apothaneitai:* 13:5 [LXX 13:6]; and forms thereof in 17:6; 17:12; 19:12; 21:21; 22:21; 24:7; cf. 13:10 [LXX 13:11]; 18:20; *teleutesousin:* 17:5); the offender shall give "life in place of life" (*psychen anti psyches:* 19:21); the neck of the heifer shall be broken (*neurokopesousin:* 21:4; *neneurokopemenes:* 21:6). On the direct correlation between the motive clause and these legal rulings calling for capital punishment, see Dion, 327; Phillips, *Deuteronomy,* 132. But note S. R. Driver (*A Critical and Exegetical Commentary on Deuteronomy* [ICC; 3rd ed.; Edinburgh: T. & T. Clark, 1902], 152) and Mayes (p. 233), who cite 19:19 as an exception with reference to the question of capital punishment. As noted in n. 59 above, there are two additional laws in Deuteronomy (13:6–11 [LXX 13:7–12]; 18:15–22) that demand the death of the offender but do not contain any form of the "removal formula."

61. Cf. Mayes, 289.

62. Thus 13:5 (LXX 13:6); 17:7; 17:12; 19:19; 21:21; 22:21; 22:22; 24:7.

63. Cf. Dion, 329–330. But note 22:21, where the accusative singular

masculine form remains inflexible even though it is spoken with reference to a woman!

64. Cf. Dion, 330 n. 43. The human agony involved in this charge is clearly alluded to in the blunt warning of 19:21: "Your eye shall not spare him."

65. Here it is not specified what form that execution shall take. Elsewhere, however (see n. 60 above), the mode of execution is explicitly defined in terms of "stoning": thus 17:6; 21:21; 22:21; 22:24; cf. 13:10 (LXX 13:11), where no "removal formula" appears).

66. Cf. the comments of Craigie (p. 251) concerning 17:2–7, another of the legal rulings containing the "removal formula": "The capital punishment of the offender removed that evil which had, by the nature of the crime, endangered the continuation of the covenant community of God." See also ibid., 224, 284–285, 307.

67. That the primary concern lies with the community is evident from the fact that it is precisely the communitarian language of the "removal formula" which concludes the ruling concerning the "unjust witness." Attention thus focuses on the life of the community as a whole and not on the question of justice at the individual level.

68. Cf. the comments of G. Ernest Wright, "Deuteronomy," *IB*, 2:417–418; Phillips, *Deuteronomy*, 95; Craigie, 293; and Elizabeth Bellefontaine, "Deuteronomy 21:18–21: Reviewing the Case of the Rebellious Son," *JSOT* 13 (1979): 24.

69. See n. 49 above. The collective involvement of the community in the execution of the offender is made explicit in 13:9 (LXX 13:10) and 17:7, where the first hands to be raised against the offender are "your hands" (*hai cheires sou*)/ "the hand of the witnesses" (*hē cheir tōn martyrōn*) and the last hands to be raised against the offender are those "of all the people" (*pantos tou laou*).

70. Cf. the comments of Patrick, 102–103: "As in all biblical law, the addressee of Deuteronomic Law is the people of Israel, but D has *collectivized* a significant portion of its law. The 'you' addressed is the people as a corporate entity. . . . The people are addressed directly in the attached motive clause ('so you shall purge the evil from the midst of you') which explains the collective orientation of the law: the community must assume collective responsibility for serious offenses that occur within it and execute the offender to remove the guilt attached to it. If it did not do so, the whole community would be subject to divine judgment."

Significant light is shed on this Deuteronomic conception of "crime and punishment" by the comparative studies of Weinfeld and Dion. Dion, who traces the "removal formula" from its Deuteronomic form to earlier formulations both within and beyond Israel, observes (p. 349) that the "innovation" of the Deuteronomist lies precisely in the "democratization" of a formula that had formerly been applied to the king as the leader of the people. Weinfeld observes (pp. 239, 242) that in Deuteronomy, by contrast with the Book of the Covenant and the Priestly Code, "the concept of sin and punishment has . . . been transferred from the divine to the human sphere. . . . In the deuteronomic view sin does not act of its own accord, nor is the malefactor cut off from his people by the natural course of events: the people themselves must purge the evil from their midst."

71. Cf. the similar formulations that occur either in conjunction with the "removal formula" (17:13: "And when the whole people hears this, it will be afraid and will no longer act impiously" [*kai pas ho laos akousas phobēthēsetai kai ouk asebēsei eti*]; 21:21c: "And when the rest of the people hear this, they will be afraid" [*kai hoi epiloipoi akousantes phobēthēsontai*]) or in conjunction with the command to execute the offender (13:11 [LXX 13:12]: "And when all Israel hears this it will be afraid; and they will no longer carry out such evil in your midst" [*pas Israel akousas phobēthēsetai kai ou prosthēsousin eti poiēsai kata to rhēma to ponēron touto en hymin*]).

72. Cf. the comments of Weinfeld, 243: "According to Deuteronomy, the death penalty does not serve a sacral need for the destruction of the malefactor who had defiled the holy state (cf. Lev. 20:3), nor is it an object in itself, that is, the removal of impurity. It serves as a deterrent 'so that all may obey and fear' (13:12; 17:13; 19:20; 21:21)."

73. While no object is supplied for the verb "fear" (*phobēthēsontai*), it would appear from the phraseological evidence of Deuteronomy that the object implied by the text is not "the punishment you have just heard about" but rather "the Lord your God." Cf. the references to "fear of God" in Deut. 4:10; 5:29; 6:2, 13, 24; 8:6; 10:12, 20; 13:4 (LXX 13:5); 14:23; 17:19; 25:18; 31:12, 13; cf. 5:5; 9:19; 25:58.

74. Thus Driver, 152; Kline, 85; Phillips, *Deuteronomy*, 119; Thompson, 174; Craigie, 252–253; Dion, 330; Patrick, 103; and Payne, 116.

75. This is evident from the fact that it is precisely this language of "doing what is good and right" (*poieō + to kalon/to areston*) which creates the verbal contrast to the warnings against "doing what is evil" (*poieō + to ponēron/ta ponēra*) which effectively bracket the text of Deuteronomy (cf. 4:25–26‖31:28–29).

76. See also Matt. 9:35–11:1; 13:1–53; 18:1–19:1; 24:1–26:1; cf. 23:1–39.

77. See p. 39 above.

78. The immediate proximity of the crowds to the disciples, however, becomes evident at the end of Jesus' address, when it is they (*hoi ochloi*: Matt. 7:28) and not the disciples who respond to the words of Jesus: "And when Jesus had finished these words, the crowds (*hoi ochloi*) were astounded at his teaching; for he was teaching them (*autous*) as one who had authority and not as their scribes" (7:28–29). If the disciples are in fact the inner circle to whom Jesus addresses his words (5:1), the crowds are nevertheless the outer circle who "listen in" from the periphery.

79. That Jesus here addresses himself to a "community" and not simply to individual "disciples" is evident from the prominent use of plural forms of address throughout the Sermon on the Mount. A prime (and relevant) example of this usage is found in the formulaic language of the "an-

titheses" themselves: "You [pl.] have heard . . . (*ēkousate*); but I say to you [pl.] . . . (*egō de legō hymin*)": 5:21/22, 27/28, 31/32, 33/34, 38/39, 43/44. But see Theissen's discussion of the antitheses (p. 176). He notes that the antitheses are divided into two groups of three antitheses, a division that becomes evident from the fact that the complete formula introduced in 5:21 ("You have heard that it was said to the people of ancient days": *ēkousate hoti errethē tois archaiois*) is repeated only once, in 5:33 ("Again you have heard that it was said to the people of ancient days": *palin ēkousate hoti errethē tois archaiois*). Theissen correctly observes that the first group of three antitheses are casuistic in their formulation: "Everyone who . . ." (*pas* + participle), while the second group of three antitheses are apodictic: "You shall/shall not . . ." (imperatival or infinitival form). Theissen's conclusion, however, that the first three antitheses are consequently directed to everyone, while the second three are addressed only to a particular group of persons, is unwarranted. The very form of Jesus' address in all six antitheses ("But I say to you [pl.]": *egō de legō hymin*) indicates that the addressees of all the antitheses are the same group of people, namely, the community of Jesus' disciples in its entirety.

80. Both of these double sayings exhibit the same syntactical structure in their two halves: (1) "Whoever . . .": *hostis* + finite verb; (2) "[And] to the one who . . . : articular participle + *thelō*. Cf. Lührmann, 418; Davies and Allison, 538; and Clavier, 49–50.

81. See p. 48 above.

82. The fact that the individual illustrations provided in 5:39b–42 are formulated in terms of a singular addressee (*sou, soi, se*) does not undermine the collective thrust of the unit as a whole. Rather, as the form of the saying makes clear, it is the collective references of 5:38–39a (*ēkousate, hymin*) which introduce and thus interpret the singular references (*sou, soi, se*), not the other way around. The individuals addressed in 5:39b–42 are called to act, accordingly, not on their own behalf but precisely as members of the community to which they belong.

83. That the grammatically ambiguous form *tō ponērō* is here to be construed as a masculine (rather than neuter; cf. 5:11; 9:4; 12:35) form and thus as a personal reference ("the one who is evil") becomes clear from the preceding statement (5:38b) as well as from the illustrations that follow (5:39b–42). On the one hand, the reference to "eye in place of eye and tooth in place of tooth" makes sense only in terms of the interactions between two individuals; and on the other hand, each of the illustrations adduced in 5:39b–42 is phrased in terms of response to "the one who . . ." Cf. R. T. France, *The Gospel According to Matthew: An Introduction and Commentary* (TNTC; Grand Rapids: Wm. B. Eerdmans Publishing Co., 1985), 126. It is as well this same context which excludes the possibility that Jesus is here making reference to Satan, "the Evil One" (cf. 5:37; 6:13; 13:19, 38). Accordingly, while 5:39a remains grammatically ambiguous, it is most naturally construed in personal terms, as a masculine singular form whose closest parallels are the unambiguous masculine plural

forms *ponērous/tous ponērous* of 5:45; 13:49; and 22:10. The verbal and contextual linkage between this Matthean text and a Deuteronomic text that makes unambiguous reference to "the one who is evil" confirms this conclusion.

84. At the same time, however, the very breadth of the examples cited in 5:39b–42 leaves room for the conclusion that the "evil one" could as well on occasion be another disciple. Horsley pushes the issue too far when he suggests (pp. 19–20) that all the illustrations cited in 5:39b–42 relate to inner-community relationships. That it is not unthinkable, however, for Jesus to identify one from among the disciple group as an "evil one" becomes clear from the text of 7:11, where Jesus classifies the entire group of addressees as "evil": "So if you who are evil people (*ei oun hymeis ponēroi ontes*) know how to give good gifts to your children, how much more will your Father who is in heaven give good things to those who make requests of him!"

85. Cf. the comments of Schlatter (p. 186), who observes that it is precisely because the disciples are not outwardly separated from the Jewish community at large that the question of how to respond to "evil" comes into sharp focus for them:

> Nur darum bekam die Frage nach dem Recht für die Jünger Wichtigkeit, weil ihre eigene Gemeinschaft sie nicht von der völkischen Gemeinschaft schied. Der Boshafte, der Ohrfeigen austeilt und einen rechtlichen Anspruch auf ihren Chiton erhebt und zum Frondienst zwingt, steht nicht im Jüngerkreis. Solches Unrecht widerfährt ihnen von ihren Volksgenossen. Weil ihr eigener Verband sie nicht von der Judenschaft trennen kann und darf und sie doch für die anderen zum Gegenstand des Hasses macht, bekam die Frage, wie das Unrecht abzuwehren sei, für sie Gewicht.

86. Thus Clavier, 49–50; and Lohfink, 240.

87. Cf. 5:11–12, where Jesus warns the disciples that they can expect people to "revile" them (*oneidisōsin*), "persecute" them (*diōxōsin*), "say all kinds of evil" about them (*eipōsin pan ponēron*), and "tell lies" about them (*pseudomenoi*) on his account.

88. That this is so can be seen from the verbal links between this text and the Servant Song of Isa. 50:4–9, where the Servant of the Lord announces (Isa. 50:6), "I offered my back to scourges and my cheeks to blows (*tas de siagonas mou eis rhapismata*)." Cf. Gundry, 95; France, 126; and Davies and Allison, 544; but note Luz's caution (p. 325) that "slaps are so widespread that it is unnecessary to awaken special reminiscences of the servant of God of Isa. 50:6, who was beaten." The character of physical assault in *rhapizō* can also be seen from the verbal links between Matt. 5:39b and Matt. 26:67, where Roman soldiers strike (*rhapizō*: cf. the noun form *rhapisma* in Mark 14:65; John 18:22; 19:3) Jesus himself. Cf. France, 126; John R. Levison, "Responsible Initiative in Matthew 5:21–48," *ExpTim* 98 (1987): 234; and Davies and Allison, 546.

89. Thus Daube, 256–257; Clavier, 53; Hill, 128; Guelich, 221–222; Gundry, 95; Lohfink, 241; Horsley, 18; Wink, 15; Davies and Allison,

543–544; and Luz, 325. The measure of insult implied by such a "back-handed" slap can be seen in the fact that the fine imposed by the Mishnah as penalty for such a slap is twice as great as the fine imposed for a slap with the open palm: "If a man slapped his fellow, he gives him 200 *zuz;* if with the back of his hand, 400 *zuz*" (*m. Baba Qamma* 8.6, cited by David Daube, "The Old Testament in the New: A Jewish Perspective," pp. 1–38 in *Appeasement or Resistance and Other Essays on New Testament Judaism* [Berkeley and Los Angeles: University of California Press, 1987], 21.

90. For a discussion of the garments in question and the legalities surrounding seizure of a garment, see Davies and Allison, 544–546. Thus also Hill, 128; Guelich, 122; Gundry, 95; Lohfink, 241; Horsley, 18; and Luz, 325–326. But note Wink (pp. 16–19), who appears to confuse the nature of the lawsuit and the type of garment demanded.

91. Thus Hill, 128; Theissen, 176–177; Guelich, 222–223; Lohfink, 240–241; Davies and Allison, 546–547; and Luz, 326. Cf. Matt. 27:32 and Mark 15:21, where soldiers "compel" (*angareuō*) Simon of Cyrene to carry Jesus' cross. But note Horsley (p. 19), who concludes that "the surrounding sayings, and especially the formulaic antithesis of 5:38–39a, force us to assume that this saying [5:41] is subordinated to the editorial framing [and thus apparently refers to inner-community rather than Roman-Jewish relations]."

92. Cf. Lohfink, 240. While many scholars view the couplet of 5:42a/42b as only tangentially related to the preceding illustrations of 5:39b; 5:40; and 5:41 (thus Guelich, 223; Davies and Allison, 547; Luz, 329), Horsley views these illustrations, conversely, as conclusive proof that the text as a whole does not concern itself with the topic of nonretaliation (p. 18).

93. Cf. the comments of Robert C. Tannehill (*The Sword of His Mouth: Forceful and Imaginative Language in Synoptic Sayings* [Philadelphia: Fortress Press, 1975], 42), who notes that "a repetitive pattern embracing a series of particulars can point us beyond the literal sense of the words by suggesting that a series is open ended, that the pattern extends to many situations which have not been named." See also Levison, 233.

94. See n. 93 above.

95. There is considerable question about the status of the *lex talionis* within Jewish society during the first century C.E. Indications from the Talmud (*Baba Qamma* 8) and Josephus (*Ant.* 4.8.35 [280]) suggest that physical retaliation had been replaced, at least in part, by monetary compensation for the harm done. Other evidence (cited by Strack and Billerbeck, 341–343) indicates that at least in certain circles the *lex talionis* was still understood in terms of physical retaliation. For a detailed discussion of this question, see Daube, *New Testament and Rabbinic Judaism,* 254–265. See also Friedlander, xxii–xxiii; Banks, 198–199; and Guelich, 219.

96. On this point, Daube (*New Testament and Rabbinic Judaism,* 258) finds it "noteworthy that when Jesus quoted the old Biblical maxim, he omitted the first clause 'Life for life' and mentioned only 'Eye for eye,

tooth for tooth.' This is highly significant. In the case of homicide, the Rabbis did not abolish retaliation, at least not in theory: a murderer was liable to capital punishment, and even he who killed a man unwittingly could save himself only by escaping into a city of refuge. Accordingly, the clause 'Life for life' was not divested by the Rabbis of its literal meaning in the way the other clauses 'Eye for eye, tooth for tooth' and so on were. The natural result was that the two parts of the maxim drifted apart, in law and in the minds of the people: the clause 'Life for life' belonged to criminal law, was connected with the death penalty; the other clauses 'Eye for eye' and so on belonged to private law, were connected with monetary compensation."

See also Daube, "The Old Testament in the New," 21–22. Such a historical development, however, does not correspond to the literary evidence at hand; since according to the Deuteronomic text the *lex talionis,* through its attachment to the "removal formula," has as its signal purpose the illustration of a law prescribing capital punishment in response to a capital crime.

97. Tannehill, 54.

98. Contra Daube (*The New Testament and Rabbinic Judaism,* 258–259), who asserts that "this part of the sermon on the mount . . . is not concerned—not even secondarily—with a certain historical system of punishment."

99. Cf. the comments of Luz (p. 329), who sees in Matt. 5:39a "a certain shift in . . . accent toward a Christian passivity," and Schottroff (p. 26), who defines the "non-resistance" of which Jesus speaks as "total surrender to the enemy's unjust demands."

100. Cf. Tannehill's discussion (p. 54) of the "imaginative shock" created by many of the Synoptic sayings: "The tension in synoptic sayings is a reflection of the fact that they seek to challenge men [*sic*] who already live in a structured personal world. New structure can arise only by attacking the old. Everything important to us has its place within our personal world, and the structures of this world are the means by which we interpret experience. We unconsciously fit whatever we experience into these structures, so experience does not ordinarily challenge them. These interpretive structures have a ravenous appetite, seeking to digest all that we encounter. If speech is to induce 'imaginative shock,' effectively challenging the old structures and suggesting new visions, it must resist such digestion. It must stick in the throat. Forceful and imaginative language can do its work only if it does not fit into our ordinary interpretive structures. The result is tension, which often finds its formal reflection within a text."

101. While the imperative "Do not reject" is, to be sure, a negative formulation, the parallelism of the two final imperatives ("give" and "do not reject") indicates that even this negative formulation is to be understood as a positive command.

102. Cf. the comments of Theissen (p. 177: "Die negative Forderung, nicht Widerstand zu leisten, wird durch eine positive ergänzt und übertroffen. So ist auch bei Mt nicht einfach an ein passives Sichfügen ge-

dacht") and Lienemann (p. 62: "Noch wichtiger aber ist, dass die Weisung Jesu durchgehend nicht auf eine passive Hinnahme des Erlittenen zielt, sondern, ganz im Gegenteil, zu einem aktiven Tun auffordert: Halte hin! Gib! Geh' mit!"). Luz, however, turns this argument on its head, arguing in precisely reverse fashion that "it signifies a new tone that [Matthew] summarizes the *positive* exhortation of vv. 39b–42 in the *negative* formulation, 'do not resist' " (p. 329).

103. Cf. Wink, 18–20.

104. Cf. the comments of Tannehill, who notes (p. 70): "In each case an *action* is commanded, and this action is the precise opposite of our natural tendency in the situation. . . . I would suggest that these almost absurd commands were conceived by the simple device of reversing man's [*sic*] natural tendency."

105. On this point, cf. Lienemann's reference (p. 61) to "konkrete Weltverhältnisse" and Lohfink's similar reference (p. 242) to "*reale* Verhaltensweisen" in contrast to those commentators who effectively disarm the imperatives of 5:39b–42 by relegating them to the realm of the metaphorical or spiritual and thus denying them the force of literal commands (thus Daube, "The Old Testament in the New," 20; and Davies and Allison, 541).

106. On this point, see Tannehill's discussion (pp. 25–27) of the distinction between "legal rule" and "text as illuminator."

107. Cf. the comments of Wink, who describes the imperatives of 5:39b–42 (p. 19) as "a practical strategic measure for empowering the oppressed" and observes with reference to the command of 5:41 (p. 21) that "the question here, as in the two previous instances, is how the oppressed can recover their initiative, how they can assert their human dignity in a situation that cannot for the time being be changed. The rules are Caesar's, but not how one responds to the rules—that is God's, and Caesar has no power over that."

108. See the comments of Davies and Allison (p. 546) and Luz (pp. 326–327) to this effect and the related comments of Tannehill (pp. 70–71). Other scholars, to the contrary, fill the apparent lacuna in this saying of Jesus with "motives" appropriate to the Matthean context: the example of the life of Jesus (Strobel, 94–98; Levison, 233–234); the awareness that judgment belongs to God alone (Hill, 127; Lienemann, 75); the desire to win over the adversary (Lohfink, 241). Even Luz, who claims to find no "motive" as such for the imperatives of 5:39b–42 (pp. 326–327), nevertheless appears to offer just such a "motive" (p. 337) when he describes the renunciation of force as "a 'contrasting sign' of the kingdom of God or a part of a new way of righteousness which has been opened up by Jesus."

3

Ethics and Exegesis: "Love Your Enemies" and the Doctrine of Nonviolence

Richard A. Horsley

The injunction "Love your enemies" and the related sayings of Jesus (Matt. 5:38–48/Luke 6:27–36) play an important role in religious ethics. These sayings provide the crucial textual basis for traditional Christian pacifism. They also are prominent in recent attempts by North Atlantic scholars to repel any suggestion that Jesus' mission had revolutionary political implications (e.g., Hengel, 1971:26; 1973:49–50). It is even argued that "the *love of one's enemy,* which he [Jesus] required in the name of the kingdom of God, places him beyond the warring political forces" (Cullmann, 1970:45). Both the traditional understanding and the more recent use of these texts, however, are highly problematic when analyzed in terms of the historical-critical approach that has dominated most modern biblical scholarship. Ironically, recent studies by biblical scholars have done little to challenge the conventional readings of these texts. In the textual analysis below, I will argue that the cluster of sayings keynoted by "Love your enemies" pertains neither to external, political enemies nor to the question of nonviolence or nonresistance.

Many social ethicists have joined a resurgent discussion of the Bible and ethics.[1] Those who practice a highly complex and sophis-

---

This essay was first published in the *Journal of the American Academy of Religion,* vol. 54, no. 1 (1986): 3–31, and is reprinted here by permission.

ticated method of moral judgment or decision making, of course, may simply reject the "way of doing ethics" implicit in both the traditional pacifist arguments and the more recent defensive discussion of Jesus. Traditional pacifists have usually understood "Love your enemies" and related sayings as divine commands or norms of Christian conduct. More recently, both pacifist theologians and scholars eagerly warding off any revolutionary implications of Jesus have pursued a broader and somewhat more sophisticated approach, finding in Jesus' ministry a more general policy of nonviolence (or nonresistance). The key texts, of course, are still the "Love your enemies" cluster, understood according to the traditional assumption that whatever Jesus said (or did) is universally and absolutely valid.[2]

Many contemporary social ethicists would raise a fundamental objection to this conception of the relation of biblical texts to ethical stance or decisions: both the concentration on absolutized rules and the pursuit of a universalized model of conduct tend to abstract the contemporary actors from their community and history. Biblical scholars might well add a parallel objection from the point of view of scripture itself, particularly the Gospels: God or Jesus asks people to respond to others in particular social contexts rather than simply to observe rules or to imitate models. Thus, a more careful consideration of the meaning of certain texts might seem beside the point to ethicists or biblical scholars who reject an approach to ethics in terms of either absolute rules or universalized models.

However, critical determination of the meaning of traditionally important texts, such as "Love your enemies," is also important for alternative ways, favored by contemporary social ethicists, of using the Bible in social ethics. For example, according to Gustafson's typology, one principal way to use the Bible in ethics is by a method of analogy. Actions are judged to be morally wrong (or right) according to their similarity to actions judged wrong (or right) in similar circumstances in scripture (Gustafson, 1970:442). Thus, careful and circumspect study of the key biblical passages (and events) potentially usable as analogies is important if the choice of analogy is not simply to be determined by some prior ethical commitment or residual interest of the decision maker.

Another understanding of the Bible's relation to ethics is based on a community's appropriation of, and identification with, the biblical story of a people. Ethics starts not with biblical commands and prohibitions but with a way of envisioning the world that is "formed by a very definite story with determinative content" (Hauerwas, 1983:29, 33). According to this approach, Jesus cannot be said to have had a social ethic; "his story *is* a social ethic" (Hauerwas, 1981:40). Faithfully remembering the biblical story, however, would mean that it cannot be summarized or reduced to a theme (such as peace) any more than it can be reduced to the centrality of "the love command" by the more principial approach to ethics. "How the story should be told" is a moral issue today just as it was in the community that produced the scriptures.[3] Those remembering the story in order to be formed by the "definite story with a determinative content" will therefore want to attend closely to the particulars of the story and not simply find there the story they are already predisposed to hear.

Yet a third (if related) way of understanding the relation of Bible and ethics is that the Bible shapes the character and orientation of moral agents. Thus, prior to the point of "decision making" the Gospels will have provided ethical agents paradigms of action, intention, and disposition that flow into and inform their manner of life and bearing toward one another (Gustafson, 1974:159). For this longer-range and deeper way in which the Bible would inform character and disposition (of persons and communities), it would seem all the more important to question traditional assumptions about the meaning of particular texts.

This last point about the importance of critical biblical study for the way in which the Bible may be shaping orientation suggests a parallel concern: the way in which biblical scholarship may be shaping or reinforcing the orientation and dispositions of contemporary social ethics and theology. For example, much of the recent portrayal of Jesus as an advocate of nonviolence depends on the assumed contrast with "the Zealots" as a supposedly militant organization agitating for violent resistance to Roman rule in first-century Palestine. Yoder, in *The Politics of Jesus*, his highly provocative attempt to relate Jesus and social ethics, assumes that Jesus had the Zealot option constantly before him (Yoder: 43–47, 56). Similarly, the portrait of Jesus' nonviolence in much Latin American liberation theology depends on the "foil" of the Zealots, which liberation theologians have picked up from European scholars (e.g., Gutiérrez: 226–231, 245–247). If critical biblical study were to open up a different reading of certain key texts, might social ethicists be induced to question their previous assumptions and to reorient their dispositions?

For all of these ways of relating the Bible to social ethics the understanding of particular passages makes a difference. But critical examination of problematic assumptions and close textual analysis suggest that "Love your enemies" and related sayings have a context and implications very different from what is assumed in most of the recent scholarly discussion.

The pertinent texts, presented below in parallel columns according to Luke's order, read as follows:

Matthew 5:38–48	*Luke 6:27–36*
[43]You have heard that it was said, "You shall love your neighbor and hate your enemy."	
[44]But I say to you, Love your enemies	[27]But I say to you that hear, Love your enemies, do good to those who hate you, [28]bless those who curse you,
and pray for those who persecute you,	pray for those who abuse you.
[38]You have heard that it was said, "An eye for an eye and a tooth for a tooth."	
[39]But I say to you, Do not resist one who is evil. But if any one strikes you on the right cheek,	[29]To him who strikes you on the cheek,
turn to him the other also;	offer the other also;
[40]and if any one would sue you and take your coat,	and from him who takes away your cloak
let him have your cloak as well;	do not withhold your coat as well.
[41]and if any one forces you to go one mile, go with him two miles.	
[42]Give to him who begs from you, and do not refuse him who would borrow from you.	[30]Give to every one who begs from you; and of him who takes away your goods do not ask them again.
[Cf. Matt. 7:12.]	[31]And as you wish that men would do to you, do so to them.
[46]For if you love those who love you, what reward have you? Do not even the tax collectors do the same?	[32]If you love those who love you, what credit is that to you? For even the sinners love those who love them.
[47]And if you salute only your brethren, what more are you doing than others? Do not even the Gentiles do the same?	[33]And if you do good to those who do good to you, what credit is that to you? For even sinners do the same.
	[34]And if you lend to those from whom you hope to receive,

what credit is that to you?
Even sinners lend to sinners,
to receive as much again.
[35]But love your enemies,
and do good, and lend,
expecting nothing in return;
and your reward will be great,
[45]so that you may be sons of your
Father who is in heaven;
and you will be sons of the Most
High;
for he makes his sun rise on the evil
and on the good,
for he is kind to the ungrateful and
the selfish.
and sends rain on the just and on the
unjust.
[48]You, therefore, must be perfect,
as your heavenly Father is perfect.
[36]Be merciful,
even as your Father is merciful.

Problematic Assumptions

Many scholarly and semipopular treatments of Jesus' teaching understand "enemies" in Matt. 5:44 and Luke 6:27 to refer to foreign or national enemies or to include national as well as personal enemies.[4] This reading appears to be rooted in at least four assumptions that invite critical examination.

1. The ordinary or common language meaning of "enemy" in English (and *Feind* in German) tends to be a political or national enemy. Hence, when the Greek word *echthros* is translated as "enemy" (*Feind*), the natural assumption is that a political, usually foreign, enemy is meant, such as the Romans for Jesus and his Jewish contemporaries (Seitz: 44; Beare: 161–162; Caird: 104; Piper: 56).

2. Bible interpreters and theologians tend to treat Jesus' sayings according to their own approach, that is, in terms of "ethics" or "ethical teachings." "Love your enemies" and such related sayings as "Do not resist one who is evil" or "Turn the other cheek" are often understood as abstract and universally applicable ethical principles (usually addressed to the individual).[5]

3. The framing of the saying in the Gospel of Matthew is usually in view and accepted. Perhaps the saying there can be understood as referring to the foreign or political enemy, for Matthew appears to move from internal community relations in the first five antitheses of the Sermon on the Mount to relations with outsiders in the sixth antithesis. However, the Matthean setting, which is a redactor's work, is often projected back to Jesus himself, or there is simply no awareness of any distinction between them (Piper: 96–99).

4. Jesus' "teachings" are often interpreted directly over against "the Zealots." Since the Zealots were supposedly an organized, religiously motivated movement of national liberation by force from their Roman overlords, "Love your enemies" is easily understood as Jesus' nonviolent stance toward the Romans—a stance diametrically opposed to Zealot teaching and action. "He excludes every use of force as it was preached by the Zealots" (Cullmann: 45).[6]

None of these four principal assumptions is valid.

On items 1 and 2: Unless we are simply to take the text at face value in translation, we must strive critically to establish not only the meaning of words in (original) literary context; we must also attempt to appreciate the meaning of Jesus' sayings and actions as understood in social-historical context (whether in the evangelists' communities or earlier). On these principles of procedure, the first two assumptions hardly require refutation. The Greek word *echthros* may mean political/foreign enemy, but that would have to be established by critical investigation. Moreover, we cannot assume without critical analysis that Jesus and/or the gospel tradition were speaking in terms of abstract, universally valid ethical principles.

On item 3: Those who reach for Matt. 5:44 as a decisive text calling for love of external enemies should consider that the framing and the context of the saying are Matthean and that Matthew has rearranged and reshaped material he found in the sayings source (Q), which both he and Luke used, apparently independently.

First, the overall literary context in Matthew is much more schematic, more highly structured, than in the corresponding appearances of some of the same sayings in Luke. As the expression of his fulfillment of the Law and the Prophets, Matthew's Jesus calls for a "higher righteousness" exemplified in the six antitheses of Matt. 5:21–48. Bultmann believed that antitheses one, two, and four were primary formulations already present in Matthew's source. But even Bultmann's form-critical analysis indicated that the other antitheses, including 5:43–44a, were Matthean formulations. More recent form-critical and redactional analysis, however, indicates that there are "no grounds that justify the notion that Matthew received the antithesis form in his tradition of the sayings of Jesus" (Suggs: 101). Matthew may well have found the phrase, "But I say to you that hear . . . ," in his source. However, that phrase in the Luke 5:27a, parallel to Matthew 5:44, can best be understood not as an introduction simply to the saying in 6:27b/Matt. 5:44a ("Love your enemies . . .") but as "a theme-bearing transition to the body of an exquisite homily, first organized in Q and edited by Luke without serious impairment of its structure" (Suggs: 100; cf. Fitzmyer: 637). The antithesis form can thus be seen as a creation of Matthew himself. "By it he intends to assert the authority of Jesus' representation of the law over against what he alleges is Pharisaic interpretation."[7]

Second, it thus is easier to understand Matt. 5:38–42 and 43–48 as Matthew's selection from, and reformulation (into two antitheses) of, what he found in Q than it is to understand Luke 6:27–36 as Luke's conflation of two semi-separate sets of sayings which he found in Q. For example, it was Matthew who made "Love your enemies" into an interpretation of Lev. 19:18—along with the contrasting "and hate your enemies," which Matthew himself added (it is not from the Hebrew Bible)—rather than Luke who deleted this specific reference to the Torah. Moreover, "the sharp polemic of the Matthean antithesis (in 5:38–42) is absent in Luke" (Furnish: 56; Beare: 161).

Third, it is much clearer that Matthew has changed certain words or phrases than that Luke has. For example, whereas "be merciful" in Luke 6:36 fits the immediate set of sayings in 6:27–35 (parallel to Matt. 5:38–47), Matthew must have substituted "be perfect" as a recapitulation looking back over the whole series of commandments from 5:21–47. The only other occurrence in the Synoptics is also in Matthew, in 19:21, in a context, moreover, in which the order of the preceding commandments is the same as in Matthew 5: on murder, adultery, false witness, and love—indicating Matthew's schematic arrangement (Furnish: 53; Stendahl, 1954:137).

Thus, even if the saying "Love your enemies" in its Matthean setting refers to outsiders, this is no indication that it referred to external, political enemies in Luke, in Q, or as an independent saying.

On item 4: The use of the Zealots as a foil for Jesus' teaching of nonviolence, recently so fashionable in New Testament studies, has been undercut by the recent realization that "the Zealots" is a modern scholarly construct without basis in historical evidence (Smith, 1971; Horsley, 1979a, 1979b). There is no evidence in Josephus, rabbinic texts, or the New Testament for an organized movement of armed opposition of Roman rule (founded supposedly by Judas the Galilean in 6 C.E. and agitating against Roman rule until the movement splintered at the outbreak of the Revolt in 66 C.E.), as supposed by many scholars since the beginning of this century (e.g., Kohler; Hengel, 1961, 1971, 1973). There may well have been some continuity, at least of leadership, between the "Fourth Philosophy" founded by Judas of Galilee in 6 C.E. and the Sicarii (but not the Zealots), who were active in the 50s and 60s C.E. If the "daggermen" were a continuation of the Fourth Philosophy, however, they apparently were dormant during the ministry of Jesus. Thus neither they, nor the Zealots proper, who originated during the Revolt in 67–68 c.e., nor any other Jewish group for which we have evidence, provides an opposition against which Jesus would have been formulating his injunction to love one's enemies. We have no evidence that armed opposition to Roman rule, or the supposedly related question of the use of violence, was prominent at the time of Jesus' ministry. Since we do not know "the popular morality of his age," we surely cannot declare that Jesus "took a rigorous position against" it in his demand for love of enemies (Hengel, 1973:49; Cassidy: 40–42).

In recent scholarly as well as popular discussion, this concept of "the Zealots" may be the most determinative false assumption. It would be well to work deliberately at removing it from our consciousness when dealing with Jesus' sayings.

Lack of Definition of "Enemies" in Recent Studies

A number of studies of "Love your enemies" have appeared in recent years, but they have given little attention to the definition of the "enemies." Perhaps this is partly because of the assumptions just described and partly because of the traditional emphasis in biblical studies on the history of ideas, without much attention to concrete social context. Some do not even raise the question of the enemies' identity (whether in Matthew, Luke, Q, or for Jesus). Furnish, for example, subsumes the command to "love enemies" into his more general quest for the love ethics of Jesus and the New Testament, with emphasis on the determinative role of the love command as the principle for interpreting the moral requirements of the whole law and on the general exhortation to everyone "to show *goodwill* towards others" (Furnish: 64–67, his emphasis). Other studies note that in Matthew, and apparently in Luke as well, the "enemies" refers to the persecutors of the Christian community, but the studies fail to explore more precisely who those persecutors may have been (and when they figured in the development of early Christian communities).[8] Yet other treatments raise the issue of the identity of the "enemies" but do not really address it. To conclude that the command requires "that we should love our enemies even though they truly are our enemies" (Schottroff: 23–24) still does not specify who those enemies may have been. Seitz raises the question implicitly (and even includes evidence that suggests other possibilities for what "enemies" may have meant) but then repeatedly reverts to the assumption that foreign political enemies were in view, specifically the Romans and their collaborators (Seitz: 43–44, 46, 48, 50, 52).

The command of loving enemies remains general, abstract, and susceptible of a variety of interpretations so long as the meaning of "enemies" remains imprecise. Specification of the enemies (whether in Matthew, Luke, Q, or for Jesus) requires investigation into the concrete social context as well as the literary context of the sayings and their transmission. Such an inquiry is not found in most recent studies of the passage. Pursuit of such an inquiry, moreover, requires attention to the context indicated by the content of the sayings. Unfortunately this is also missing from most recent studies. In the few studies that note the context indicated in the sayings themselves, the interpreters still jump to the foreign/political interpretation (Manson: 50–51; Seitz: 46–52).

The Text of the Sayings in Matthew, Luke, and Q

It is crucial for exploration of "what is characteristic of the preaching of Jesus" (Bultmann: 105) to establish the content and form of the sayings on "love of enemies," and so forth, in Q or the material used by Q. There is no point, however, in entertaining illusions about being able to reconstruct the original sayings of Jesus, especially in some sort of sequence that could have been an original "sermon." As noted above, there are compelling reasons to believe that Matthew (rather than Luke) has rearranged the order of the sayings in order to fit his grand scheme of fulfillment of "the Law and Prophets" delineated in six antitheses. Matthew 5:38–39a and 5:43, to which there are no Lukan parallels, are clearly schematic Matthean additions (Bultmann: 91). Thus, the Lukan order of the sayings is likely closer to what stood in Q. The "But I say to you who hear" of Luke 6:27a, moreover, is likely a phrase that connected not simply 6:27 but the whole complex of sayings from 6:28 to 6:45 with the preceding blessings (or blessings and curses) already in the sayings source (Suggs: 100–101).

Both Matthew and Luke have altered particular words in pursuit of their respective concerns. "Pray for *those who persecute you*" (Matt. 5:44b) is Matthew's special interpretation to identify the "enemies" of 5:44a. This wording in Matthew fits a pattern evident in 5:10; 5:11–12; and 10:23, contexts in which Matthew establishes a theme either by the insertion of his special material or by altering the wording he found in the saying's source. This Matthean specification of the enemies as "those who persecute you" might also explain why Matthew would have deleted the other two parallel phrases still found in Luke 6:27–28 and would fit well with form critics' judgment that Luke 6:27–28 represents the original form of these lines because of the synonymous parallelism.[9] Whereas Luke may be less likely to alter the order and the length of sayings from Q, he apparently felt free to make changes in the wording. Matthew's wording in 5:39b–40 and 42 (contra Luke 6:29–30) would appear to retain the more concrete, even legal, terminology specific to the backhanded blow on the right cheek and the procedure of loaning/borrowing and the security posted for the loan. The wording in Luke, in 6:29b and 30b, makes the illustrations more general or makes the situations appear to be those of theft rather than claiming the security on a loan and borrowing.[10]

Misconceptions in Interpretation of Luke 6:27–36/Matthew 5:38–48

Before we focus directly on the question of who the "enemies" were, it is necessary to clear away a curious assortment of misreadings and misconceptions that have often decisively influenced treatment of Luke 6:27–36 and Matt. 5:38–48. Apparently some of these result from the practice of applying questions current in the modern world to these sayings.

1. On the assumption that the concepts of nonviolence (or nonresistance) and love of enemy are the same or integrally linked, both are found in Matt. 5:38–48 and Luke 6:27–36.[11] The basis of this interpretation is a puzzle. All the illustrative sayings are grouped under the theme of love of enemy in the Lukan and Q versions, but none suggests the concept of nonviolence (or nonresistance). The saying that might suggest nonresistance (nonviolence) stands in the Matthean version (5:39a), but Matthew has divided the material into two separate antitheses, with Jesus "fulfilling" (not abolishing!) the *lex talionis* in 5:38–42 and then addressing love of enemies as a separate issue in 5:43–47.

2. Prominent in recent interpretations is the belief that the issue in Matt. 5:38–48 and Luke 6:27–36 is violence and nonviolence. This is reflected dramatically in the titles of articles and tracts and is simply assumed in some recent commentaries (e.g., Schottroff; Hengel, 1973; Talbert: 73–75; Tinsley: 70; Daly: 52, 41). Perhaps the most extreme form of this claim is that "the heart of the proclamation of Jesus, the conscious rejection of violence . . . is unequivocally represented in the oldest sayings-traditions of the logia (Q) source (Luke 6:27–36 par Matt 5:38–48)" (Hengel, 1971:26). Many

of these interpretations suppose that these sayings were shaped in conscious opposition to the "Zealots." But "the Zealots" is a modern scholarly fiction, not a historical reality, and without it there is nothing in either Matthew or Luke (or Q) to suggest the issue of violence/nonviolence in these sayings. Matthew's placing of 5:41 indicates that the foil of the Zealots was hardly in mind (Stendahl, 1962a:777). This saying about going two miles instead of one, supposedly in response to the imperial requisition of labor, thus stands in a section dealing with interpersonal relations, 5:38–42, and not in the section on love of enemies. That Jesus' disciples or the Matthean community may have experienced persecution (Matt. 5:44) does not necessarily imply violence. The only "violence" in the Lukan version (and its only suggestion in the potentially Q version) is merely verbal, the cursing in Luke 6:28.[12] In Matthew's version one could find the issue of violence only by implication from comparative material in Romans 12 and 1QS 9–10: the violence God might do to evildoers or persecutors in his wrathful judgment. The only suggestion of the issue of personal violence in Matthew appears in the illustration of the *lex talionis,* and this is in the quotation provided by Matthew in his framing of the material. In short, the issue of political violence for liberation from oppression (contra Hengel, 1971, 1973; Cullmann), or even violence in interpersonal relations (except in the quotation of illustrations of the *lex talionis* by Matthew), is wholly absent from these sayings. Nonviolence is not the issue or the message in these texts (Mott: 171–173).

3. Matthew 5:38–48 and Luke 6:27–36 are also sometimes understood as a commandment of nonresistance to evil (Piper: 89, 91; Rausch; Caird: 104; Tannehill: 377). This interpretation very likely reflects the continuing influence of the King James Version of Matt. 5:39a: "Resist not evil." More recent versions have corrected the impression that evil in general is not to be resisted by translating instead with phrases such as "one who is evil" (RSV) or "the wicked man" (JB). Clearly Matt. 5:39–41, and principally 5:39a, is the only portion of the overall set of sayings that could possibly be understood as focused on a command of nonresistance to an evildoer. However, since the context in Matt. 5:38–42 (in contrast perhaps with Matt. 5:43–47) is not relations with outsiders, nonresistance as a stance toward oppression or persecution is not the subject in focus. Rather, the context is interpersonal relations. Moreover, the illustrations in 5:39a and 40 show that "resistance" does not connote physical force, but testimony against the "evildoer." Matthew's Greek term (*antistēnai*) would be better translated "protest" or "testify against" (Currie). Although (in the English-speaking world) "Turn

the other cheek" may well have become an admonition of nonresistance, it is difficult to see how stretching the original phrase metaphorically to mean nonresistance to evil in general can possibly meet the criteria of acceptable biblical exegesis. There would have to be some other parallel saying or some clear injunction in the immediate literary context that clearly indicates that this meaning was intended.

4. It is also assumed, finally, that Matt. 5:38–48 and Luke 6:27–36 provide a teaching on nonretaliation (Furnish: 56, 61; Beare: 158; Piper: 56, 58), which surely is a more appropriate label for the subject of these sayings than either nonviolence or nonresistance. Nevertheless that judgment is justified only by Matthew's redactional framing of some of the sayings, that is, 5:38–39a, in which the new righteousness is set over against the old *lex talionis* in the fifth antithesis. It is perhaps conceivable that the loving response to the "enemies," who are specified as the persecutors in Matt. 5:43–44, is also a sort of nonretaliation. Thus Matt. 5:43–47 could be read as a prohibition of revenge, parallel to Paul's exhortation in Rom. 12:19–21. Matthew, however, must have some reason for dividing this material into two different antitheses, only the first of which had Jesus' response to the *lex talionis* explicitly in mind. Even within Matthew's fifth antithesis, moreover, as in the Lukan parallel, the individual sayings (such as giving to one who begs and not refusing a request for a loan) do not fit the topic of nonretaliation very well. Matthew's own addition of the saying on going the second mile is a poor illustration of nonretaliation in the sphere of interpersonal relations; the saying must stem originally from the sphere of imperial political-economic relations. The only saying whose content approaches nonretaliation is Matt. 5:39b (Luke 6:29a). Still, whereas the *lex talionis* dealt primarily with cases of personal injury, it is highly doubtful that Matt. 5:39b can be read as referring to physical "blows" and "physical abuse" (Piper: 58; Beare: 158). For the discussion that follows, it is important to observe that neither in Luke nor in Q is there any connection between turning the other cheek and the *lex talionis* (cf. Fitzmyer: 638). The connection, which only Matthew makes with his framing of the sayings in the fifth antithesis, remains to be clarified.

The Character of the Sayings

To appreciate the subject and concern of the "Love your enemies" passage, it is essential to consider the character of the sayings themselves. These sayings do not constitute new law in the broad sense, certainly not to the point of abolishing the old, Mosaic law (contra Piper: 89, 90, 95; Furnish: 56). Like many other assumptions and conclusions about these sayings, this misconception is rooted in the acceptance of the Matthean framing of the material into antitheses. Since the early redaction criticism on Matthew and the Sermon on the Mount, it has been clear that Matthew implies no abolition of the old law in favor of the new. Jesus has come to fulfill the law, to restore the proper functioning of the law to the true righteousness originally intended by God in giving the Torah (Stendahl, 1962a: 776; Davies:101–102).

Nor are many of the individual sayings to be understood as laws or commands. A number of commentators have noted that sayings such as those in Luke 6:29–30 are exaggerated ways of stating or illustrating the injunction about loving. As Dodd (51–52) noted sometime ago, "the Gospels do not give directions for conduct in the same sense as do the ethical precepts of the Epistles." Using illustrations from Romans 12 and Matt. 5:39–42 and Luke 14:12–13, he points out that "the precepts in Romans are perfectly straightforward general maxims which you could transfer directly to the field of conduct. . . . That could hardly be said of the Gospel precepts. . . . You could not possibly go about applying these precepts directly and literally as they stand." T. W. Manson had previously explained the absurdity of taking Luke 6:29 (Matt. 5:40) literally, which would have meant relinquishing one's inner as well as one's outer garment to the thief (Luke) or the creditor (Matthew): "In either case the issue would be nudism, a sufficient indication that it is a certain spirit that is being commended to our notice—not a regulation to be slavishly carried out" (Manson: 51). Besides being extreme, all the sayings in Luke 6:29–30 and Matt. 5:39b–42 deal with specific situations and have a very limited application if taken literally (Tannehill: 377). The special features of such sayings have provoked hypotheses about their characteristics and function, such as that of the "focal instances." In distinction from a "legal rule," which deals with a general area of behavior, is manageable in its literal sense, and permits a clear deduction as to the range of its application, the "focal instance" is both specific and extreme and, supposedly, refers to everything up to and including the literal sense. A series of "focal instances," such as Luke 6:29–30, challenges the hearer to responsible behavior in a whole field of situations by giving a few extreme illustrations (Tannehill: 381–382).

Of course, not all the sayings in the passage are "focal instances." The principal saying ("Love your enemies," and so forth, in Luke 6:27; cf. Matt. 7:12), its repetition with variation in 6:35a, the

"Golden Rule" in 6:31, and the concluding "Be merciful" are all broad general commands or exhortations regarding social relations. They are similar in form and content to traditional proverbial commands or exhortations, such as those found as far back as Babylonian and Akkadian literature (Klassen: 34–35). The sayings that fill out the rest of the passage, Luke 6:32–34, 35b (Matt. 5:45–47), constitute further exhortation to motivating and sanctioning behavior according to the principal commands to love and be merciful. The love of enemies is set over against the love of neighbor only in Matthew's framing (vs. Piper: 55). In both Luke and Q, "Love your enemies" and "Be merciful" are exhortations to transcend ordinary reciprocal love. This is clear whether one concludes that the Golden Rule (and Luke 6:34) stood in Q as well as in Luke (6:31) or whether one reads the Golden Rule as itself transcended or simply clarified by the sayings in Luke 6:32–34 and 35b (Matt. 5:46–47 and 45b). The rhetorical questions of Luke 6:32–33 (Matt. 5:46–47) clearly invite the conclusion that love of enemies transcends the reciprocity between those who love each other.

Although Matthew may have shaped his material formally into antitheses that present new law in fulfillment of the old, the character of the sayings he used, as they can be determined from comparison with the discourse apparently adapted by Luke from Q, is not that of law. The love of enemies passage is rather composed of broad general commands regarding social relations illustrated by several extreme instances and further motivated by comparative exhortations.

The Social-Economic Context Indicated by the Content of the Sayings

Let us now examine the content of the sayings to see what it reveals about their context and the probable meaning of "enemies" and "Love your enemies" in Matthew, Luke, Q, and even in the earliest communities of the Jesus movement. As we shall see, the content of nearly all the sayings indicates a context of local interaction with personal enemies, not one of relations with foreign or political foes.

Luke 6:27–28: In the Septuagint, which strongly influenced the Greek usage of the early churches, *echthros* can be used both for foreign, political enemies and for personal (and more local) enemies. More decisive for determining the meaning of this and other terms, however, is the usage in the individual Gospel writers, the synoptic tradition generally, and especially in the immediate context. In two passages in Luke (the Song of Zechariah, 1:71, 74; and the lament over Jerusalem, 19:43) the term refers to national enemies. In the other occurrences in both Matthew and Luke, none of the cases is a reference to foreign national or domestic political enemies. The "enemy" is, rather, a local adversary, for example, one who sabotages a farmer's crop by sowing weeds among the grain (Matt. 13:25, 28). The crucial decision required in response to Jesus' preaching of the kingdom (bringing not peace but a sword) means that the members of one's own household may become "enemies" (Matt. 10:34–36). Herod Antipas and Pilate had been personal enemies, although there may have been an element of political rivalry involved (Luke 23:12). Even Satan is conceived as a personal enemy, especially in the analogy drawn from the parable (Matt. 13:39; cf. 13:25, 28; cf. Luke 10:19). The other principal passage, Matt. 22:44/Luke 20:43, is a quotation from Ps. 110:1 and is formulaic. In the immediate context of the saying in Luke 6:27–28 and in Q, there is nothing to suggest that foreign or political enemies are in view. Standing in isolation, "your enemies" is vague. Taken in connection with the parallel sayings in Luke (and in Q probably), the phrase surely means those with whom one is in personal, local interaction. Although "those who hate" and "those who curse" could be anyone, whether local or distant, "those who mistreat (*epēreazontōn* in Luke 6:28) you" would have to be local. But, with a few exceptions (song of Zechariah and synoptic apocalypse, Luke 1:71 and Matt. 24:9), "those who hate," although outside the community of Jesus' followers, are within the local sphere of social interaction. The "hatred" could even be between family members, precisely as the result of response to Jesus (Luke 14:26). Similarly, while one could bless and pray for people at a distance, "doing good" presupposes direct interaction. Even in Matthew's specification of enemies as persecutors, the latter appear to be in local interaction with the community members.

Luke 6:29a: Far from being a symbol for violence or evil (to which Jesus then counsels passive nonretaliation or nonresistance), the slap on the cheek was simply a formal insult, not a spontaneous act of violence (Perrin: 147). It was a serious insult (as in *m. Baba Qamma* 8:6), but there is only insult and "no damage to person" (Daube: 257). If we also consider the principle of "focal instance," in which an extreme example is used to cover similar actions up to and including the literal case, then the insulting slap in the face (the formal insult) is the most extreme case envisaged in the saying.

Thus, if the content of the saying concerns the insulting slap in the face and other lesser but similar actions, then the context is local village or town interaction.

Luke 6:29b/Matt. 5:40: While Luke may be imagining a case of theft, Matthew's wording makes intelligible the case of the seizure of a garment in pledge. According to the Torah (Ex. 22:25–26; Deut. 24:10–13; cf. Amos 2:8), "If ever you take your neighbor's garment in pledge, you shall restore it to him before the sun goes down; for that is his only covering. . . . In what else shall he sleep?" The Torah thus covers the outer garment (cloak/*himation*), but not the undergarment (*chitōn*). The saying (in Matthew's wording) thus appears to envisage a situation in which the creditor seizes a person's undergarment, and Jesus counsels rendering up the outer garment (which cannot legally be taken away) as well—thus leaving the poor person in the ridiculous situation of standing naked before the unmerciful creditor and any onlookers. The content of the saying clearly indicates a local interaction between creditor and debtor over a loan.

Luke 6:30/Matt. 5:42: That these exhortations do "not fit the topic of non-retaliation very well" (Furnish: 56) indicates that non-retaliation is not the subject of the passage as a whole. In 6:30b, Luke may have a situation of theft in mind (Fitzmyer: 639). In the more original wording (Matt. 5:42), the sayings are straightforward exhortations to give to one who begs and to loan to one who seeks to borrow. The exhortation to lend is repeated in Luke 6:34 and 35a. It thus has a certain prominence in the passage as a whole, at least in Luke, and perhaps in Q as well (depending on one's reconstruction). The context and the content of the sayings clearly presuppose local social-economic relationships. Only without this concrete social-economic context do the references to "lending" appear to be "somewhat clumsy illustrations" (contra Schottroff: 25).

Luke 6:32–33 (–34)/Matt. 5:46–47: In these sayings Jesus challenges his hearers to transcend reciprocal love, "doing good," and so forth. Matthew 5:46 may well reproduce the more original wording from Q: "sinners" occurs often in Luke, and Matthew has the term only where clearly following Q or Mark. But the "gentiles" in Matt. 5:47 is clearly a distinctive Matthean term, occurring elsewhere only in another Sermon on the Mount text (6:7) and in the church-discipline discourse (18:17). Thus it is only Matthew who uses non-Jews (outsiders) as a contrast for the transreciprocal relations Jesus is calling for. In Luke and Q the sayings draw their comparison and contrast within the broader Jewish community (with "sinners" and/or "toll collectors"). And, in the case of either "sinners" or "toll collectors," the contrast is drawn from people with whom the hearers would have been familiar in their local communities. (Indeed, some of the Jesus followers were probably former sinners or toll collectors).

Luke 6:36/Matt. 5:48: Luke's "merciful" is surely closer to Q (the term occurs only here; to Matt. 5:48, cf. Matt. 19:21). As the concluding exhortations, both terms "be merciful" and "be perfect," in imitation of God, however, indicate that the context of the whole group of sayings is the covenant people who are called to practice justice in imitation of God's justice.

Thus far we have been dealing with the sayings in Q, with occasional comparative comments regarding Matthew's or Luke's redactions. When we shift the focus to Matthew and Luke, we find little change from what we have seen. For Luke we have few cases of definite editorial changes, principally alterations in wording, on which to base deductions. We have already noted that there is no evidence that in 6:27–36 Luke has in mind only persecutors from outside the Christian communities. With "enemies," "those who curse," and so forth, he may have in mind either community members or noncommunity members or both. Especially if the formulation of 6:35 is Luke's and was not originally in Q, then his focus is clearly local intracommunity social-economic relations. He appears to envision situations less specific than local borrowing and lending in 6:29b and 30b, perhaps situations of theft, but the context is still local social interaction. Certainly there is no indication of foreign enemies.

We must treat the Matthean interpretation according to the framing into two different antitheses. The saying in Matt. 5:41 appears to refer to relations between the occupying imperial power and the population subject to forced labor (*angariae*). But the surrounding sayings, and especially the formulaic antithesis of 5:38–39a, force us to assume that this saying is subordinated to the editorial framing. The *lex talionis,* of course, referred not to imperial-subject relations but to domestic Jewish social relations. Moreover, by Jesus' time, and certainly by Matthew's, the *lex talionis* was interpreted not in terms of cases of violence and personal mutilation but "as signifying the claim to accurate, nicely calculated compensation" for personal humiliation (Daube: 255–258). Matthew's framing in terms of not opposing or going to court against an evildoer is appropriate to the sayings he used from Q, all but one of which refer to local personal social-economic relations. In 5:38–42 he has in mind the internal relations of members of the church.

Matthew 5:43–44a has decisively influenced the interpretation of the whole passage (Matt. 5:38–48/Luke 6:27–35). Jeremias, attempting to reconstruct the Aramaic behind the Greek, suggests that the original saying, 5:43, should read, "You shall love your compatriot, but you need not love your adversary." Matthew may well still be thinking of local adversaries. The adversaries, however, are now persecutors outside the church communities. Moreover, perhaps precisely because the adversaries are now outsiders to the Christian community, Matthew backs away from suggesting any concrete social-economic responsibility as the meaning of "love." In the context indicated by Matthew's content in 5:43–47, the "enemy" may still be a local adversary, but the Christian has no specific duty to do good or to lend to that adversary.

This analysis of the sayings in Luke 6:27–36/Matt. 5:38–48, whether in the Q form or in the Matthean or Lukan adaptations, suggests that the context indicated by the content of the individual sayings is that of social-economic relations in a village or town. It is easy to understand the "enemies, haters, cursers, abusers" in the context of local interaction but difficult if not impossible to understand them as referring to national or political enemies. This interpretation is confirmed simply by the kinds of relationships assumed in the following sayings: the insulting slap in the face, the local creditors' seizure of the token pledge given by the debtor, borrowing and begging among local community members, or doing good and lending to those who may be local adversaries. Matthew evidently reinterpreted the thematic saying he found in Q, "Love your enemies," to refer to persecutors of Jesus' followers. But he also took most of the other sayings to refer to the internal relations of the local community. Finally, in the Lukan Sermon on the Plain, as well as in the sayings source Q, whether in this passage or in the sermon as a whole, "Jesus' words . . . touch on the concerns of daily existence, poverty, hunger, grief, hatred, and ostracism" (Daube: 255–258).

The Background of the Sayings and the Situation They Addressed

In addressing social-economic relationships in the local community, these Jesus sayings (and many others) draw on, and bring renewal of, long-standing Jewish (Israelite) covenantal Torah and wisdom teachings. Allusions to Leviticus 19 are even evident in the sayings themselves, as noted above: "Be merciful as God is merciful (perfect)" clearly is an allusion to and/or restatement of the principle found in Lev. 19:2; and prior to Matthew's reformulation into a quotation in the antithesis of 5:43–44a, "Love your enemies" was likely related to Lev. 19:17–18. The immediate scriptural context, Lev. 19:17–18—and perhaps other injunctions in Leviticus 19 as well (esp. 19:9–16)—indicates the kind of covenantal concerns that Jesus is addressing (and intensifying or sharpening):

> You shall not hate your brother in your heart,
> but you shall reason with your neighbor,
>   lest you bear sin because of him.
> You shall not take vengeance or bear any grudge against
> the sons of your own people,
> but you shall love your neighbor as yourself.

Mosaic covenantal Torah, moreover, was formulated not simply in terms of giving aid to one's brother or neighbor but also in terms of aiding one's personal local "enemy":

> If you meet your enemy's ox or his ass going astray, you shall bring it back to him. If you see the ass of one who hates you lying under its burden, you shall refrain from leaving him with it, you shall help him to lift it up. (Ex. 23:4–5; cf. Deut. 22:1–4)

The wisdom of (Jesus) ben Sirah is much closer to New Testament times and substantively similar to Jesus' teaching. It understands mercy as manifested concretely in local covenantal economic relations:

> He that shows mercy will lend to his neighbor, and he that strengthens him with his hand keeps the commandments. (Sir. 29:1)

The sayings of Jesus, however, as has often been observed, sharpen or intensify, as well as renew, such covenantal teachings and wisdom. It is well, therefore, to examine more carefully the general social-economic situation indicated by the content of "Love your enemies" and the related sayings along with that indicated by other aspects of Jesus' teachings.

The sayings in Luke 6:27–36/Matt. 5:38–48 depict circumstances of severe economic hardship among those addressed. It assumes that some in the local village community are asking for loans for which they have genuine need. Some to whom the sayings are addressed, already in debt, are unable to repay and fear that their creditors may seize the security they have posted. Still others have been reduced to begging. It is not surprising that in such desperate economic circumstances, some people are at each other's throats, hating, cursing, and abusing. The picture given by the blessings and the woes, which must have immediately preceded the "Love your enemies" passage even in Q, is similar; those addressed are apparently poor, hungry, and in despair. What is more, they stand opposite others (their urban creditors?) who are wealthy, well fed, and satisfied with life.

This picture of peasant village life in Galilee/Palestine accords with that depicted in other Synoptic Gospel material and with the conclusions of scholarly analyses. Among the latter, A. N. Sherwin-White found in the Galilee portrayed by the Gospels a society characterized by the extremely poor masses over against the extremely wealthy upper class (Sherwin-White: 139–142). It has long since been observed, on the basis of Jesus' parables, that many of the peasants in Galilee were heavily in debt (Matt. 18:23–33; Luke 16:1–7) and that many had become day laborers, either because they found it necessary to supplement the inadequate sustenance gained from their own small parcel of land or because they had already forfeited their land to their creditors. At least since the Roman conquest of Palestine, the reduction in Jewish territory, and the devastating civil wars that ended in Herod's conquest of Palestine as the client king of Rome, the Jewish peasantry had come under severe economic pressure. Decades of heavy demand for "surplus" production in the form of Jewish tithes, Herodian taxes, and Roman tribute had driven many into debt. As indebted peasants forfeited their land, the beneficiaries were the wealthy (Herodian families, high-priestly families, etc.), thus able to add to their already large landed estates and income (see further Applebaum: 657–667; Goodman).

These sayings of Jesus appear to be addressed to people caught in precisely such a situation. In such circumstances one would expect a high degree of resentment of the wealthy. Indeed, the woes against the wealthy reflect just that. The sayings beginning with "Love your enemies," however, do not have the exploitative ruling class in mind. These sayings of Jesus, rather, call people in local village communities to take economic responsibility for each other in their desperate circumstances. Those addressed may have little or nothing themselves. But they are called upon to share what they have willingly with others in the community, even with their enemies or those who hate them. They are not to seek damages from a formal insult. They are even to render up the pledge for a loan that the unmerciful creditor has no right to take. (Do they thus avoid being taken into the court and taking each other into court, as Jesus admonishes in the related sayings in Luke 12:57–59/Matt. 5:24–26?) The message seems to be: take responsibility for helping each other willingly, even your enemies, in the local village community.

This reading of the "Love your enemies" passage involves a clear shift of focus toward the concrete situation of Jesus and his followers. The implications of a failure to appreciate this concrete situation are illustrated in a statement of Johannes Weiss, cited by Schottroff (p. 12):

> [It is not] the pathetic squabbles of day-to-day life which we survive more or less unruffled, that provide the battleground to prove our love for our enemies. . . . Only when we have to fight with our backs to the wall for the supreme values of life, for our faith and convictions, and deadly enmity comes our way, do we have the chance to show whether we are really capable of that spiritual freedom which Jesus expects of his disciples.

Perhaps this is true for the well-off members of industrial society. For most peasants in early-first-century Galilean and Judean villages, however, the "squabbles of day-to-day life" were integrally related to externally determined circumstances in which they had "to fight with [their] backs to the wall." Most peasants are economically marginal, living at little more than a subsistence level. At times of acute pressure on their already marginal situation their problem is simply to survive. "The supreme values of [their] life," moreover, are closely related to their fight to survive in the traditional way of life. For the ancient Jewish peasantry, life's fundamental values were articulated in the covenantal Torah, which attempted to protect the Israelite/Jewish peasant against undue exploitation by others (cf. Exodus 21–23 and the stories and oracles of the prophets, who protested against ruling class abuses). The "supreme values of life" were expressed precisely in social-economic relations. Exploitation of the people by the Jewish priestly aristocracy and the Romans may well have been addressed in other sayings of Jesus. The focus of "Love your enemies" and the related sayings, however, is not on the Romans or even on domestic political enemies. Rather, they call for realization of the will of God and for imitation of the mercy of God in dealing with precisely those "squabbles of day-to-day life" which were integrally related to the struggle for supreme values and which took place in circumstances where people had "[their] backs to the wall." When the people have achieved such solidarity with regard to the supreme values of life focused on concrete social-economic relations, however, it has usually been highly threatening to the ruling groups. The movement gathered around Jesus appears to have been no exception.

Implications for the Various Approaches
to Ethics

Perhaps Jesus advocated nonviolence. Yet there is little or no evidence that he ever directly or explicitly addressed this issue of violence versus nonviolence. Surely nonviolence was not the primary focus or purpose of his praxis and preaching. Two principal keystones of the argument that Jesus was an advocate of nonviolence, at least in recent discussions, have been "the Zealots" as a foil for Jesus' position and the sayings in Matt. 5:38–48 as evidence for Jesus' own view. We now recognize, however, that there was no such long-standing resistance movement of "the Zealots," which advocated violent rebellion against the Romans. Since the sayings grouped with "Love your enemies" do not refer to foreign or political enemies and do not focus on the question of violence, the lesser components of the usual picture of Jesus as advocate of nonviolence will not hold together (Mott: 178–183). Rather, the primary focus of Jesus' recorded preaching and praxis was the coming of the kingdom of God and the appropriate personal and community response to God's initiative. In the Gospels, Jesus appears as the agent of God's rule in his exorcism, healing, forgiveness, and table fellowship as well as in his prophecies, parables, and teachings. "Love your enemies" and the related sayings apparently were understood by his followers, certainly in Q, and apparently also in the Lukan community, to refer to local social-economic relations, largely within the village community, which was still probably coextensive with the religious community in most cases. In Matthew, "Love your enemies" itself, but apparently not the other sayings, apparently referred to persecutors outside the religious community but still in the local residential community—and certainly not the national or political enemies (Romans).

If "Love your enemies" and related sayings did not proclaim some noble principle of nonviolence but pertained instead to the squabbles of local life, what is their relevance for ethics? Space prohibits an extensive exploration of how the "Love your enemies" saying(s) might be used in the various ways of relating scripture and ethics. Yet a few preliminary thoughts, confined in this case to the ways of doing ethics mentioned at the outset, may be in order.

According to the ethics of character development, the Bible provides contemporary ethical agents with paradigms of disposition, intention, and action that inform their manner of life. It is evident that the teachings of Jesus and other biblical paradigms are not simply "spiritual" counsels but are concerned with the whole of communal and personal life, including concrete economic and community relations. Insofar as contemporary ethical agents discern that such concrete and comprehensive concerns are at least implicit and often even explicit in sayings such as "Love your enemies," they are likely to think and act to form alternative economic and social patterns when the established ones block the pursuit or realization of such paradigms. To a considerable extent, some of the early churches did exactly this (Dodds: 136–138).

Ethics based in a faithful remembering and appropriation of the biblical story will surely depend significantly on the position of those who are reading and remembering. Indeed, it may be difficult for many contemporary readers to appropriate or identify with a story that is so foreign to their experience. The story, including Jesus' sayings, is alien not only in the sense that Jesus presupposed and addressed a traditional agrarian society. Almost certainly more important is the difficulty for those in positions of privilege to respond to a story that is oriented toward the poor and is judgmental of the rich and powerful.[13] In the Gospel story itself there are telling episodes in which the wealthy or the intellectuals (scribes and Pharisees) were unable to respond to certain aspects of the coming of God's rule. It seems, according to the Gospels at least, that such people never even heard Jesus sayings such as "Love your enemies." It is difficult to see how those who have not even been "hearers" of Jesus' words can become "doers of his words" (see Luke 6:47–49/ Matt. 7:24–27). Nevertheless there may be some possibilities for an understanding of "Love your enemies" and other Jesus sayings in the context of a faithful remembering of the biblical story. The readers must first of all be critically aware of their own situation in relation to the story and its orientation. Also, the story should not be reduced to manageable proportions or read in highly selective fashion. With these precautions, it should be possible to appropriate the love of enemies and related sayings in the context of other parts of the overall story, such as Caesar's decree of tribute from subject peoples, Herod's "massacre of the innocents," the inability of the intellectuals and ruling groups to respond to the coming kingdom, and the passage concerning why (and by whom) Jesus was crucified.

An ethics of analogy may be easier to pursue because it calls for a sharper focus on particular events, issues, and sets of relationships and thus is less susceptible to a transformation of the story into what one can (or wants to) hear. Nevertheless this method has its share of difficulties, among which is the "control" of the analogy (Gustafson, 1970:442–443). The problems of the analogy method are well illustrated by the recent interpretation of the "Love your enemies" saying. Understanding it to be Jesus' admonition to his followers to assume a nonviolent stance vis-à-vis their Roman imperial rulers (perhaps even in conscious opposition to the resistance movement of "Zealots"), contemporary North Atlantic Christians could argue by analogy that third world Christians should remain pacifist in the face of imperial oppression and even persecution.[14] The closer reading of the "Love your enemies" and related sayings suggested above, of course, makes such an analogy impossible. The more serious difficulty in this method, however, may be the scope and complexity with which one enters into the analogy. If the analogy is drawn, for example, between ancient Jewish society and the contemporary church, then professional ethicists and biblical interpreters correspond more to the scribes and Pharisees in the Gospels than to the common people to whom "Love your enemies" and other sayings were directed. If the analogy is broadened to more comprehensive proportions, then professionals are analogous to intellectuals of imperial Roman society, while the poor of the third world correspond to those who heard Jesus' sayings more directly. This does not mean, however, that such sayings are irrelevant to members of a modern imperial society. Jesus also calls for an identification with the poor and a voluntary humility, relinquishment, and sharing by the wealthy and powerful (and educated). Thus perhaps an analogous application of the "Love your enemies" set of sayings is possible through a sufficiently comprehensive scope and analysis. The analogy to doing good, lending (without interest!), and sharing what little one has with those who have nothing in a simple agrarian community could be sought in the more sophisticated and complex social-economic response to the needy in the complicated modern international capitalist economy where the investment of one's retirement funds or the availability of bananas and coffee for one's breakfast has an indirect but decisive effect upon the poverty of the campesinos who picked the bananas or the coffee beans.

Even those who want to stay with the principial approach to ethics, whether of the deontological or the teleological type, can still use the "Love your enemies" group of sayings. These sayings were not understood as universal ethical principles at the early stages of the gospel tradition or in the Gospels of Matthew and Luke. Yet already by early in the second century Christians apparently were not only widely acquainted with the "Love your enemies" teaching (Koester: 44, 75–76, 220–230, 263–265) but understood it as a general ethical principle. Hence Christians today should feel the same freedom to broaden the implications and applications of such Jesus sayings into universal ethical rules or ideals. The difference, of course, is that we moderns are aware that as a universal ethical principle "Love your enemies" is not a dominical command (i.e., of Jesus himself) but a Christian ideal and that the Jesus saying on which the ideal is based referred to a community's concrete social-economic relations. To take responsibility for broadening the saying of Jesus into a universal principle, however, entails the corresponding responsibility for broadening the concrete social-economic context in which the principle would be applied. Thus, "Love your enemies," "Turn the other cheek," "Do good and lend," and others, understood as pertaining to (complex) social-economic relations (and not to nonviolent behavior), could be applied to the use of economic resources for the benefit of the needy and oppressed. Christians who took the ideal seriously would be likely to find serious implications for their own involvement in the structural exploitation inherent in many social-economic institutions. It may be worth noting, finally, that although this investigation has been critical of the presuppositions and exegesis of studies (such as Yoder, 1972) that articulate an absolute pacifist position,[15] it reaches fundamentally similar conclusions about the serious implications of these sayings of Jesus for ethical judgments regarding political-economic structures.

Notes

1. E.g., Yoder; Gustafson (1970); Mott; Hauerwas (1983); and Ogletree. The list of relevant books and articles grows yearly.

2. The principal difference appears to be whether one directly applies the norm/policy to every situation (Yoder, etc.) or follows the ideal as far as possible depending on the circumstances (Hengel).

3. Hauerwas articulated some highly appropriate critical principles (1981: e.g., 56, 67) but would appear not to have followed them himself (1983).

4. E.g., Foerster (814). This understanding of "enemies" persists and is prominent especially in recent treatments: e.g., Klassen (86, 108 n. 17); Piper (91, 95); Riches (134); Schottroff (9); and Theissen (177–178, 191–195). Ferguson (1977:86) even refers to Jesus' "embracing the Romans within the community of love" (Matt. 5:38–48).

5. See the interpretation criticized by Schottroff (9–11); and see Perrin (109).

6. Cullmann (45). Similarly many other interpreters, such as Hengel (1973:49–50); Hoffmann (76); Klassen (45, 47–48, 65, 94–100); Riches (172, 175–176); and Yoder (1972: chs. 1 and 2).

7. Piper (esp. 151–152) appears to ignore the structure of Matthew 5, which goes far to determine how we can discern Matthew's understanding of 5:44–47.

8. Fitzmyer (637–638) presents principally a concise history of ideas.

9. Manson (50); Seitz (52), where it is not clear that he had read Bultmann (79) correctly. Also, it would thus seem that the "enemies" to be loved were not identified as the persecutors already at the Q stage, contra Schottroff (22).

10. Lührmann (418) argues that Matthew has the more original wording in 5:42b (par. Luke 6:30b) because the occurrence of *daneizō* in Luke 6:34, 35 seems to indicate that Luke had read Matthew's form of 5:42b and because *apo tou airontos* in Luke 6:30b provides a formal parallel with 6:29b and smooths the contrast between the content of 6:29 and 30.

11. Piper (95; cf. 91) even asserts that "Jesus' command of enemy love abolished the *lex talionis.*" Schottroff (26) ironically not only objects to the linking of these concepts but also exemplifies this problematic interpretation. For a clear differentiation in treatment of New Testament and related texts, see Stendahl (1962b).

12. Perhaps the taking away of one's garment or goods, understood as theft in Luke, might suggest a certain private interpersonal violence—but such "violence" would thus pertain to local interaction, not to relations with the Romans or other political foes.

13. Sociologists of knowledge have long recognized an "elective affinity" or "associative relationship" between people's beliefs or behavior and their social location (Gager, 1982:263). Perhaps contemporary ethical actors in positions of power and privilege are capable of breaking with this social-historical pattern.

14. Would this be the implication, for example, of Hengel's tracts (1971 and 1973) if read in third world communities? The comments of Reinhold Niebuhr (166–167) are pertinent and hardly dated.

15. By religious disposition and conviction I too have been a pacifist and a practitioner of nonviolence since my mid-teens.

References

Applebaum, S.
1976   "Economic Life in Palestine." In *The Jewish People in the First Century,* 2:631–700. Edited by S. Safrai and M. Stern. Philadelphia: Fortress Press.

Beare, F. W.
1981   *The Gospel According to Matthew.* Oxford: Basil Blackwell.

Bultmann, R.
1963   *History of the Synoptic Tradition.* Oxford: Basil
                 Blackwell.

Caird, G. B.
1963   *Saint Luke.* Philadelphia: Westminster Press.

Cassidy, R. J.
1978   *Jesus, Politics and Society: A Study of St. Luke's Gos-
                 pel.* Maryknoll, N.Y.: Orbis Books.

Cullmann, O.
1970   *Jesus and the Revolutionaries.* New York: Harper &
                 Row.

Currie, S. D.
1964   "Matthew 5:39a—Resistance or Protest?" *HTR* 57:
                 140–145.

Daly, R. J.
1982   "The New Testament and the Early Church." In *Non-
                 Violence—Central to Christian Spirituality: Perspec-
                 tives from Scripture to the Present,* pp. 34–62. Edited
                 by J. T. Culliton. Toronto Studies in Theology 8. To-
                 ronto: Edwin Mellen.

Daube, D.
1956   *The New Testament and Rabbinic Judaism.* London:
                 Athlone Press.

Davies, W. D.
1964   *The Setting of the Sermon on the Mount.* Cambridge:
                 Cambridge University Press.

Dodd, C. H.
1951   *Gospel and Law.* New York: Columbia University
                 Press.

Dodds, E. R.
1965   *Pagan and Christian in an Age of Anxiety.* Cam-
                 bridge: Cambridge University Press.

Ferguson, J.
1977   *The Politics of Love: The New Testament and Non-
                 violent Revolution.* Nyack, N.Y.: Fellowship of
                 Reconciliation.

Fitzmyer, J. A.
1981   *The Gospel According to Luke I–IX.* AB 28. Garden
                 City, N.Y.: Doubleday & Co.

Foerster, W.
1964   *"Echthros."* In *TDNT,* 2:811–815. Grand Rapids:
                 Wm. B. Eerdmans Publishing Co.

Furnish, V. P.
1972   *The Love Command in the New Testament.* Nashville:
                       Abingdon Press.

Gager, J. G.
1979   "Sociological Description and Sociological Explana-
                       tion in the Study of Early Christianity: A Review Es-
                       say." *Religious Studies Review* 5:174–180.
1982   "Shall We Marry Our Enemies? Sociology and the
                       New Testament." *Int* 36:256–265.

Goodman, M.
1982   "The First Jewish Revolt: Social Conflict and the
                       Problem of Debt." *Journal of Jewish Studies* 33:417–
                       427.

Gustafson, J.
1970   "The Place of Scripture in Christian Ethics: A Meth-
                       odological Study." *Int* 24:430–455.
1974   "The Relation of the Gospels to the Moral Life." In
                       Theology and Christian Ethics. Philadelphia: United
                       Church Press.

Gutiérrez, G.
1973   *A Theology of Liberation: History, Politics and Sal-
                       vation.* Translated by C. Inda and J. Eagleson. Mary-
                       knoll, N.Y.: Orbis Books.

Hauerwas, S.
1981   *A Community of Character.* Notre Dame, Ind.:
                       University of Notre Dame Press.
1983   *The Peaceable Kingdom.* Notre Dame, Ind.:
                       University of Notre Dame Press.

Hengel, M.
1961   *Die Zeloten.* Leiden: E. J. Brill.
1971   *Was Jesus a Revolutionist?* Philadelphia: Fortress
                       Press.
1973   *Victory Over Violence.* Philadelphia: Fortress Press.
Hoffmann, P.
1972   *Studien zur Theologie der Logienquelle.* NTAbh, n.F.
                       8. Münster: Verlag Aschendorff.

Horsley, R. A.
1979a   "Josephus and the Bandits." *Journal for the Study of
                       Judaism* 10:37–63.
1979b   "The Sicarii: Ancient Jewish 'Terrorists.' " *JR*
                       59:435–458.

Klassen, W.
1984   *Love of Enemies: The Way to Peace.* Philadelphia: Fortress Press.

Koester, H.
1957   *Synoptische Überlieferung bei den apostolischen Vätern.* Berlin: Akademie-Verlag.

Kohler, K.
1905   "The Zealots." In *Jewish Encyclopedia.* New York: Funk & Wagnalls. Reprinted in Cullmann, pp. 73–82.

Lührmann, D.
1972   "Liebet eure Feinde (Lk 6,27–36/Mt 5,39–48)." *ZTK* 69:412–438.

Manson, T. W.
1950 (1937)   *The Sayings of Jesus.* London: SCM Press.

Mott, S. C.
1982   *Biblical Ethics and Social Change.* Oxford: Oxford University Press.

Niebuhr, R.
1956 (1935)   *An Interpretation of Christian Ethics.* New York: Meridian Books.

Ogletree, T. W.
1983   *The Use of the Bible in Christian Ethics.* Philadelphia: Fortress Press.

Perrin, N.
1967   *Rediscovering the Teachings of Jesus.* New York: Harper & Row.

Piper, J.
1979   *"Love Your Enemies": Jesus' Love Command in the Synoptic Gospels and in the Early Christian Paraenesis.* Cambridge: Cambridge University Press.

Rausch, J.
1966   "The Principle of Nonresistance and Love of Enemy in Mt. 5:38–48." *CBQ* 28:31–41.

Riches, J.
1980   *Jesus and the Transformation of Judaism.* London: Darton, Longman & Todd.

Schottroff, L.
1978   "Non-Violence and the Love of One's Enemies." In *Essays on the Love Commandment,* Luise Schottroff et al., pp. 9–39. Philadelphia: Fortress Press.

Seitz, O. J. F.
1969   "Love Your Enemies: The Historical Setting of Matthew V.43f.; Luke VI.27f." *NTS* 16:39–54.
Sherwin-White, A. N.
1963   *Roman Society and Roman Law in the New Testament.* Oxford: Clarendon Press.
Smith, M.
1952   "Mt. 5:43: 'Hate Thine Enemy.' " *HTR* 45:71–73.
1971   "Zealots and Sicarii, Their Origins and Relations." *HTR* 64:1–19.
Stendahl, K.
1954   *The School of St. Matthew and Its Use of the New Testament.* Lund: W. K. Gleerup.
1962a   "Matthew." In *Peake's Commentary on the Bible.* London: Thomas Nelson & Sons.
1962b   "Hate, Non-Retaliation and Love: 1QS X, 17–20 and Romans 12:19–21." *HTR* 55:343–355.
Suggs, M. J.
1978   "The Antitheses as Redactional Products." In *Essays on the Love Commandment.* Philadelphia: Fortress Press.
Talbert, C. H.
1982   *Reading Luke.* New York: Crossroad.
Tannehill, R. C.
1970   "The 'Focal Instance' as a Form of New Testament Speech: A Study of Matthew 5:39b–42." *JR* 50:372–385.
Theissen, G.
1979   "Gewaltverzicht and Feindesliebe (Mt 5, 38–48/Lk 6, 27–38) und deren sozialgeschichtlicher Hintergrund." In *Studien zur Soziologie des Urchristenums.* WUNT 19. Tübingen: J. C. B. Mohr [Paul Siebeck].
Tinsley, E. J.
1964   *The Gospel According to St. Luke.* Cambridge: Cambridge University Press.
Yoder, J. H.
1972   *The Politics of Jesus.* Grand Rapids: Wm. B. Eerdmans Publishing Co.

4

Neither Passivity
nor Violence:
Jesus' Third Way
(Matt. 5:38–42 par.)

Walter Wink

Jesus' statement about violence in Matt. 5:38–42 has itself been
the victim of unusual violence. There are those who reduce the text
to a pietistic exhortation: "rather suffer injustice than impose their
rights through violence."[1] "His disciples are to be so free of self that
they do not even desire human justice."[2] Others believe that Jesus
taught nonretaliation because God would imminently wreak vengeance on the wicked,[3] or, coming at revenge by another indirect
route, we are to suffer evil and leave it to the civil rulers to see that
justice gets done after all.[4] Or the passage has been seen as encouraging flattery and sycophantism toward those in power: "Politicians,
government officials and rich men are always friendly and kind
toward those who willingly carry their burdens without complain-
ing"—written without the slightest trace of irony.[5]

A host of writers, from Chrysostom to the present, stress the spiritual benefits to be gained by voluntarily undergoing humiliation and
the mortification of the ego.[6] Such views justify the contempt of
Herbert Marcuse when he writes, "With the Sermon on the Mount
one cannot revolt. . . . Nothing is more abominable than the
preaching of love: 'Do not hate your opponent'—this in a world in
which hate is everywhere institutionalized."[7]

Revision of a paper that first appeared in *SBL Seminar Papers,* 1988, pp.
210–224, by permission of the Society of Biblical Literature.

It is all very well for those of us who are used to receiving justice to surrender it voluntarily, because we are normally treated fairly. A bit of renunciation might even do us good. But to ask the poor and powerless to acquiesce in injustice when that is all they have ever known is itself an act of complicity in injustice. For those who are struggling for a more human world, these readings of the text are themselves laden with political repression and demagoguery. Jesus never intended anything of the sort. I will argue that the radicalism of Jesus' message can be recovered by a closer examination of his audience and context and that his message was not one of nonresistance, as almost all commentators have argued, but rather of active nonviolent resistance.

Matthew's Version of the Discourse
(Matthew 5:38–42)

[38]You have heard that it was said, "An eye for an eye and a tooth for a tooth." [39]But I say to you, Do not resist an evildoer. But if anyone strikes you on the right cheek, turn the other also; [40]and if anyone wants to sue you and take your coat, give your cloak as well; [41]and if anyone forces you to go one mile, go also the second mile. [42]Give to everyone who begs from you, and do not refuse anyone who wants to borrow from you. (NRSV)

The core of Matthew's logion is 5:39b–42, though v. 42 may not belong to the original cluster.[8] In vs. 39b–41 the focus is first on what an oppressor does and then on what the hearers can do back; in v. 42 the focus shifts to the hearers and what they should do when another would beg or borrow. The more original version of v. 42 is probably preserved in Luke 6:35: "and lend, expecting nothing in return," and in *Gos. Thom.* 95: "If you have money do not lend at interest, but give . . . from whom you will not get them [back]." What in Matthew seems to be the bland encouragement of almsgiving and moneylending appears in Luke and *Thomas* in a form as shocking as the injunctions that precede it in Matthew: lend without hope even of interest, lend even to those who cannot pay it back at all. "The follower of Jesus is not merely to lend without interest, but to *give*. If this be so, the very radicalism of the saying might suggest its authenticity."[9] Matthew has not quite succeeded in integrating v. 42 into the rest of the saying. I will therefore treat v. 42 as a secondary addition of a (probably authentic) saying of Jesus as represented by the Lukan and *Thomas* version.

Luke's Version of the Saying
(Luke 6:29–30)

[29]If anyone strikes you on the cheek, offer the other also; and from anyone who takes away your coat do not withhold even your shirt. [30]Give to everyone who begs from you; and if anyone takes away your goods, do not ask for them again. (NRSV)

Luke's version lacks Matthew's introduction, thesis statement, and the saying about forced labor. Luke has made a number of alterations to the Q version. He mistakes the striking as armed robbery[10] and the response as submission: offer the other cheek to be pommeled. Consequently, he drops Matthew's "right" cheek, apparently not recognizing that "right" specifies the type of blow and that it is intended, not as attack or injury, but as humiliation. In the same way, he regards the taking of the coat as theft; disciples are supposed to offer to the thieves their last remaining covering. In v. 30 he preserves Matthew's injunction to give to beggars, but in the second half of the saying he returns to the theme of brigandage: if anyone forcibly seizes your goods, do not seek to recover them— as if one could! Since he has read virtually the whole passage as a response to armed robbery, Luke simply has no use for the saying about how to respond to the enforced carrying of imperial Roman baggage, so he drops that altogether. Luke correctly preserves the original sequence of the taking of garments, however: first the *himation* (outer garment, cloak), then the *chitōn* (undergarment, shirt).

The Q version included, at the very least, Luke 6:29–30 and probably also the saying on forced labor (Matt. 5:41).[11]

In the analysis that follows, I treat Matthew's version of the core of the discourse (Matt. 5:39b–42) as substantially original and regard Luke 6:35‖*Gos. Thom.* 95 as more authentic than Matthew's v. 42. I assume that Jesus is the source of these sayings, but only the plausibility of the interpretation will bear that out.

Interpreting the Core Sayings

Turn the Other Cheek. "If anyone strikes you on the right cheek, turn the other also." Why the *right* cheek? A blow by the right fist in that right-handed world would land on the *left* cheek of the opponent. An openhanded slap would also strike the left cheek. To hit the right cheek with a fist would require using the left hand, but in that society the left hand was used only for unclean tasks. Even to gesture with the left hand at Qumran carried the penalty of ten days' penance.[12] The only way one could naturally strike the right cheek with the right hand would be with the back of the hand. We are dealing here with insult, not a fistfight. The intention is clearly not to injure but to humiliate, to put someone in his or her "place." One normally did not strike a peer thus, and if one did, the fine was exorbitant. *M. Baba Qamma* specifies the various fines for striking an equal: for cuffing (slugging with a fist), 4 *zuz* (a *zuz* was a day's wage); for slapping, 200 *zuz;* but "if [he struck him] with the back of his hand he must pay him 400 *zuz.*" But damages for indignity are not paid to bondmen (8:1–7).[13]

A backhand slap was the usual way of admonishing inferiors. Masters backhanded slaves; husbands, wives; parents, children; men, women; Romans, Jews. *We have here a set of unequal relations, in each of which retaliation would be suicidal.* The only normal response would be cowering submission.

Part of the confusion surrounding these sayings arises from the failure to ask who Jesus' audience was. In all three of the examples in Matt. 5:39b–41, Jesus' listeners are not those who strike, initiate lawsuits, or impose forced labor, but are their victims ("If anyone strikes *you* . . . wants to sue *you* . . . forces *you* to go one mile . . ."). There are among Jesus' hearers people who were subjected to these very indignities, forced to stifle their inner outrage at the dehumanizing treatment meted out to them by the hierarchical system of caste and class, race and gender, age and status, and as a result of imperial occupation.

Why, then, does Jesus counsel these already humiliated people to turn the other cheek? Because this action robs the oppressor of the power to humiliate. The person who turns the other cheek is saying, in effect, "Try again. Your first blow failed to achieve its intended effect. I deny you the power to humiliate me. I am a human being just like you. Your status (gender, race, age, wealth) does not alter that fact. You cannot demean me."

Such a response would create enormous difficulties for the striker. Purely logistically, how would he now hit the turned other cheek? He cannot backhand it with his right hand (one almost needs to try this physically to see the problem).[14] If he hits with a fist, he makes the other his equal, acknowledging him as a peer. But the point of the back of the hand is to reinforce the caste system and its institutionalized inequality. Even if the superior orders the person flogged for such "cheeky" behavior (this is certainly no way to *avoid* conflict!), the point has been irrevocably made. He has been given notice that this underling is in fact a human being. In that world of honor and shaming, he has been rendered impotent to instill shame in a subordinate.[15] He has been stripped of his power to dehumanize the other.

Give the Undergarment. The second example that Jesus gives is set in a court of law. Someone is being sued for his outer garment. Who would do that, and under what circumstances? The Hebrew scriptures provide the clues.

> If you lend money to any of my people with you *who is poor,* you shall not be to him as a creditor, and you shall not exact interest from him. If ever you take your neighbor's garment (*himation*) in pledge, you shall restore it to him before the sun goes down; for that is his only covering, it is his mantle (*himation*) for his body; in what else shall he sleep? And if he cries to me, I will hear, for I am compassionate. (Ex. 22:25–27; LXX 22:24–26)

> When you make your neighbor a loan of any sort, you shall not go into his house to fetch his pledge. You shall stand outside, and the man to whom you make the loan shall bring the pledge out to you. *And if he is a poor man,* you shall not sleep in his pledge; when the sun goes down, you shall restore to him the pledge that he may sleep in his cloak (*himatiō*) and bless you. . . . You shall not . . . take a widow's garment (*himation*) in pledge. (Deut. 24:10–13, 17)

> They that trample the head of the poor into the dust of the earth . . . lay themselves down beside every altar upon garments (*himatia*) taken in pledge. (Amos 2:7–8; see also Ezek. 18:5–9)

Only the poorest of the poor would have nothing but a garment to give as collateral for a loan. Jewish law strictly required its return every evening at sunset.[16]

Matthew and Luke are at odds as to whether it is the outer garment (Luke) or the undergarment (Matthew) that is being seized. But the Jewish practice of giving the outer garment as a pledge (it alone would be useful as a blanket for sleeping) makes it clear that Luke's order is correct, even though he does not preserve the legal setting. According to Liddell-Scott, *himation* is "always an outer garment . . . worn above the *chitōn*," whereas the *chitōn* is a "garment worn next to the skin." Consistent with this usage, the LXX reads *himation* in the passages just cited. S. Safrai and M. Stern describe normal Jewish dress: an outer garment or cloak of wool and an undergarment or tunic of linen.[17] To avoid confusion, I will simply refer to the "outer garment" and the "undergarment."

The situation to which Jesus speaks is one with which his hearers would have been all too familiar: the poor debtor has sunk ever deeper into poverty, the debt cannot be repaid, and his creditor has summoned him to court (*krithēnai*) to wring out repayment by legal means.

Indebtedness was one of the most serious social problems in first-century Palestine. Jesus' parables are full of debtors struggling to salvage their lives. Heavy debt was not, however, a natural calamity that had overtaken the incompetent. It was the direct consequence of Roman imperial policy. Emperors had taxed the wealthy so stringently to fund their wars that the rich began seeking nonliquid investments to secure their wealth. Land was best, but it was ancestrally owned and passed down over generations, and no peasant would voluntarily relinquish it. Exorbitant interest, however, could be used to drive landowners ever deeper into debt until they were forced to sell their land. By the time of Jesus we see this process already far advanced: large estates owned by absentee landlords, managed by stewards, and worked by servants, sharecroppers, and day laborers. It is no accident that the first act of the Jewish revolutionaries in 66 C.E. was to burn the temple treasury, where the record of debts was kept.

It is in this context that Jesus speaks. His hearers are the poor ("if anyone would sue *you*"). They share a rankling hatred for a system that subjects them to humiliation by stripping them of their lands, their goods, and finally even their outer garments.

Why, then, does Jesus counsel them to give over their undergarments as well? This would mean stripping off all their clothing and marching out of court stark naked! Imagine the hilarity this saying must have evoked. There stands the creditor, covered with shame, the poor debtor's outer garment in the one hand, his undergarment in the other. The tables have suddenly been turned on the creditor. The debtor had no hope of winning the case; the law was entirely in the creditor's favor. But the poor man has transcended this attempt to humiliate him. He has risen above shame. At the same time, he has registered a stunning protest against a system that spawns such debt. He has said in effect, "You want my robe? Here, take everything! Now you've got all I have except my body. Is that what you'll take next?"

Nakedness was taboo in Judaism, and opprobrium fell not on the naked party but on the person viewing or causing one's nakedness (Gen. 9:20–27).[18] Nonobservant Jews apparently took this taboo lightly, however. By stripping, the debtor has brought the creditor under the same prohibition that led to the curse of Canaan. We can imagine him parading naked into the street. His friends and neighbors, startled, aghast, inquire what happened. He explains. They join his growing procession, which now resembles a victory parade. The entire system by which debtors are oppressed has been publicly unmasked. The creditor is revealed to be not a "respectable" money-lender but a party to the reduction of an entire social class to land-lessness and destitution. This unmasking is not simply punitive, therefore; it offers the creditor a chance to see, perhaps for the first time in his life, what his practices cause, and to repent.

The "powers that be" literally stand on their dignity. Nothing de-potentiates them faster than deft lampooning. By refusing to be awed by their power, the powerless are emboldened to seize the initiative, even where structural change is not immediately possible. This message, far from being a counsel to perfection unattainable in this life, is a practical, strategic measure for empowering the op-pressed, and it is being lived out all over the world today by pow-erless people ready to take their history into their own hands.

Jesus provides here a hint of how to take on the entire system in a way that unmasks its essential cruelty and to burlesque its preten-sions to justice, law, and order. Here is a poor man who will no longer be treated as a sponge to be squeezed dry by the rich. He accepts the laws as they stand, pushes them to the point of absurdity, and reveals them for what they have become. He strips nude, walks out before his compatriots, and leaves this creditor, and the whole economic edifice that he represents, stark naked.

Go the Second Mile. Jesus' third example, the one about going the second mile, is drawn from the relatively enlightened practice of limiting the amount of forced or impressed labor (*angareia*) that Roman soldiers could levy on subject peoples to a single mile.[19] The term *angareia* is Persian and became a loan word in Aramaic, Greek, and Latin. Josephus mentions it in reference to the Seleucid ruler Demetrius, who, in order to enlist Jewish support for his bid to be king, promised, among other things, that "the Jews' beasts of burden shall not be requisitioned (*angareuesthai*) for our army" (*Ant.* 13.52). In the passion narrative, Simon of Cyrene is "com-pelled" (*angareuousin*) by the soldiers to carry Jesus' cross (Mark 15:21; Matt. 27:32). Such forced service was a constant feature of Palestine from Persian to late Roman times, and whoever was found on the street could be compelled into service.[20] Most cases of im-pressment involved the need of the postal service for animals and the need of soldiers for civilians to help carry their packs. The sit-uation in Matthew is clearly the latter. It is not a matter of requisi-tioning animals but people themselves.

This forced labor was a source of bitter resentment by all Roman subjects. "*Angareia* is like death," complains one source.[21] The sheer frequency, even into the late empire, of reiterated legislation proscribing the misuse of the *angareia* and limiting its legal employment shows how regularly the practice was used and its regulations violated. An inscription of 49 C.E. from Egypt orders that Roman "soldiers of any degree when passing through the several districts are not to make any requisitions or to employ forced transport (*angareia*) unless they have the prefect's written authority"[22]—a rescript clearly made necessary by soldiers abusing their privileges. Another decree from Egypt from 133–137 documents this abuse: "As I have learned that many soldiers without written requisition are travelling about in the country, demanding ships, beasts of burden, and men, beyond anything authorized, sometimes seizing things by force . . . to the point of *showing abuse and threats to private citizens,* the result is that the military is associated with arrogance and injustice."[23] In order to minimize resentment in the conquered lands, at least some effort was made by Rome to punish violators of the laws regarding impressment.

The Theodosian Code devotes an entire section to *angareia.*[24] Among its ordinances are these:

> If any person while making a journey should consider that he may abstract an ox that is not assigned to the public post but dedicated to the plow, he shall be *arrested with due force* by the rural police . . . and he shall be haled before the judge [normally the governor]. (8.5.1, 315 C.E.)

> By this interdict We forbid that any person should deem that they may request packanimals and supplementary posthorses. But if any person should rashly act so presumptuously, *he shall be punished very severely.* (8.5.6, 354 C.E.; italics added)

> When any legion is proceeding to its destination, it shall not hereafter attempt to appropriate more than two posthorses (*angariae*), and only for the sake of any who are sick. (8.5.11, 360 C.E.)

Late as these regulations are, they reflect a situation that had changed little since the time of the Persians. Armies had to be moved through countries with dispatch. Some legionnaires bought their own slaves to help carry their sixty- to eighty-five-pound packs (not including weapons).[25] The majority of the rank and file, however, had to depend on impressed civilians. There are vivid accounts of whole villages fleeing to avoid being forced to carry soldiers' baggage, and of richer towns prepared to pay large sums to escape having Roman soldiers billeted on them for winter.[26]

With few exceptions, the commanding general of a legion person-ally administered justice in serious cases, and all other cases were left to the disciplinary control of his subordinates. Centurions had almost limitless authority in dealing with routine cases of discipline. This accounts for the curious fact that there is very little codified military law, and what we have is late. Roman military historians are agreed, however, that military law changed very little in its es-sential character throughout the imperial period.[27] No account of the penalties to be meted out to soldiers for forcing a civilian to carry his pack more than the permitted mile survives to us today, but there are at least hints. "If in winter quarters, in camp, *or on the march,* either an officer or a soldier does injury to a civilian, and does not fully repair the same, he shall pay the damage twofold."[28] This is about as mild a penalty, however, as one can find. Josephus's com-ment is surely exaggerated, even if it states the popular impression: Roman military forces "have laws which punish with death not merely desertion of the ranks, but even a slight neglect of duty" (*J.W.* 3.102–108). Between these extremes was deprivation of pay, a ration of barley instead of wheat, reduction in rank, dishonorable discharge, being forced to camp outside the fortifications, or to stand all day before the general's tent holding a clod in one's hands, or to stand barefoot in public places. But the most frequent punish-ment by far was flogging.[29]

We must also reckon, however, with an ancient version of the "old boys network"; a centurion would be unlikely to impose pun-ishment for minor infractions unless there was personal animosity between him and his subordinate. The sheer frequency with which decrees were issued to curb misuse of the *angareia* indicates how lax discipline on this point was. Perhaps the soldier might receive only a rebuke. But the point is that the soldier *does not know what will happen.*

It is in this context of Roman military occupation that Jesus speaks. He does not counsel revolt. One does not "befriend" the soldier, draw him aside and drive a knife into his ribs. Jesus was keenly aware of the futility of armed insurrection against Roman imperial might and minced no words about it, though it must have cost him support from those whose hatred of Rome was near to flaming into violence.[30]

But why carry his pack a second mile? Is this not to rebound to the opposite extreme: aiding and abetting the enemy?[31] Not at all.

The question here, as in the two previous instances, is how the oppressed can recover the initiative, how they can assert their human dignity in a situation that cannot for the time being be changed. The rules are Caesar's, but how one responds to the rules is God's, and Caesar has no power over that.

Imagine then the soldier's surprise when, at the next mile marker, he reluctantly reaches to assume his pack, and the civilian says, "Oh no, let me carry it another mile." Why would he want to do that? What is he up to? Normally, soldiers have to coerce people to carry their packs, but this Jew does so cheerfully, and *will not stop!* Is this a provocation? Is he insulting the legionnaire's strength? Being kind? Trying to get him disciplined for seeming to violate the rules of impressment? Will this civilian file a complaint? Create trouble?

From a situation of servile impressment, the oppressed have once more seized the initiative. They have taken back the power of choice. The soldier is thrown off balance by being deprived of the predictability of his victim's response. He has never dealt with such a problem before. Now he has been forced into making a decision for which nothing in his previous experience has prepared him. If he has enjoyed feeling superior to the vanquished, he will not enjoy it today. Imagine the hilarious situation of a Roman infantryman pleading with a Jew to give back his pack. The humor of this scene may escape those who picture it through sanctimonious eyes, but it could scarcely have been lost on Jesus' hearers, who must have been regaled at the prospect of thus discomfiting their oppressors.

One could easily misuse Jesus' advice vindictively; that is why it must not be separated from the command to love enemies so integrally connected with it in both Matthew and Luke. But love is not averse to taking the law and using its oppressive momentum to throw the soldier into a region of uncertainty and anxiety where he has never been before.

Jesus is inviting those whose lifelong pattern has been to cringe before their masters to liberate themselves from both servile actions and a servile mentality. But he is doing something else as well: he asserts that they can do this *before* there is a revolution. There is no need to wait until Rome has been defeated or peasants are landed and slaves freed. They can begin to behave with dignity and recovered humanity *now,* even under the unchanged conditions of the old order. Jesus' sense of divine immediacy has social implications. The reign of God is already breaking into the world, and it comes, not as an imposition from on high, but as the leaven slowly raising the dough (Matt. 13:33‖Luke 13:20–21). Jesus' teaching on nonviolence is thus of a piece with his proclamation of the dawning of the reign of God.

In the conditions of first-century Palestine, a political revolution against the Romans could only be catastrophic, as the events of 66–70 c.e. would prove. Jesus does not propose armed revolution. But he does lay the foundations for a social revolution, as Richard Horsley has pointed out. And a social revolution becomes political when it reaches a critical threshold of acceptance, and this in fact did happen to the Roman Empire as the Christian church overcame it from below.[32]

Nor were peasants and slaves in a position to transform the economic system by frontal assault. But they could begin to act from an already recovered dignity and freedom, and the ultimate consequences of such acts could only be revolutionary. To that end, Jesus spoke repeatedly of a general remission of debts.[33]

It is entirely appropriate, then, that the saying on debts in Matt. 5:42‖Luke 6:30‖*Gos. Thom.* 95 has been added to this saying block. Jesus counsels his hearers not just to practice alms and lend money, even to bad-risk debtors, but actually to lend without expecting interest or even the return of the principle. Such radical egalitarian sharing would be necessary to rescue impoverished Palestinian peasants from their plight; one need not contemplate an imminent end of history as a limit on the need for such astonishing generosity. Yet none of this is new; Jesus is merely issuing a prophetic summons to Israel to observe the commandments pertaining to the sabbatical year enshrined in Torah, adapted to a new situation.[34]

Such egalitarian sharing would be necessary in order to restore true communitarian impulses cleansed of narrow calculations of who owes what. For the risky defiance of the "powers that be" that Jesus advocates would inevitably issue in punitive economic sanctions and physical punishment against individuals. They will need economic support; Matthew's "Give to everyone who *asks* [*aitounti*—not necessarily *begs*] of you" may simply refer to this need for mutual sustenance. Staggering interest rates and taxes work to isolate peasants, who go under one by one. This is a standard function of imperial "divide and rule" strategy.[35] Jesus' solution was neither utopian nor apocalyptic. It was realistic in the extreme. Nothing less could halt or reverse the avalanche of defaults through indebtedness than a complete suspension of usury and debt and a rebalancing of economic equality through outright grants, a pattern actually implemented in the earliest Christian community, according to the book of Acts.[36]

The Introductory Setting
(Matthew 5:38–39a)

On the basis of the criterion of dissimilarity, the examples of un-armed direct action in Matt. 5:39b–41 appear to have originated with Jesus. No one, not only in the first century but in all of human history, ever advocated defiance of oppressors by turning the cheek, stripping naked in court, or jeopardizing a soldier by carrying his pack a second mile. For three centuries, the early church obediently observed the injunction to nonviolence implicit in Jesus' teaching and example. But nowhere in the early church, to say nothing of the early Fathers, do we find statements similar to these in their humor and originality. These sayings are, in fact, so radical, so unprece-dented, and so threatening, that it has taken all these centuries just to begin to grasp their implications.

The introduction to the passage (Matt. 5:38–39a) is more prob-lematic, however. The six antitheses in Matt. 5:21–48 are probably Matthean additions.[37] Matthew's introduction of the *lex talionis* in 5:38 is not altogether successful; that law dealt with the principle of proportionality in punishment for crimes and serves as the basis of every legal system. In the examples that follow (5:39b–42), how-ever, Jesus does not nullify, supersede, or add to the old law. He is not even attempting to formulate new legislation. His examples *as-sume* the continuation of existing laws and customs and in each case represent a surprising new strategy the poor can use to win dignity and recover moral initiative even when the legal system is unjust and works against them.

The nub of the problem is v. 39a. The "But I say to you" is echoed in Luke 6:27, and the clause that follows in Matthew, "Do not *antistēnai* one who is evil," provides a summary of the three core sayings that follow. "Evil" (*ponēros*) is a typically Matthean term (26 out of a total of 78 times in the New Testament), yet ten of the occurrences have parallels in Q. Luke, however, does not have the word in his version of this passage.

The critical issue is the meaning of *antistēnai*. Virtually all trans-lators and interpreters have taken it in a general sense: do not *resist*. That meaning of the word is certainly well attested, but its use in this passage is insupportable. Purely on logical grounds, "resist not" does not fit the aggressive nonviolent actions described in the three following examples. Since in these three instances Jesus provides strategies for resisting oppression, it is altogether inconsistent for him to counsel people in almost the same breath not to resist it.

Likewise the alternatives are false: one either resists evil or resists not. No other possibility appears to exist; if then Jesus commands us not to resist, then the only other choice would appear to be supine submission, passivity, complicity in our own oppression, surrender to evil, acquiescence. *And this is precisely the way most Christians have interpreted this saying.* "Turn the other cheek" is taken to enjoin becoming a doormat for Jesus, to be walked over without protest. "Give your undergarment as well" has encouraged people to go limp in the face of injustice and hand over the last thing they own. "Going the second mile" has been turned into a platitude meaning nothing more than "extend yourself." Rather than encourage the oppressed to counteract their oppressors, these revolutionary statements have been deliberately transformed into injunctions to collude in one's own despoiling.

The court translators working in the hire of King James, like most of their predecessors, knew that the king did not want people concluding that they had any recourse against his or any other sovereign's tyranny. In fact, James had explicitly commissioned the new translation because of what he regarded as "seditious" tendencies in the Geneva Bible.[38] Therefore the public had to be made to believe that there are two alternatives, and only two: flight or fight. And Jesus is made to command us, according to these king's men, to resist not. Jesus appears to authorize monarchical absolutism. Submission is the will of God. Most modern translators have meekly followed in that path.[39]

What these translators have not noted, however, is how frequently *anthistēmi* is used as a military term. Resistance implies "counteractive aggression," a response to hostilities initiated by someone else. Liddell-Scott defines *anthistēmi* as to "*set against* esp. in battle, *withstand.*" Ephesians 6:13 is exemplary of its military usage: "Therefore take the whole armor of God, that you may be able to withstand [*antistēnai,* literally, to draw up battle ranks against the enemy] in the evil day, and having done all, to stand [*stēnai,* literally, to close ranks and refuse to retreat]." The term is used in the LXX primarily for armed resistance in military encounters (44 out of 71 times).[40] Josephus uses *anthistēmi* for violent struggle 15 out of 17 times; Philo, 4 out of 10.

Stasis, the noun form of *stēnai,* means "a stand," in the military sense of facing off against an enemy. By extension, it came to mean a "party formed for seditious purposes; sedition, revolt." The NRSV translates *stasis* in Mark 15:7 as "insurrection" (so also Luke 23:19, 25), in Acts 19:40 as "rioting," and in Acts 23:10 as "violent dissension." *Anistēmi,* which is virtually interchangeable with *anthistēmi,* is used militarily in the LXX 94 times in the sense of "rise up against someone" in revolt or war.[41]

In short, *antistēnai* means more in Matt. 5:39a than simply to "stand against" or "resist." It means to resist *violently,* to revolt or rebel, to engage in an insurrection. The logic of the text requires such a meaning: on the one hand, do not continue to be supine and complicit in your oppression; but on the other hand, do not react violently to it either. Rather, find a third way, a way that is neither submission nor assault, neither flight nor fight, a way that can secure your human dignity and begin to change the power equation, even now, before the revolution. Turn your cheek, thus indicating to the one who backhands you that his attempts to shame you into servility have failed. Strip naked and parade out of court, thus taking the momentum of the law and the whole debt economy and flipping them, jujitsu-like, in a burlesque of legality. Walk a second mile, surprising the occupation troops with a sudden threat to their safety. These are, of course, not rules to be followed literally but examples to spark an infinite variety of creative responses in new and changed circumstances. They break the cycle of humiliation with humor and even ridicule, exposing the injustice of the system. They recover for the poor a modicum of initiative that can force the oppressor to see them in a new light.

How, then, did a series of sayings that encouraged subversive assertiveness among the poor get turned into a command to submit to every indecency? The problem surely did not begin with the English translators; Jerome and the early theologians had already fallen under the spell of the "eat humble pie" interpretation.[42] The problem may go back to Matthew himself and his construction of the antitheses. In casting about for an Old Testament verse to serve as a foil to Jesus' sayings on nonviolent direct action, Matthew hit upon the *lex talionis* (Ex. 21:22–25; Lev. 24:19–20; Deut. 19:18–21). Superficially, the law of proportionate revenge fits: do not seek revenge (as the old law allowed); rather, return evil with good. But Jesus' sayings in vs. 39b–41 envision the rejection of both passivity and violence for a third way which seeks to recover the humanity of both oppressed and oppressor through acts of defiant vulnerability. Matthew's *lex talionis,* on the other hand, introduces a quite different set of contrasts: rejection of massive retaliation (which the *lex talionis* was devised to stop), rejection even of proportionate retaliation (the *lex talionis* itself) for—the logic proceeds inexorably toward this conclusion—rejection of retaliation of any kind.

To put it differently, the logic of Jesus' examples in Matt. 5:39b–

42 goes beyond both inaction and overreaction, capitulation and murderous counterviolence, to a new response, fired in the crucible of love, that promises to liberate the oppressed from evil even as it frees the oppressor from sin. Matthew's introduction of the *lex talionis* skewed that focus, shifting it to seeking no revenge or reparations whatever. As a result, Jesus' militant strategies came to be read as passive acquiescence in oppression, and the radical intent of these sayings was virtually buried.

On the other hand, the problem may be one of translation. There is good reason to believe that the earliest form of Matt. 5:39a is to be found in the New Testament epistles. In Romans 12 we find the densest concentration of dominical sayings in the entire Pauline corpus:

Romans
   12:14   "Bless those who persecute you; bless and do not curse
              them" = Matt. 5:44‖Luke 6:28.
   12:15   "Rejoice with those who rejoice, weep with those who
              weep" = Matt. 5:4, 12‖Luke 6:21, 23.
   12:17   "Do not repay anyone evil for evil," and 12:21—"Do not be
              overcome by evil, but overcome evil with good" = Matt.
              5:39a.

Both 1 Thess. 5:15 ("See that none of you repays evil for evil") and 1 Peter 3:9 ("Do not return evil for evil or abuse for abuse; but, on the contrary, repay with a blessing") preserve the same saying as Rom. 12:17. We appear to have here an extremely early fixed catechetical tradition, predating even the earliest preserved epistle.[43] The teaching on nonviolence thus clearly antedates the Jewish War and was not a reaction to it.

The expression "Repay no one evil for evil" conveys precisely the sense we have found in Matt. 5:39a: Do not mirror evil. The examples that follow in 5:39b–41 in fact presuppose some such sense. Could this ancient catechetical tradition have originally stood, then, in Matthew's tradition? If "Do not repay evil for evil" and "Do not forcibly resist evil" have equivalent meanings, could they simply be translation variants of the same saying?

We can now, for the first time, answer a cautious yes to that question. George Howard has recently published what he regards as an early Hebrew text of the Gospel of Matthew, which reads at 5:39a, "But I say to you, *do not repay evil for evil.*"[44] If this remarkable find is indeed as ancient as Howard argues, it reinforces our suspicion that Matt. 5:39a and the catechetical saying in Rom. 12:17; 1

Thess. 5:15; and 1 Peter 3:9 are indeed derived from the same Aramaic *Vorlage*. It is Matthew who has skewed its translation by adjusting it to the *lex talionis* in the opening antithesis (v. 38).[45]

If this line of argument is correct, then the original version of 5:39a was something closer to, "Do not repay evil for evil." This is the sense that 5:39b–42 requires. "Do not react violently to evil, do not counter evil in kind, do not let evil dictate the terms of your opposition"—this is a revolutionary principle that fits Jesus' own logic too closely to have been introduced by someone who clearly did not fully grasp it. Perhaps, then, Jesus used this phrase as a thesis statement to preface the three examples that follow. Together, thesis statement and examples form the charter for a way of being in the world that at last breaks the spiral of violence. Jesus here reveals a way of fighting evil with all one's power but without being transformed into the very evil we fight. It is a way of not becoming what we hate. Do not counter evil in kind—this insight is the distilled essence, stated with sublime simplicity, of the experience of those Jews who had, in Jesus' very lifetime, so courageously and effectively practiced nonviolent direct action against Rome.[46]

Jesus, in short, abhors both passivity and violence. He articulates, out of the history of his own people's struggles, a way by which evil can be opposed without being mirrored, the oppressor resisted without being emulated, the enemy neutralized without being destroyed. Those who have lived by Jesus' words—Leo Tolstoy, Mohandas K. Gandhi, Martin Luther King, Jr., Dorothy Day, César Chavez, Adolfo Pérez Esquivel—point us to a new way of confronting evil whose potential for personal and social transformation we are only beginning to grasp today.[47]

Notes

1. Gerhard Lohfink, *Jesus and Community: The Social Dimension of Christian Faith* (Philadelphia: Fortress Press, 1984), 55. So also Georg Strecker, *The Sermon on the Mount: An Exegetical Commentary* (Nashville: Abingdon Press, 1988), 82–83: Jesus commands "not struggle with evil but submission to hostile power."

2. A. H. McNeile, *The Gospel According to St. Matthew* (London: Macmillan & Co., 1961), 69.

3. David L. Dungan, "Jesus and Violence," in *Jesus, the Gospels and the Church* (ed. E. P. Sanders; FS W. R. Farmer; Macon, Ga.: Mercer University Press, 1987), 136—Jesus did not advocate resistance. " 'Do not resist evil; turn the other cheek' simply means: do not resist—at all." Leave it to the vengeance of God.

4. William Tyndale, *Expositions and Notes on Sundry Portions of the Holy Scriptures* (Cambridge: Cambridge University Press, 1849), 58–63.

5. George M. Lamsa, *Gospel Light* (Philadelphia: A. J. Holman Co., 1936), 40.

6. Chrysostom, *Homilies on the Epistle to the Romans,* Hom. 12 on Rom. 6:19 (NPNF 1st series, 11:426); Eduard Schweizer, *The Good News According to Matthew* (trans. David E. Green; London: SPCK, 1976), 130—"Jesus' concern again is to destroy self-consciousness, here the self-pity of the persecuted." "It is better to surrender everything and go through life naked than to insist on one's legal rights."

7. Herbert Marcuse, cited without reference by Pinchas Lapide, *The Sermon on the Mount: Utopia or Program for Action?* (Maryknoll, N.Y.: Orbis Books, 1986), 96.

8. For a structural analysis of this logion, see J. Dominic Crossan, "Divine Immediacy and Human Immediacy," in *Semeia* 44 (1988): 121–140. On the Q form of this unit, see John Kloppenborg, *The Formation of Q* (Philadelphia: Fortress Press, 1987), 173–180.

9. R. McL. Wilson, *Studies in the Gospel of Thomas* (London: A. R. Mowbray & Co., 1960), 128.

10. *Typtō* is used in Homer mostly with weapons of war (Liddell-Scott); in the LXX it usually has the sense "to smite, kill, slaughter"; and in the New Testament, ten out of thirteen times it refers to a violent beating.

11. Luke's focus on robbery may indicate that he is applying the saying to the rigors of the life of wandering preachers in the early church, on the order of 2 Cor. 11:23–27.

12. 1QS 7:15. "Right" must not be regarded as an insertion into Matthew's text, whatever other tendencies one may find in the tradition (contra Crossan, "Divine Immediacy"). Otherwise the type of blow is not specified, and it is wrongly regarded as a slug, not a backhand (Luke). "Hit on the right cheek" here is effectively a technical term; it is not merely descriptive of anatomy. (So also Lapide, *The Sermon on the Mount,* 121, whose work independently confirms some of the conclusions of this analysis.)

The *Didache* has generally been regarded as dependent on Matthew and/or Luke. But Aaron Milavec has presented compelling evidence that the writer(s) had access to the Jesus tradition independent of the Synoptics ("The Didache as Independent of the Gospels," Paper for the Jesus Seminar, Sonoma, Calif., March 1–3, 1991). For this saying, in fact, *Didache* preserves the best and quite possibly earliest version extant: (1) he specifies the right cheek, following Matthew; (2) yet he follows Luke (correctly) in the order "cloak/shirt"; and (3) he agrees with Matthew against Luke by including the saying about the second mile.

13. The Code of Hammurabi decrees in par. 202, "If a man has smitten the cheek of a man who is his superior, he shall be given sixty lashes with an ox whip in the assembly" (Thorkild Jacobsen, *Toward the Image of Tammuz* [Cambridge: Harvard University Press, 1970], 161).

14. The TEV translation, excellent in this passage in other respects,

misses when it reads, "Let him slap your left cheek too." But this is precisely what he *cannot* do, unless he abandons the backhand altogether.

15. "Landowners look for respect since what counts to them as well as to their tenants is honor; landowners need the 'status support' that only their tenants can give them" (Bruce J. Malina, "Patron and Client: The Analogy Behind Synoptic Theology," *Forum* 4 [1988]: 3).

16. The rights of the poor debtor are thus protected by scripture. On the other hand, the creditor is permitted to harass and shame the debtor by demanding the outer garment each morning. The *Mekilta de R. Ishmael* on Ex. 22:25–27 shows creditors intensifying their demand by taking a night garment by day and a day garment by night. See also *T.b. Tem.* 6a; *T.b. B. Mes.* 31b, 113ab, 114ab; *T.b. San.* 21a.

17. S. Safrai and M. Stern, *The Jewish People in the First Century* (Philadelphia: Fortress Press, 1987), I.2. 797–798. See also J. M. Myers, "Dress," *IDB*, 1:869–871. Matthew is not the only evangelist who confuses these terms. Mark, e.g., uses *chitōnas* for the high priest's mantle in 14:63 where Matthew (following LXX usage) has *himatia*. In its citation of Matt. 5:39b//Luke 6:29b, *Didache* 1:4 correctly agrees with Matthew against Luke by referring to the "right" cheek, and with Luke against Matthew on the garments: "If any one takes your coat (*himation*), give your shirt (*chitōna*) also" (*Apostolic Fathers* [LCL; Cambridge: Harvard University Press, 1959], 310–311). See also *Mekilta de R. Ishmael* on Ex. 22:27—"*For That Is His Only Covering.* This refers to the cloak. *It Is the Garment for His Skin.* This refers to the shirt."

18. Augustine understood Jesus to be speaking of nudity: "Whoever wishes to take away thy tunic, give over to him *whatever clothing thou hast*" (*Sermon on the Mount* 1.19.60). The *Pseudo-Clementine Homily,* which in 15.5 cites Matt. 5:40, changes the word here for "undergarment" in order to avoid the suggestion that the person becomes naked. For, comments the translator, A. Cleveland Coxe, the person who lost both cloak and tunic would be naked altogether; and "this, the writer may have imagined, Christ would not have commanded" (ANF, 8.310). Another indication that Matt. 5:40 refers to nakedness is provided by *Gospel of Thomas* 21, which appears to be a gnosticizing development of Jesus' saying about stripping naked. When the owners of the field come to reclaim it, the children take off their clothes before the owners and "are naked in their presence"—an excellent nonviolent tactic, here unfortunately distorted to mean stripping off the body after death in the presence of the evil Archons.

Nudity is so abhorrent because it violates the classification system by which one can identify a person's place on the social map. Without clothes, the boundaries by which society is ordered and guarded are dissolved. Clothing signifies one's social location, gender, and status (Jerome H. Neyrey, "A Symbolic Approach to Mark 7," *Forum* 4/3[1988]: 72). Thus Jesus depicts the wounded person by the side of the road as naked, so that the priest and the Levite have no claim laid on them by his social rank or status but only his humanity (Luke 10:30). Therefore, to strip naked voluntarily before the creditor and magistrate, precisely in a context intended to shame the poor into repayment, is to defy the hierarchical system of classification in its entirety.

19. See B. H. Isaac and I. Roll, "A Milestone of A.D. 69 from Judaea: The Elder Trajan and Vespasian," *Journal of Roman Studies* 66 (1976): 15–19. There is, so far as I can tell, no surviving Roman law limiting *angareia* to one mile, but scholars have almost universally inferred from the wording of the text (correctly, I believe) that some such rule was in force.

20. M. Rostovtzeff, "Angariae," *Klio. Beiträge zur alten Geschichte* 6 (1906): 249–258. In one Aramaic version of the book of Tobit, Tobit is unable to go fetch the gold deposited in Rages because "in those days the *angareia* had increased," and therefore "the travelers had disappeared from the streets out of fear" (*The Book of Tobit: A Chaldee Text from a Unique MS in the Bodleian Library* [ed. A. Neubauer; Oxford: Clarendon Press, 1878], 4, lines 7–9; mistranslated "tribute," p. xxviii). Other early references to *angareia* are found in *Pap. Teb.* I 5, 178ff. and 252ff. (2nd cent. B.C.E.). The former commands soldiers and others who are on official business neither to impress (*engareuein*) any of the inhabitants of the province or their beasts of burden for their own personal needs nor to requisition calves, etc. Similarly also *Orientis Graeci Inscr. Selectae* I 665.21 (ed. W. Dittenberger).

21. *j. B. Mes.* 6.3, 11a, cited by Paul Fiebig, "*angareuō*," *ZNW* 18 (1918): 64–72. For additional Jewish references, see "*angaria*" in Gustaf Dalman, *Aramäisch-neuhebräisches Handwörterbuch* (2nd ed.; Frankfurt: J. Kauffmann, 1897–1901), 105; and Marcus Jastrow, *A Dictionary of the Targumim* (New York: Pardes, 1950), 81; for Greek, "*angareia*" in Liddell-Scott; for Latin, "*angaria, angario*" in *Thesaurus Linguae Latinae* (Leipzig: B. G. Teubner, 1940–1946), 2.43. See also August Wünsche, *Neue Beiträge zur Erläuterung der Evangelien aus Talmud und Midrasch* (Göttingen: Vandenhoeck & Ruprecht, 1878), 64–65; L. Goldschmid, "Impôts et droits de douane en Judée sous les Romains," *Rev. d. it. juives* 34 (1897): 207–208; Friedrich Preisigke, "Die ptolemäische Staatspost," *Klio* 7 (1907): 275–277; Ulrich Wilcken, "Transport-Requisitionen für Beamte und Truppen," in *Grundzüge und Chrestomathie der Papyruskunde* (L. Mitteis and U. Wilcken; Leipzig/Berlin: B. G. Teubner, 1912), 1:374–376); Vincente Garcia de Diego, "Notas etimológicas: Angaria," *Boletín de la Real Academia Española* 40 (1960): 380–399; T. Henckels and H. G. Crocker, *Memorandum of Authorities on the Law of Angary* (Washington, D.C.: Government Printing Office, 1919), 25–30; J. Le Clère, *Les mesures coercitives sur les navires de commerce étrangers* (Paris: Librairie générale de droit et de jurisprudence, 1949), 19–21, 35–36; Ạ.-H. Schröder, *Das Angarienrecht* (Hamburg: Forschungsstelle für Völkerrecht und ausländisches öffentliches Recht der Universität Hamburg, 1965), 15–18; Joshua Gutmann and Daniel Sperber, "Angaria," *Encyclopaedia Judaica*, 2 (1971), cols. 950–951; D. Sperber, *Nautica Talmudica* (Ramat-Gan: Bar-Ilan University, 1986), 115–118; Sperber, "Angaria in Rabbinic

Literature," *L'Antiquité Classique* 38 (1969): 164–168; and Iu. A. Solo-
dukho, "Podati i povinnosti v Irake v III–V vv. nashï'ery" ("Taxes and
Obligations in Iraq in the Third to Fifth Centuries of Our Era"), *Sovetskoe
vostokovedenie* 5 (1948): 69, sec. 9 and n. 1.

22. *Corp. Insc. Gr.* No. 4956, A21, cited by Edwin Hatch, *Essays in
Biblical Greek* (Amsterdam: Philo, [1889] 1970), 37. Hatch suggested that
Matt. 5:41 should not be translated "whosoever shall compel thee to *go*
one mile" but "whosoever shall compel thee to *carry his baggage* one
mile," but few versions have followed his sage advice. TEV, however, ably
renders it, "If one of the occupation troops forces you to carry his pack
one mile."

23. *PSI* 446 (133–137 C.E.), cited by Ramsay MacMullen, *Soldier and
Civilian in the Late Roman Empire* (Cambridge: Harvard University Press,
1963), 89 n. 42, italics added.

24. *The Theodosian Code* (ed. Clyde Pharr; Princeton: Princeton University Press, 1952), secs. 8.5.1, 2, 6, 7; 8.1, 11, 66. See in addition *The
Digests of Justinian* (ed. Th. Mommsen; Philadelphia: University of Penn-
sylvania Press, 1985), secs. 49.18.4; 50.4.18.21–22 and 29; 50.5.10, 11;
and Justinian's *Novellae* (Constitutions), 16.9, 10; 17.1, 9, 22 (*The Civil
Law* [trans. S. P. Scott; Cincinnati: Central Trust, 1973]).

25. According to Tacitus (*Hist.* 2.70), slaves and camp followers actually outnumbered the soldiers in the army that Vitellius marched to Rome.
In Acts 10:7, the centurion Cornelius counts at least two servants and a
soldier "among those that waited on him." See for a later period Mac-
Mullen, *Soldier and Civilian*, 106 n. 29, 126–127.

26. Michael Grant, *The Army of the Caesars* (London: Weidenfeld &
Nicolson, 1974), xxi–xxx; Fiebig, "*angareuō*," esp. *Lev. R.* par. 12; *b.
Sanh.* 101b; *b. B. Qam.* 38b; *b. Sota* 10a; *b. Ber.* 9b; *b. Yoma* 35b; *b.
Ned.* 32a. Vegetius, *De re militari*, gives a graphic picture of the contents
of a Roman soldier's pack and the rigors of a forced march (translated in
Roots of Strategy [ed. T. R. Phillips; Harrisburg, Pa.: Military Service
Publ., 1955], 76–88).

27. "It was the centurion who formed the backbone of Roman military
discipline, and he did so by intensely personal coercion" (C. E. Brand,
Roman Military Law (Austin: University of Texas Press, 1968), 81, 42.
See also Robert R. Evans, *Soldiers of Rome* (Washington, D.C.: Seven
Locks Press, 1986), 74; G. W. Currie, *The Military Discipline of the Ro-
mans from the Founding of the Empire to the Close of the Republic*
(Bloomington, Ind.: Indiana University Press, 1928), 10, 12, 161; Abel
H. J. Greenridge, "The *Provocatio Militiae* and Provincial Jurisdiction,"
Class Rev 10 (1896): 226; Richard E. Smith, *Service in the Post-Marian
Roman Army* (Manchester: Manchester University Press, 1958).

28. Marius, *Strategica* 7:3, italics added; cited by Brand, *Roman Military Laws*, 21. See also 4.10, p. 195.

29. Brand, *Roman Military Laws*, 104–106. In any case, military law
was always more severe in its punishments than civil. Of the 102 instances
in which the punishment of a soldier is mentioned, 40 resulted in the death

penalty (Currie, *Military Discipline*, 38).

30. Matt. 5:38–42 is the *locus classicus* for Jesus' attitude toward violence. Nonviolence is implied by Jesus' teaching on the love of enemies as well (Matt. 5:43–48 par.). His rejection of political messiahship and his refusal to ignite armed rebellion in Jerusalem are also to the point. His view of the reign of God as coming from below, as attested by the parables, also reflects a nonviolent approach. His eschatology, significantly, though it does envision the end of Roman hegemony, does not include extermination of the Romans. Historical memory of his position on violence is also preserved in passages whose historicity is in doubt, such as John 18:36 ("if my kingship were of this world, my servants would fight"); Matt. 26:52 ("Put your sword back into its place; for all who take the sword will perish by the sword"; similarly Luke 22:51); and the absence of charges of armed revolt before Caiaphas and Pilate (Mark 14:55–15.5 par.). See also Luke 23:25; Acts 3:14–15; and Acts 13:28. The saying about two swords (Luke 22:35–38), whatever its meaning (possibly arming against robbers), is most certainly not about insurrection! For a significant study of nonviolence in the gospel message of Mark, see Ched Myers, *Binding the Strong Man* (Maryknoll, N.Y.: Orbis Books, 1988).

31. Epictetus provides an example of passive submission to impressment that is the polar opposite of Jesus' advice in Matthew. "You ought to treat your whole body like a poor loaded-down donkey . . . and if it be commandeered (*angareia*) and a soldier lay hold of it, let it go, do not resist (*antiteine*) or grumble. If you do, you will get a beating and lose your little donkey just the same" (*Disc.* 4.1.79). For the degeneration of *angareia* to plain extortion by soldiers, see MacMullen, *Soldier and Civilian*, 85–86; and M. Rostovtzeff, *The Social and Economic History of the Roman Empire* (2nd ed.; Oxford: Clarendon Press, 1957), 1.424 and 2.721–723 nn. 45–47.

32. Richard A. Horsley, *Jesus and the Spiral of Violence: Jewish Resistance in Roman Palestine* (San Francisco: Harper & Row, 1987), 318–326.

33. See Sharon H. Ringe, *Jesus, Liberation, and the Biblical Jubilee* (Philadelphia: Fortress Press, 1985).

34. That Jesus proposed such behavior in concrete situations is illustrated by the story of the rich young man (Mark 10:17–22 par.). The same kind of liberating generosity is envisioned in Luke 7:41–42; 10:35; Mark 10:23–31 par. See Douglas E. Oakman, *Jesus and the Economic Questions of His Day* (Lewiston, N.Y.: Edwin Mellen Press, 1986), 166, 215–216.

35. Horsley, *Jesus and the Spiral of Violence*, 32.

36. Acts 2:43–47; 4:32–5:11; 6:1. These reports may be idealized, but they are by no means pure fiction. The well-established poverty of the Jerusalem church may have been one of the unintended results of mixing Jesus' stringent program of redistribution of wealth with the church's apocalyptic belief in an immediate end of history. Hence the early community *liquidated* capital and lived off the proceeds, rather than sharing in communitarian economic arrangements, and quickly found itself destitute.

37. See M. Jack Suggs, "The Antitheses as Redactional Products," in *Jesus Christus in Historie und Theologie: Neutestamentliche FS Hans Conzelmann zum 60. Geburtstag* (ed. G. Strecker; Tübingen: J. C. B. Mohr [Paul Siebeck], 1975), 441; Crossan, "Divine Immediacy," 11–12.

38. James I (d. 1625) considered the Geneva Bible of 1560 the "worst" of the English translations and called it "very partiall, vntrue, seditious, and savouring, too much, of dangerous, and trayterous conceipts" (David Daiches, *The King James Version of the English Bible* [Chicago: University of Chicago Press, 1941], 65). On Rom. 13:5, e.g., the Geneva Bible margin justified disobedience of an unjust ruler: "So farre as lawfully wee may: for if unlawfull things be commanded us, we must answere as Peter teacheth us, It is better to obey God, then men."

39. Coverdale, Cranmer, and the Geneva Bible rendered the Vulgate's *resisto* in Matt. 5:39a as "resist not euell." Tyndale (d. 1536) translated "resist not wrong(e)." The sole British exception to this general pattern was the first translator of the scriptures into English, John Wycliffe (d. 1384), who rendered Matt. 5:39a, "ayenstonde not an yuel man." *Ayenstonden,* like *antistēnai,* literally means to "stand against." *The Middle English Dictionary* (ed. H. Kurath and S. M. Kuhn; Ann Arbor: University of Michigan Press, 1956), I.1.593–594 gives as meaning c "to fight against, offer resistance, defend oneself," and cites under it Wycliffe's translation of Matt. 5:39. The term is frequently used of rebellion and warfare (Wycliffe also uses it of Jannes and Jambres's revolt against Moses, 2 Tim. 3:8). Wycliffe's preaching was a root cause of the Peasants' Revolt of 1381; his works were burned in 1415.

40. Sjef van Tilborg grasps the proper sense of *antistēnai:* "A manly word is used: if you fight do it as a soldier who stands fast in war" (*The Sermon on the Mount as an Ideological Intervention* [Assen: Van Gorcum, 1986], 71). *Anthistēmi* is used militarily in Lev. 26:37; Deut. 7:24; 25:18; Josh. 7:13; 23:9; Judg. 2:14; 3 Macc. 6:19, to cite but a few. The verbal stem *histēmi* ("to stand") is compounded in a wide variety of terms denoting violent warfare, attack, revolt, rebellion, insurrection, and revolution: *aphistēmi* (Acts 5:37); *ephistēmi* (Acts 17:5; 6:12); *epanistēmi* (Matt. 10:21; Mark 13:12); *katephistēmi* (Acts 18:12); *exanistēmi* (Josh. 8:7); *enistēmi* (1 Macc. 8:24); *antikathistēmi* (Heb. 12:4); and *synephistēmi* (Acts 16:22).

The following compounds of *histēmi* are sometimes used as technical terms for military formations and strategy: *kathistēmi* (1 Macc. 10:32); *apokathistēmi* (2 Macc. 15:20); *periistēmi* (2 Macc. 14:9); *synistēmi* (Num. 16:3).

41. See, e.g., Gen. 4:8; Num. 16:2; Josh. 24:9; Judg. 9:43; 20:5; 1 Sam. 25:29; Obad. 1; Hab. 2:7. *Stasis* is also compounded in myriad ways frequently associated with war, violent uprisings, insurrection, sedition, rebellion, and revolution: *stasiōtēs, stasiōdēs* (Josephus, *Ant.* 13.403; *J.W.* 1.198); *stasiōteia, stasiarchia; stasiarchos; stasiastichos; stasiasis; stasiastēs; stasiasmos; stasiopoiia; stasiopoios* (Josephus, *Life* 134); *stasiopoieō* (Josephus, *Ant.* 17.117); *stasiazō* (Judith 7:15); *akatastasia*

(Luke 21:9); *hypostasis* (1 Sam. 13:23); *epistasis* (2 Macc. 6:3); *epistatēs* (2 Kings 25:19); *prōtostatēs* (Acts 24:5); *apostatis* (1 Esdras 2:18); *apostasia* (2 Thess. 2:3); *apostasis* (Josh. 22:22); *apostatēs* (2 Macc. 5:8); *apostatikos; apostatein* (1 Macc. 11:14); *dichostasia* (Rom. 16:17); *systasiazō* (Josephus, *Ant.* 17.285); *systasiastēs* (Josephus, *Ant.* 14:22); *systasis; prostatēs* (1 Macc. 14:47).

42. Jerome follows Luke (above, p. 104) in seeing seizure of the cloak as robbery and treats turning the cheek as patient submission to injustice and calumny (*Letter 53, To Paulinus* 11; *Letter 84, To Pammachius and Oceanus* 1; *Letter 123, To Ageruchia* 13; *Letter 54, To Furia* 12 [NPNF, 6.102, 176, 235, 106]).

43. Victor Paul Furnish, *The Love Command in the New Testament* (Nashville: Abingdon Press, 1972), 106; C. E. B. Cranfield, *The Epistle to the Romans* (ICC; Edinburgh: T. & T. Clark, 1979), 645. For non-Christian parallels, see William Klassen, *Love of Enemies: The Way to Peace* (Philadelphia: Fortress Press, 1984), 115–116 and 130 nn. 5–8. The actual verbal parallelism is remarkable:

> *mēdeni*　　　*kakon anti kakou apodidontes*—Rom. 12:17
> *mē . . .*　　　*kakon anti kakou . . . apodō*—1 Thess. 5:15
> *mē apodidontes kakon anti kakou*—1 Peter 3:9

44. George Howard, *The Gospel of Matthew According to a Primitive Hebrew Text* (Macon, Ga.: Mercer University Press, 1987), 20–21. Howard notes in addition ("The Textual Nature of Shem-Tob's Hebrew Matthew," *JBL* 108 [1989]: 253–254) that the sayings of Jesus in Shem-Tob's Hebrew version of Matthew are interrupted sixteen times by words like "Jesus said to his disciples" precisely at those points where Luke's parallel is found in a different place in Luke's Gospel or where Luke has no parallel. It appears then that this Hebrew Matthew reflects an *earlier* form of Matthew than our canonical Greek Matthew, which has omitted all these *Gospel of Thomas*-like introductions in order to create a smooth, homogeneous whole. This provides further confirmation that the earliest form of the saying was, in fact, "Do not return evil for evil."

45. Calvin had already hit upon this reading intuitively (*On a Harmony of the Evangelists* [Grand Rapids: Wm. B. Eerdmans Publishing Co., 1949], 1: 298). Pseudo-Chrysostom also equated "Resist not evil" and "Do not render evil for evil" (cited by Thomas Aquinas, *Commentary on the Four Gospels* [Oxford: James Parker, 1894], 197), as do the modern commentators Pinchas Lapide (*The Sermon on the Mount*, 134) and G. H. C. Macgregor, *The Relevance of an Impossible Ideal* (London: Fellowship of Reconciliation, 1960), 48. So also, the Christian Common Bible (Quezon City, Philippines: Claretian Publications et al., 1988) reads, "Do not oppose evil with evil." David Wenham, on carefully argued exegetical grounds, concludes that Matthew's "Do not resist evil" and the Pauline/ Petrine "Do not return evil for evil" should be seen as differing versions of the same saying of Jesus and that the latter is the more original ("Paul's Use of the Jesus Tradition: Three Samples," in Wenham, ed., *Gospel Perspectives*, vol. 5: *The Jesus Tradition Outside the Gospels* [Sheffield: JSOT Press, 1985], 18–19).

46. See Josephus, *J.W.* 2.169–174; *Ant.* 18.55–59; *J.W.* 2.230–231; Philo, *Leg.* 299–305; and later, Josephus, *Ant.* 18.261–309 and Philo, *Leg.* 225–229; and Horsley's excellent discussion, *Jesus and the Spiral of Violence,* 90–120. I am baffled, however, by the way Horsley depicts Jews initiating popular nonviolent protests and then portrays Jesus and Matt. 5:38–42 as virtually irrelevant to that setting. He denies that "enemies" referred to outsiders, but rather applied only to fellow peasants. But we can accurately specify the enemies Jesus has in mind in this passage: "enemies" are masters and overlords who backhand peasants, women, and Jews generally (v. 39); "enemies" are landlords who humiliate sharecroppers and the unemployed by seizing their outer garments (v. 40); "enemies" are Roman soldiers who compel Jews to carry their baggage (v. 41). On p. 303, Horsley contradicts his own argument when he speaks of the destruction of Jerusalem "by its enemies, who, at the time of Jesus, would obviously have been the Romans." He compellingly sketches a society in the birth pangs of discovering nonviolence and then creates a Jesus, with much questionable argumentation, who is a dreamer no different from Theudas. It seems to me that the argument of this paper fits the sociopolitical setting that Horsley has so admirably reconstructed far better than his own!

47. I have attempted to apply Jesus' teaching on the "third way" to the situation in South Africa (*Violence and Nonviolence in South Africa* [Philadelphia: New Society Pubs., 1987]) and plan to explore these themes more fully in the third volume of my trilogy on the Powers, *Engaging the Powers* (Minneapolis: Fortress Press, 1992). It would be anachronistic to regard "nonviolence" as a full-blown philosophical option in first-century Palestine. Gandhi seems to have been the first person to develop nonviolence into a total way of life, philosophy, and strategy for social change. But all the elements of that synthesis were present in Jesus' life and teaching. See Ched Myers, *Binding the Strong Man,* 47.

5

Response to Walter Wink, "Neither Passivity nor Violence: Jesus' Third Way"

Richard A. Horsley

Walter Wink finds "neither passivity nor violence," but "Jesus' third way," in Matt. 5:38–42:

> ³⁸You have heard that it was said, "An eye for an eye and a tooth for a tooth." ³⁹But I say to you, Do not resist one who is evil. But if any one strikes you on the right cheek, turn to him the other also; ⁴⁰and if any one would sue you and take your coat, let him have your cloak as well; ⁴¹and if any one forces you to go one mile, go with him two miles. ⁴²Give to him who begs from you, and do not refuse him who would borrow from you. (RSV)

Although he takes Luke's version of the sayings into account, Wink takes Matthew's version of 5:39cd–42 as "substantially original," except for substituting *Gos. Thom.* 95 for v. 42, and assumes that Jesus is the source of the sayings.

Wink sharply rejects traditional interpretations that hold that Jesus here taught nonretaliation or nonresistance, and particularly those, as in the KJV, which turned the sayings into exhortation to passivity and submission in the face of the ruling authorities. Such traditional interpretations have been rooted largely in the antithesis form imposed by Matthew, particularly by the introduction of the *lex talionis,* which transforms the other sayings into a rejection even of proportional retaliation.

In the remaining sayings, 5:39cd to 42, Wink finds the situation to be one of the oppressed people facing their oppressors. The saying to turn the other cheek in response to a backhanded insult concerns slaves or Jews who are being humiliated by masters or Romans respectively. The saying about rendering up the inner garment along with the outer garment pertains to destitute debtors being taken to court by their wealthy creditors. The saying about going the second mile refers to Jews forced to carry the heavy gear of Roman soldiers.

Once the Matthean framing in terms of an antithesis in v. 38 is stripped away, and the verb *antistēnai* seen to mean "to revolt" or "to resist violently," then v. 39a appears to be Jesus' admonition against violent resistance. The implicit logic of the saying, suggests Wink, is, on the one hand, do not acquiesce in your own oppression, but, on the other hand, do not react violently to it either. Rather, find a third way that can secure your human dignity and begin to change the power equation even now before the impending revolution. The sayings in vs. 39cd, 40, and 41, then, are not laws but "examples to spark an infinite variety of creative responses in new and changed circumstances." Turning the other cheek robs the oppressor of the power to humiliate (for if he hits again, with a fist, he acknowledges the other as a peer). Rendering up the inner garment along with the outer would mean standing stark naked in the court, thus embarrassing the creditor and registering "a stunning protest against the system that spawns such debt." Carrying the soldier's gear a second mile in a situation in which there were sharp sanctions against soldiers exploiting the occupied people would throw him off balance in his anxiety that he might possibly be severely disciplined. Jesus is thus inviting those whose lifelong pattern has been to bow and scrape before their masters to liberate themselves from both servile actions and a servile mentality, and to do this now even before the revolution has changed the conditions of the old order. The saying about lending to the would-be borrower, finally, provides for the economic support of those who would be subjected to punitive economic sanctions for defying the "powers that be" in ways such as those indicated in vs. 39cd, 40, and 41. In this "third way" opened up by Jesus, "the oppressor can be resisted without being emulated, the enemy neutralized without being destroyed. Those who have lived by Jesus' words, such as Gandhi, Martin Luther King, Dorothy Day, or César Chavez, point us to a new way of controlling evil.

Wink's paper is a paradigmatic and provocative essay in consciously engaged biblical scholarship. Having been actively involved with anti-apartheid movements in South Africa, he has discerned in Matthew 5 a possible strategy of nonviolent resistance to the intransigent forces of oppression and dehumanization. I say *consciously* engaged because any and all scholarship occupies, hence assumes, a social-political position. Even those who claim to be neutral or apolitical thus tacitly accept or acquiesce in the system in which they live and work. Nor can anyone still naively claim that biblical literature belongs to some sort of "religious" realm separate from political-economic life. Certainly there is nothing particularly "religious" in the texts that Wink is exploring. They deal with political-economic relations. And the situation portrayed is one of conflict.

In this consciously engaged analysis Wink continues a long-standing assumption that the sayings of Jesus are directly applicable to political-economic-religious situations and issues today. In the tradition of the modern Western liberal culture of individualism and voluntarism, the sayings of Jesus are accepted as ethical principles directly applicable to individuals' decisions and positions, as in the way most of us pacifists have understood "Love your enemies" and "Do not resist evil" and "Turn the other cheek" to mean that we cannot engage in violence, whether in military combat or as a means of effecting social justice. Following Gandhi and Martin Luther King, Wink has moved this reading and application of Jesus' sayings to a higher level of sophistication by discerning in the texts a strategy of response to oppression, and not simply abstract ethical principles.

But what if we turn a critical eye on the context, structure, and presuppositions by which we proceed in biblical studies or in Bible reading generally?

1. Understanding Jesus' traditions as ethical principles addressed to the individual has something to do with centuries of having read the Bible in the KJV as individual verses of propositional truth. Even when we broaden our focus to a whole "pericope" (note the meaning in Greek), as in the way the RSV and the Jerusalem Bible are organized into paragraphs, and the way the Bible is read in church services in separate "lessons," we take texts out of context. But it was not Jesus (nor the evangelists, for that matter) who organized his preaching and practice into nice neat pericopes or lessons corresponding to the patterns of our professional and devotional life. As Wink insists, Jesus' sayings are concerned with concrete situations. But Jesus appears to have been more comprehensive in his approach to a whole historical situation than we can deal with when we isolate particular biblical sayings and paragraphs. By the very structure of our procedure we block consideration of the whole situation.

2. Even if we wanted "to do as Jesus did" (often the motivation

of direct application of Jesus' sayings to today), then we must change the approach. Fairly clearly, Jesus did not "live by Moses' words" (which I take would be the parallel to our "living by Jesus' words"). Rather, he discerned the will of God for his situation and practice, and he invited his contemporaries to do the same, no longer bound to religious authority in an alienated form, that is, to the scripture, particularly as interpreted by the learned official interpreters.

3. It is highly doubtful that Jesus' sayings can be adequately understood as directed (directly) to us. As Wink sees, peoples in colonial situations, such as oppressed South Africans, are far more appropriate candidates than are we, comfortable intellectuals in the imperial metropolis who correspond more to the intellectuals of the Roman Empire (even more than we do to the scribes and Pharisees castigated in the Gospels). So it is necessary not only to get the texts straight critically but to attain as comprehensive and precise as possible a sense of the contexts—literary, social-historical, then and now—in order to understand how particular sayings of Jesus may be placed in his overall strategy and practice.

Critical analysis of the texts in fact already points to a context somewhat different from that posited by Wink. Most analyses of these sayings suggest not only that Matthew imposed the form of antithesis on the material but that the Lukan arrangement is closer to Q, even though Matthew may have followed the Q wording more closely. It thus also seems more likely that Matthew inserted the saying about going the second mile than that Luke deleted it, and especially that Matthew is responsible for the presence of "Do not resist evil" as the completion of the antithesis (rather than that Luke deleted it). But that means that there is little or no reason to believe that Matt. 5:39cd, 40, and 41 were three illustrations of the general principle "Do not resist evil (violently)," all of which Jesus himself used to articulate a "third way."

Establishment of the earliest arrangement of the sayings we can discern reinforces a close reading of the individual sayings in pointing to a *local* social-economic context for the sayings in Q = Luke 6:27–28, 29, 30, rather than the direct face-off between oppressor and oppressed suggested by Wink. The latter reading seems to depend heavily on "go the second mile" with the presumed immediate presence of a Roman occupation army. But that saying was apparently added by Matthew, making its connections with other sayings of Jesus thus unclear. It is highly doubtful that Roman soldiers would have been much of a presence in Galilee, which was ruled by the client king Antipas, who had his own security forces. For

Wink's reconstruction, much depends on the backhanded insult being an insult by a superior to an inferior. But the backhanded insult was not confined to such relations and could have been part of local quarrels and conflicts as well. Moreover, the creditor asking for the cloak would more likely have been a local than a wealthy absentee official or landowner. I suggest a broader and looser approach that accords with the probable broader political-economic situation, on the one hand, and with more precise local social-economic relations on the other. That is, briefly stated, the people addressed were indeed in oppressive conditions of poverty and debt; hence the resultant local tensions. But in these and related sayings, Jesus was exhorting them to respond positively to each other and to be supportive of one another rather than divisive.

Such local cooperation and renewal of local community relations, however, were part of a broader strategy. Once we no longer pretend that Jesus was somehow apolitical or that there were no serious structural conflicts between the Herodian or high-priestly rulers and the ordinary people (or between Galilee and Jerusalem), we must take seriously the Gospel materials indicating that Jesus stood against the oppressive institutional structures that dominated Palestine. The kingdom of God was not some cosmic catastrophe but meant the renewal of the people of Israel and the imminent divine judgment of the oppressive rulers. Roman domination itself was remote from the immediate experience of Galileans. It may not be surprising that the only time Caesar is mentioned in Jesus' sayings is in Jesus' response to the question about the tribute, that is, in connection with *the way* Roman domination directly affected the people: the tribute collected from the people. Rome dominated, but through client rulers. Hence, it is not surprising that Jesus' strategy focused on the concrete ruling institutions in Palestine. We must take seriously the traditions of Jesus' prophecies against the temple, his prophetic lament about the destruction of Jerusalem, and his prophetic parable against the high priests. The imminent divine judgment against these ruling institutions proclaimed by Jesus constituted what might be called the "political revolution," the elimination of the old order. In the confidence that such divine judgment was imminent, Jesus proceeded with what might be called the "social revolution," which is ordinarily not possible, as Wink points out, prior to the removal of oppressive structures. But Jesus proceeded to catalyze the renewal of local communities in the conviction that "the kingdom of God" was "among them" or "in the midst of them." Of course, the organization of local communities over against the established ruling institutions is itself a serious challenge to the legitimacy and viability of the latter.

Thus I agree with Wink that Jesus' strategy can be discerned in sayings such as Matt. 5:39cd, 40, 42, and his strategy was socially revolutionary. But the strategy cannot be discerned in those sayings apart from an analysis of the whole Jesus tradition in broad social-historical context. And those sayings give evidence, not of whether the strategy was violent or nonviolent, but of the kind of social relations that Jesus advocated and of his focus on renewal of local communities. We must look elsewhere for indications of whether Jesus' approach was nonviolent. Aside from his announcement of imminent divine judgment, it appears to have been nonviolent. But I see no solid evidence, textual or contextual, for asserting confidently that "Jesus was keenly aware of the futility of armed insurrection against Roman imperial might and minced no words about it."

For some time now, (colonized) third world peoples have been discerning that the traditions about Jesus' teachings and practice, along with the exodus traditions, stand firmly against oppressive structures and provide prototypes of revolutionary action against rulers and ruling institutions. This happened in the European Middle Ages when priests translated Gospel passages into vernacular languages. It happened again in twentieth-century African and Asian colonies when missionaries introduced the Bible in the people's languages. What is not clear, to me at least, is how (on what basis) we biblical scholars in the first world can argue that such revolution must be nonviolent—or whether we have any right to so argue. It is much clearer, from the sayings and practice of Jesus, that oppressive institutions and political-economic-religious relations generally stand under divine indictment.

Finally, there is the question of how *directly* we can apply the results of our historical analysis of Jesus' practice understood in its broader context. Perhaps it is still viable to apply Jesus' words directly to today's situations in social contexts where people's faith and discipleship take the general form of such direct application. That was surely the case for many of those organized by the Southern Christian Leadership Conference in the 1960s and may well be the case for many in South Africa today. But there are surely some significant differences between the historical situation of Jesus and situations today, and there are surely also differences from situation to situation today. Martin Luther King's strategy of publicly embarrassing respectable white southerners, somewhat in the way Wink's

Jesus suggested embarrassing respectable overlords and creditors, may have worked in the United States in the 1960s, with a federal government at least somewhat sensitive to the principles stated in its own Constitution. But it is unclear what remains to be "unmasked" in South Africa, where the apartheid regime makes no pretense of concern for the "civil" rights, let alone the humanity of its black subjects. There are surely some broad analogies to be drawn between Jesus' situation and that of today, such that North Atlantic intellectuals can discern their own social location and interests in the dominant metropolis. And discernment of what the word of God was in the paradigmatic, revelatory situations in which Jesus operated surely can and should inform discernment of the will of God for today's situation. But direct application of Jesus' words today may be an unwarranted shortcut in the process by which our own broader situation is analyzed and the will of God for our situation is discerned.

6

Counterresponse to Richard Horsley

Walter Wink

If any two persons ought to agree on the subject at hand, it is Horsley and Wink. We are both committed to a kind of scholarship that is involved in the urgent questions of our time. We are both wary of pacifism, especially that form of pacifism which is more concerned with the purity of the pacifist than winning justice for the oppressed. Neither of us is disposed to take Jesus' teachings as a law that says a follower "cannot" engage in violence, though neither of us can really get away from Jesus' nonviolence as in some sense normative. We both believe that we cannot be delivered from having to discern the will of God for our own quite unique modern situations and that Jesus' teaching cannot be simply transferred to our problems today in an unmediated way.

Furthermore, I find myself in substantial agreement with much of Horsley's reconstruction of the social context of first-century Judaism in his *Jesus and the Spiral of Violence*. Yet when he begins to relate Jesus to that setting, our paths suddenly and sharply part.

Horsley believes that Jesus' teachings about turning the cheek and walking out of court naked are directed, not at Rome or absentee landlords, but at local compatriots. However, these sayings cannot have been directed against peers but against those in the hierarchical structures of village life who were masters and creditors. He throws out the business of walking the second mile, arguing simply that Luke does not have it. But Luke, all through this pericope, has emptied it of its Palestinian context and applied it to the situation of

wandering preachers in the early church. He therefore understands
the hitting (*typtō*) to be armed robbery and interprets the taking of
the cloak likewise as seizure of goods by bandits. In this situation the reference to carrying the soldier's pack makes no sense, so
Luke drops it altogether.

It won't do simply to jettison the soldier's pack, then, simply
because it doesn't fit one's reconstruction. I have provided exhaustive documentation for the practice of *angareia,* and we know that
it was actively employed in Palestine, as the reference to Simon of
Cyrene proves (Mark 15:21, *angareuousin*). It is true that Romans
were not quartered in Galilee, but they had to pass through it on
their way elsewhere and may also have had to step in occasionally
to assist Herod Antipas's militia. And that militia was itself modeled
along Roman lines, even to the aping of Roman military terms.
There is no doubt that the *angareia* was imposed by Herod Antipas's
soldiers as well. And Rome's clients represented Rome in the
people's minds.

Here is where I become really befuddled, because I consider myself a better Horsleyan than Horsley. He wants to deny that Jesus
taught love of enemies in reference to Romans and their puppets,
and reserved this love only for fellow peasants in the local community. But there is nothing noteworthy in such a teaching. Even the
tax collectors do the same. Does Horsley really wish to justify hatred of the oppressor? In order to get rid of the damaging evidence
that Jesus had fellowship with tax collectors and harlots, Horsley
mounts a highly tendentious argument denying that Jesus ever did
such a thing. But why would the church have made up Jesus' table
fellowship with sinners, since the church itself from a time well in
advance of the writing of the Gospels had ceased to practice the
radical table fellowship of Jesus, did not permit harlots into the fellowship, and was already treating the Lord's Supper as a mystery
rite open only to baptized Christians? Thus, on Horsley's reading,
two of the most distinctive aspects of Jesus' ministry—loving and
forgiving enemies and fellowshiping with outcasts—bite the dust.

Horsley himself, having gone to much trouble to deny that Jesus
meant "Romans" by enemies, gives away his whole case when he
later speaks of the destruction of Jerusalem "by its enemies, who at
the time of Jesus, would obviously have been the Romans" (p. 303).

Horsley's ambivalence persists to the very end of *Jesus and the
Spiral of Violence.* Jesus was not a pacifist, but Horsley says "he
actively opposed violence, particularly institutionalized oppressive
and repressive violence, and its effects on a subject people. Jesus

was apparently a revolutionary but not a violent political revolutionary" (p. 326). How does he know this, if he has robbed Jesus of the very passage that best shows how Jesus opposed counterviolence against oppressors? Horsley believes that, as love of local peasant enemies is translated into mutual support and transformed socioeconomic relations, the social revolution Jesus sought to spark would become a political revolution. But the Jesus he depicts is just as much an apocalyptic dreamer as Theudas and others, who were "acting precisely out of a *fantasy* that God is about to deliver them from reality" (p. 36). For his Jesus also believes that "God was imminently to complete the restoration of Israel and judge the institutions that maintained justice" (p. 321), and it never happened. If Jesus did not teach a *nonviolent* method of opposition, then he taught none at all; and his "social revolution," if it did not include table fellowship with the marginalized and outcast, as Horsley argues, becomes just one more form of quietistic sectarianism.

Most bewildering of all, Horsley concludes his *JAAR* essay, "Ethics and Exegesis: 'Love Your Enemies' and the Doctrine of Non-Violence" (54 [1986]: 3–31), with the comment that it is still possible to universalize Jesus' teachings on love of enemies in a way that ends up fundamentally similar to John Howard Yoder's absolute pacifism as far as its implications for political-economic structures are concerned. In a final footnote, Horsley acknowledges that he has been "a pacifist and a practitioner of nonviolence" since his teens (p. 27 n. 15; see p. 97 n. 15 above). So why the polemic against pacifism? And if we come out where pacifists have been all along, why has he gone to so much trouble to demolish the ethical grounds of the pacifist position?

So here I am, a person who does not consider himself a pacifist, arguing for nonviolence against a person who declares himself a pacifist and yet denies that Jesus, in this pericope, taught nonviolence. If this strikes you as confusing, join the club!

I think I understand something of this confusion, because it is inside a lot of us. We look at the Nicaraguan revolution as a fundamental success, if only it had been allowed to flower in its own way, and that revolution included violence. We look at South Africa and don't see how nonviolence can succeed against such a violent regime. And we have been sensitized to the arrogance of white Western male Americans telling the oppressed how they ought to fight their battles. We are all keenly aware that many have championed nonviolence as a way of avoiding conflict rather than as a way of inciting and aggravating conflict and precipitating confrontation. We are also aware, as I mentioned earlier, that pacifists have sometimes seemed to place their own purity above the need to defend the innocent.

All this can create a kind of ethical paralysis. Some of us break it by opting for revolutionary violence, under one form or another of the just war theory or so-called Christian realism. Others cannot quite ignore the shadow of Jesus that still falls across our lives, and we waffle. We may talk revolution, but when pressed, we can't quite seem to take up guns. Or we say we are committed to using non-violence as long as it seems viable, as our preferred course of action, but reserve the option of violence if nonviolence seems to have failed. These are what one observer calls the "not-yet-violent." In short, I wonder if some of the confusion I find in Horsley's position is not a reflection of the times in which we find ourselves.

I have already mentioned that I consider myself a better Horsleyan than Horsley. My paper is the proper corrective, it seems to me, for understanding not only how Jesus lived in the midst of a spiral of violence but how he developed a strategy for stopping it.

7

Who Is My Enemy?
The Parable
of the Good Samaritan
and the Love of Enemies

John R. Donahue, S.J.

Scarcely any parable of the Gospels is more familiar to both Christians and non-Christians than Luke's story of the Good Samaritan (Luke 10:29–37). Luke locates this parable in the context of Jesus' journey to Jerusalem which begins in 9:51 and terminates at 19:28 with the approach to Jerusalem. In this section Luke departs from his Markan source and includes material taken either from his own tradition (generally designated L) or from the sayings source (Q), which he shares in common with Matthew. Under the motif of a journey (way), the Lukan Jesus instructs his disciples on the way of discipleship.[1] The most important and most distinctive concerns of Luke's theology occur in this section. One of these is Luke's universalist vision which is dramatized most forcibly in the Samaritan stories.[2]

As the section begins, Jesus sends his disciples to prepare a place for him in a Samaritan village (Luke 9:52; see 19:30 for a similar motif at the end of the journey). The people of the village, however, will not receive him, "because his face was set toward Jerusalem" (9:53). Upon returning, James and John ask "the Lord" if he wants them to "command fire to come down from heaven and consume them" (9:54). Jesus simply turns and rebukes them (*epetimēsen*, a term often used when Jesus rebukes demons or hostile powers) and moves on to another village.[3]

In the light of the Samaritan reaction, it seems somewhat surprising that the first parable of the journey narrative is that of the Good Samaritan (Luke 10:29–37).[4] Since Luke places most of the parables distinctive to his Gospel in the journey narrative, this parable occupies a prominent place in both the literary structure and, as we shall see, the theological program of Luke. Though the geography of the journey is somewhat confused and disorganized, the major portion takes place in Samaritan territory, which lay between Galilee and Judea and extended roughly forty-five miles north-south and thirty-five miles east-west.[5] The third major Samaritan incident occurs near the end of the journey when Jesus heals ten lepers (Luke 17:11, "On the way to Jerusalem Jesus was going through the region between Samaria and Galilee"), only one of whom returns to praise God for the cure. Luke remarks crisply, "And he was a Samaritan" (17:16), and Jesus states (17:18), "Was none of them found to return and give praise to God except this foreigner (*allogenēs*)?"[6]

Apart from the command of Jesus to his disciples in Matt. 10:5 ("and enter no town of the Samaritans"), the long narrative of the meeting of Jesus with the Samaritan woman in John 4, and the brief reference in John 8:48, all the references to the Samaritans in the New Testament are found in the Gospel of Luke or in the Acts of the Apostles. The positive evaluation of a Samaritan in Luke 10 and Luke 17, as well as the mission to the Samaritans in Acts 8, is in stark contrast to the prevailing attitudes of Jews toward Samaritans in the first century C.E., which are reflected in Luke 9:51–55; Matt. 10:5; John 4:9 ("How is it that you, a Jew, ask a drink of me, a woman of Samaria?"); and John 8:48, where Jesus' opponents say, "Are we not right in saying that you are a Samaritan and have a demon?" For first-century Jews, the "Samaritan" was both foreigner and enemy. To understand better both the shock of the parable of the Good Samaritan and the impact of Jesus' teaching on the emerging church, I will offer a brief review of the relations between Jews and Samaritans and then comment in more detail on the parable of the Good Samaritan.[7] Suggestions will then be offered on the impact of Jesus' radical reinterpretation of the concept "enemy" both on the church of Luke's day and on contemporary theology.

Jews and Samaritans

Samaria is the name of the ancient capital of the Northern Kingdom (Israel), roughly forty-two miles north of Jerusalem and twenty-five miles east of the Mediterranean Sea.[8] It is also used of a territory, the boundaries of which fluctuated, but it was originally the locale of the tribes Ephraim and Manasseh.[9] Its principal cities are Samaria itself and Shechem (Sychar, in John 4:5–6), located in the pass between Mt. Ebal and Mt. Gerizim, near the traditional site of Jacob's well.[10] Tension between this region, which became part of Israel, and Judah (Judea in New Testament times) is rooted in the division of the kingdom after the death of Solomon (922 B.C.E.). The remote history of the Samaritans begins with the conquest of the Northern Kingdom by Assyria in 722 B.C.E.

The origin of the Samaritans as a "schismatic" movement within Judaism is disputed. J. D. Purvis provides a handy overview of the four distinct views of this origin: (1) the Samaritan view that their movement is a perpetuation of ancient Israelite faith as practiced in premonarchic Shechem; (2) the counterclaim of Orthodox Judaism that Samaritanism is a heresy derived from a corrupt Yahwism introduced after the Assyrian conquest in the eighth century B.C.E.; (3) a view on the basis of Ezra and Nehemiah collated with material from Josephus that Samaritanism originated during the Persian period; and (4) the view of Josephus himself that the schism occurred early in the Greek period (see below).[11] In a recent study of Samaritan history, Menachem Mor remarks, "The origin and early history of the Samaritan sect is vague and problematic."[12] Three principal theories have emerged to explain their origin. First, they are an Israelite remnant in the north, "because only an insignificant number of the inhabitants were deported to Assyria. Thus the Samaritans would be called the true Israelites who were the 'keepers' (*smrim*) of the Mosaic law."[13] "Another tradition might find Samaritan origins linked to the captives whom the Assyrians had transferred from Babylon, Cuthah, Avva, Hamatah and Sepharvaim to Israel's north to repopulate the land," so that the ancestors of the Samaritans would be syncretistic pagans (cf. Luke 17:18, "this foreigner").[14] The third theory of Samaritan origins combines the previous two: "The Assyrian exile of the ten tribes was not total, and significant numbers of the Israelite population were left behind. Simultaneously, the Assyrians brought a group of exiles to the regions of what had been the Israelite northern kingdom. These diverse populations living together side-by-side intermingled, forming a new people who were eventually called Cuthaeans or Samaritans."[15]

While the remote origins of the Samaritans are obscure, their real history begins in the postexilic period, during the time of Ezra and Nehemiah (ca. 464–358 B.C.E.).[16] Ezra and Nehemiah represent stages in the return of the people from Babylon under the Persian kings Artaxerxes I (464–423 B.C.E.) and Artaxerxes II (404–358 B.C.E.). Mor argues that both Ezra and Nehemiah represent an ideology of Babylonian Jewry that considered itself to be the "holy seed" (Ezra 9:2) or remnant (Ezra 9:15) which stood in opposition to intermarriage with those who had remained in Israel and who were thought to be "unclean with the pollutions of the peoples of the lands, with their abominations" (Ezra 9:11). The program of the returning reformers involved the rebuilding of the temple, codification of the law, strong prohibitions of intermarriage, and building a wall around Jerusalem. This program was resisted both by groups within Judean Jewry and especially by the Samaritan Sanballat, the Persian governor of Samaria (Neh. 6:1–14). Characteristic of this period, then, according to Mor, was the conflict within Judean Jewry between those who held a separatist ideology and those who held a universalist ideology.[17] Against the ideology of the "holy seed" was a second group, who were interested in bringing together all the different neighboring groups and whose theology is reflected in texts such as Isaiah 52 and 63, and the books of Jonah, Ruth, and Judith, which are the literary work of the universalist stream. This fundamental tension will characterize Jewish thought well into the New Testament period.

While there existed serious tensions between Samaritans and Jews during the Persian period (538–330 B.C.E.), the real roots of the final separation emerge after the conquest of Palestine by Alexander the Great (330 B.C.E.) and during the subsequent centuries when Palestine was often caught in a tug of war between Alexander's successors (the Ptolemies, who ruled in Egypt, and the Seleucids of Syria).

The specific events that explain the final rupture between the Jews and the Samaritans are a matter of some dispute among contemporary experts on Samaritan studies. This is partly due to confusion in Josephus, who remains the principal ancient literary source for the Samaritans. Mentioned above was Josephus's view that the Samaritans were semipagan. Later in the *Antiquities,* Josephus roots the Samaritan schism in the permission given to the Samaritans by Alexander the Great to erect the Samaritan temple and in the absorption of disenfranchised Jerusalem priests by the Samaritan community.[18] This account of Josephus was generally judged suspect because of his known anti-Samaritan bias and also because there is yet no conclusive evidence of a Samaritan temple on Mt. Gerizim that dates to this period.[19]

Information on the relations between Jews and Samaritans (as well as on Jewish history in general) is sparse during the Greek period (323–165 B.C.E.). One important text that shows the growing antipathy is Sir. 50:25–26, which dates from ca. 180 B.C.E. This reference occurs in the final section of the book, immediately preceding the author's postscript (Sir. 50:27–29). In coded language it reads:

> Two nations my soul detests, and the third is not even a people: Those who live in Seir [Edomites], and the Philistines [Hellenists], and the foolish people that live in Shechem [the Samaritans]. (Sir. 50:25–26)

The Septuagint is even more explicit. Instead of "those who live in Seir," it reads "those dwelling on the mountain of Samaria," seeming to equate the Samaritans with the Edomites.

The final split between Samaritans and Jews occurs, however, only after the Maccabean revolt in 165 B.C.E. and during the reign of the Hasmonean kings (145–65 B.C.E.). The territorial expansion of these kings reached its peak during the reign of John Hyrcanus (134–104 B.C.E.). According to Mor, John's policies were divided into two approaches: cruel behavior toward the Hellenistic cities in the land of Israel which were burned to the ground and their populations deported, and one of sympathy toward other groups who accepted circumcision.[20] Mor notes further that, though the Samaritans fulfilled this important condition, John treated them as he did the Hellenistic cities. In 128 B.C.E. "he burned their temple on Mount Gerizim, and late in 107 B.C.E., he destroyed Shechem."[21] Mor goes on to remark that the main reason for the division between Jews and Samaritans was the existence of the temple on Mt. Gerizim. Whether an actual temple or a shrine existed on Mt. Gerizim, the harsh, expansionist policies of John Hyrcanus contributed to the hatred between Jew and Samaritan in the first century B.C.E. and the first century C.E.

Josephus and the New Testament are the principal sources for the antipathy between Jew and Samaritan at the time of Jesus, which continued throughout the first century. During the time of the Roman prefect Coponius, 6–9 C.E., when the Jews were celebrating the Festival of Unleavened Bread, some Samaritans scattered human bones in the temple.[22] According to accounts in Josephus (*Ant.* 18.4.1–2, §85–89), near the end of the governorship of Pontius Pilate (26–36 C.E.) a man persuaded a number of Samaritans to accompany him to Mt. Gerizim after he had promised them that, when they arrived there, he would show them certain sacred vessels.[23] Josephus recounts that a number of those assembled were armed and that when Pilate prevented their ascent to the mountain, in the fighting that ensued a number of Samaritans were killed or taken prisoner. Pilate subsequently executed the leaders of the Samaritans.

Josephus goes on to report that the Samaritans sent a delegation to L. Vitellius, the legate of Syria, which accused Pilate of the murder. Again, according to Josephus, Pilate was subsequently recalled to Rome, not only for this incident but for other cruelties as well.[24]

Though the origins of the Samaritans are murky, and though the precise points of dispute are often unclear, both the anti-Samaritan bias of Josephus and the fragmentary New Testament evidence mentioned above show that there was a serious split between Jews and Samaritans during the first century c.e. While Menachem Mor stresses that the basis of the split was primarily religious, that is, the existence of a rival temple in Samaria, Ferdinand Dexinger argues for a complex of religious and political reasons.[25] The latter include different views on mixed marriages among the returning exiles, political and economic rivalry between Samaria and Jerusalem, and the presence of a Gentile ruling class in Samaria.

While recognizing differences, Samaritans and Jews shared much in common. Both recognized the authority of scripture, even though the Samaritans gave absolute priority to the Pentateuch. Both practiced circumcision and enforced strict Sabbath observance.[26] Nonetheless the Samaritans possessed distinctive theological ideas. Prime among these was the importance of Moses. John MacDonald describes this belief as follows: "It [Samaritanism] developed a belief in Moses, its only prophet, as the pre-eminent one of all humanity, the specially endowed of God. Like Christianity, it elevated its chief historical figure to the highest degree, but unlike Christianity it did not accredit him with divine sonship."[27] Samaritan eschatology is characterized by the hope for a *Taheb* (lit., "restorer") who fulfills the promise of Deut. 18:18, "I will raise up for them a prophet like you [Moses] from among their own people." The hope for a Mosaic prophet also appears in the Dead Sea Scrolls (1QS 9:11) and in the New Testament (Acts 3:22; see also Acts 1:6). In Samaritan traditions this "restorer" will appear at the time of the second kingdom to restore the temple on Mt. Gerizim and reinstitute the sacrificial cult.[28]

This admittedly somewhat oversimplified survey of Jewish-Samaritan relationships shows that at the time of Jesus there were serious grounds for hatred and suspicion between Jews and Samaritans. Though the term "sect" is often used to describe the Samaritans, the diversity in first-century Judaism that embraced groups as divergent as the Essenes and the Sadducees is a caution against overemphasizing the differences. In fact, the antipathy between Jew and Samaritan arose as much out of their shared heritage as from their differences. As religious wars throughout history have shown, there is no struggle more bitter than between groups with a common heritage who are claiming to be the authentic bearers and interpreters of this heritage.

The Parable of the Good Samaritan

Set against this historical background is the parable of the Good Samaritan, which is found only in Luke (Luke 10:29–37). In the early church, this parable, like most of the parables, was seen as an allegory. Augustine's allegorical interpretation is perhaps the best known. Adam (i.e., every human) is the traveler on the way from Jerusalem, the city of heavenly peace, which means the garden from which he is expelled. The thieves are the devil and his angels who strip Adam of his immortality. The priest and the Levite symbolize the Old Testament, while the Samaritan (which can mean "guardian" or watcher in Hebrew) symbolizes Christ. The beast on which the wounded man is placed is the flesh of Christ, and being placed on the beast is belief in the incarnation. The inn to which the man is brought is the church, and the innkeeper is the apostle Paul.[29]

With the advent of historical criticism and the consequent rejection of allegorical exegesis, the Good Samaritan was seen in the context of the teaching of Jesus. Still, its significance was lost in the debate over whether it was a *Beispielerzählung* (example story) or a parable strictly speaking. Example stories lacked the paradox and surprise connected with parables and were used mainly to illustrate some particular aspect of Jesus' teaching. It was assumed that the Good Samaritan was simply an illustration of the command to love one's neighbor in Luke 10:25–28.

A major breakthrough in interpretation of the Good Samaritan came as a result of the debate between Dan O. Via and J. Dominic Crossan, two major figures of modern parable exegesis, over whether it was an example story or a parable. Crossan argued strongly and persuasively that it is truly a parable. He notes that the narrative would serve as an example story if the third person who stops and tends the wounded man were a Jewish lay person. He argues, then, that the narrative is truly a parable in virtue of the choice of the Samaritan as a central figure. The paradox and shock come when the reader is forced to put together "good" and "Samaritan." Crossan writes:

> The literal point confronted the hearers with the necessity of saying the impossible and having their world turned upside down. . . . The metaphorical point is that *just so* does the Kingdom of God break

abruptly into human consciousness and demand the overturn of prior values, closed options, set judgments and established conclusions. . . . The hearer struggling with the contradictory dualism of Good/Samaritan is actually experiencing in and through this the in-breaking of the Kingdom.[30]

Crossan's position has remained most influential among those scholars who use the Good Samaritan as an entree to the teaching of the historical Jesus. In his major new commentary Bernard Brandon Scott agrees with Crossan that the shock comes from the introduction of the Samaritan, but with an interesting variation.[31] He argues that the expected "mytheme" would be a narrative of a priest, a Levite, and an Israelite lay person, which would have functioned in the social world of first-century Palestine as an attack on the clerical establishment.[32] In its present form "the story subverts the effort to order reality into the known hierarchy of priest, Levite and Israelite. Utterly rejected is any notion that the kingdom can be marked off as religious: the map no longer has boundaries."[33] He notes that in the parable the Samaritan is not converted (and thus remains an "enemy"), so that "gone is the apocalyptic vision of ultimate triumph over one's enemies. The world with its sure arrangement of insiders and outsiders is no longer an adequate model for predicting the kingdom."[34]

In this parable Jesus thus challenges both the historical reality of viewing the Samaritan as enemy and the deeper religious attitude that divides the world into outsiders and insiders.

In its Lukan context there are further subtle nuances to the parable.[35] Luke is certainly responsible for the present context of the parable as an answer to the debate over the greatest commandment which is found in a different context without a parabolic illustration in Mark and Matthew.[36] In effect, Luke is the first one to use the parable as an illustration. Since allusions to the Old Testament are rare in the authentic parables of Jesus, the subtle allusion to Hos. 6:6 in Luke 10:37 (see below) may also be due to Luke.

By placing it in the context of the lawyer's question, Luke subtly alters the thrust of the parable. While the lawyer in Luke 10:29 asks, "And who is my neighbor?" the parable itself describes what it means to be a neighbor, which then becomes the substance of Jesus' counterquestion in Luke 10:36, "Which of these three, do you think, was a neighbor to the man who fell into the hands of the robbers?" While retaining the paradox of the "good" Samaritan, Luke gives content to the paradox by stating that it is the religious and social outsider who illustrates what it means to act as neighbor, which is brought out clearly by the final words of the pericope, "Go and do likewise" (Luke 10:37).

In response to the question of Jesus in Luke 10:36, as to who proved to be neighbor, the lawyer responds, "The one who showed him mercy" (Luke 10:37). This is a subtle but significant allusion to Hos. 6:6, "I desire mercy (*eleos*) and not sacrifice" (my trans.), and perhaps to Micah 6:8, "to do justice and to love kindness [or mercy]" (*agapan eleon*, in the Greek Old Testament). Since the Samaritans did not recognize the authority of the prophetic books, the answer of the lawyer is doubly ironic. Not only is the Samaritan a neighbor but he acts according to those scriptures which the lawyer himself recognizes as authoritative. Luke relativizes the value of a sacred and canonical text as the sure guide for fulfilling the command to love God and neighbor. Such a perspective fits in with the universalist strain of Luke-Acts, most evident in Paul's Areopagus speech with its claim that the pagan nations have worshiped the true God.[37]

The Grateful Samaritan Who Returns to Praise God

As noted earlier, only Luke and John contain significant material and favorable pictures of the Samaritans. Allied to the parable of the Good Samaritan is the story of the ten lepers, also found only in Luke.

Just as the parable of the Good Samaritan occurs during the initial stages of Jesus' journey to Jerusalem, the healing of the ten lepers (Luke 17:11–19) occurs at the beginning of the third and final phase of this journey (Luke 17:11a; see 9:51; 13:22). The narrative seems to be modeled on the earlier story of the healing of the leper, which Luke takes over from his Markan source (Mark 1:40–45 = Luke 5:12–16). Though showing traces of the traditional form of miracle story (e.g., the request for healing; healing by powerful word; the demonstrative sign, i.e., showing one's self to the priest; the simple mention of healing), the Lukan focus is clearly on the second part of the narrative, the actions of the Samaritan in Luke 17:15–18.[38]

The first part of the narrative (Luke 17:11–14) is virtually a self-enclosed unit marked off by two typically Lukan phrases, *kai egeneto en tō* (17:11, 14), so that the hearers' attention is drawn to the second half of the narrative. Here for the first time it is mentioned that one of these healed was a Samaritan, even though the reader has been alerted by the introductory verse that Jesus is on the border of Samaria. Suspense builds in vs. 15–16, especially in the Greek word order: one of those who has been healed returns; he is "glorifying God (*doxazōn*) in a loud voice" (my trans.); in a gesture of worship he falls with face bowed at the feet of Jesus, and only then is it stated: and he was a Samaritan.[39] As in the parable of the Good Samaritan, where the Samaritan is the third passerby, the suspense builds to highlight the presence of the Samaritan. The major thrust of the narrative then unfolds in the pronouncements of Jesus in vs. 17–18: "Were not ten made clean? But the other nine, where are they? Was none found to return and give glory (*doxan*) to God except this foreigner (*allogenēs*)." The postponement of the reference to "this foreigner" to the final words of Jesus' saying is similar in structure to the word order of vs. 15–16, so that the reference to the Samaritan again stands out. Jesus' final words of the story are a praise of the faith of the Samaritan.

Often overlooked in the interpretation of the parable is the double reference to the Samaritan glorifying God (vs. 15, 18). Though "glorifying God" is a standard motif of the acclamation due to God at the end of a mighty work (Mark 2:12), Luke accentuates the notion of glory in his Gospel. At the announcement of the birth of Jesus, the heavenly host proclaims, "Glory to God in the highest heaven" (Luke 2:14), and the shepherds return from the manger "glorifying and praising" God (Luke 2:20). While Luke repeats Mark's comment that after the healing of the paralytic all the people glorify God (Mark 2:12 = Luke 5:26), he adds that the man who was healed also glorifies God (Luke 5:25). In the L narrative of the raising of the son of the widow at Nain the people glorify God (Luke 7:16), and in the narrative of the woman crippled for eighteen years (Luke 13:10–17; also L), when healed, the woman "glorifies God" (Luke 13:13). Though Luke follows Mark 10:46–52 in the story of the blind beggar at Jericho (Luke 18:35–43), only Luke notes that the beggar, when given his sight, follows Jesus, "glorifying God" (v. 43). When Jesus finally enters Jerusalem where he will be "taken up" (see Luke 9:51), only in Luke do the crowds cry, "glory in the highest heaven" (Luke 19:38), which recalls 2:14. Both Jesus' birth and his entry into the city where he will be crucified and raised are highlighted by praise of God. Finally, only in Luke is it mentioned that at the death of Jesus the centurion "glorifies God" (Luke 23:47).

Two things are noteworthy. First, Luke clearly sees "glorifying God" as a fundamental response to the presence of God in the actions of Jesus. Second, in significant places those who give such glory are people on the margin of Jesus' society. Shepherds (along with tax collectors) are listed among those occupations which no observant Jew should pursue.[40] Illness was often thought to be a sign of divine disfavor, and beggars were scorned. Samaritans, as we noted, were hated and suspect, and a leper who was a Samaritan was doubly scorned, both for his disease and for his religious and ethnic identity. A Gentile centurion is *allogenēs,* like the Samaritan leper, as well as a representative of an occupying power. Samaritans are thus among those outsiders in Luke who respond in a special way to the presence of God manifest in Jesus.

The actions of the Samaritan in the parable and of the Samaritan leper also comprise two religious attitudes that are fundamental to both Judaism and the teaching of Jesus. At the time of Jesus, Jewish teachers defined the two fundamental obligations as worship of God (*eusebeia* or *dikaiosynē*) and love of neighbor (*philanthrōpia*).[41] Worship of God was shown especially through offering praise and glory to God. The Samaritan leper who twice gives glory to God embodies the first of these fundamental dispositions, while the Good Samaritan is a model of love of neighbor. Luke forcefully says that those who are called enemy and scorned as outsiders are fulfilling fundamental religious attitudes expected of Jews and of followers of Jesus.

The Samaritan Mission in Acts

At the beginning of Acts, Luke's sequel to his Gospel, which recounts the spread of the gospel throughout the Roman Empire, the risen Jesus says that the gift of the Holy Spirit will make of his disciples "witnesses in Jerusalem, in all Judea and Samaria, and to the ends of the earth" (Acts 1:8). This provides the basis for the structure of Acts, where the church spreads centrifugally from Jerusalem, most often as a result of persecution or opposition. The initial narratives deal with the coming of the Spirit and the early days of the Jerusalem church (Acts 1:12–8:1a). After the martyrdom of Stephen a severe persecution breaks out (Acts 8:1b–2), and "those who were scattered went from place to place, proclaiming the word" (Acts 8:4). First among the missions of the disciples is Samaria. Philip (one of the Hellenists, Acts 6:5) "goes down" (from Jerusalem) to a city of Samaria and the crowds eagerly accept his message and witness his mighty works, so "there was great joy in that city" (Acts 8:8).

The Samaritan mission in Acts 8 seems to be a combination of at least two traditions and two distinct attitudes toward the Samaritans. Acts 8:4–8 recounts the successful mission of Philip, with a subsequent successful mission of Peter and John in Acts 8:14–17 and 8:25. Luke's theological and editorial concerns are evident in these sections.[42] The gospel spreads outward, but the gift of the Spirit is assured by the arrival of representatives of the Jerusalem church. A second tradition deals with the presence of Simon Magus.[43] Simon is first introduced in Acts 8:9 as a man who practiced magic, who was called "the power of God that is called Great" (Acts 8:10), and who is convinced by Philip's mighty works, is baptized, and becomes a believer (Acts 8:9–13). Simon reappears after the arrival of Peter and John, and, after observing that the Holy Spirit came through the laying on of hands by Peter and John, he offers to buy the power of conferring the Spirit (Acts 8:15–19). Peter responds strongly, "May your silver perish with you, . . . for your heart is not right before God" (Acts 8:20–21), and summons Simon to repent (Acts 8:22). Simon seems to repent and asks the apostles to pray for him (Acts 8:24).[44]

The relation of Simonian Gnosis to the Simon of Acts 8 is a very much debated issue. The clear identification goes back to Irenaeus of Lyons, who also said that from Simon of Samaria "all sorts of heresies derive their origin" (*Adv. Haer.* 23:1–2).[45] To pursue this would lead us too far afield. What is important is that *in Luke's perspective* there was a successful mission to the Samaritans that followed the establishment of the church in Judea and preceded the Gentile mission. This success is reflected also in Acts 9:31, in a summary statement about the growth of the church after the conversion of Paul: "Meanwhile the church throughout Judea, Galilee, and Samaria had peace and was built up. Living in the fear of the Lord and in the comfort of the Holy Spirit, it increased in numbers." In Acts 15:3, on their return to Jerusalem for the Apostolic Council, Paul and Barnabas pass through Samaria and report to the peoples there the conversion of the Gentiles. According to Acts, a flourishing Christian community exists in Samaria.

The acceptance of Christianity by the Samaritans is the counterpart in the Acts of the Apostles to the favorable picture of the Samaritans in the parable of the Good Samaritan and the story of the ten lepers. In each case the enemy and the outsider embody major theological themes of the respective books. In the Gospel, the Samaritans fulfill the love command and praise God; in Acts, they are models of response to the postresurrection proclamation of the gospel. Even Simon Magus repents of his sins (Acts 8:22–24). The Acts of the Apostles is a narrative demonstration that the teaching of Jesus breaks through those categories by which people are classed as enemies and outsiders. This vision of Acts is to lead the church to break through those ethnic and religious boundaries which divide the world into friend and enemy. When this occurs, as Acts 9:31 states, the church has peace and is built up.

A Brief Look at the Samaritans in the Gospel of John

We called attention earlier to John 8:48 as evidence of the hatred between Jew and Samaritan. All the more remarkable, then, is the long narrative of Jesus' meeting with the Samaritan woman in John 4. Like other major dramatic narratives in John (e.g., John 9), this becomes a major vehicle of Johannine theology. The narrative is set in the Samaritan city of Sychar (Shechem), near Jacob's well. Jesus, "tired out by his journey," sits by the well at noon. When a Samaritan woman comes to draw water, Jesus asks her for a drink. As the readers might expect, the woman answers: "How is it that you, a Jew, ask a drink of me, a woman of Samaria?"(John 4:9). For the audience of John, this woman is triply disenfranchised: she is a Samaritan, a woman who converses freely with a man in public, and she is living, according to John 4:18, in an adulterous relationship. Though the thrust of the whole narrative is the dialogue on true worship and on living water, the important thing for our investigation is that the woman becomes a believer in the Messiah (John 4:25) and that she goes forth as a missionary and witness: "Many Samaritans from that city believed in him because of the woman's testimony" (John 4:39), and then because of her testimony the Samaritans themselves come to Jesus (John 4:40–41).[46]

This narrative from John combines in a single incident from the life of Jesus the double attitude toward the Samaritans found in Luke-Acts. By his dialogue with and acceptance of the Samaritan woman, Jesus shocks even his own disciples (John 4:27) and thus breaks down the barrier between neighbor and enemy. When the Samaritan woman becomes a missionary and the Samaritans come to believe, they both serve as symbols of the conversion of the Samaritans and the success of the early Christian mission among them.

In his evocative study of the Johannine community Raymond Brown has argued that a second major group who entered the original Johannine community "consisted of Jews of peculiar anti-Temple views [see Stephen's speech in Acts 7] who converted Samaritans and picked up some elements of Samaritan thought, including a Christology not centered on a Davidic Messiah."[47] Drawing on the research of scholars such as Wayne Meeks, Brown then argues that Samaritan theology has left a distinct imprint on Johannine theology, especially in areas such as its anti-temple bias and its stress on Jesus as a Mosaic (rather than Davidic) figure.[48]

Since Samaritan studies themselves have been in considerable ferment in the last two decades, major historical questions remain somewhat unsolved. For example, some authors argue that the statement of Justin in his *First Apology* (ch. 53) that there were not many converts to Christianity from the Jews or the Samaritans is evidence that the mission to the Samaritans was not very successful or significant.[49] The history of the Samaritans themselves in the early centuries of our era is so obscure that little can be said with certainty about whether many became Christian converts. For the first century, however, the New Testament remains the best source, and John and Luke-Acts provide independent witness that such a mission was initially successful and left its imprint on the theology of the early church.

Samaritans, Peace, and the Love of Enemies

Jesus' parable of the Good Samaritan, the other traditions about the Samaritans in Luke-Acts, and John's narrative of the Samaritan woman offer alternate images of the Samaritans to those found in other parts of the New Testament and in other ancient sources, principally Josephus. In Luke and John, the Samaritan is not the outsider whose territory must be avoided, nor the sectarian heretic. The Samaritan fulfills the commands of God, gives praise and glory to God, and in John and Acts accepts the proclamation of Jesus as Messiah.

These alternate images must influence people today who read and ponder these same New Testament narratives. Amid a period of unprecedented international readjustment due to the breakup of monolithic Marxism and the transformations under way in the former Soviet Union, people in the West, and especially in the United States of America, should not forget the hold that the myth of "the enemy" has exercised on our national consciousness. A generation grew up with fear about "the enemy within," understood as Communist subversion of our government, and a recent President was the delight of many Christians when he spoke of "the evil empire." In an important study on the images of the enemy, Robert W. Rieber and Robert J. Kelly have analyzed those qualities which people attribute to enemies and which become the presupposition of violent action toward them.[50] They write:

From a religious point of view, the enemy becomes nothing less than evil incarnate, a "fake person," an impostor, a malefactor pretending to be human. In more general terms, the enemy may be characterized as racially, linguistically, ethnically, or physically different; but the difference is held to be both fundamental and noxious.[51]

Such observations about the images of enemy in contemporary life are hauntingly similar to the images of the Samaritan gleaned from ancient sources. Jesus is considered to be a Samaritan and have a demon, "evil incarnate" (cf. John 8:48). The Samaritan is "a foreigner" (Luke 17:18), *allogenēs,* literally "of another kind," that is, not fundamentally sharing the same humanity. The woman says to Jesus in John 4:9, "For Jews have no dealings with Samaritans."[52] The meaning of this verse has long puzzled exegetes and is omitted in some manuscripts of the New Testament. The principal problem is that the main verb, *sygchrōntai,* can mean "use in common" or "associate on friendly terms." In the context of Jesus' request for a drink of water, many commentators argue that it means, "For Jews do not use vessels in common with Samaritans."[53] Here the issue would be different conceptions of ritual purity by the two groups. In the light of the well-known Johannine propensity for deliberate double meanings of phrases (e.g., the Son of Man will be lifted up in reference to both the crucifixion and the exaltation of Jesus, see John 3:14; 8:28; 12:32, 34), I would argue that both the contextual meaning and the larger meaning are true. On the narrative level the woman may be saying that Jews and Samaritans may not drink from the same vessels, but the readers of the Gospel know that the division is much deeper. They share little in common and treat each other, in the words of Rieber and Kelly, as "ethnically or physically different," with a difference that is fundamental and noxious.

One lasting value, then, of the Samaritan stories of the New Testament is that they challenge continually the tendency to dehumanize people by classifying them as enemies. The legacy of these narratives is that the Jesus of Luke and John offers alternate images and a different way of thinking about people who are not only different, and with whom one may share a common history and heritage, but who have grown apart for religious, social, and ethnic reasons.[54] In our contemporary world, the most bitter disputes seem to arise among such groups—Christian versus Christian in Northern Ireland, Moslem versus Moslem in the Middle East, along with disputes between related groups in the newly independent countries of Eastern Europe.

The charter of UNESCO states: "Since wars begin in the minds of men [and women] it is in the minds of men [and women] that we must erect the ramparts of peace."[55] The question that faces the Christian churches today is whether they can plant the alternate vision offered by the New Testament into the minds and imaginations of people today. Followers of Jesus today are not different from James and John in Luke 9:54. Rejection and hostility are met with a desire for punishment and vindication—or the modern equivalent of invoking divine power to rain fire down from heaven and consume enemies. Yet the same Jesus who begins his journey to Jerusalem by rebuking the violent tendency of his disciples welcomes these same Samaritans. When the journey is complete, having himself become the hostile outsider, he prays for his enemies: "Father, forgive them; for they do not know what they are doing" (Luke 23:34).[56] Sadly, however, Christianity has often thrived more on the polarization between insiders and outsiders, and on crusades against enemies, than on an inclusive and reconciling vision. As William Klassen stated, writing on the love of enemies, "Christianity has not so much been tried and found wanting, as it is still wanting to be tried."[57]

Notes

1. On the theological importance of this journey, see J. A. Fitzmyer, *The Gospel According to Luke I–IX* (AB 28; Garden City, N.Y.: Doubleday & Co., 1981), 169–171; and David P. Moessner, *Lord of the Banquet: The Literary and Theological Significance of the Lukan Travel Narrative* (Minneapolis: Fortress Press, 1989), esp. 290–325.

2. On universalism in Luke, see Fitzmyer, *Luke*, 187–192.

3. On *epetimēsen,* see Luke 4:35; 8:24; 9:42.

4. Morton Enslin ("The Samaritan Ministry and Mission," *HUCA* 51 [1980]: 38) suggests that the whole "great interpolation" (Luke 9:51–18:14) should be called "The Samaritan Ministry."

5. B. J. Roberts, "Samaritan, Territory," *IDB,* 4:188–190.

6. *Allogenēs* is found on the Jerusalem temple inscription to designate non-Jews who were excluded from the court of Israel. For the text of the inscription, see J. H. Moulton and George Milligan, *The Vocabulary of the Greek Testament* (Grand Rapids: Wm. B. Eerdmans Publishing Co., 1974), 23; on its significance, see J. D. Purvis, "Samaritans," *Harper's Bible Dictionary* (ed. Paul J. Achtemeier; San Francisco: Harper & Row, 1985), 896.

7. There has been a great expansion of Samaritan studies in the last two decades, so that major debates rage on fundamental issues, such as the origin of the Samaritans, the cause and precise time of the split between

Samaritans and Jews, and the existence of a Samaritan temple on Mt. Gerizim. Since it is beyond the scope of this essay to discuss all the major problems, I will draw selectively on recent studies. The principal ones are the important essays on all aspects of Samaritan belief and practice by leading experts in Alan D. Crown, ed., *The Samaritans* (Tübingen: J. C. B. Mohr [Paul Siebeck], 1989); also F. Dexinger, "Limits of Tolerance in Judaism: The Samaritan Example," in *Jewish and Christian Self-Definition*, vol. 2: *Aspects of Judaism in the Greco-Roman Period* (ed. E. P. Sanders with A. I. Baumgarten, and Alan Mendelson; Philadelphia: Fortress Press, 1981), 88–114; Sergio Noja, "The Last Decade in Samaritan Studies," in Crown, *Samaritans*, 802–813; R. Pummer, "The Present State of Samaritan Studies, I," *Journal of Semitic Studies* 21 (1976): 39–61; 22 (1977): 27–47; idem, *The Samaritans* (Leiden: E. J. Brill, 1987); J. D. Purvis, "The Samaritans and Judaism," in *Early Judaism and Its Modern Interpreters* (ed. R. A. Kraft and G. W. E. Nickelsburg; The Bible and Its Modern Interpreters; Philadelphia: Fortress Press, 1986), 81–98; and Nathan Schur, *History of the Samaritans* (Frankfurt am Main: Verlag Peter Lang, 1989).

8. G. W. van Beek, "Samaria," *IDB*, 4:182.

9. Roberts, "Samaritan, Territory," 188–190.

10. W. L. Reed, "Shechem (City)," *IDB*, 4:313–315.

11. J. D. Purvis, *The Samaritan Pentateuch and the Origin of the Samaritans* (HSM 2; Cambridge: Harvard University Press, 1968), 4–5.

12. Menachem Mor, "The Persian, Hellenistic and Hasmonaean Period," in Crown, *Samaritans*, 1.

13. Ibid. Mor lists as evidence for an Israelite remnant in the north 2 Kings 21:19; 23:26; 2 Chronicles 30; 34:1–7 and cites R. J. Coggins, *Samaritans and Jews: The Origins of Samaritanism Reconsidered* (Atlanta: John Knox Press, 1975), 13–28, and, for a Samaritan account, Wayne A. Brindle, "The Origin and History of the Samaritans," *Grace Theological Journal* 5 (1984): 50–54.

14. Mor, "Persian, Hellenistic and Hasmonaean Period," 1. This explanation is offered by Josephus in *Ant.* 9.14.3 §288–291.

15. Ibid., 1.

16. Dexinger ("Limits," 92–93) argues that during the period of Ezra and Nehemiah there was not yet a religious break between Jerusalem and Samaria, and advocates the adoption of more precise terminological distinctions between "Samarians," i.e., the Gentile inhabitants of Samaria and "proto-Samaritans," the Jewish population of the north, from which the "Samaritans" developed.

17. Mor, "Persian, Hellenistic and Hasmonaean Period," 3.

18. Josephus, *Ant.* 11.7.2–8.4 §302–325; 11.8.7 §346–347; see Purvis, "Samaritans and Judaism," 85.

19. See esp. R. T. Anderson, "The Elusive Samaritan Temple," *Biblical Archaeologist* 54 (1991): 104–107; and Reinhard Pummer, "Samaritan Material Remains and Archaeology," in Crown, *Samaritans*, 172: "No traces of a temple have been found so far. But first of all, as was said

above, the excavations are still in their beginning stages. Secondly, the Samaritan sources are virtually silent about such a temple." Even those, however, who deny that there is evidence for a temple admit some type of Samaritan shrine in Mt. Gerizim. The statement in John 4:20, "Our ancestors worshiped on this mountain," is inconclusive, since it could refer to a temple, a shrine, or simply a sacred place.

20. Mor, "Persian, Hellenistic and Hasmonaean Period," 16; also F. M. Cross, "Aspects of Jewish and Samaritan History in Late Persian and Hellenistic Times," *HTR* 59 (1966): 210–211. For a contrary view see Bruce Hall, "From John Hyrcanus to Baba Rabbah," in Crown, *Samaritans,* 33–54, who states (p. 34): "We do not really know how the conquests of Hyrcanus and the subsequent Jewish control of Samaria affected the Samaritans."

21. Mor, "Persian, Hellenistic and Hasmonaean period," 16. Clearly Mor is among those scholars who feel that the literary evidence (principally Josephus) is adequate to speak of a Samaritan *temple* on Mt. Gerizim.

22. Josephus, *Ant.* 18.2.2 §29–30. Though Coponius and Pilate are often called "procurators," until the time of Claudius (41–54 C.E.) the Roman governors of Judea were called "prefects." See A. H. M. Jones, "Procurators and Prefects in the Early Principate," in *Studies in Roman Government and Law* (Oxford: Basil Blackwell, 1960), 115–125; and J. A. Fitzmyer, "From Pompey to Bar Chochba," in *The New Jerome Biblical Commentary* (ed. R. E. Brown; J. A. Fitzmyer; and R. E. Murphy; Englewood Cliffs, N.J.: Prentice-Hall, 1991), 1248.

23. See Hall, "From John Hyrcanus to Baba Rabbah," in Crown, *Samaritans,* 38–40.

24. For a fine reassessment of the ancient sources dealing with Pilate (esp. Josephus, Philo, and the New Testament), see G. McGing, "Pontius Pilate and the Sources," *CBQ* 53 (1991): 416–438, esp. 433–434 on the incident at Mt. Gerizim.

25. Dexinger, "Limits," 112–114.

26. See Purvis, *Samaritan Pentateuch, 8–9.*

27. John Macdonald, *The Theology of the Samaritans* (London: SCM Press, 1964), 147. See also Wayne Meeks (*The Prophet-King: Moses Traditions and Johannine Christology* [NovTSup 14; Leiden: E. J. Brill, 1967], 216–257) for a fine discussion of Moses in Samaritan sources.

28. Theodore Gaster, "Samaritans," *IDB,* 4:194–195.

29. *Quaestiones Evangeliorum* II, 19, as summarized in C. H. Dodd, *The Parables of the Kingdom* (New York: Charles Scribner's Sons, 1961), 1–2.

30. J. Dominic Crossan, *In Parables: The Challenge of the Historical Jesus* (New York: Harper & Row, 1973), 65–66; see also idem, "Parable as a Religious and Poetic Experience," *JR* 53 (1973): 330–358.

31. Bernard Brandon Scott, *Hear Then the Parable: A Commentary on the Parables of Jesus* (Minneapolis: Fortress Press, 1989), 189–202.

32. As Scott notes (ibid., 199), the proposal that in the original parable

the third passerby was an "Israelite" goes back to J. Hálevy, "Sens et origine de la parabole évangélique dité du bon samaritain," *Revue des Etudes Juïves* 4 (1882): 249–255. Scott (p. 428) defines "mytheme" as "the bundles or sets of traditional narrative elements that are combined by myth tellers to form a coherent mythical story."

33. Scott, *Hear Then the Parable,* 201–202.

34. Ibid., 202.

35. See John R. Donahue, *The Gospel in Parable: Metaphor, Narrative, and Theology in the Synoptic Gospels* (Philadelphia: Fortress Press, 1988), 126–139.

36. Mark 12:28–34 = Matt. 22:34–40 appear in the polemical context of Jesus' disputes with scribes (Mark) or Pharisees (Matthew) after Jesus' arrival in Jerusalem.

37. See n. 2 above.

38. On the form of miracle stories, see esp. Gerd Theissen, *The Miracle Stories of the Early Christian Tradition* (Philadelphia: Fortress Press, 1983), 47–72.

39. In Luke 17:15, 18 the *NRSV* translates *doxazōn* as "praising" and *doxa* as "praise." This is inaccurate and does not capture the true meaning of the Greek terms. Nor is the translation consistent; see Luke 2:14, 20. In citing places where the terms occur, I render the Greek as "glory" or "glorify."

40. Joachim Jeremias, *Jerusalem in the Time of Jesus* (London: SCM Press, 1969), 304–305.

41. Klaus Berger, *Die Gesetzesauslegung Jesu: Ihr historischer Hintergrund im Judentum und im Alten Testament; I: Markus und Parallelen* (WMANT 40; Neukirchen-Vluyn: Neukirchener Verlag, 1972), 143–165; and Reginald H. Fuller, "The Double Commandment of Love: A Test Case for the Criteria of Authenticity," in *Essays on the Love Commandment* (Luise Schottroff et al.; Philadelphia: Fortress Press, 1978), 41–56.

42. Gerd Lüdemann (*Early Christianity According to the Traditions in Acts* [Minneapolis: Fortress Press, 1989], 98) argues that behind Acts 8:5–8 is the tradition of a spirit-filled activity of the preacher, Philip, in Samaria, and that 8:14–17 is redactional in both language and content.

43. Lüdemann (ibid., 98) argues that behind Acts 8:9–13 is a tradition about Simon Magus that reported the clash between the supporters of Simonian and Christian religion.

44. This section also manifests considerable Lukan redaction, esp. within the emphasis on the activity of apostles in Jerusalem (8:14–17, 25–26) which embodies the familiar theme of Acts that the mission churches are bound closely to the mother church in Jerusalem; see H. Conzelmann, *The Acts of the Apostles* (Hermeneia; Philadelphia: Fortress Press, 1987), 65.

45. See also Gerd Lüdemann ("The Acts of the Apostles and the Beginnings of Simonian Gnosis," *NTS* 37 [1983]: 420–426), who roots Simonian Gnosticism in the New Testament period. R. Bergmeier ("Die Gestalt des Simon Magus in Act 8 und in der simonianischen Gnosis," *ZNW* 77

[1986]: 267–275) denies such early dating of Simonian Gnosis. For a recent and thorough discussion, see Jarl Fossum, "Samaritan Sects and Movements," in Crown, *Samaritans*, 357–389.

46. Raymond E. Brown ("Roles of Women in the Fourth Gospel," in *Community of the Beloved Disciple* [New York: Paulist Press, 1979], esp. 186–189) points out that the woman fulfills the Johannine concept of a missionary and calls attention to the similarity between John 4:39, 42 and 17:20.

47. Brown, *Community*, 36–40.

48. It is not surprising that the influence of Samaritan theology on John is itself a debated issue. See esp. E. D. Freed, "Did John Write His Gospel Partly to Win Samaritan Converts?" *NovT* 12 (1970): 241–256; M. Pamment, "Is There Convincing Evidence of Samaritan Influence on the Fourth Gospel?" *ZNW* 73 (1982): 221–230; and J. D. Purvis, "The Fourth Gospel and the Samaritans," *NovT* 17 (1975): 161–198.

49. Bruce Hall ("From John Hyrcanus to Baba Rabbah," in Crown, *Samaritans*, 41) argues that if Justin is accurate, there were not many converts to Christianity from among the Samaritans. Justin's *First Apology* is a defense of Christianity made to the emperor Antonius Pius and the Roman senate. Given the Roman suspicion of both Christianity and Judaism, Justin stresses the appeal of Christianity to pagans. His statement is not totally accurate in the case of the Jews, so may be suspect also in respect to the Samaritans.

50. "Shadow and Substance: Images of the Enemy," in *The Psychology of War and Peace: The Image of the Enemy* (ed. Robert W. Rieber; New York and London: Plenum Publ. Corp., 1991), 3–39; see also Sam Keen, *Faces of the Enemy: Reflections of the Hostile Imagination* (San Francisco: Harper & Row, 1986).

51. Ibid., 15.

52. Translation here is mine. The NRSV translates as "(Jews do not share things in common with Samaritans)," indicating by the parentheses that it is an editorial comment rather than a statement of the woman.

53. See Raymond E. Brown, *The Gospel According to John I–XII* (AB 29; Garden City, N.Y.: Doubleday & Co., 1966), 170; and G. Sloyan, "The Samaritans in the New Testament," *Horizons* 10 (1983): 16. On the two possible meanings, see Walter Bauer, *A Greek-English Lexicon of the New Testament* (2nd rev. ed. by F. W. Gingrich and F. Danker, Chicago: University of Chicago Press, 1979), 775.

54. Keen (*Faces*, 12) writes: "Creative thinking about war will always involve considering both the individual psyche and social institution. Society shapes the psyche and vice versa. Therefore, we have to work at the tasks of creating psychological and political alternatives to war, changing the psyche of *homo hostilis* and the structure of international relations."

55. Quoted in Keen, *Faces*, 10.

56. This is found only in Luke.

57. William Klassen, *Love of Enemies: The Way to Peace* (Philadelphia: Fortress Press, 1984), 88.

8

Luke's Transforming of Tradition: Eirēnē and Love of Enemy

Willard M. Swartley

In 1955, C. F. Evans advanced the view that Luke's travel narrative (Luke 9:51–19:44) is structurally modeled on the book of Deuteronomy, a view he again espouses in his 1990 TPINTC commentary on Luke.[1] In 1989, David P. Moessner, in *Lord of the Banquet,* argued at length that Luke's theology is shaped by four major thematic emphases derived from Deuteronomy, thus providing broader literary connections for Luke's identification of Jesus as a prophet like Moses (Acts 3:22).[2]

Within the context of these contributions this essay draws attention to several rarely noticed compositional emphases in the journey narrative that also echo influence from Deuteronomy, a part of Israel's larger "way to the land" and "conquest" traditions. These thematic accents appear to develop Luke's social ethic enunciated already in the Nazareth proclamation of 4:16–21. Specifically, Luke develops the themes of peace (*eirēnē*), justice *(dikaiosynē),* and the gospel's conquest of evil, as well as God's judgment of evil.[3] These themes play roles of major importance in the narrative unity of Luke's central section, even in its structural design.[4]

Evans's view that the content of the section is modeled on Deu-

---

This chapter is an adapted form of a section in chapter 4 of Willard M. Swartley, *Story Shaping Story: Israel's Scripture Traditions in the Synoptic Gospels* (Peabody, Mass.: Hendrickson Publishers, forthcoming in 1993).

teronomy merits careful analysis. His study shows remarkable textual connections but fails to enter into an analysis of the possible theological and moral dimensions of this literary phenomenon. He does not take up the question of whether Luke's central section contains a theology of "conquest" that is in some way analogous to, or different from, that of Deuteronomy. Evans, however, does say that Luke's journey follows that of Deuteronomy to the Promised Land "by way of correspondence and contrast."[5] Designated as an *analēmpsis*, this section echoes in both form and content the *Assumption of Moses*, clearly modeled on Deuteronomy.[6]

James L. Resseguie observes that relatively few criticisms of Evans's ingenious contribution have been made and that those put forward are minor in comparison to the weight of evidence presented.[7] Indeed, James A. Sanders has regarded Evans's thesis positively.[8] In assessing Evans's proposal, it is important for one to observe not only the vast number of correspondences but the fact that the parallels are in sequential order. This testifies to design and intention; it is hardly a matter of happenstance.[9] In my judgment, at least twenty-one text correspondences are substantial, either in word or conceptual connection. In order to assess the data and their significance, I have summarized the more persuasive correspondences in a table (see end of chapter). Some of Evans's textual correspondences are omitted in this tabulation; other scholars who examine his work carefully may regard other correspondences as or more convincing than the ones I selected. The evidence is much too weighty for Evans's thesis to be discounted. The correspondences that show either transformation (9) or contrast (7) total 60 percent, significantly more than those that are only conceptually parallel (11).

This phenomenon in which Luke uses Deuteronomy as a literary model calls for analysis at the level of theological-ethical significance.[10] For here we have a New Testament use of the Old Testament that shows both continuity and change between the orders of Moses and Jesus. Borrowing Marcus Borg's holiness category,[11] we note that in every case where Deuteronomy prescribed death for what might contaminate the community, Luke's Jesus calls for a reversal of values: the enemy Samaritan is the neighbor who models the Shema; repentance of sinners is the new way to prohibit evil from consuming the community; and laws on clean and unclean are stood on their head. When the peace greeting is refused, demolishing the village and killing the people are replaced by wiping off the dust from one's feet as one leaves. Also, in the primary conceptualization of the "enemy" we see a major transformation. People are not the enemy; rather, Satan is the one dethroned in Jesus' vision of victory. At the same time, we see basic parallel thought structures against oppression of the poor, for obedience to God's word, the primacy of the love command, and the call to put loyalty to the Lord over all other loyalties.

Another significant link to Deuteronomy's "way-conquest" tradition is Luke's twofold use of the question, "What must I do to inherit eternal life?" (Luke 10:25; 18:18). By placing the story of the lawyer close to the beginning and the story of the ruler close to the ending of his special section—thus functioning as an inclusio—Luke is underlining the entire section's thematic linkage with Deuteronomy's emphasis on inheriting the land. In my fuller study I propose a connection between the Deuteronomic formula "entering into the land" and "entering the kingdom of God" in Mark's journey narrative.[12] Here Luke seems to be making a connection between "inheriting the land" and "inheriting eternal life." The way to inherit eternal life is marked specifically by love for the neighbor, even the enemy, and using wealth for the benefit of the poor. This moral directive reflects the same accent on discipleship found in Mark's story of Jesus' teaching "on the way," leading to the kingdom of God.

With the many endeavors to discern what Luke sought to do in this section, it is surprising that several distinctive features of the narrative have not been adequately considered. These themes, which I present here in three pairs, are prominent in the structural design and disclose the influence of the Deuteronomic "entrance" and "conquest" traditions.[13] The first of these three dual thematic emphases sets the context for the second and third doublets, which contribute directly to the topic of these essays in that they address the relation between peace and love of enemy as well as the gospel's conquest of evil in relation to God's judgment of evil.

Jesus as Journeying Guest and Rejected Prophet

As David Moessner has amply demonstrated, the Lukan journey narrative echoes Deuteronomy in portraying Jesus as a journeying guest and a rejected prophet like Moses. As journeying guest, Jesus speaks of banquets and calls for proper response to the banquet that he himself will host (Luke 22 and 24). Further, the narrative echoes the Deuteronomic themes of resisting God, stubborn unbelief, and failure to enter the land. As the people rejected Moses, so they reject Jesus, and thus they will miss out on the banquet and rejoicing before the Lord in the land, that is, in Luke the banquet of messianic celebration. In Luke 9:51ff., "Jesus, like Moses, sends out messengers to secure food and hospitality for them," but, as "if on cue, they are flatly rejected."[14] Moessner has helpfully identified many texts that either depict Jesus as a journeying guest or rejected prophet. He links these to one another *and* to the theme of Jesus as Lord of the banquet.[15] While this correlation is not as strong as he suggests,[16] it cannot be denied that these emphases permeate the narrative. These themes are also not confined to this section but tone Luke-Acts more broadly. The distinctive feature of this section consists of the relationship between these themes and their occurrence in Deuteronomy which functions as a literary archetype for this section. Hence, Luke's travel narrative witnesses in a special way to Jesus as a prophet like Moses.

Not only is *rejection* of the prophet integral to both units of literature, both literarily and theologically, but the analogical emphasis on Israel's journeying to the promised land of milk and honey and Jesus' journeying to the banquet which he will host (Luke 14:15–24; 22:7–27; 24:13–35) is most important. Further, as Moessner notes, the correspondence has within it also a contrast: in Deuteronomy, the people will be dispersed into households as they come into the land of feasting; in Luke, those who heed the invitation of and celebrate with the journeying guest will be gathered together as a new household at the banquet.[17] Another correspondence, as a parallel, may also be noted: the journeying Israelites in Deuteronomy are expected to attend three major feasts annually and to celebrate with thanksgiving and joy (Deuteronomy 16). Luke portrays Jesus frequently feasting and speaking about feasting (esp. Luke 14–15). The fault with the Pharisees—and the elder brother (Luke 15)—is that they refuse to celebrate, feast, and *rejoice* upon the finding of the lost, the homecoming of the sinner. Further, following the sections that speak of feasts in Deuteronomy and of banquets in Luke's central section, strong injunctions to do justice that prevents oppression of the poor and the socially marginalized occur. Precisely those kinds of people, who in the older story were barred from the holy space (Lev. 21:17–21) and who the Qumran covenanters proscribed from the war preceding the messianic banquet (see below), are those welcomed to the banquet which Jesus as journeying guest will host (Luke 14:21–24).

The Lukan journey narrative then, in its echo of the Deuteronomic "land entrance" and "conquest" traditions, develops a twin theme of journeying guest/Lord of the banquet and rejected prophet. This twin theme is closely intertwined with the next, that of peace and justice, for the journeying guest offers to people the gospel of peace. Responses to this offer set up a lockstep sequence: if the people respond by accepting the peace, they prepare for the banquet which Jesus as Lord will host. If they reject the offer, they reject the journeying prophet. Further, this twin theme of journeying guest—who is also incognito Lord of the banquet—and rejected prophet can be rightly and fully assessed by viewing this dual emphasis as the context for both Luke's *peace and justice* emphases *and* his treatment of the gospel's conquest of evil and God's judgment of evil, the second and third couplets.

Peace (*Eirēnē*) and Justice (*Dikaios*) as Primary Motifs

The second of Luke's twin themes lies in his accent on peace (*eirēnē*) and justice (*dikaios*). If one regards Luke 9:51–62 as introductory to the central section, then the first (10:1ff.) and last (19:28ff.) narratives in the section are laced with Luke's peace accent. The word occurs three times in 10:5–6, including the phrase "son of peace," and thrice again in 19:28–42. Each occurrence is crucial and strategic both in Luke's literary design and in his theological intention. In the mission of the seventy, which prefigures the church's later mission to the Gentiles, the first word of address is " 'Peace be with you.' " If a "child of peace" is there, the door will be open; you shall enter, heal the sick, and say, "The kingdom of God has come near to you" (10:9). If the peace is refused, it "shall return to you" and you shall wipe off the dust of your feet against them and say, "Nevertheless know this, that the kingdom of God has come near" (10:11). Ulrich Mauser has shown the close relationship between the greeting of peace and the announcement of the kingdom's advent in the structural parallelism between 10:5–6 and 10:8–11. Imparting peace to the child of peace is matched by healing the sick and announcing that the kingdom of God is near.[18] Indeed, this appears to capsulize Luke's peace theology: the proclamation of the gospel of the kingdom is the advent of peace and the reception of that gospel is the realization of peace. If, on the other hand, peace is refused, then also the kingdom is refused.

Further, the seventy are "sent (*apesteilen*)," the same word used for Jesus' mission in 4:18 and 43; Jesus *sends* out the seventy before his face (*pro prosōpou autou,* 10:1). While Luke's favorite verb *euangelizomai* does not occur here, the same activity is carried forward by the seventy under the gospel's salutation, "Peace be to this house!" A peace response becomes the criterion by which the people receive either the kingdom of God or condemnation. Certainly this emphasis, heading up Luke's special section, carries forward his narrative intentions in 2:14 where the angelic choir heralds the meaning of Jesus' birth as "glory in heaven" and "peace on earth."

Paul Minear has suggested a direct correlation between "glory in heaven" and "peace on earth," in Luke's thematic intentions: "the more glory the more peace, and the more peace the more glory."[19] Similarly, Minear correlates the seventy's rejoicing that their names are written in heaven (10:20) with their *shalom-eirēnē* shout to the homes they visited; joy in heaven matches the peace, joy, and wholeness experienced on earth (15:7, 10, 20–24).[20]

By introducing the peace motif prominently again in the ending of his special section, Luke wants his readers to see that Jesus' entire mission was one of bringing peace.[21] The multitude of disciples that followed Jesus as he descended the Mount of Olives to enter Jerusalem "began to praise God joyfully with a loud voice for all the deeds of power that they had seen, saying, 'Blessed is the king who comes in the name of the Lord! Peace in heaven, and glory in the highest heaven!' " (19:37–38). This shout of "Peace in heaven" is clearly an antiphonal response to 2:14 in the larger Lukan narrative. The proclamation of the heavenly host is now complemented by the shout of the multitude of disciples. Earth answers heaven. It is urgent that the praise be given, for when the Pharisees try to hush it, Jesus says, "If they don't shout it, the very stones will cry it out" (my rendering). Luke's narrative exclaims: Jesus comes as earth's true king ringing heaven's bells of peace; a vast multitude of followers have confessed it. But the outcry shows also an abortive dimension: the peace has not been welcomed by all on earth. Hence, in sharp contrast to the mood of the praising multitude, Jesus laments over Jerusalem and pronounces judgment: "If you, even you, had only recognized on this day the things that make for peace! But now they are hidden from your eyes" (v. 42). The harsh words of judgment upon the city end with the sad explanatory comment: "because you did not recognize the time of your visitation from God" (v. 44). Thus the section ends. God has sent divine peace through Jesus, but the response pattern has been full of surprises. Those with standing invitation to the banquet have refused; those previously barred from the banquet have accepted.

John Donahue has pointed out an arresting parallel between Israel's holy war regulations in Deuteronomy 20 and Luke's great banquet parable in 14:16–24.[22] This connection is also one of the correspondences cited by C. F. Evans. The excuses of the guests with first invitation to the banquet echo the same reasons why male

Israelites were exempted from responding to the call to holy war (Deuteronomy 20), as follows:

Deuteronomy War Exemptions	*Luke's Banquet Excuses*
1. Built a new house	1. Bought a piece of land
2. Planted a vineyard	2. Bought five yoke of oxen
3. Engaged to a woman	3. Just married a wife

The parallelism is indeed striking. The first are property excuses; the second, work excuses—the oxen tilled the vineyard; and the third, excuses arising from marital obligations. Donahue observes that in the Old Testament and later Jewish literature the feast of the messianic age is inaugurated by great violence or war to crush the enemies.[23] Indeed, in Luke, Jesus tells this parable in response to earlier banqueting instructions (14:7–14) and in response to the exclamation in v. 15, "Blessed is the one who will eat bread in the kingdom of God." Jesus' parable of the great banquet comes next and ends with the words, "For I tell you, none of those who were invited will eat of my banquet" (v. 24)!

Luke's portrayal of Jesus, says Donahue, departs from the standard Jewish eschatological anticipations in that "he omits those violent elements (cf. Matt. 10:39) normally associated with the eschatological banquet."[24] Stressing nonviolence and peace, Luke's Jesus takes the parable into a second dimension in which substitute guests are invited: the poor, the crippled, and the lame—precisely those who in the Qumran literature (1QM 7:4–6; 1QSa 2:5–10) were excluded from the expected messianic banquet.[25] Even after these ritually unclean people are gathered into the feast, a third invitation compels more to come from the highways and hedges. Thus Luke accents the inclusiveness of the kingdom banquet. In this echo and new version of the earlier war tradition, the human enemy has disappeared.

This textual transformation of the holy war tradition shows thus another link between Luke's travel narrative and Israel's "conquest" warfare traditions; at the same time, it contributes also to Luke's narrative intention to depict Jesus' journey as God's gracious offer of peace, an offer rejected by those called first, but accepted by those formerly barred from the banquet.

Complementing Luke's portrait of Jesus' gospel as God's offer of peace is his emphasis on true justice. Luke uses either the verb or noun forms of justice (*dikaios, dikaioō, ekdikeō, ekdikēsis*) twelve times, and none has parallels in either Matthew or Mark. Four uses describe specific persons or groups who pretend justice or seek to justify themselves (the lawyer in 10:29; the Pharisees in 16:15; likely the Pharisees in 18:9 who "trusted in themselves that they were righteous"; and the scribes and chief priests in 20:20 in setting the tax trap). Four texts either call for justice (12:57) or designate someone or some group as just: the resurrection of the just in 14:14; the ninety-nine righteous in 15:7—which has an ironic edge to it; and the tax collector for his prayer of contrition who was "justified rather than the other [Pharisee]" in 18:14. A second group of four uses occur in the parable of the Unjust Judge. Twice the woman pleads for justice (18:3, 5) and twice Jesus assures the listener that God will grant justice (18:7, 8). Here God's own character is the standard that defines justice. Another four uses describe specific persons or groups who pretend justice or seek to justify themselves: the lawyer in 10:29; the Pharisees in 16:15; likely the Pharisees in 18:9 who "trusted in themselves that they were righteous"; and the scribes and chief priests in 20:20 in setting the tax trap. These counterfeit portraits of justice provide a narrative foil for the Gospel's climactic christological confession, "Truly this was a righteous man," in 23:47, a bold alternative to Mark and Matthew. Thus in Luke's theology, Jesus, like God, emerges as the standard of true justice (here both the RSV and NRSV obscure Luke's point by translating *dikaios* as "innocent").

Luke's special section echoes Deuteronomy's widely recognized emphasis on justice, especially 16:18–20, where God tells Israel to appoint judges to render just decisions and then calls for justice: "Justice, and only justice, you shall pursue, so that you may occupy the land that the Lord your God is giving you." In Evans's work this particular text corresponds to Luke 14:1–14, a text that promises a reward "at the resurrection of the just" to those who host banquets the Jesus way—inviting in the poor, the maimed, the lame, and the blind.[26] Luke's justice text in 18:1–8 corresponds to Deuteronomy 24:6–25:3, a passage containing numerous injunctions against oppressive treatment of the poor, the resident alien, the orphan, and the widow. Deuteronomy 24:17 uses the word "justice" (*mishpat*) only once: "You shall not deprive a resident alien or an orphan of justice; you shall not take the widow's garment in pledge." The widow's persistent pleas for justice in Luke 18 clearly echo the Deuteronomic parallel, and thus again Evans's thesis has remarkable support.

Beyond these specific connections between Luke's central section and Deuteronomy, Luke's pervasive emphasis on social justice matches that of Deuteronomy's (see, e.g., Deut. 8:11–18, where the prophet Moses warns Israel against allowing prosperity in the land to seduce them into forgetting God). In two parables, the rich fool in Luke 12:16–20 and the rich man and Lazarus in Luke 16:19–31, Luke warns against wealth's blinding of people to the kingdom's call and its justice. Noting that these parables are distinctive to Luke and expressive of his extensive treatment of the apparent gap between rich and poor in the churches, Donahue summarizes Luke's special contribution on this topic. The travel narrative includes not only these two parables but Zacchaeus's giving of half his goods to the poor (19:8), other teaching on almsgiving (11:41; 12:33), and a strong Deuteronomic echo of social justice: "Luke presents Jesus in the form of an OT prophet who takes the side of the widow (7:11–17; 18:1–8), the stranger in the land (10:29–37; 17:16), and those on the margin of society (14:12–13, 21)."[27] Indeed, this aspect of social justice as one portion of Israel's "way to the land" and "conquest" traditions resonates loudly in Luke's journey narrative, so loudly that we may assuredly accept that Luke used Deuteronomy imitatively as a literary model.[28]

In the light of the contemporary urgent need to correlate peace with justice, Luke creatively and profoundly speaks to our needs as well as to those of his time. The meaning of justice in both Deuteronomy and Luke is not to be confused with the Greek notion of rendering to everyone their due but must be understood as expressive of mercy as shown in God's covenant relationship to Israel. Seeing the needs of the poor and marginalized, justice responds with compassion. As Millard Lind has put it, "Both justice and mercy arise out of the covenant relationship of God and people." Further, Israel's "law is an expression of that [mercy and justice] norm."[29] Just as law and justice show the design of life within the people's covenant relationship with God, so the Gospel's portrayal of Jesus proclaiming peace and justice reflects also the good news of the kingdom and its pattern for life. It is the way of the Jesus community. It calls people to stop feigning justice, that is, pretending to be righteous, but to actually live the way of God's kingdom, brought near in Jesus. Failing this, God's justice means judgment, for God's peace and justice mean that evil's power is broken.

The Gospel's Conquest of Evil;
God's Judgment of Evil

A third crucial feature in Luke's journey narrative is the gospel's conquest of evil[30] and God's judgment of evil, including especially those who failed to respond to God's offer of peace and justice. In

Luke, Jesus' interpretive declaration on the mission of the seventy is most striking. From the sequence of the narrative, Luke clearly intends to show that the gospel of peace goes out as victorious power over evil. In the oracle put between the sending out and the return of the seventy, Jesus speaks woes upon Chorazin and Bethsaida for failure to receive God's peace mission—God's *missio Dei* (Luke 10:13–16). Jesus' words of judgment echo the downfall of earlier self-exalted and oppressive kings (Isaiah 14; Ezekiel 28): "And you, Capernaum, will you be exalted to heaven? No, you will be brought down to Hades" (Luke 10:15). Despite the extensive scope of rejection and judgment, Jesus *sees* also another result of the kingdom's peace mission: "I saw Satan fall like lightning from heaven" (v. 18, RSV). As people accepted the gospel of peace, the demons lost their hold on them. When the seventy proclaimed the gospel of peace, they in effect also bound and expelled the demons in the name of Jesus. This event marked the end of an era: Satan's rule ended; Jesus' rule began! This victory has also even more enduring consequence in that "your names are written in heaven" (v. 20).

The next paragraph's startling jubilation—with Jesus' rejoicing in the Holy Spirit and outcry to God as Father—appears to be Jesus' celebration of this cosmic exorcistic victory: the hidden things have been revealed not to the wise and understanding but to babes. This ejaculation voices the simple truth and sheer joy experienced when the gospel word of peace liberates from Satan's bonds. The outburst continues by underscoring the basis of authority for all this to have happened: "All things have been handed over (*paredothē*) to me by my Father; and no one knows who the Son is except the Father, or who the Father is except the Son and anyone to whom the Son chooses to reveal him" (v. 22). Then follows instruction to the disciples on seeing and hearing and their privileged position: "Blessed are the eyes that see what you see!"

Next comes a testing (*ekpeirazōn*) from a lawyer on the question of inheriting eternal life (v. 25). Will the lawyer see what the disciples have seen? No, for in the face of God's love commands, he seeks self-justification (*thelōn dikaiōsai*). In contrast, the gospel of peace (so defined earlier in Luke 10) shows love compassionately aiding not only an unknown neighbor but a known enemy—and the hands of love are those of a Samaritan! The narrative shifts from the question, "Who is the neighbor whom I am commanded to love?" to another, "Am I a loving neighbor even to the enemy?" To be such a neighbor ensures one of eternal life, and it does not test with evil intent the Teacher of truth and life. The Good Samaritan story climaxes Luke's first segment which is thus framed by the Samaritan theme, for in 9:54 the disciples wanted to rain fire down upon a Samaritan village because of its rejection of the journeying prophet Jesus (cf. 2 Kings 1:10, 12). But Jesus rebuked (*epetimēsen*) them, thus expelling their evil desire.

This first segment (9:51–10:37) of Luke's central section thus develops the theme of the gospel's overcoming of evil through its proclamation of peace and its deeds of love, even to the enemy. As people receive the kingdom's gospel of peace, Satan falls from his throne of power. Enemies are saved from death through love that risks life for life. The gospel of peace and love has conquered.

Since the mission of the seventy appears to be a narrative follow-up to Jesus' sending messengers ahead to Samaritan towns (9:51–53, 56), another point, blending the two above, comes also into view. The two themes, the peace of the kingdom and the "conquest" of evil, are developed in the narrative by actions that are located squarely in the territory of the religious and sociopolitical enemy, the despised Samaritans.[31] In the light of the older story, this has double significance, for Samaria matches geographically the place where Joshua's or Yahweh's first battles against the Canaanites occurred. Thus another powerful link to and transformation of Israel's "conquest" tradition comes into focus. But now, rather than eradicating the enemy, the new strategy eradicates the enmity. The Samaritans receive the peace of the kingdom of God. Instead of killing people to get rid of idolatry, the attack through the gospel is upon Satan directly. Instead of razing high places, Satan is blown off his throne! Hence the root of idolatry is plucked from its source (see Deut. 18:9–14 for the rationale, i.e., idolatry, for destroying the people in the Promised Land).

Other pericopes also highlight Jesus' "conquest" and judgment of evil. These are the Beelzebul controversy, which Luke alone places in this section of the synoptic structure; recurring pronouncements of judgment upon "this evil generation" (Luke 12); and the release of a woman bound by Satan for eighteen years (13:10–17). The Beelzebul controversy contains Jesus' famous claim of authority and word of victory: "But if it is by the finger of God that I cast out the demons, then the kingdom of God has come to you" (11:20). Again, the theme of the kingdom is correlated directly with victory over the evil hosts. The next verses portray Jesus as the one stronger than the strong man, one who has successfully assailed Satan and rescued those under his dominion. In this context of Jesus' assault and victory over Satan's goods, an earlier saying (9:50) is reversed, "Whoever is not with me is against me, and whoever does not gather with me scatters" (11:23). Even though the statement appears reversed from its other synoptic uses, the shift in context makes its meaning the same in both uses: it is important to be on the side of Jesus in the battle against evil, for Jesus and the gospel of the kingdom will triumph. By placing this pericope in this section, Luke further accents Jesus' "conquest" over evil.

Some themes in this section fit well as subthemes of peace and victory over evil. Much of the teaching guards against sin or evil threatening to creep into the Christian life or accents rescue of people from sin and evil (esp. Luke 15). The climax of the Lord's Prayer, "Lead us not into temptation," calls on God's power to protect against evil's seductive power;[32] the contrast between evil and good in the subsequent exposition (11:13) shows the pervasiveness of the theme. The extensive warnings against wealth, noted above, exemplify further the point. To be a lover of money is to resist Jesus and his way (16:13–15). By placing close to the end of the section the contrasting stories of the rich ruler (18:18–30) and Zacchaeus (19:1–10), Luke regards attachment to wealth as a hindrance to the peace-gospel's overcoming of evil (cf. 16:13).[33]

The central section also contains two crucially placed pericopes that accent Jesus' judgment of those who fail to respond to the gospel's peace. According to Kenneth Bailey's and Michael Goulder's chiastic analyses,[34] the strategic center of the section is 13:31–35. In this tightly crafted saying Jesus describes his ministry—to the Pharisees and Herod who seeks to kill him—as one of casting out demons and performing cures. This he must do today, tomorrow, and the next day; then he will accept the prophet's destiny in Jerusalem. An evil-good opposition emerges: Jerusalem will kill and stone Jesus as they did the other prophets; Jesus then voices the two-sided reality of his mission, both yearning love and judgment upon spurned opportunity:

> How often would I have gathered your children together as a hen gathers her brood under her wings, and you were not willing! See, your house is left to you. And I tell you, you will not see me until the time comes when you say, "Blessed is the one who comes in the name of the Lord." (13:34b–35)

The final segment of Luke's special section sounds a similar note. Luke's parable of the pounds (19:11–27) contains two levels of story: the nobleman's response to the servants who used the pounds or talents in different ways and the nobleman's response to "the citizens of his country [who] hated him" (19:14) The final punch of the parable falls upon them:

> But as for these enemies of mine who did not want me to be king over them—bring them here and slaughter them in my presence. (19:27)

Even though Luke shows unambiguously that his followers are called to befriend and love the enemy, thus destroying the enmity, the category of "enemy" is not altogether eliminated. While, in Luke, Jesus' ethic for humans regards the enemy as opportunity for neighbor love, those who refuse the kingdom's gospel of peace fall under divine judgment. The parable indicates that the citizens set up the "enemy" stance by their hatred of the nobleman; Jesus' word thus responds to that stance. In keeping with the older story, judgment falls upon those who hate the God of peace and love. Verse 27 is stark and chilling. The segment's final words reinforce the same reality on a socionational corporate level, because the city refused the peace proffered by the humble one seeking royal coronation in God's holy city (19:29–40). Because they did not recognize the things that make for peace, things hidden from their eyes, they now hear:

> Indeed, the days will come upon you, when your enemies will set up ramparts around you and surround you, and hem you in on every side. They will crush you to the ground, you and your children within you, and they will not leave within you one stone upon another; because you did not recognize the time of your visitation from God. (19:43–44)

Though the end of the narrative carries this somber pronouncement, one detail in the segment especially intrigues the reader: "The whole multitude of the disciples began to praise God joyfully with a loud voice for all the deeds of power that they had seen, saying, '. . . Peace in heaven, and glory in the highest heaven!' " (19:37b–38). Who were all those people in the multitude—hardly many from Jerusalem (vs. 41–44)—who sang the praises of peace? In the light of the narrative's progression from Galilee through Samaria and the judgment upon Jerusalem, the composition of this multitude depends on the swelling crowd that follows the journeying guest to the promised banquet. It is for these for whom the walls of Jericho have fallen anew, through the gospel of peace, love, and justice.

David Tiede rightly says that Luke writes a narrative that enters "into a complex contemporary discussion of divine justice and grace, faithfulness and abandonment, vengeance and providence in Israel's recent history."[35] He concurs with Norman Petersen: *"The rejection of God's agents by God's people in connection with God's sanctuaries (synagogues and temples) is the plot device by which the narrative as a whole is motivated.*"[36] While this is poignantly true in Luke's narrative, another side must be equally emphasized: The Luke 10 narrative indicates that the announced peace on earth has found some takers and God's gospel of salvation will triumph in its peace gift, despite the massive rejection.[37] Both the acceptance and the rejection of the gospel of peace are present in these inclusio narratives of Luke's central section. Thus the journey from the transfiguration to Jerusalem, the place of humiliation, was a journey of "conquest" disarming the power of Satan and evil by bringing peace to those who received the peace of God's kingdom and "a desolate house" to those who refused it (13:35).[38]

Conclusion

In both form and content Luke's journey narrative reflects influences in its content and emphases from Israel's earlier story of journey on the way to and "conquest" within the land of promise. In form, Luke's narrative is a journey, like the older story, and Deuteronomy does appear to be its literary model. In content, six themes permeate the narrative, here developed as three couplets. Echoing the older narrative, Luke's story discloses Jesus as the journeying guest/Lord of the banquet and rejected prophet, the bringer of peace and justice, and the disarmer of evil and agent of divine judgment. It is important to note that the first themes in each of the three couplets are tightly interlinked to one another, as are the second themes in each of the three couplets closely linked also. The journeying guest/Lord of the banquet brings the gospel of peace, a power that depowers Satan and his arsenal of evil. The rejected prophet is the prophet of justice whose word is judgment for those who refuse the banqueting guest, spurn the gospel of peace, and court evil. In the light of the above exposition, the journey motif functions primarily, we propose, to signal the reader to hear Luke's story of Jesus in the central section against the memory of the older story—and, among other things, see what happens to the enemy (Canaanites and Samaritans) in the center of the land and story. That the healed Samaritan leper returns to give thanks is both paradigmatic and parabolic (17:11–19).

Jesus' command, "Love your enemies, do good to those who hate you" (Luke 6:27), has, then, its narrative expression in Luke's central section. Its sharpness of depiction emerges as the various episodes of the Jesus story are compared to what appears to be the narrative's literary archetype, the book of Deuteronomy. By casting

Samaritans in paradigmatic roles, Luke "converts" stock strands of enmity, from Jewish perspectives, and thus shows concretely what love for the enemy entails in socioethnic terms. By portraying the advance of the gospel of the kingdom as the offer and making of peace, Luke forges an indissoluble link between salvation and ethics. By joining the peace-gospel's advance with the dethronement of Satan and the confrontation and defeat of evil, Luke presents also a realistic peace ethic, not a peace that closes its eyes to evil, but a peace that forces a choice: God's favor and saving power or God's judgment.

Correspondences Between
Luke 9:51–19:44 and Deuteronomy

A correspondence of parallel thought is designated (P); one of transformation in thought (T); and reversal of the thought structure, that is, contrast (C). Brackets indicate Swartley's additions to Evans's content.

Texts	*No.*	*Correspondence*	*Rela-tion-ship*
Deut. 1/Luke 10:1–3, 17–20 [really 9:51–53]	1.	Israel *journeys* under Moses to Promised Land / Jesus and disciples to Jerusalem:	C
		If Jesus' destiny is viewed as glory, then:	P
	2.	The land set "before your face" and Twelve sent out / Jesus sends out seventy. Nature of mission:	T
	[3.	People in land are too great and tall; can't conquer, and then Lord prevents going / Mission is success; Jesus sees Satan falling from heaven]:	C
Deut. 2:1–3:22/Luke 10:4–16	4.	Messengers sent to Sihon and Og with word of peace / Seventy sent out with word of peace:	P
	5.	If rejected, destroy / If rejected, wipe the dust off your feet and leave:	T
	6.	What the Lord did to two kings / Jesus prophesies judgment upon Chorazin, Bethsaida, and Capernaum:	P
Deut. 3:23–4:40/Luke 10:21–24	7.	Moses is servant mediator / Jesus is revealer mediator. Both texts contain similar terms: "in that hour," "wisdom

		and understanding," "seeing and hearing" God's disclosure:	P
Deut. 5–6/Luke 10:25–27	8.	Shema and "inherit the land . . . in order to live" / Lawyer asks about inheriting eternal life, answers with Shema:	P/T
Deut. 7/Luke 10:29–37	9.	Destroy the foreigner; show no mercy / Parable of Good Samaritan; show mercy:	C
Deut. 8:1–3/Luke 10:38–42	10.	Living by word of God in both:	P
Deut. 8:4–20/Luke 11:1–13	11.	Father to son instruction / Son to Father prayer. "Eating" occurs in both:	T
Deut. 9:1–10:11/Luke 11:14–26	12.	Lord drives out strong fierce nations / Jesus drives out strong demons. Term "finger of God/*en (tō) daktylō (tou) Theou*" in both:	T
Deut. 10:12–11/Luke 11:27–36	13.	Lord requires only keeping Torah / Jesus, "hear word of God and do it." Also a "stiff-necked people who saw great wonders in Egypt" / An "evil generation" who seeks a sign:	P
Deut. 12:1–16/Luke 11:37–12:12	14.	Clean and unclean in both: reject / accept:	C
Deut. 12:17–32/Luke 12:13–13:34	15.	The Lord prospers; keep commands to gain inheritance; rejoice in wealth / Life is more than possessions; seek kingdom, sell, give alms, and gain eternal life:	C
Deut. 13:1–11/Luke 12:35–53	16.	Death to those who go after other gods; don't let family members entice you /Reward and punishment as the Lord's stewards; give up family members to follow Jesus, thus division:	P/T
Deut. 13:12–32/Luke 12:54–13:5	17.	Destruction of city for apostasy / Jesus' teachings on discernment and judgment; group calamity, were they worse sinners? No, all must repent:	T

Deut. 15:1–18/Luke 13:10–21	18. Release from debts and slavery / Jesus releases a woman from bondage:	P/T
Deut. 20/Luke 14:15–35	19. Excused from Lord's battle for new wife, house, vineyard / Similar excuses of invited guests to great banquet who miss the feast:	P/T
Deut. 21:15–22:4/Luke 15	20. How father handles rebellious son—stone to death / Father seeks prodigal son—celebrates return:	C
Deut. 23:15–24:4/Luke 16:1–18	21. Treatment of fugitive slave; law against usury; granting bill of divorce / Unjust steward forgives oppressed debtors; Pharisees—lovers of money; against divorce—adultery:	P/C
Deut. 24:6–25:3/Luke 16:19–18:8	22. Injunctions against oppressing poor and needy / Lord judges those who oppress poor:	P

Notes

1. C. F. Evans, "The Central Section of Luke's Gospel," in *Studies in the Gospels* (ed. D. E. Nineham; Oxford: Basil Blackwell, 1955, 1967), 37–53; also in C. F. Evans, *Saint Luke* (TPINTC; London: SCM Press, and Philadelphia: Trinity Press International, 1990), 34–36.

2. David P. Moessner, *Lord of the Banquet: The Literary and Theological Significance of the Lukan Travel Narrative* (Minneapolis: Fortress Press, 1989).

3. My development of this latter theme draws upon Susan Garrett's study of Luke-Acts, *The Demise of the Devil: Magic and the Demonic in Luke's Writings* (Minneapolis: Fortress Press, 1989).

4. In my larger work from which this essay draws I propose and argue that Israel's "way to the promised land" and "conquest" traditions influenced both the genre and the emphases of this section.

5. Evans, "Central Section," 51.

6. Whether Luke knew of the *Assumption (Testament) of Moses* cannot be determined; its date of origin is uncertain.

7. James L. Resseguie, "Interpretation of Luke's Central Section (Luke 9:51–19:44) Since 1856," *Studia Biblica et Theologica* 5 (1975): 13.

8. James A. Sanders, *Canon and Community: A Guide to Canonical Criticism* (Philadelphia: Fortress Press, 1984), 63–67.

9. My first impression of this was to dismiss it. But after a third careful reading of the evidence, I concluded that 60–70 percent of the correspondences are substantial. But there are weaknesses: five Deuteronomy sections (Deut. 14:1–21; 19; 21:1–14; 22:5–23:14; 25:4–19) have no Lukan parallels. Surprisingly, Deut. 18:15–18, containing a key Lukan theme—Jesus is a prophet like unto Moses—has no parallel (Evans ["Central Section," 47] explains this omission by the connection already made in Luke 9:35, the voice at the transfiguration). Also I note that the chiastic center of Luke's central section, 13:31–35 (as proposed by Kenneth E. Bailey, *Poet and Peasant* [Grand Rapids: Wm. B. Eerdmans Publishing Co., 1976], 80–83), has no particular thought correspondence in Deuteronomy. Nonetheless the evidence for Luke's use of Deuteronomy for his composition is too strong for the thesis to be dismissed.

10. This point needs more attention in David Moessner's recent study of Luke's use of Deuteronomy. In my judgment, the theme of "rejected prophet" (see tenets B and C, *Lord of the Banquet*, 84) characterizes Luke's accent more broadly and is not restricted to the journey narrative. Similarly, the Lukan emphasis on Jesus as "Journeying Guest" and Lord of the Banquet is also not restricted to the journey narrative, for Luke 24 contains a finale to this emphasis, as Moessner observes in showing the continuation of the theme in the passion narrative (22:7–38) and climactically in the Emmaus account (24:13–53). In this respect it is important to maintain, to some extent, the literary dependence of the travel narrative on the content of Deuteronomy, as Evans has shown. By slighting this feature, Moessner has not shown the dependence of the travel narrative on Deuteronomy in a way distinctive from the rest of Luke-Acts. His summary of correspondences between the travel narrative and Deuteronomy on pp. 280–285 offers more persuasive evidence, but this appears not to play a crucial role in his contribution as a whole.

11. See Marcus J. Borg, *Jesus: A New Vision; Spirit, Culture and the Life of Discipleship* (San Francisco: Harper & Row, 1987), 86–93, 183–184; and his earlier more extensive treatment of holiness in *Conflict, Holiness and Politics in the Teaching of Jesus* (Toronto: Edwin Mellen, 1983).

12. Willard M. Swartley, *Story Shaping Story: Israel's Scripture Traditions in the Synoptics* (Peabody, Mass.: Hendrickson Publishers, forthcoming in 1993).

13. David Moessner's and Susan Garrett's recent works have opened the door to at least some of these perceptions.

14. Moessner, *Lord of the Banquet*, 273.

15. Ibid., 3–4, 174–176, 211.

16. Luke 11:37–54 is the only text that explicitly joins the rejected prophet with the banquet theme, and there the positions are reversed: the Pharisee throws the banquet and Jesus rejects the Pharisees and lawyers. Only in 10:38–42 and 19:1–10 are the journey and banqueting themes linked. Moessner's diagram (p. 176) shows how he must choose different texts and hook them together to make his point. True, the texts are all in this section, but the joining of the journeying guest or rejected prophet

themes with the banquet theme is not as clear in Luke as it is in Moessner. There simply is not tight textual correlation between the journey motif and the banqueting motif, even though the two flow together in broad narrative strokes.

17. Moessner (*Lord of the Banquet*, 273) puts this a little differently; he speaks of Jesus gathering households for the banquet. But Luke 14:26 requires a different conception.

18. Ulrich Mauser, *The Gospel of Peace* (SPS 1; Louisville: Westminster/John Knox Press, 1992), 55.

19. Paul Minear, *To Heal and to Reveal: The Prophetic Vocation According to Luke* (New York: Seabury Press, 1976), 50. Indeed, glory also is a major thematic accent of Luke's Gospel.

20. Ibid., 50–55; Minear uses the Hebrew word *shalom*. For evidence that it is appropriate to link *eirēnē* with *shalom* in Luke, see Willard M. Swartley, "Politics and Peace (*Eirēnē*) in Luke's Gospel," in *Political Issues in Luke-Acts* (ed. R. J. Cassidy and P. J. Scharper; Maryknoll, N.Y.: Orbis Books, 1983), 35–37.

21. John R. Donahue ("The Good News of Peace," *The Way* 22 [1982]: 88–89) has suggested we read the Lukan journey narrative as "a path to peace."

22. John R. Donahue, *The Gospel in Parable: Metaphor, Narrative, and Theology in the Synoptic Gospels* (Philadelphia: Fortress Press, 1988), 140–146.

23. Donahue, *Parable*, 142. Donahue cites in n. 27 Isa. 25:6–8; 55:1–2; 65:13–14; *1 Enoch* 62:14; *2 Apoc. Bar.* 29:4; Revelation 20–21.

24. Ibid., 142.

25. Ibid., 144.

26. Evans lifts Deut. 16:18ff. out of 16:1–17:7 and puts it with 17:8–18:22 so that this judicial law section is parallel to Luke's parable of the Great Banquet in Luke 14:1–14. By connecting the banqueting and justice themes in this way Luke fuses together the first and second thematic couplets explicated here in my discussion of Luke's travel narrative.

27. Donahue, *Parable*, 175.

28. Of the four intertextual relationships that a literary work might bear to a predecessor—imitative, eclectic, heuristic, or dialectical, according to Thomas Greene—Luke's central section is related to Deuteronomy imitatively on this point of justice. However, where he transforms the Deuteronomic thought, not slaying the Canaanites but forming friendship between Jews and Samaritans, the relationship is dialectical, in conversation with but transforming the emphases also. See Thomas M. Greene, *The Light in Troy: Imitation and Discovery in Renaissance Poetry* (New Haven, Conn.: Yale University Press, 1982), 38–46.

29. Millard C. Lind, "Transformation of Justice: From Moses to Jesus," in *Monotheism, Power and Justice: Collected Old Testament Essays* (Text-Reader 3; Elkhart, Ind.: Institute of Mennonite Studies, 1990), 82–83.

30. Susan Garrett, *The Demise of the Devil;* see especially her treatment of Luke 10:17–20 (pp. 46–56). While Garrett argues that this text is pro-

leptic of the victory of Jesus' resurrection and exaltation in Luke's narrative, the effort to understand this text in its present narrative location merits attention. If one makes 10:17–20 proleptic, then one must do the same for 10:1–12, anticipating the later mission of the church. The essential connection between the seventy's proclamation of the gospel of peace and the dethronement or disempowerment of Satan cannot be slighted, in faithfulness to the narrative purpose. Cf. Mauser's treatment of Luke 10:17–20 (*Gospel,* 42–45). Mauser also fails to treat this text in respect to its narrative unity with 10:1–12, but rather connects it to Matt. 10:34 and related conflictual emphases.

31. The entire segment of 9:51–10:37 then has Samaria as its locational context.

32. Though the later copyists' addition, "deliver us from evil," was influenced by Matthew's text, the petition certainly fits also the larger Lukan emphasis.

33. On this topic, see Walter E. Pilgrim, *Good News to the Poor: Wealth and Poverty in Luke-Acts* (Minneapolis: Augsburg Publishing House, 1981), esp. 109–133.

34. Kenneth Bailey, "The Literary Outline of the Travel Narrative (Jerusalem Document): Luke 9:51–19:48," in *Poet and Peasant,* 80–83. Bailey's chiastic analysis extends the earlier work of Michael D. Goulder, "The Chiastic Structure of the Lucan Journey," in *Studia Evangelica* II, 195–202.

35. David Tiede, *Prophecy and History in Luke-Acts* (Philadelphia: Fortress Press, 1980), 15.

36. Norman Petersen, *Literary Criticism for New Testament Critics* (Philadelphia: Fortress Press, 1978), 83. Cited by Tiede, *Prophecy and History,* 14.

37. Note Jesus' postresurrection greeting to his disciples, " 'Peace be to you' " (24:36). Peace vocabulary but, more significantly, peace-making events continue through Acts. See Swartley, "Politics and Peace," 18–37; Joseph Comblin, "La paix dans la théologie de saint Luc," *ETL* 32 (1956): 439–460, and Mauser, *The Gospel of Peace,* 89–102.

38. As David P. Reid puts it, "If there is a journey to discipleship, there is also a journey to refusal" ("Peace and Praise in Luke," in *Blessed Are the Peacemakers* [ed. Anthony J. Tambasco; Mahwah, N.J.: Paulist Press, 1989], 106).

9

Paul's Ethic
of Nonretaliation
and Peace

Gordon Zerbe

Paul often faced the realities of conflict and enmity, both within his churches and in relation to outsiders hostile to him and the church. Such realities were so significant that references to proper Christian behavior in response to injury or persecution appear in nearly all his extant letters and in a variety of genres.[1] First, in paraenetic contexts we find explicit exhortations on this topic. Romans 12:14, 17–21, the longest passage on this theme, is addressed to relations with outsiders, particularly persecutors:[2]

> Bless those who persecute you;[3] bless and do not curse. . . .
> Repay no one evil for evil,
>> but take forethought for noble conduct in the sight of all.
>> If possible, so far as it depends on you, live peaceably with all.
> Do not avenge yourselves, beloved, but leave room for wrath;
>>> for it is written, "Vengeance is mine, I myself will repay, says the Lord."
> But, "if your enemy is hungry, feed him; if he is thirsty, give him drink;

This chapter is an adapted form of chapter 6 of Gordon Zerbe's doctoral dissertation, *Non-Retaliation in Early Jewish and New Testament Texts: Ethical Themes in Social Contexts*, to be published by Sheffield Academic Press in the *Journal for the Study of the Pseudepigrapha* Supplement Series.

for by doing so you will heap coals of fire upon his head."
Do not be conquered by evil, but conquer evil with good.

The exhortation of 1 Thess. 5:13b–15 is addressed initially to internal conflict but is extended to refer to relations with all people, implicitly including the persecutors of the community:[4]

> . . . Be at peace among yourselves.
> And we exhort you, . . . admonish the idlers, encourage the faint-hearted, help the weak, be forbearing with all.
> See that nobody repays evil for evil,
> but always pursue good toward one another and toward all.

The context of Phil. 4:5 indicates that Paul here also exhorts non-retaliatory conduct in relation to all, including persecutors:[5]

> Let your forbearance be known to all people. The Lord is at hand.

Colossians 3:12–15a, representing the continuing Pauline tradition, addresses relations within the church:

> Put on, then, . . . forbearance, enduring one another and forgiving one another if someone has a complaint against another;
> just as the Lord has forgiven you, so also you must forgive.
> And upon all of these put on love, which is the bond of perfection.
> And let the peace of Christ rule in your hearts, to which indeed you were called in the one body.

Second, nonretaliatory themes appear in catalogs of hardships describing Paul's behavioral credentials as an apostle. First Corinthians 4:12–13a describes Paul's response to persecutors:

> When reviled we bless, when persecuted we endure,
> when slandered we conciliate.

In the catalog of 2 Cor. 6:3–10, Paul commends his "great endurance" (*hypomonē pollē*) in afflictions (2 Cor. 6:4), his "forbearance" (*makrothymia*), and his "genuine love" (*agapē anypokritos*, 2 Cor. 6:6).

Third, in the virtue and vice lists of Gal. 5:16–24, the vices of enmity, strife, and jealousy (*echthrai, eris, zēlos*, Gal. 5:20) are countered by the virtues of love, peace, and forbearance (*agapē, eirēnē, makrothymia*, Gal. 5:22).

Fourth, the nonretaliatory acceptance of abuse is promoted in the ad hoc exhortation of 1 Cor. 6:1–8. Paul exhorts his readers not to take their disputes to the pagan courts but either to find a Christian mediator or, better, to accept abuse instead of pursuing judicial vindication:

> Actually, it is already a defeat for you that you have lawsuits with one another. Why not rather be wronged? Why not rather be defrauded? (1 Cor. 6:7)

Fifth, the hymn to love in 1 Corinthians 13, which in its context addresses relations within the church, includes the following nonretaliatory themes:

> Love is forbearing. (1 Cor. 13:4)
> It does not reckon evil. (13:5)
> It bears all things . . . , endures all things. (13:7)

Finally, in the fool's speech of 2 Cor. 11:1–12:13, Paul implicitly presents the ideal conduct of slaves in response to abuse:

> You endure it if someone enslaves you, if someone devours you, if someone takes advantage of you, if someone acts presumptuously, if someone strikes you in the face. (2 Cor. 11:20)

While ironically ridiculing the community for taking upon themselves a servile position in relation to the enslaving false teachers, Paul implies that endurance is the proper behavior of a slave in the context of abuse (cf. *kalōs anechesthe*, 2 Cor. 11:4; *hēdeōs anechesthe*, 2 Cor. 11:19). What Paul derides is their acceptance of a servile position in relation to the false teachers. The later Pauline tradition of Col. 3:22–25 expresses the same ideal for slaves, based on deferring justice to God:

> Slaves, obey your earthly masters in everything. . . .
> For the wrongdoer will be paid back for the wrong committed, and there is no partiality. (Col. 3:22a, 25)[6]

To summarize, we find the following themes included in the field of proper responses to injury or persecution. Passive responses include:

1. "Not repaying evil for evil" (*mē apodidonai kakon anti kakou*, 1 Thess. 5:15a; Rom. 12:17a)
2. "Not taking vengeance for oneself" (*mē heautous ekdikountes*, Rom. 12:19a)
3. "Not cursing" (*mē katarēsthai*, Rom. 12:14)
4. "Forbearance" (*epieikes*, Phil. 4:5; *makrothymia*, 1 Thess. 5:14; 1 Cor. 13:4; Gal. 5:22; 2 Cor. 6:6)
5. "Endurance" (*anechesthai*, 1 Cor. 4:12; 2 Cor. 11:20; cf.

Col. 3:13; 2 Thess. 1:4; *hypomenein*, Rom. 12:12; 2 Cor. 6:4;
1 Cor. 13:7; cf. Rom. 5:3–4; 2 Cor. 1:6)

6. "Not litigating" (1 Cor. 6:1–8)
7. "Not reckoning evil" (*mē logizesthai*, 1 Cor. 13:5)[7]

Active responses include:

8. "Responding with good/kind deeds (1 Thess. 5:15b; Rom. 12:17b, 20–21)
9. "Blessing" (*eulogein*, Rom. 12:14; 1 Cor. 4:12)
10. "Conciliating" (*parakalein*, 1 Cor. 4:13)[8]
11. "Being at peace" (*eirēneuein*, 1 Thess. 5:13; Rom. 12:18; cf. Gal. 5:20, 22)[9]
12. "Forgiving" (*charizesthai*, 2 Cor. 2:7–10; Col. 3:13)[10]
13. "Loving" (1 Cor. 13:4–7; cf. 2 Cor. 6:6; Rom. 12:9; 1 Thess. 3:13)

The purpose of this essay is to identify the coherence fundamental to these exhortations and themes, particularly as regards their various explications, implicit or explicit warrants, motivations/goals, and social applications. For the sake of this essay, we will term this coherence Paul's "ethic of nonretaliation and peace."[11] Such a treatment of these exhortations and themes is necessary, since the terminology of "vengeance" or "retaliation" in antiquity has multiple lexical meanings[12] and since nearly identical formulations on the topic of nonretaliation in antiquity can range so markedly in social setting, meaning, and function as to be hardly comparable.[13] We must, then, necessarily ask the following questions. (1) What kind of "vengeance" does Paul prohibit in different cases? (2) Do the exhortations apply equally to different types of abuse and abusers? Are the abusers viewed as friends, fellow church members, personal adversaries, or as sinners and the enemies of God? Is it significant that in the previous survey of texts "love" and "forgiving" are not explicitly exhorted in relation to hostile outsiders (cf. Matt. 5:44)? (3) What motivations or warrants characterize or ground the exhortations, and do they differ in accordance with different social settings? What hopes are expressed as to the eventual fate of the opponents: their reconciliation with the injured party, or their punishment or demise? If the latter, how is the agency of divine vengeance anticipated?

In the following pages we will investigate these issues by focusing on Rom. 12:14, 17–21, since this is Paul's most extensive treatment on the proper response to injury and conflict and since this text is the subject of considerable scholarly debate. But in order to place the discussion in the context of Paul's thought as a whole, particu-

larly since Paul's ethical vision is fundamentally related to his redemptive vision,[14] we will begin with a summary of Paul's vision of
cosmic peace.

Paul's Vision of Cosmic Peace

At the core of Paul's gospel is his vision of cosmic restoration—
the eschatological redemption of the entire created order. This coming order of peace and righteousness (*a*) will be fully realized by the
final triumph of God over the hostile and destructive powers of this
age,[15] which includes judgment and wrath against all unrighteousness and opposition to God,[16] (*b*) has been proleptically inaugurated
by God in Christ through the resurrection, and (*c*) is realized provisionally in the life of the believer and the church where Christ already reigns as Lord.[17]

"Peace" is one of the essential characteristics of this coming order
of salvation.[18] While the language of "peace" in Paul sometimes
refers to eschatological salvation as a whole,[19] terms such as "the
reconciliation of the cosmos/all things"[20] and "the subjection of all
things" to Christ and God[21] also express the vision of cosmic peace.
The numerous texts in which Paul characterizes God as "the God of
peace"[22] also indicate that "peace" is a central attribute of God's
salvation.

For Paul, then, "peace" refers fundamentally to the eschatological
salvation of the whole person, all humanity,[23] and the entire universe.[24] It refers to the normal state of all things—the *order* of God's
creative and redeeming action versus the *disorder* of the chaotic
powers of Satan.[25]

The many other specific uses of "peace" in Paul appear to be
founded on this basic notion: peace with God,[26] peace of soul,[27]
peace as a fruit of the Spirit in the believer,[28] peace among people,
especially in the church,[29] and peace as divinely wrought well-being
and wholeness.[30]

Against the backdrop of this vision of cosmic peace, then, we
proceed to discuss Paul's ethic of nonretaliation and peace, as expressed especially in Rom. 12:14, 17–21.

The Debate Regarding
Romans 12:14, 17–21

Structurally, the exhortation of Rom. 12:14, 17–21 consists of a
series of paired contrasts, comprised of negative prohibitions balanced by positive prescriptions:

Bless persecutors/Do not curse. (12:14)

Do not retaliate/Maintain noble conduct and live in peace.
(12:17–18)

Do not avenge for yourselves/Give food and drink to the enemy.
(12:19–20)

Do not be conquered by evil/Conquer evil with good. (12:21)

The exhortations of vs. 19 and 20 are grounded by parallel motivational clauses:

for God will avenge/
for doing good will heap coals of fire upon the opponent's head

One of the critical issues of scholarly debate on this text focuses on the character and motivational structure of the exhortation.[31] Is Paul's exhortation best characterized as an ethic of nonretaliation understood as an apocalyptic restraint in deference to God's impending wrath against persecutors or as an ethic of love aimed at reconciliation with opponents? Are kind deeds to enemies of the church (vs. 20–21) to be interpreted as contributing to the enemies' repentance and reconciliation or as the means to appease the church's abusers while contributing to the punishment stored against them in the day of wrath?[32]

Interpretations of Rom. 12:14, 17–21 can be grouped into three types despite variations in regard to details. These can be termed the "standard," "apocalyptic," and "mediating" approaches.

The standard interpretation holds that Rom. 12:14, 17–21 expresses an ethic of "love" (12:9) toward one's enemies, the goal of which is the conversion and reconciliation of the opponent.[33] Unconditional love toward the other is not only the content of behavior enjoined but also its grounding motivation. On this interpretation, "heaping coals of fire" in v. 20c refers either (1) to the pangs of shame and remorse, which either lead to conversion and reconciliation or leave the opponent with a bad conscience[34] or (2) to the simple resolve of the adversary to pursue reconciliation.[35] Verse 21b ("but conquer evil with good," *alla nika en tō agathō to kakon*) is thus taken as a reference to the power of love to influence evil and to effect conversion and reconciliation. The theme of leaving wrath and vengeance in God's hands (v. 19bc), which is often downplayed, means that Christians ought not to be occupied in any way with God's vengeance and the last judgment.[36] The call is simply to trust in God's sovereignty[37] or to hope that God's educative wrath will lead adversaries to repentance.[38]

By contrast, the apocalyptic interpretation, as articulated especially by Krister Stendahl,[39] reads this text in the context of persecution. Nonretaliation and good deeds are simply the right responses in times of trouble, when enmity is inevitable and insurmountable. "Heaping coals of fire" is understood as a reference to eschatological judgment, which the enemies of the church are storing up against themselves. Good deeds are not to be understood as a type of love and not intended necessarily to have any reconciling effect; rather, they actually contribute to the culpability of the enemies on the day of wrath. Nonretaliation, then, is essentially an apocalyptic restraint, motivated primarily out of deference to God's judgment. It is not only the conviction that God is the rightful arbiter of justice but also the conviction of the imminent realization of the eschaton which motivates or permits nonretaliation.[40] Verse 21b ("but conquer evil with good") does not refer to the power of love to influence evil but to the assured eschatological victory over evil; doing good while deferring to God is the way ultimately to defeat evil. Some scholars see here a distinct desire for revenge against opponents.[41] But others focus rather on the notion of deferment as primarily offering an eschatological hope and a theodicy of evil.[42]

A mediating position, as articulated recently by John Piper, stands between the standard and apocalyptic interpretations.[43] With the apocalyptic interpretation, Piper argues that both v. 19c and v. 20c refer to eschatological judgment. "Heaping up coals of fire" is essentially the same as "storing up wrath" against impenitent unbelievers (Rom. 2:4–5).[44] Nevertheless Piper still seeks to understand the exhortation as a "love command." First, the call to bless the persecutor in Rom. 12:14 governs the thought of the entire passage and rules out the possibility that the exhortation entails any desire for one's neighbors' destruction; there is no revenge motif here.[45] Second, v. 20 implies the condition of *persistent* disobedience and enmity in the face of good deeds. Third, Piper argues that "enemy love" *requires* complete confidence in the future wrath against the enemies of the church:

> The two *gar* clauses (Rom. 12:19c, 20c) are intended to give assurance that God is not unrighteous: "God will render to every man according to his works" (Rom. 2:6). Rom. 12:20c does not present the conscious aim of the believer, but states the framework of justice in which enemy love becomes possible and good—a framework founded on God's own righteousness (Rom. 2:4, 5). To be aware of this framework will motivate to genuine enemy love just as much as God's consciousness of his own righteousness moves him to kindness.[46]

Piper, then, differs from the "apocalyptic" interpretation and sides with the standard interpretation in the following ways. (1) Paul's exhortation is indeed a command of enemy love in content and motivation. (2) The exhortation does not forgo hope for the enemies' conversion and reconciliation.[47] (3) The motivation of deferring to God's righteous judgment "is subordinate to, but not inconsistent with, the overarching ground of enemy love which is expressed in Rom. 12:1—'the mercies of God.' "[48]

In what follows, then, we will clarify the character of Paul's ethic in Rom. 12:14, 17–21 by observing the implications of the literary context for interpreting this text and then by discussing the social setting and application of the exhortation, the substantive meaning of the individual exhortations, and the warrants for the exhortation.

Implications of the Literary Context of Romans 12:14, 17–21

When Rom. 12:14, 17–21 is seen within the literary context of the two larger units of which it is a part (Rom. 12:9–21; 12:1–13:14), two things become apparent: the exhortation (1) is related to the theme of love and (2) is set within the framework of the apocalyptic struggle and choice between the two aeons, the powers of good and evil.

In contrast to Rom. 14:1–15:13, a sustained argument on a specific topic, Rom. 12:1–13:14 is comprised of a series of independent thematic units.[49] In the absence of any overall logical structure or thematic development, 12:1–13:14 is tied together by catchwords,[50] by recurring themes,[51] and by two units (12:1–2; 13:11–14) which bracket the entire exhortation and place it in the context of the conflict and choice between two aeons.[52]

As a series of terse, loosely connected exhortations, Rom. 12:9–21 is a microcosm of 12:1–13:14. In contrast to the rest of the units that comprise 12:1–13:14, it is thematically diverse as an assembly of both independent (12:9a, 9bc, 14) and formally grouped (12:10–13, 15–16, 17–21) exhortations. Nevertheless it can be distinguished as a unit by thematic inclusion (vs. 9bc, 21), by the use of parallelism, including doublets (vs. 10–13) and paired contrasts (vs. 9bc, 14–21), and by the use of imperatival participles, adjectives, and infinitives.[53] Three recurring topics within the unit are relations within the community (vs. 10, 13, 15–16), steadfastness in piety (vs. 11–12), and relations with abusers (vs. 14, 17–21).[54] Both v. 9a ("Let love be genuine," *hē agapē anypokritos*)[55] and v. 9bc function to introduce the unit, formally and thematically.

Verse 9a functions partially as a bridge between 12:3–8 and 12:9–21, two units that cannot be sharply separated.[56] Nevertheless, v. 9a also functions as a heading for 12:9–21. (1) While love cannot account for all the contents of 12:9–21 (cf. 12:9bc, 11–12),[57] a good portion of 12:9–21 deals with the topic of harmonious relations among all people, which naturally falls under the category of love. (2) While "love" in Paul and in the present context is articulated especially in terms of relations within the Christian community (12:10; 13:8–10),[58] 1 Thess. 3:12 confirms that, for Paul, love also extends to outsiders:

> And may the Lord make you increase and abound in love to one another and to all (*eis allēlous kai eis pantas*).

The fact that Paul's only other use of the phrase *eis allēlous kai eis pantas* clarifies the horizon of nonretaliation and goodness later in 1 Thess. 5:15 suggests that nonretaliation and goodness conform to the category of love.[59] (3) In 2 Cor. 6:6, the only other occurrence of this phrase in Paul, *agapē anypokritos* is a key theme alongside other key themes of Paul, expressing the commendable character of his ministry:

> In the Holy Spirit, in genuine love,
> in truthful speech, in the power of God . . .

Though *agapē anypokritos* is not explicitly related to nonretaliatory conduct in this passage (2 Cor. 6:3–10), the fact that Paul's catalog of virtues arises in the context of persecution (2 Cor. 6:4–5) and includes forbearance (*en hypomonē pollē, en makrothymia*, 2 Cor. 6:4, 6) suggests that *agapē anypokritos* includes the nonretaliatory conduct that he describes.[60] In Paul's vocabulary, then, *agapē anypokritos* is appropriate as a heading for proper human conduct and for nonretaliatory conduct in particular (Rom. 12:14, 17–21).

Romans 12:9bc also functions as an introductory heading for 12:9–21.[61] It has a general character, it introduces the forms of the imperatival participle and the paired contrast, and with v. 21 encloses the unit:

> Abhor the evil (*to ponēron*), be united with the good. (12:9bc)
> Do not be conquered by evil (*tou kakou*), but conquer evil with good. (12:21)

Moreover, the theme of the struggle between good and evil in vs. 9bc and 21 is a component of the theme that encloses and grounds the entire segment of Rom. 12:1–13:14, the apocalyptic conflict and choice between the two aeons (12:1–2; 13:11–14). Accordingly, the exhortation of 12:14, 17–21 is also grounded in "the mercies of God" (12:1), which mark the victory of the coming age over the present age through Christ (cf. 5:1–11; 8:31–39). The apocalyptic framework of the choice between good and evil is expressed also at the close of the letter:

> For I wish that you be wise as to the good, but innocent as to the evil;
> and then the God of peace will soon crush Satan under your feet.
> (16:19b–20a)

The literary context of Rom. 12:14, 17–21, then, indicates that the exhortation must be interpreted both within the context of the theme of love and within the context of the apocalyptic conflict between the aeons of good and evil.

The Social Setting and Application of Romans 12:14, 17–21

A judgment regarding the social setting and application of Rom. 12:14, 17–21 is also critical for its interpretation. It is necessary, first, to clarify the nature of the abuse to which these verses are addressed.

The following factors indicate that Rom. 12:14, 17–21 is addressed to relations with outsiders, particularly those hostile to the community. (1) Verse 14 is directed specifically to the situation of persecution. *Diōkein* in the sense of "persecute" elsewhere in Paul and the New Testament refers only to hostility from outsiders, never from insiders.[62] (2) In vs. 17–21, which pick up the theme of v. 14, the exhortation is emphatically directed to relations with "all" (*mēdeni*, v. 17a; *enōpion pantōn anthrōpōn*, v. 17b; *meta pantōn anthrōpōn*, v. 18). Verse 18b, "be at peace with all people," is set in direct contrast to the internal focus of v. 18a, "if possible, so far as it depends on you" (*ei dynaton to ex hymōn*). The implication is that the conflict is so serious that it may not be resolved. (3) The battle imagery of v. 21 implies serious conflict, particularly the apocalyptic conflict between the two ages. Besides picking up the theme of the struggle between good and evil in 12:1–2; 12:9; and 13:11–14, the verse also continues the theme of apocalyptic conflict and victory against powers hostile to the church in 8:31–39.[63] (4) The grounding theme of deferring vengeance to God is especially appropriate for nonretaliatory conduct in relation to outsiders. As we shall see, in Paul's view, Christians must make justice a reality in their own midst but leave the judgment of outsiders to God (1 Cor. 5:9–

13).[64] A further factor (5) does not provide direct evidence for, but accords with a focus on, difficult relations with outsiders. The exhortation to nonretaliation and good deeds in relation to hostile outsiders (Rom. 12:14, 17–21) complements the exhortation to submission in relation to ruling authorities (Rom. 13:1–7). The two passages are linked thematically; both passages address the question of responding to and minimizing conflict with the surrounding world.[65]

The question that now emerges is whether or not Rom. 12:14, 17–21 presupposes a particular setting, either one in Paul's experience or one in Rome to which the exhortation is addressed.

Paul is apparently preoccupied with the problem of suffering and persecution when writing Romans. This is indicated by the centrality of the themes of persecution, suffering, endurance, and the eschatological victory over evil earlier in the letter. This topic is introduced in Rom. 5:1–11. By virtue of God's act of salvation in Jesus Christ, Christians can "boast in our hope of sharing in the glory of God" (5:2). But,

> more than that, we boast in our sufferings (*thlipsesin*), knowing that suffering produces endurance (*hē thlipsis hypomonēn katergazetai*), and endurance produces character, and character produces hope, and hope does not disappoint us, because God's love has been poured into our hearts through the Holy Spirit which has been given to us.(5:3–5)

It is not until Rom. 8:17–39, however, that Paul can elaborate on these themes. Indeed, Rom. 8:17–39 demonstrates that suffering and persecution are critical issues in both Paul's life and thought.[66]

Romans 8:17–39 explicates the necessary but temporary and surmountable experience of suffering on the road to glory. The climax comes in 8:31–39, the confession of ultimate victory over the powers of evil through Christ. The passage is focused by four rhetorical questions: (1) Who is against us? (v. 31) (2) Who will bring a charge against the elect of God? (v. 33) (3) Who is to condemn? (v. 34) (4) Who will separate us from the love of Christ? (v. 35) These questions are indeed rhetorical, but they are not hypothetical. They express the crises faced recently by Paul and his churches: (1) there are indeed many adversaries;[67] (2) there are many who bring charges; (3) there are some who condemn. The point is that none of this opposition will ultimately prevail. Even the last question (4) is elaborated by trials that come directly out of Paul's recent experience: "tribulation, or distress, or persecution, or famine, or nakedness, or peril, or sword?" (*thlipsis ē stenochōria ē diōgmos ē limos*

ē gymnotēs ē kindynos ē machaira, 8:35). Paul has used each of
these terms, except for "sword" (machaira),[68] in his account of recent troubles.[69] Romans 8:31–39, then, is a personal confession, not
just a theological and hypothetical confession. No one can gain victory over and destroy Christians. Rather, "in all these things [the
crises listed] we overwhelmingly conquer (hypernikōmen) through
him who loved us" (8:37).

This confession seems to have both a backward and a forward
look. Facing backward, Paul sees his recent survival of a most serious persecution in Asia, which he recounts in 2 Corinthians,[70] and
the recent persecution of his churches in Macedonia.[71] The parallels
between the accounts in 2 Corinthians and Rom. 8:35 confirm that
the issue of persecution preoccupies Paul's current reflection. But
facing ahead, Paul also sees the prospect of opposition to himself
and his gospel. He thus asks the Romans "to strive together with me
in your prayers to God on my behalf, that I may be delivered from
the unbelievers in Judea" (Rom. 15:30–31). It is quite clear, then,
that part of the social setting behind Paul's exhortation in Rom.
12:14, 17–21 is the experience of persecution facing Paul and his
churches.

Is Rom. 12:14, 17–21 also intended to address a current or imminent crisis facing the Roman church?[72] The following arguments
can be made in favor of this possibility. (1) The "convergence of
motivations" that occasioned the letter to Rome included an interest
in speaking to specific problems in the Roman church.[73] (2) Other
pieces of the exhortation in Rom. 12:1–13:14 were chosen because
of their special relevance to the situation of the Roman church.[74]
(3) Explicit exhortations to nonretaliation in other Pauline letters
were directed to the situation of persecution facing the church.[75]
(4) Suetonius's account of the expulsion of the Jews from Rome in
49 C.E. implies some degree of conflict between Jews and Christians.[76] (5) Jewish Christians were undoubtedly susceptible to the
same anti-Semitism that Jews encountered in Rome during this
time.[77] (6) The seeds of the popular alienation, which gave Nero the
occasion to make Christians scapegoats of Rome's destructive fire
ten years later in 64 C.E., were quite possibly already developing.[78]

This evidence, however, is largely circumstantial and inconclusive. Particularly problematic for the assumption of a persecuted
Roman church at the time of Paul's writing is the lack of any explicit
reference to such a crisis elsewhere in his letter (cf. 1 Thess. 3:1–5;
Phil. 1:27–30). The more probable scenario is that Paul, preoccupied with the opposition to the gospel and his churches in various
parts of the world, sees the prospect of persecution in Rome as a

very real possibility. Thus Paul seeks to prepare his readers, so that they might respond properly if hostile opposition from outsiders should arise.

Features of the text itself indicate that the question of responding to hostile opposition is particularly urgent and important for Paul. (1) He recapitulates his exhortation (12:14) not just once (12:17–18) but twice (12:19–21). (2) His exhortation on this topic is more extensive here than in any other passage. (3) The exhortation is carefully grounded and articulated through explicit appeals and allusions to the scriptures.[79] (4) Paul recapitulates the exhortation in 12:19 with the address "beloved," which signifies its importance.[80]

Romans 12:14, 17–21, then, is not only addressed especially to the problem of responding to abuse from outsiders but also reflects Paul's own preoccupation with this problem in the face of his own and his churches' experience of persecution. While there is inconclusive evidence to sustain the notion that the Roman church is currently facing hostility, it is likely that Paul sees the prospect of persecution in Rome as a real possibility and thus seeks to prepare his readers for that eventuality.

The Substance of the Exhortation

Having clarified the literary and social contexts of Rom. 12:14, 17–21, we turn to an examination of the substance and warrants of the exhortation.

Verse 14. The question in regard to this verse is what precisely the command "bless" (*eulogeite*) means here. It might imply "simply a friendly disposition towards the enemy."[81] In this case, "blessing" would entail the same sort of response as to "do good" to one's abuser (1 Thess. 5:15; Rom. 12:20a; cf. 1 Peter 3:10–11). But with most commentators, it is better to hold that blessing here has its full biblical sense, namely, to call down God's gracious power on someone.[82] In favor of this interpretation are (1) the consistent use of *eulogeō* in the Septuagint with this meaning and (2) the parallels in Matt. 5:44b and Luke 6:28b, which tie the command to bless to the command to pray on behalf of persecutors.[83] Parallels to v. 14 in early Jewish texts indicate that "blessing" may have included prayer for leniency or forgiveness from God, for their repentance, or for their salvation.[84]

Verse 17a. At the heading of vs. 17–21, "To no one repay evil for evil" (*mēdeni kakon anti kakou apodidontes*) presents the fundamental nonretaliatory principle. Its basic meaning is clear, though its precise application remains unspecified. Does it prohibit judicial vindication in addition to vindication by self-help?[85] We will return to this question with the parallel injunction in v. 19a.

The meaning of v. 17b (*pronooumenoi kala enōpion pantōn anthrōpōn*), which is based on the Septuagint text of Prov. 3:4,[86] is a matter of debate. Some interpreters see a reference to good deeds *done to* all people.[87] It is better, however, to interpret v. 17b as referring to good conduct *evident to* all.[88] A similar use of Prov. 3:4 (LXX) in 2 Cor. 8:21 clarifies the meaning of v. 17b: ("for we aim at what is honorable not only in the Lord's sight but also in the sight of men" [RSV], *pronooumen gar kala ou monon enōpion kyriou alla kai enōpion anthrōpōn*). Paul's concern in 2 Cor. 8:20–22 is to preclude suspicion, reproach, or opposition that may arise in connection with the offering he is collecting for Jerusalem. The citation of Prov. 3:4 establishes his interest in ensuring that the collection *is evident* as honorable in the sight of God and people. Similarly, in v. 17b Paul counsels his readers to take "forethought" (*pronoeomai*) for good behavior before all people. Christians should preclude any occasion for slander and hostility by exhibiting noble behavior. This interpretation is confirmed by other texts of Paul that exhort Christians to display good behavior in front of outsiders to forestall any negative reactions.[89] An adequate translation of v. 17b is thus: "Take forethought for noble conduct in the sight of all."

Verse 18 extends the theme of v. 17b with the call to "live in peace with all" (*meta pantōn anthrōpōn eirēneuontes*). The exhortation is, however, introduced with a proviso, *ei dynaton to ex hymōn*, which is best translated, "if possible, so far as it depends on you." What we have here is a realistic acknowledgment that hostility from the opponent may preclude the establishment of true peace. Nevertheless the proviso implies a unilateral readiness to be at or to pursue peace with all: from your side, do what you can to be at peace.[90] First Corinthians 7:15, the only other text in which Paul refers directly to "peace" with outsiders, also implies this unilateral readiness.[91] For life in the church, however, where peace and righteousness are to be present realities under Christ's lordship,[92] the exhortations to peace are modified by no such proviso.[93] What this indicates is that Paul's ethic of "peace" is closely tied to his redemptive vision and his ecclesiology. In summary, then, vs. 17b–18 stress, as a counterpart to v. 17a, that Christians must take care to prevent and to minimize conflict by exemplary and conciliatory behavior in relation to abusers outside the church.

Verse 19a, "Do not avenge yourselves" (*mē heautous ekdikountes*), recapitulates v. 17a, recasting the Septuagint text of Lev. 19:18a.[94] At minimum, this command prohibits one from avenging injury through personal self-help. The reflexive *heautous* indicates that this prohibition focuses primarily on personal vengeance.[95] The question is whether the injunction goes beyond this focus to prohibit the pursuit of judicial vindication.[96] The fact that the counterpart to the prohibition is the command to defer vindication to God indicates either (*a*) that judicial vindication is included in the prohibition or (*b*) that judicial vindication is not a realistic option for the alienated victim.[97]

In order to answer this question, it is appropriate to examine another text in Paul that refers to the pursuit of judicial right. In 1 Cor. 6:1–8, Paul exhorts his readers not to take their legal disputes[98] to the civic courts. Rather, they should either solve their disputes through judicial procedures inside the church (1 Cor. 6:1–6) or accept abuse instead of pursuing judicial vindication (vs. 7–8). Paul favors the latter option of desisting from the pursuit of legal right, though this does not mean the renunciation of all rights as a general rule.[99]

The likelihood that Paul would also have rejected litigation against non-Christians, were they in a position to undertake it,[100] is suggested by his beliefs (*a*) that civic courts are unjust (*adikoi,* 1 Cor. 6:1),[101] (*b*) that the better way is to endure than to litigate (6:7), (*c*) that the judgment of outsiders is to be left to God (5:12–13), and (*d*) that Christians will ultimately judge the world (6:2–3). Moreover, the basic similarity in the substance of conduct as applied to relationships within and outside the church[102] would also point in this direction. If this is so, it would follow that Rom. 12:19a means not only that one ought not to take the law into one's own hands but also that one ought not to pursue legal action against outside abusers in court. In both cases, judgment must be left to God. In other words, if renunciation of legal right is preferable even in the church where justice is achievable (cf. 1 Cor. 5:12–13), how much more in relation to hostile outsiders, a situation in which justice is even more elusive.

Another situation in Paul's life, however, might stand in tension with Paul's command to desist from vengeance. As can be inferred from 2 Cor. 2:1–11 and 7:8–11, Paul was apparently offended by a member of the congregation, most likely in the form of slander, during a painful and abortive visit to Corinth.[103] Instead of ignoring or passively accepting the insult, Paul wrote a "painful letter" to the congregation, commanding them to punish the offender and in so doing to show their loyalty to Paul. Now, following the obedient response of the majority in punishing the offender (*epitimia,* 2:6; *ekdikēsis,* 7:11), Paul is encouraged by their renewed loyalty. He exhorts the congregation to forgive (*charizesthai*) and to conciliate (*parakalein*) the offender, and to reaffirm their love for him (2 Cor. 2:6–11). The question that arises is: why does Paul not take a forgiving stance, refusing to pursue vengeance, but instead pursues justice against the offender? How can Paul, on the one hand, exhort his readers "not to avenge themselves" (*mē heautous ekdikountes*, Rom. 12:19a) and, on the other hand, still claim that it is his role in the church "to be ready to avenge every disobedience" (*en hetoimō echontes ekdikēsai pasan parakoēn*, 2 Cor. 10:6)?

The answer lies in Paul's understanding of his apostolic role and in distinguishing types of "vengeance" (*ekdikēsis*). Most likely, the slander suffered by Paul was directed at his apostolicity; and for that reason Paul argues that the injustice was not simply against himself but against the entire congregation (2 Cor. 2:5). Moreover, it is the apostle's legitimate role to execute justice in the church in the name of the Lord Jesus for matters pertaining to internal relations and conduct (2 Cor. 10:5; 1 Cor. 5:3; cf. 5:12–13).

In Paul, then, we must distinguish various meanings of *ekdikēsis*. First, vengeance through self-help is prohibited (Rom. 12:19). Second, judicial vindication for injury suffered is discouraged, though not categorically prohibited (1 Cor. 6:1–8; Philemon 18–19). Such a pursuit of justice, however, may take place only in the case of conflict between church members and must be adjudicated by court procedures within the church (1 Cor. 6:1–6). For general unrighteousness within the church, it is the responsibility of the congregation to mete out justice through judicial procedure (1 Cor. 5:12). Judicial vindication is probably not an option in the case of injury suffered from hostile outsiders. Third, executive vindication is realized (*a*) through the deferment of justice to God in the case of injuries suffered from outsiders (Rom. 12:19; Phil. 4:5; cf. 1 Cor. 5:12–13)[104] and in the case of slaves who have no other recourse (Col. 3:22–25) and (*b*) through the agency of apostolic leaders in the case of unrighteousness within the church (1 Cor. 5:3–4, 9–13; 2 Cor. 10:5).

Verse 20ab ("but 'if your enemy is hungry, feed him; if he is thirsty, given him drink'") is cited from Prov. 25:21 and requires little explanation. The call to give food and drink is an illustrative example of the general exhortation to do good to one's abuser (cf. Rom. 12:21b; 1 Thess. 5:15b).

Verse 21 brings vs. 17–21 to a close with economy of word: "Do not be conquered by evil, but conquer evil with good" (*mē nikō hypo tou kakou alla nika en tō agathō to kakon*). The brevity of this verse creates some difficulties for determining its meaning. What does it mean to "be conquered by evil"? What is the force of *nika* ("conquer") in v. 21b? Does v. 21b imply the influencing of evil toward the good; that is, does it mean achieving the abuser's repentance and reconciliation? Or does it imply the ultimate mastery of good over the evil power of the present age?

The imagery of the verse is that of the believer standing in the middle of a battle with "evil."[105] The neuter *to kakon* in v. 21b indicates that the reference is not to an evil person. Rather, "evil" here is the evil power of the present age manifested both in immorality and in the injurious hostility toward the church.

This meaning is evident from the context. First, as we observed earlier, the theme of good versus evil in v. 21 connects with the theme of the conflict and choice between the ages which brackets 12:1–13:14 (12:1–2; 13:11–14; cf. 12:9bc; 16:20). Second, the theme of victory in v. 21 is related to the theme of overwhelming victory over the powers of this age through Christ's love (8:31–39; cf. 1 Cor. 15:24–26). Third, the conflict imagery of 12:21 links both literarily and conceptually with the theme of "weapons" appropriate for the battle between light and darkness (13:11–14). As other "armament" texts demonstrate, for Paul it is only the spiritual weapons of the new age that have power to gain victory in the eschatological battle already invading the present (2 Cor. 10:2–4; 6:7; 1 Thess. 5:5–8). These "weapons," as described in texts addressed to the situation of hardship, are the new stance and conduct (*erga*, Rom. 13:12) of the believer: faith, love, hope (1 Thess. 5:8), and righteousness (2 Cor. 6:7).[106] Similarly, then, in Rom. 12:21 the chief weapon in the conflict with the powers of evil is "good," implicitly not physical, retaliatory, or destructive force.[107]

We return, then, to the meaning of v. 21a. "To be conquered by evil" might be understood in a general sense, namely, to grow weary and faithless in the context of the struggle between the powers of the two ages.[108] But the immediate context, particularly the series of paired contrasts in 12:14, 17–21 and the contrast with v. 21b, suggests that "to be conquered" has the more focused meaning of capitulating to the normal means of battle by retaliating and seeking vengeance.[109] Verse 21a can thus be paraphrased: "Do not become faithless in the struggle with evil by resorting to retaliatory measures."[110]

Verse 21b, on the other hand, calls the believer to conquer the evil of the present age with the power of good. This final call is not focused on the goal of the abuser's conversion or reconciliation.[111] Nor is it a matter of mastery over one's abuser.[112] The emphasis is simply on the proper conduct with which one battles evil, the method by which Christians gain ultimate victory. "Conquering evil with good" might, but will not necessarily, effect a change in the abuser.[113]

The victory in v. 21, then, has both a present and an eschatological aspect, just as the affirmation of victory in 8:37–39 does. For Paul, the present struggle has an eschatological character (13:11–14), and ultimate victory will arrive imminently (cf. 16:20a). But the victory implied in v. 21b also has a present focus, especially since the call of v. 21a, to which v. 21b is contrasted, is oriented to the present situation. This present aspect is founded on Paul's belief that the powers of the coming age have already invaded the present age.

The Warrants of the Exhortation

We turn now to an examination of the warrants of the exhortation. In particular, we will focus on the meaning of "heaping coals of fire" in v. 20, since this is a crux.

As we noted earlier, vs. 19 and 20 are parallel exhortations, presenting the proper passive behavior (v. 19) and active behavior (v. 20) in response to hostility. Both exhortations contain supporting reason clauses introduced with *gar*:

> Do not avenge yourselves, beloved,
>> but leave room for wrath,
>>> for it is written, "Vengeance is mine, I myself will repay, says the Lord."
> But "if your enemy is hungry, feed him,
>> if he is thirsty, give him drink,
>>> for by doing so you will heap coals of fire upon his head."

The following exegetical questions arise. Does v. 20c have a parallel significance to v. 19c and refer to eschatological punishment which is stored against the enemies for the day of vengeance? If so, are both nonretaliation and kind deeds to persecutors grounded in an ulterior motive which really anticipates the punishment of the enemies of the church? Or does v. 20c, as in the standard interpretation, refer either (1) to the pangs of shame and remorse, which either lead to conversion and reconciliation or leave the opponent with a bad conscience, or (2) to the resolve of the adversary to pursue reconciliation?

The standard interpretation is based on four arguments.[114] First, the main argument is that the interpretation of "coals of fire" as eschatological punishment, which supposedly implies the pursuit of revenge, is incompatible with the positive exhortations in the context which promote love, peace, doing good, and blessing toward the abuser.[115] Incompatibility with an eschatological interpretation is further argued on the grounds that the exhortation is based on the teachings of Jesus and breathes the spirit of the Sermon on the Mount.[116]

The following points, however, mitigate the decisiveness of this argument. (1) A tension, though not necessarily an incompatibility, already exists between the positive exhortations and the motif of retribution in v. 19c. (2) "Heaping coals of fire" as denoting punishment does not necessarily imply a desire for revenge. Verse 20c need not mean anything more than v. 19c in expressing the reality of God's justice in the cosmos, not necessarily the hope for the abuser's punishment. Moreover, as we shall see, the prospect of punishment noted here probably implies the condition of unrepentant hostility, persistent disbelief. (3) The presence of a tension between positive exhortations for the abuser's well-being and the affirmation of God's punishment of the abuser, in spite of its harshness from a modern point of view, must be seen at least as a possible interpretation, since such a tension occurs elsewhere in Early Judaism and early Christianity.[117] (4) The appeal to the Jesus tradition is inconclusive, since *(a)* dependence does not rule out accommodation, and *(b)* the Jesus tradition also exhibits a tension between nonretaliatory exhortations, including blessing, and proclamations of judgment upon abusers.[118]

A second argument in favor of the standard interpretation is the presence of a rabbinic interpretation of Prov. 25:22, in which the last phrase יְשַׁלֶּם לָךְ ("and he [God] will reward you") is read as יַשְׁלִימֶנּוּ לָךְ ("and he will make him [the adversary] to be at peace with you," or "and he will surrender him to you").[119] It is argued that this reading indicates that "heaping coals of fire" symbolizes the hope for reconciliation. The presence of this reading in the Targum is sometimes used to argue for its antiquity and availability to Paul.[120]

This rabbinic interpretation, however, is of dubious value for interpreting Rom. 12:14, 17–21. (1) It is not certain that the Targums follow this reading.[121] (2) There is no evidence that this reading was current before the second century C.E.[122] (3) Retributive interpretations of Prov. 25:21–22 were also extant.[123] (4) The rabbinic interpretation, as allegorically applied to conflict with the evil impulse, emphasizes the notion of the *mastery* of the good impulse over the evil impulse, not simply reconciliation.[124] (5) If Paul was aware of the alternative reading of Prov. 25:22b, and considered it decisive for the interpretation of 25:21–22, he could have included it in the citation to remove any ambiguity.

Third, appeal is made to an Egyptian penitential ritual from the third century B.C.E. involving a forced change of mind. The injurer is required to come back to the injured party carrying a staff in his hand and a tray of burning coals on his head.[125] Some scholars claim that this text provides the background and interpretive clue to the original image of "heaping coals of fire" in Prov. 25:21–22.[126] Others go so far as to assert that this parallel also controls the meaning of the image in Rom. 12:20, symbolizing either the humiliation and remorse of the injurer,[127] or simply his change of mind and desire for reconciliation.[128]

This argument is also not conclusive. This ritual may help to elucidate the original meaning of Prov. 25:22. But there is no evidence that Paul was acquainted with this Egyptian practice, as many interpreters favoring the standard interpretation concede.[129] If this parallel is used as an interpretive clue for Rom. 12:20, it must be acknowledged that the ritual entails *(a)* the forced repentance of the injurer, *(b)* the moral victory and satisfaction of the injured, and *(c)* the public humiliation and penance of the injurer.[130] The parallel thus rules out the interpretation of "heaping coals of fire" as symbolizing simply the realization of reconciliation and actually suggests an interpretation of v. 20c as "and so you will put your opponent to public shame."[131] Finally, Paul's understanding of this image is much more likely shaped by its usage in the Old Testament, which we will examine shortly.

The fourth argument is that Paul's deletion of Prov. 25:22b ("and the Lord will repay you with good," *ho de kyrios antapodōsei soi agatha*) from the citation is read as a rejection of the notion of revenge and private advantage seeking.[132] But an argument about the meaning of any passage on the basis of what is omitted is not very weighty. Even if Paul omitted Prov. 25:22b from the citation because it might foster a faulty attitude, one can say no more than that Paul sought to avoid any notion of personal reward or private advantage for particular deeds of goodness. This does not mean that Paul meant to preclude a general affirmation of vindication and punishment.[133]

The arguments in favor of the standard interpretation, then, appear to be inconclusive. On the other hand, there are conclusive arguments in favor of the interpretation of "coals of fire" as referring to divine punishment. Four main arguments can be adduced: (1) the Old Testament background of the image of "coals of fire"; (2) the usage of "fire" elsewhere in Paul; (3) the parallel structure of vs. 19 and 20;[134] and (4) Paul's attitude regarding the fate of enemies of the gospel.

1. In the Old Testament, "coals" and "coals of fire" symbolize divine anger and vengeance, divine punishment on the wicked, a medium for destruction, or an evil passion.[135] Moreover, retribution and culpability are often spoken of as coming upon or being on someone's head.[136] "Heaping coals of fire" nowhere in the Old Testament symbolizes the pain of shame leading to repentance.[137] Since Paul's understanding of this image was likely shaped more than anything else by the usage of this image in the Old Testament, these observations are weighty.

2. The other uses of *pyr* (fire) in Paul's letters all refer to eschatological punishment (1 Cor. 3:13, 15; cf. 2 Thess. 1:8).[138] While this evidence is somewhat equivocal because of the infrequency of occurrence, its import must not be dismissed.[139]

3. As we have already observed, vs. 19 and 20, and particularly the motivational clauses in vs. 19c and 20c, display a parallel structure. This structuring, when taken together with the meaning of "coals of fire" in the Old Testament, suggests that "heaping coals of fire" in v. 20 refers to the same prospect of judgment as that expressed in v. 19.[140]

At this point, however, we must clarify the meaning of v. 19bc. Complementing the prohibition *mē heautous ekdikountes* (v. 19a) is the command *dote topon tē orgē*, that is, "give the wrath [of God] an opportunity to work out its purpose" (v. 19b).[141] Here we have an affirmation of God's wrath against the enemies of God, which has primarily an eschatological focus,[142] but probably also a temporal aspect within history.[143] This exhortation is next grounded through a citation of Deut. 32:35 (v. 19c):[144] "For it is written, 'Vengeance is mine, I myself will repay, says the Lord' (*gegraptai gar, emoi ekdikēsis, egō antapodōsō, legei kyrios*)." This citation emphasizes the Lord's prerogative for vengeance (*emoi, egō*), and the added *legei kyrios* reinforces its authoritative character in the manner of prophetic pronouncements.[145] Here we have a specific promise of retribution (*antapodōsō*), not a simple appeal to God's sovereignty to judge as God pleases. There is also here no intimation that wrath is to be understood in terms of a disciplinary effect that leads to repentance.

Verse 19, then, already grounds nonretaliation and good deeds in an eschatological framework that affirms the punishment of the enemies. The expectation of eschatological "coals of fire" is not essentially different from the expectation of "wrath" and "repayment."

4. The expressions of judgment upon the enemies of the church elsewhere in Paul's letters confirm and clarify the meaning of "coals of fire" as eschatological punishment.

a. Phil. 4:5; 1:27–30; 3:18–21. Philippians 4:5 provides an important parallel to Rom. 12:17–21: "Let your forbearance (*to epieikes*) be known to all people. The Lord is at hand." This text speaks to the problem of hostility from enemies of the church,[146] exhorts the response of nonretaliation or endurance,[147] and grounds this response with a reference to the imminence of the Lord's return. It is clear from Phil. 1:27–30 that this hope in the Lord's return entails both salvation for believers and punishment for opponents:

> [27]Only let your manner of life be worthy of the gospel of Christ, so that . . . I may hear of you that you stand firm in one spirit, with one mind striving side by side for the faith of the gospel, [28]and not frightened in anything by your opponents (*antikeimenōn*). This is a clear omen in regard to them of destruction, but of your salvation, and that from God. [29]For it has been granted to you that for the sake of Christ you should not only believe in him but also suffer for his sake, [30]engaged in the same conflict which you saw and now hear to be mine.[148]

Both the constancy of the believers under trial and the fact of hostility and persecution are a clear sign (*endeixis*) of the opponents' destruction and the believers' salvation.[149] In context, Phil. 1:28–29 provides the readers with a theodicy to help them understand and endure their suffering and the need to act with "forbearance" before outsiders (Phil. 4:5).

While Phil. 3:18–21 probably has a different group of opponents in view, [150] the expectation is the same. Here it is said of "many . . . who live as enemies (*echthrous*) of the cross of Christ," and "whose God is the belly and whose glory is in their shame, and who set minds on earthly things" that "their end is destruction" (*hōn to telos apōleia*, 3:18–19). By contrast, true believers ("we") can anticipate the salvation and *politeuma* of heaven (3:20). For Paul, the rightful end of any "enemy of the cross" is "destruction" (as in 1:28).[151]

b. Romans 2:5 also illustrates Paul's thinking on the fate of those who display persistent enmity against God:

> But by your hard and impenitent heart you are storing up wrath for yourself on the day of wrath when God's righteous judgment will be revealed. (RSV)

Paul is arguing here against those who pass judgment upon another but are impenitent for their own sins (Rom. 2:1–4). There is some uncertainty as to whom Paul has in mind in this passage.[152] In any event, a fundamental principle is expressed that helps elucidate Rom. 12:19–20: while God's kindness and forbearance aim at repentance (2:4), continued impenitence stores wrath against a person for the day of judgment. Both Rom. 2:5 and 12:19–20 express the themes of "wrath" and the "storing up" of punishment against the impenitent.[153]

c. 1 Thess. 2:16. The present investigation assumes the authenticity of 1 Thess. 2:13–16.[154] Here the Jews' consistent opposition to the gospel has this result: "so as always to fill up the measure of their sins" (*eis to anaplērōsai autōn tas hamartias pantote*, v. 16b).[155] This notion is essentially the same as that expressed in Rom. 2:5: that opposition to the gospel stores up punishment against a person for the day of judgment. Thereupon follows v. 16c: "God's wrath has come upon them unto the end" (*ephthasen de ep' autous hē orgē eis telos*).[156] Like the previous texts, then, 1 Thess. 2:16 expresses the idea of accumulated eschatological culpability and judgment upon persecutors of the church.

d. Paul's statements about "false teachers" also express the expectation of judgment upon these opponents. Similarly to Phil. 3:18–19, Paul says of the "false apostles" against whom he must defend himself in 2 Corinthians 10–13 and whom he describes as "servants of Satan": "Their end will correspond to their deeds" (*hōn to telos estai kata ta erga autōn*, 2 Cor. 11:15). Of those who charge Paul of antinomianism, Paul says: "Their condemnation is just" (*hōn to krima endikon estin*, Rom. 3:8). Of the anonymous instigator of the Galatian heresy Paul says, "and he who is troubling you will bear his judgment" (*ho de tarassōn hymas bastasei to krima*, Gal. 5:10; cf. 1:8, 9, *anathema estō*). As for his own justification and vindication in the face of attempts to undermine his apostolic authority, he defers his case ultimately to God and the final judgment (1 Cor. 3:12–15; 4:1–5; 2 Cor. 10:18; cf. Rom. 14:10–13).

It is clear, then, that Paul expects destruction upon the opponents and persecutors of the church. Sometimes this expectation appears as a wish (Phil. 3:18–19; 2 Cor. 11:15; Rom. 3:8; Gal. 5:10; 1:8, 9). In some cases, it functions primarily to offer the readers a theodicy to help them understand their suffering and the need to act with forbearance (Phil. 1:27–30; cf. 2 Thess. 1:4–10).[157] Indeed, the church's own faithfulness in suffering is part of the "signal" (*endeixis*) of the persecutors' punishment and the elect's salvation (Phil. 1:27–30; cf. 2 Thess. 1:4–6). This expectation accords with Paul's conception of outsiders as being on the road to destruction (*apollymenoi*, 1 Cor. 1:18; 2 Cor. 2:15; 4:3; cf. 2 Thess. 2:10). In particular, the sins of the impenitent, including persecutors, are mounting up and being stored against them for the day of vengeance (Rom. 2:5; 1 Thess. 2:16.)

This perspective confirms and clarifies the meaning of "coals of fire" as eschatological judgment upon persecutors of the church. Faithful conduct in persecution, including nonretaliation and good deeds, is part of the "signal" of judgment upon the persecutor. In this sense, continued impenitence in the face of good deeds increases the persecutor's culpability. This notion does not, however, express the conscious intention of the believer's response of good deeds toward persecutors. It is not that good deeds directly increase the opponent's punishment. Rather, the affirmation of the persecutor's punishment functions as a theodicy to encourage faithfulness and the nonretaliatory conduct. Verse 20, then, like v. 19, grounds nonretaliatory behavior in the prerogative of God for justice.[158]

One final text helps to clarify Paul's notion of deferring vengeance to God. First Corinthians 5:9–6:6, though not referring specifically to the problem of hostile outsiders, presents two ideas relevant to the present topic. First, judgment upon outsiders must be deferred to God, while judgment upon insiders is the responsibility of the church. This notion appears in 1 Cor. 5:9–13, which clarifies Paul's call not to associate with immoral insiders (vs. 9–10) and stresses the need to maintain discipline within the church (cf. 5:1–8):

> For what have I to do with judging outsiders? Is it not those inside the church whom you are to judge? God judges those outside. "Drive out the wicked person from among you." (1 Cor. 5:12–13, RSV)

This text emphasizes the need to judge insiders, apparently on the assumption that righteousness can be achieved within the Christian community (cf. 5:6–8, 6:9–11). In this case, the judicial procedures of the church are an instrument of God's justice.[159] On the other hand, the church desists from judging outsiders, since it is God's prerogative and role to do so.

A second notion in 1 Cor. 6:1–6 is that Christians will participate in the eschatological judgment of the non-Christian world (*kosmos*).[160] While this notion is used to support the main point that Christians should mediate their own disputes and not go to the unjust civic judges, its basic validity for Paul can be seen in the way he introduces it twice: "Do you not know . . ." (vs. 2, 3). Although this notion appears nowhere else in Paul, it is a common theme in apocalyptic thought[161] and apparently one that was shared by Paul. Thus, while Christians must defer the judgment of outsiders to God at least for the present (5:9–13), they will eventually participate in the eschatological judgment of outsiders.[162] This judgment would supposedly include the judgment of persecutors, though such a specific notion does not appear in Paul.[163] When Paul refers to the judgment of persecutors, he emphasizes God's role in judgment (Rom. 12:19–20; cf. Phil. 1:27–30; 4:5; 1 Thess. 2:16).

To conclude, both v. 19c and v. 20c ground the exhortation to nonretaliation and good deeds in Rom. 12:17–21 with the notion of God's retribution of the abusers. It is God's prerogative to avenge, especially in the case of those outside the community of faith. God will indeed repay evil (v. 19c), and continued impenitence in the face of good deeds increases the opponents' culpability (v. 20c). Thus Christians must trustingly defer their cases to God (v. 19b), while responding with nonretaliation and good deeds.

The question that emerges, however, is how one is to understand the tension between the affirmation of God's punishment of the abusers (vs. 19–20) and the call to bless the persecutor, that is, to call down God's gracious power upon them (v. 14). How can the call to bless be anything but insincere when an affirmation of the abuser's punishment is maintained? This tension might be explained in terms of Paul's citation of different traditions, namely, the Jesus tradition (v. 14) and a separate paraenetic tradition (vs. 17–21). But this explanation is inadequate. Paul presents both notions apparently without seeing any contradiction. Moreover, a similar tension appears elsewhere in the New Testament. In 1 Peter 3:9–12, the call to nonretaliation and to blessing is grounded eschatologically in both the vindication of the elect and the punishment of the persecutors. And at the Q level of the gospel tradition, the call to bless abusers is countered by the proclamation of judgment upon the enemies of the community.[164]

Ultimately, this tension represents a fundamental theological tension between God's mercy and justice (e.g., Rom. 2:1–11; 11:22). On the one hand, the believer calls upon God's gracious power on behalf of the abuser, a blessing that aims ultimately at the abuser's repentance and salvation. At the same time, Paul affirms God's righteous rule of the universe, in which wrongs will ultimately be righted and good will prevail. This affirmation provides the framework of justice, a theodicy, in which nonretaliatory conduct can be grounded. The believer prays for the best possible fate of the abuser but leaves the final realization of justice to God. The notion of deferment (v. 19b) provides the key to the tension, even though it does not completely resolve it.

It is noteworthy to observe what possible warrants are lacking here. First, there is no intimation that nonretaliation and good deeds are intended to effect, or will effect, the conversion and reconciliation of the opponents (cf. *Did.* 1:3). A pragmatic motive of reducing tensions through the display of noble conduct emerges only slightly (vs. 17b–18). Second, Paul does not ground his exhortation by appealing to the authoritative commandments of "the Lord."[165] Paul probably does not know the commands on nonretaliation and good deeds as dominical sayings. Indeed, the substance of the exhortations and their warrants were probably known to Paul from his pre-Christian Jewish ethical heritage.[166] Third, and more surprising, there is no christological grounding through a reference to Christ's paradigmatic model of endurance, his path from suffering to glory. We must look at this last point more closely.

The Christological Ground of Nonretaliation

Despite the lack of any direct connections between nonretaliation and Christology as there are in 1 Peter 2:21–25, should one suppose a fundamental connection in Paul's thought? An examination of Paul's theology of suffering seems to point in this direction.

For Paul, suffering is an experience that the Christian essentially shares with Christ,[167] just as Christians participate salvifically and sacramentally in Christ's death.[168] This participation extends to Christ's entire passion, so that Christians also experience this passion in life.[169] Paul interprets his own hardships as an experience of Christ's passion.[170] Moreover, Paul's suffering, like Christ's, has a vicarious effect upon his converts.[171] As for Christ, so for the Christian, suffering is the necessary prelude to glory; indeed, tribulation produces for Christians an eternal weight of glory.[172]

The way of Christ's passion, then, is by necessity the way for the Christian. But more than this, it constitutes a model that one ought to follow. For instance, Christ's pattern of humiliation and exaltation is held up as the model for relationships within the community in Phil. 2:3–11.[173] In "receiving the word in much affliction with joy from the Holy Spirit," the Thessalonians "became imitators (*mimē-tai*) of us and of the Lord" (1 Thess. 1:6).[174] In 2 Cor. 8:9, Christ's way of becoming poor, even though rich, for the sake of Christians is presented as a model to follow in contributing to needy Christians. Paul describes his own hardships in the same way: "as poor, yet making many rich" (2 Cor. 6:10).[175]

Given this prototypical and exemplary role of Christ in suffering, it is curious that Paul does not appeal to it explicitly in the context of Rom. 12:14, 17–21. Since the problem of responding to hostility is so critical from Paul's perspective, a christological reference could have provided the clinching argument. Perhaps the best explanation is that the traditional materials on which Paul was dependent here lacked a specific appeal to Christ's teaching or prototypical role.

Nevertheless one must assume a fundamental connection between nonretaliation and Christology in Paul's thought. We have already observed the role of Christology for Paul's understanding of tribulation. In addition, Christology connects with nonretaliation as the theoretical ground for the Christian's new life (Rom. 12:1–2; 6:1–7:6; 8:1–13).[176] If good instead of retaliation is the means to ultimate victory (v. 21), this victory is founded on the "mercies of God" (12:1–2), specifically on Christ's love (8:31–39) and God's love in Christ (5:1–11). Moreover, in the battle against evil, the weapon of "good" (v. 21) comes from "clothing oneself with the Lord Jesus Christ" (13:12–14). Paul's Christology, then, provides Paul not only a theoretical ground for his ethic of nonretaliation but also a material ground, insofar as Christ is the prototype and exemplar in suffering.

Conclusion

In the various references to the issue of responding to abuse in Paul's writings a fundamental continuity in the conduct enjoined is evident. Whether the problem concerns conflict within the church or hostility from outsiders, Paul exhorts (a) nonretaliation, including the stance of endurance and the refusal to litigate, (b) kind actions, including the pursuit of peace, and (c) kind words, including blessing and conciliating. But a distinction in exhortations directed to these two situations can be observed in the grounding motivation, a distinction based on Paul's understanding of the apocalyptic character of persecution and his redemptive vision. On the one hand, Paul assumes that righteousness, reconciliation, and peace can be realized, at least provisionally, within the context of the church; for this context the exhortations to nonretaliation and peace stand unqualified, extending to the call "to forgive." On the other hand, Paul realizes that some hostility toward the church will continue until the eschaton, when universal peace and righteousness will finally be achieved; for this context, the calls to nonretaliation and peace are grounded especially in the notion of deferment to God's judgment (Phil. 4:5; Rom. 12:14, 17–21). It is perhaps not accidental that the responses enjoined for this situation do not include calls "to forgive," which is ultimately God's prerogative, although the call to "bless" may likely include prayers for the persecutors' forgiveness from God.

Romans 12:14, 17–21, the lengthiest passage expressing Paul's ethic of nonretaliation and peace, represents the latter category of exhortations. This passage is addressed especially to the problem of responding to persecutors of the church. It is apparent from other passages in Romans and Paul's recent letters, especially 2 Corinthians, that the problem of hostility against Paul and his churches is becoming acute. The formulation and inclusion of 12:14, 17–21 in Romans seems to reflect Paul's own preoccupation with this issue. At the same time, Paul sees the prospect of persecution in Rome as a definite possibility and seeks to prepare his Roman readers for such a situation. Ten years later under Nero, this very crisis would be realized.

The question we have addressed is whether Rom. 12:14, 17–21 expresses a nonretaliatory ethic of apocalyptically motivated restraint, as argued especially by Stendahl, or a reconciling ethic of love, as argued by a majority of interpreters. The answer to this question is a qualified both.

On the one hand, the exhortation has a definite apocalyptic character, though not as a mere restraint in the face of God's impending judgment. The warrants in vs. 19–20 emphasize the certainty of God's righteous judgment. Verse 19 grounds the prohibition against vengeance in the deferment of wrath to God, based on God's prerogative for retribution. Verse 20 grounds the call to good deeds in the notion that the sins of the impenitent are being stored against them for the day of wrath (cf. 2:5). In addition, v. 21 frames the call to do good within the context of the eschatological battle of the power of good versus the power of evil. Assured and imminent victory will come through the weapons of good and through God's love in Christ (cf. Rom. 5:1–11; 8:31–39; 13:11–14; 16:19–20). The christological pattern of weakness as the means of power and victory is fundamental here.

On the other hand, the exhortation is related to the theme of love (12:9a). In relation to abusers, Christians are called not simply to desist from retaliation but to bless, to do good, to be at peace, and to take forethought for noble conduct. Indeed, Christians are called to the unilateral pursuit of peace. The preoccupation of Paul is not with the retribution of the abusers, which is to be deferred to God, but with the proper stance and conduct within the eschatological conflict. Although the exhortation is not aimed primarily at the conversion and reconciliation of the abusers, Paul does not relinquish this hope (v. 18a).

These two aspects, however, stand in tension. On the one hand, Paul calls his readers to bless their persecutors, to call down God's gracious power upon them. On the other hand, Paul affirms God's righteous rule of the universe wherein unrepentant persecutors will ultimately be punished. This affirmation functions mainly as a theodicy that provides the framework for the call to nonretaliatory conduct. Personal vengeance and the pursuit of judicial vengeance in pagan courts are prohibited. The pursuit of judicial vengeance for offenses suffered by fellow believers is discouraged and can take place only in the church courts. In all cases, vengeance is properly deferred to the executive vengeance of God, whose prerogative it is as ruler of the universe. Some role for Christians in the final judgment is hinted at (1 Cor. 6:2–3), in continuity with Jewish apocalyptic beliefs, but never defined or emphasized. In other words, Paul never diminishes his belief in justice. Rather, the issue is one of agency. Vindication and vengeance belong to God.

Notes

1. Besides the seven undisputed letters, I will also refer to 2 Thessalonians, Colossians, and Ephesians, since they represent the continuing Pauline tradition. Translations are mine, unless otherwise indicated.

2. For the focus on outsiders, and especially persecutors, see pp. 186–189.

3. The *hymas* ("you") is somewhat dubious textually, omitted in several key manuscripts; see, e.g., Bruce M. Metzger, *A Textual Commentary on the Greek New Testament* (London: United Bible Societies, 1971), 528. Because *hymas* makes explicit what is implicit, it seems appropriate to translate, "Bless those who persecute you." P[46] omits the second *eulogeite*, an attempt to polish the sequence of paired contrasts.

4. Since the Thessalonians are suffering some sort of opposition (1 Thess. 1:6–7; 2:14–16; 3:1–5), the application of the exhortation to "all" implicitly extends to persecutors.

5. The facts that the Philippians are experiencing hostility from outsiders (Phil. 1:27–30), that Phil. 4:4–7 is an exhortation to perseverance in suffering, and that 4:5 is directed to relations with "all" indicate that 4:5 exhorts a nonretaliatory stance particularly in relation to persecutors. See further, p. 198.

6. Cf. 1 Peter 2:18–25; Eph. 6:5–9.

7. For this usage of *mē logizesthai*, cf. 2 Cor. 5:19.

8. For this meaning of *parakalein* here, see BAGD, s.v. "*parakaleō*," #5. This meaning is also evident in 2 Cor. 6:7, parallel with *charizesthai*; 2 Macc. 13:23; Luke 15:28; Acts 16:39.

9. For other references to being at peace in Paul that refer particularly to relations within the community, see Rom. 14:17, 19; 1 Cor. 7:15; 2 Cor. 13:11; cf. Col. 3:15.

10. For *charizomai* in the sense of "forgive," see also 2 Cor. 12:13; Col. 2:13.

11. "Ethic" here is used in its colloquial, nonphilosophical sense as "a set of moral principles and values." "Nonretaliation and peace" are, it seems to me, the best general way of summarizing the substance of these exhortations, without prejudging their specific interpretation. I quite deliberately avoid the term "love of enemy" as a descriptive term, since the language of "loving enemies" is not found in Paul's letters and since it already assumes a certain interpretation of the texts.

12. See esp. George E. Mendenhall, *The Tenth Generation: The Origins of the Biblical Tradition* (Baltimore: Johns Hopkins University Press, 1973), ch. 3: "The 'Vengeance' of Yahweh," pp. 69–104. Mendenhall identifies three uses of the Hebrew root *nqm* that accord with the uses of the Greek *ekdikein* and the Latin *vindicatio*: (1) to avenge through socially sanctioned executive action by royal or divine power; (2) to avenge or to litigate through judicial action; and (3) to take revenge through self-help, i.e., extralegal self-redress. All of these are distinguished from defensive vindication, which takes place at the moment of the offending action, whereas the former three are subsequent in time to the offense.

13. See esp. Luise Schottroff, "Non-Violence and the Love of One's Enemies," in *Essays on the Love Commandment* (Luise Schottroff et al.; Philadelphia: Fortress Press, 1978), 16–22. She identifies three attitudes or types of renunciation of revenge in the Greco-Roman world. (1) Nonretaliation as the proper ethic of the underdog, whether exhorted by the powerful or the powerless: the dependent, especially a slave, must accept injustice and has no other recourse than to make a virtue of necessity, since it simply does not pay to attempt to avenge injustice. Here, nonretaliatory acceptance of injustice springs from a position of dependence or alienation. She notes 1 Peter 2:18–25; Col. 3:25 in this category, to which 2 Cor. 11:19–21 could be added. (2) Nonretaliation and clemency as the ethic of the powerful, appropriate for superiors, rulers in relation to their subjects, or defeated opponents. This ethic is motivated especially by the interest to preserve harmony in the family, body politic, or empire. Here, nonretaliation means the exercise of one's own power. (3) Nonretaliation as the protest of the powerless, based especially on the Socratic prototype: the philosopher is abused by society because of his disturbing teaching but desists from retaliation, declaring himself to be a victim of injustice, in order to proclaim the rottenness of society. See, e.g., Epictetus, *Discourses* 3.22.54, perhaps the only example of the explicit use of love to an enemy in Greco-Roman philosophy: "For this too is a very pleasant strand woven into the Cynic's pattern of life; he must needs be flogged like an ass, and while he is being flogged he must love (*philein*) the men who flog him, as though he were the father or brother of them all" (LCL).

14. See esp. Victor Paul Furnish, *Theology and Ethics in Paul* (Nash-

ville: Abingdon Press, 1968), 207–227; and J. C. Beker, *Paul the Apostle: The Triumph of God in Life and Thought* (Philadelphia: Fortress Press, 1980), 255–302.

15. E.g., 1 Cor. 15:20–28; Rom. 8:18–39; 11:36; 16:20. For references to the eschatological "kingdom," see 1 Cor. 6:9–10; Gal. 5:21; 1 Thess. 2:12.

16. E.g., 1 Thess. 1:10; 5:9; Rom. 2:5, 8; 5:9.

17. For treatments of Paul's redemptive vision along these lines, see esp. Furnish, *Theology*, 115–206; and Beker, *Paul*, 11–19, 135–367.

18. For the eschatological framework of "peace" in Paul, see esp. Ulrich Luz, "Eschatologie und Friedenshandeln bei Paulus," in *Eschatologie und Friedenshandeln* (Ulrich Luz et al.; Stuttgart: Verlag Katholisches Bibelwerk, 1981), 153–194.

19. BAGD, s.v. *"eirēnē"*; e.g., Rom. 2:10; 8:6; 14:17; cf. Eph. 6:15, "the gospel of peace."

20. 2 Cor. 5:19; Rom. 11:5; cf. Col. 1:20.

21. E.g., Phil. 3:21; 1 Cor. 15:21, 24–28; Rom. 8:28–39; 11:36. Cf. also the language of "new creation" (2 Cor. 5:17; Gal. 6:15) and the notion of the renewal of the image of God (Rom. 8:29; 1 Cor. 15:29; 2 Cor. 3:18; cf. Col. 3:10; Eph. 4:24).

22. Rom. 15:33; 16:20; 2 Cor. 13:11; Phil. 4:9; 1 Thess. 3:16; cf. 2 Thess. 3:16.

23. For the eschatological reconciliation of all people (Jews and Gentiles), see esp. Rom. 11:25–32. See also Eph. 2:14–18 for the notion of the eschatological arrival of peace between Jew and Gentile, through the redemptive work of Christ, who is "our peace."

24. See, e.g., W. Foerster, *"eirēnē,"* TDNT, 2:410–420.

25. See, e.g., 1 Cor. 14:33. Rom. 16:20 is particularly noteworthy, since it is "the God of peace" who will "soon crush Satan under your feet."

26. Rom. 5:1, related to "reconciliation" in 5:10–12; cf. Col. 1:20. Note also Eph. 2:14–18.

27. Rom. 15:13.

28. Gal. 5:22.

29. See n. 9 above, and p. 190.

30. Expressed in salutations (Rom. 1:7; 1 Cor. 1:3; 2 Cor. 1:2; Gal. 1:3; Phil 1:2; 1 Thess. 1:1; Philemon 3: cf. Col. 1:2; 2 Thess. 1:2; Eph. 1:2) and benedictions (1 Cor. 16:11; Gal. 6:16; Rom. 15:33; 2 Cor. 13:11; Phil. 4:7, 9; 1 Thess. 5:23; cf. 2 Thess. 3:16; Eph. 6:23).

31. The other debated issue concerns the sources and traditiohistorical background of Paul's exhortation. Does Paul's exhortation derive directly from the teachings of Jesus and express a distinctly Christian ethic, or does it derive mainly from early Jewish ethical traditions, with some influence from Greco-Roman moral philosophy? On this debate, see further Gordon Zerbe, *Non-Retaliation in Early Jewish and New Testament Texts: Ethical Themes in Social Contexts* (Ph.D. diss., Princeton Theological Seminary, 1991), 12, 304–316. In this work I argue that Paul's exhortation does not derive directly from Jesus and does not represent a distinctly Christian

theme: that the one saying that derives substantively from Jesus (Rom. 12:14) is not known by Paul as a dominical saying; that the substance of Paul's exhortation is best seen as dependent on a broad tradition of non-retaliatory ethics in Early Judaism, with affinities especially to *Joseph and Aseneth*, the *Testaments of the Twelve Patriarchs*, and the community of the Dead Sea Scrolls; that while some affinities to the ethics of Greek moral philosophy must be noted, the particularly Jewish and biblical flavor of Paul's exhortation is unmistakable; and that Paul's text is dependent on traditional associations (not fixed codes or formulations) of paraenetic materials in early Christian circles.

32. For these basic options, see, e.g., Victor Paul Furnish, *The Love Command in the New Testament* (Nashville: Abingdon Press, 1972), 107–108. For a fuller account of the debate, see Zerbe, *Non-Retaliation*, 1–16.

33. C. E. B. Cranfield (*A Critical and Exegetical Commentary on the Epistle to the Romans* [2 vols.; 6th ed.; Edinburgh: T. & T. Clark, 1975–1979], 2:647 n. 4) and Otto Michel (*Der Brief an die Römer* [13th ed.; Göttingen: Vandenhoeck & Ruprecht, 1966], 278) suppose that this text refers to both personal enemies and enemies of the church.

34. E.g., Origen, Pelagius, Augustine (references in Cranfield, *Romans*, 2:649); C. H. Dodd, *The Epistle of Paul to the Romans* (8th ed.; London: Fontana Press, 1959), 200; J. Knox, *IB*, 9:596; Michel, *Römer*, 279, asserting that "coals of fire" is a paradoxical image of judgment and repentance; Heinrich Schlier, *Der Römerbrief* (Freiberg: Herder, 1977), 383; Ernst Käsemann, *Commentary on Romans* (Grand Rapids: Wm. B. Eerdmans Publishing Co., 1980), 349; and Cranfield, *Romans*, 2:649 n. 5, emphasizing in the true Augustinian tradition the psychological dimension of the shame. J. E. Young ("Heaping Coals of Fire on the Head," *Expositor*, 3rd series, 2 [1885]: 158–159) and J. Steele ("Heaping Coals on the Head [Pr 25:22; Ro 12:20]," *ExpTim* 44 [1932/1933], 141) appeal to the imagery of metallurgy, so that the text refers to the melting and softening of anger.

35. William Klassen, "Coals of Fire: Sign of Repentance or Revenge?" *NTS* 9 (1962/1963): 349; idem, *Love of Enemies: The Way to Peace* (Philadelphia: Fortress Press, 1984), 36, 120; F.-J. Ortkemper, *Leben aus dem Glauben: Christliche Grundhaltungen nach Röm 12–13* (Münster: Verlag Aschendorff, 1980), 122–123; and Ulrich Wilckens, *Der Brief an die Römer* (EKK; Zurich: Benzinger Verlag, 1982), 3:26.

36. E.g., Cranfield, *Romans*, 2:648; and Käsemann, *Romans*, 349.

37. Emphasizing that Rom. 12:19bc aims to provide a general theodicy are Cranfield, *Romans*, 2:647–648; and Michel, *Römer*, 278–279.

38. Esp. Klassen, "Coals of Fire," 349 n. 1; cf. idem, *Love of Enemies*, 121, 131 n. 12; Cranfield, *Romans*, 2:648; and S. Travis, *Christ and the Judgment of God: Divine Retribution in the New Testament* (Basingstoke, Hants: Marshall Pickering, 1986), 41–42, 49. Ortkemper in an excursus on the wrath and vengeance of God (*Leben aus dem Glauben*, 112–119) acknowledges that Paul's notion of wrath and vengeance cannot be minimized but suggests that Paul moderates a rather negative Jewish view.

39. Krister Stendahl, "Hate, Non-Retaliation and Love: 1QS x, 17–20 and Romans 12:19–21," *HTR* 55 (1962): 343–355.

40. Also emphasizing this aspect, though generally taking the traditional interpretation, is Knox, *IB*, 9:597: "Still, it is doubtful that Paul would have been able to define the human responsibility for dealing with evil if he had not entertained vivid expectations of the 'wrath of God.' " Eschatological imminence "made it easier to regard the individual as having no responsibility for judgment."

41. Emphasizing this aspect of Rom. 12:20, though not elaborating a broader apocalyptic interpretation, are Herbert Preisker, *Das Ethos des Urchristentums* (Gütersloh: C. Bertelsmann, 1949), 184; and M. Black, *Romans* (London: Oliphants, 1973), 157. Cf. Friedrich Nietzsche, *The Anti-Christ*, #45: "Paul was the greatest of all apostles of revenge."

42. This aspect is emphasized by Stendahl, "Non-Retaliation," 348–349, 354–355.

43. John Piper, *"Love Your Enemies": Jesus' Love Command in the Synoptic Gospels and in the Early Christian Paraenesis* (SNTSMS 38; Cambridge: Cambridge University Press, 1979), 114–119; similar is C. Spicq, *Agape in the New Testament*, vol. 2 (trans. M. A. McNamara and M. H. Richter; St. Louis: B. Herder Book Co., 1965), 207–208. Black (*Romans*, 157) sees a revenge motif in Rom. 12:20 but otherwise interprets 12:14, 17–21 in terms of a love command; Michel (*Römer*, 279) sees in "coals of fire" a paradoxical image of judgment and repentance. Others who admit some secondary notion of eschatological vengeance in v. 20 are F. Lang, *"pyr,"* TDNT, 6:944, following Adolf Schlatter; and E. Synofzig, *Die Gerichts- und Vergeltungsaussagen bei Paulus: Eine traditionsgeschichtliche Untersuchung* (Göttingen: Vandenhoeck & Ruprecht, 1977), 48–49.

44. Piper, *"Love Your Enemies,"* 118. Cf. the interpretation of some patristic writers (Cranfield, *Romans*, 2:648–649): "coals of fire" refers to future punishment; the notion is that "doing good to one's enemy will cause his punishment, in the event of his not repenting, to be the greater"; but one should not do good to one's enemy with this intention.

45. Ibid., 116–117.

46. Ibid., 118. Cf. Spicq, *Agape*, 2:208: "*Agapē* hates evil as much as it loves good (v. 9). It is forbidden to execute justice itself, and it must treat even the most obstinate and wicked person with respect and kindness, for 'it takes no note of injury' (1 Cor. 13:5). Yet its sense of justice, which is like God's own, refuses to accept that evil should go unpunished."

47. Piper (*"Love Your Enemies,"* 215 n. 47) admits a proximity to Stendahl except for these first two points; he does not discuss Rom. 12:21.

48. Ibid., 119.

49. Rom. 12:1–2, programmatic introduction; 12:3–8, on harmony and gifts within the community; 12:9–12, loosely connected exhortations; 13:1–7, on subordination to ruling authority, 13:8–10, on love for one another as the fulfillment of the law; 13:11–14, on the apocalyptic urgency of choosing between evil and good.

50. E.g., *diōkontes, diōkontas*, Rom. 12:13, 14; *opheilas, opheilete*, 13:7, 8.

51. E.g., *(a)* the contrast between good and evil, Rom. 12:1–2, 9bc, 21; 13:11–14; *(b)* harmony and love within the community, 12:3–8, 9a, 10, 13, 15–16; 13:8–10; and *(c)* relations with outsiders, 12:14, 17–21; 13:1–7. Some of these themes extend to other passages in Romans; cf. the use of the harmony theme using *phronein* in 12:3, 16 and in 11:20, 25; 15:5; and the use of "love" also in 14:15.

52. Rom. 12:1–2 functions as the introduction to both 12:1–13:14 and the entire paraenetic segment of 12:1–15:13. On the bracketing and grounding function of 12:1–2 and 13:1–4, see esp. O. Merk, *Handeln aus Glauben: Die Motivierung der paulinischen Ethik* (Marburg: Elwert Verlag, 1968), 157–158, 166–167; Furnish, *Theology*, 98–106, 215–227; and Schlier, *Römerbrief*, 350.

53. For participles, see Rom. 12:9–14, 16–19; for adjectives, see 12:9–11; for infinitives, see 12:15.

54. Rom. 12:14 stands alone formally and thematically but links with v. 13 through the catchword *diōkein* and with v. 12 thematically ("Be patient in tribulation"). On first impression, vs. 15–16 seem to be out of place between v. 14 and vs. 17–21, reverting to the theme of harmony and love within the church (12:3–9a, 10, 13). But vs. 15–16 are probably meant as an exhortation to harmony specifically in the situation of abuse, thus naturally following v. 14; so, e.g., Stendahl, "Non-Retaliation," 345; J. D. G. Dunn, *Romans 9–16* (Dallas: Word Books, 1988), 738. Verse 15 clearly implies the situation of suffering (*klaiontōn*), and v. 16 probably implies the situation of the "lowly" and "humiliated" (*tapeinoi*) in the church, not simply the "humble-spirited"; see Cranfield, *Romans*, 2:644; cf. esp. Phil. 4:12, where *tapeinousthai* refers to Paul's physical abasement in persecution. On this view, the *tapeinoi* of v. 16 are the "weepers" of v. 15. The likelihood of this interpretation is enhanced by other paraenetic texts that also promote harmony specifically in the situation of suffering and persecution (Phil. 1:27–30; 1 Peter 3:8–9). Verses 15–16, therefore, by implying the situation of suffering, are not completely out of place between v. 14 and vs. 17–21. The thematic linkage between v. 15 and v. 16 is confirmed by the linkage of the same themes in 1 Cor. 12:25–26.

55. Given the continuity of implied imperative from 12:6–8 to 12:9b–13, it is probably best to construe *anypokritos* imperativally (e.g., Michel, *Römer*, 288; Schlier, *Römerbrief*, 350; Wilckens, *Römer*, 3:18; Cranfield, *Romans*, 2:628–629), although some prefer to take it adjectivally, translating the phrase as "genuine love" (so, e.g., Dunn, *Romans 9–16*, 737–738).

56. Formally it continues the asyndetic construction of implied imperatives in Rom. 12:6–8 and anticipates the imperatival participles and adjectives in 12:9b–13. Thematically it extends the theme of harmony in the community which occurs in 12:3–5, 10, 13, 15–16. Emphasizing the loose boundary are Käsemann, *Romans*, 344; Ortkemper, *Leben aus dem Glau-*

ben, 8, 17; and Schlier, *Römerbrief*, x, 364. Cf. Furnish (*Love Command*, 103) and P. Achtemeier (*Romans* [Atlanta: John Knox Press, 1985], 198), who unite 12:3–13 as dealing with the life within the Christian community. C. K. Barrett (*The Epistle to the Romans* [New York: Harper & Brothers, 1957], 233–243) sees 12:3–21 as a single unit. The parallel of 1 Corinthians 13 in relation to 1 Corinthians 12 also suggests continuity between Rom. 12:3–8 and 9a.

57. Käsemann, *Romans*, 343–344, 352. Also admitting that love is not the theme of everything in this section are Michel, *Römer*, 308; and Ortkemper, *Leben aus dem Glauben*, 9.

58. E.g., Wolfgang Schrage, *The Ethics of the New Testament* (Philadelphia: Fortress Press, 1988), 212, 215; Käsemann, *Romans*, 360; and Barrett, *Romans*, 250. In Gal. 5:13–14 and Rom. 13:8–10, Lev. 19:18b is interpreted especially in terms of "one another" (*allēlous*); cf. also *allēlous* in Rom. 12:10; "neighbor" (*plēsion*) in Rom. 15:2 also refers to fellow Christians. On one extreme, some scholars argue that Rom. 13:8–10 articulates a universal horizon to love on the basis of the *mēdeni* in v. 8; see, e.g., Cranfield, *Romans*, 2:675; Black, *Romans*, 162; Ortkemper, *Leben aus dem Glauben*, 128; and Furnish, *Love Command*, 109. Also inadequate is the view that Paul restricts the love command; see, e.g., C. H. Ratschow, "Agape, Nächstenliebe und Bruderliebe," *ZST* 21 (1950): 160–182; and Hugh W. Montefiore, "Thou Shalt Love the Neighbour as Thyself," *NovT* 5 (1962):157–170, esp. 161.

59. Cf. 1 Cor. 13:4–7, where nonretaliatory themes are associated with love, and 1 Thess. 5:8, where "love" is one of the "weapons" for battle with evil.

60. Cf. the third strophe of credentials (2 Cor. 6:7b–8a): Paul uses the "weapons of righteousness" in response to conflict. On "weapons" in Paul, see further, p. 193.

61. Cf. the concluding function of a similar injunction (1 Thess. 5:21b–22) in a series of loosely related injunctions in 1 Thess. 5:12–22.

62. Regarding Paul the persecutor, see 1 Cor. 15:9; Gal. 1:13, 23; Phil. 3:6; on persecution from outsiders, see 1 Cor. 4:12, 2 Cor. 4:9; Gal. 4:29; 5:11; 6:12.

63. See pp. 182–183; note esp. the use of *hypernikaō* in Rom. 8:37.

64. See p. 200–201.

65. Cf. 1 Peter, where nonretaliation in relation to persecutors (1 Peter 2:18–25; 3:9–12) and submission to the ruling authorities (2:13–17) are also found in close proximity. Note also 1 Peter 2:23, where nonretaliation is articulated as an aspect of submission. It is likely, on the basis of the parallels between Romans and 1 Peter, that the exhortations to nonretaliation and submission were found in close proximity in early Christian catechesis; see, e.g., A. Verhey, *The Great Reversal: Ethics and the New Testament* (Grand Rapids: Wm. B. Eerdmans Publishing Co., 1984), 61–71. On the thematic unity of Rom. 12:14–21 and 13:1–7, see also J. Moiser, "Rethinking Romans 12–15," *NTS* 36 (1990): 576.

66. See, e.g., J. C. Beker, *Suffering and Hope* (Philadelphia: Fortress Press, 1987), 57–79.

67. Cf. 1 Cor. 16:9, *antikeimenoi polloi*.

68. *Machaira* may refer to (1) violent death (BAGD) or (2) the power of Roman authorities; cf. Rom. 13:4, the only other use in Paul; cf. Acts 12:2. The likelihood of the latter is suggested by Paul's recent imprisonment under Roman authorities. See 2 Cor. 6:5; 11:23; Paul's imprisonment in Philippians, Philemon, and Colossians (?) also in all likelihood date to an Asian circumstance in the recent past.

69. *Thlipsis*: 2 Cor. 1:4, 8; 2:4; 4:17; 6:4; 7:4; 8:2; Phil. 1:16; 4:14; Col. 1:24; 1 Thess. 1:6; 3:3, 7; 2 Thess. 1:4. *Stenochōria*: 2 Cor. 6:4; 12:10; cf. Rom. 2:9. *Diōgmos*: 2 Cor. 12:10; 2 Thess. 1:4; cf. *diōkein*, 1 Cor. 4:12; 2 Cor. 4:9; Gal. 4:29; 5:11; 6:12. *Limos*: 2 Cor. 11:27. *Gymnotēs*: 2 Cor. 11:27; cf. *gymnos*, 2 Cor. 5:3–4; *gymniteuesthai*, 1 Cor. 4:11. *Kindynos*: 2 Cor. 11:26; cf. 1 Cor. 15:30.

70. 2 Cor. 1:3–11; 4:7–12; 6:3–10; 7:5; 11:23–28. If Romans is dated in the summer/fall of 56 C.E., 2 Corinthians 1–9 and 10–13 date to fall 55/spring 56 C.E. The Asian crisis of Paul probably occurred in the summer of 55 C.E. Paul also refers to his experience of persecution in 1 Thess. 1:6; 2:2, 14–16 (ca. 50–51 C.E.); 1 Cor. 4:12 (ca. 54 C.E.); and Gal. 4:29; 5:11; 6:12 (ca. 56 C.E.). For these dates, see esp. Victor Paul Furnish, *II Corinthians* (AB 32A; Garden City, N.Y.: Doubleday & Co., 1984), 54–55.

71. See 2 Cor. 8:2; cf. Phil. 1:27–30, probably written in the summer of 55 C.E. during Paul's Asian imprisonment. Cf. the earlier experience of the Thessalonians: 1 Thess. 1:6; 2:14–16; 3:3.

72. See, e.g., Dunn, *Romans 9–16*, 738: the exhortation reflects the church's status as an "endangered species, vulnerable to further imperial rulings against Jews and societies." Similarly Moiser, "Rethinking Romans 12–15," 576–577.

73. See, e.g., Beker, *Paul*, 59–74; Käsemann, *Romans*, 402–406; P. Stuhlmacher, "Der Abfassungszweck des Römerbriefes," *ZNW* 77 (1986): 180–193; and J. Marcus, "The Circumcision and Uncircumcision in Rome," *NTS* 35 (1989): 67–81.

74. E.g., Rom. 12:3–8, 10, 13, 15–16, on harmony in the community; so, e.g., Käsemann, *Romans*, 332. This theme, as articulated with the *phronein* word group, emerges at rhetorically important points in Rom. 11:20, 25 and 15:5. Similarly, 13:1–7 is probably included because of its special relevance for the Roman church; so, e.g., Käsemann, *Romans*, 364; argued esp. by M. Borg, "A New Context for Romans XIII," *NTS* 19 (1972/1973): 205–218; P. W. Meyer ("Romans," *HBC*, 1163) grants the "possibility" that 13:1–7 is intended to quiet tumults. For a balanced treatment of the extent to which Romans 12–13 should be read in the light of the Roman situation, see Ortkemper, *Leben aus dem Glauben*, 13–15.

75. E.g., 1 Thess. 5:14–15; Phil. 4:5.

76. See Suetonius's reference (*Claudius*, 25) to the expulsion of Jews from Rome in 49 C.E. because of "disturbances at the instigation of Ches-

tus" (*tumultuantes impulsore Chresto*), which implies conflict between Jews and Christians. See, e.g., W. Wiefel, "The Jewish Community in Ancient Rome and the Origins of Roman Christianity," in *The Romans Debate* (ed. K. P. Donfried; Minneapolis: Augsburg Publishing House, 1977), 109–110.

77. On Roman anti-Semitism, see, e.g., Wiefel, "The Jewish Community in Ancient Rome," 100–119.

78. See Tacitus, *Annals* 15.44; cf. the references to popular persecution possibly in Rome in Heb. 10:32–34. See further P. Lampe, *Die stadtrömischen Christen in der ersten beiden Jahrhunderten* (Tübingen: J. C. B. Mohr [Paul Siebeck], 1987).

79. Paul cites Deut. 32:35 and Prov. 25:21–22a in Rom. 12:19–20. He alludes to Lev. 19:18a in Rom. 12:19a, and to Prov. 3:4 (LXX) in Rom. 12:17b.

80. *Agapētoi* occurs especially for emphasis in paraenetic contexts: 1 Cor. 10:14; 15:58; 2 Cor. 7:1; 12:19; Phil. 2:12; 4:1; cf. 1 Cor. 4:14.

81. E.g., H.-G. Link, "Blessing," *NIDNTT*, 1:215. The predominant usage of *eulogeō* in secular Greek is to speak well of or to extol someone; see BAGD, s.v. "*eulogeō*," 1. Cf. the usage of *eulogia* in Rom. 16:18 to denote fine, flattering speech.

82. E.g., BAGD, s.v. "*eulogeō*," #2; H. W. Beyer, "*eulogeō*," *TDNT*, 2:754–765; Schlier, *Römerbrief*, 379; Dodd, *Romans*, 200; Cranfield, *Romans*, 2:640; Klassen, *Love of Enemies*, 114; and C. Westermann, *Blessing in the Bible and the Life of the Church* (Philadelphia: Fortress Press, 1978), 90–99. Nevertheless the only other occurrence of this meaning of *eulogeō* in the New Testament, besides those dealing with abuse (Luke 6:28; 1 Peter 3:9; Rom. 12:14; 1 Cor. 4:12), is in Luke 2:34.

83. Cf. Acts 7:60; Luke 23:34. Cf. the call to greet (*aspazomai*) one's abuser in Matt. 5:46–47, apparently with *shalom*, cf. Matt. 10:12–13.

84. Note, e.g., prayer that God not hold abusing brothers accountable (*T. Jos.* 18:2; *T. Benj.* 3:6–7), prayer for abusers' repentance instead of cursing them (*b. Ber.* 10a, attributed R. Meir), prayer for forgiveness of the abuser (*t. B. Qam.* 9:29/*m. B. Qam.* 8:7; possibly 1QapGen 20.28–29). See further Zerbe, *Non-Retaliation*, 307–308, 317.

85. For these categories, see n. 12 above.

86. Prov. 3:4 (LXX): *pronoou kala enōpion kyriou kai anthrōpōn*.

87. E.g., Michel, *Römer*, 308; Schlier, *Römerbrief*, 381–382; Käsemann, *Romans*, 348; Klassen, *Love of Enemies*, 116; Ortkemper, *Leben aus dem Glauben*, 107–110; and Wilckens, *Römer*, 3:23–24. It is argued that a direct counterpart best suits the context, esp. v. 17a.

88. The meaning required of *enōpion* in the alternative interpretation is unprecedented. Similar uses of *enōpion* in a "dative" sense are used to denote the persons "to whom" something appears or is pleasing, never persons "to whom" something is done; see BAGD, s.v. "*enōpion*"; BDF, #187 (2), #214 (5, 6). Some interpret the verse as referring to that conduct which all see as good and honorable; e.g., Furnish, *Love Command*, 107; Black, *Romans*, 157; and NEB. Cranfield (*Romans*, 2:645–646) in-

terprets the verse as referring to that peculiar Christian behavior defined by the gospel. But this distinction is probably not a concern of Paul's here; cf. Barrett, *Romans*, 242: "Plan to lead an honest life before all men."

89. See esp. 1 Thess. 4:10b–12; Rom. 13:13; Phil. 2:15; 1 Cor. 10:32–33; 2 Cor. 6:3; cf. Rom. 13:3–4; Col. 4:5–6; W. C. van Unnik, "Die Rücksicht auf die Reaktion der Nicht-Christen als Motiv in der altchristlichen Paränese," in *Judentum Urchristentum Kirche* (ed. W. Eltester; Berlin: A. Töpelmann, 1960), 227–229.

90. There is no need to suppose that this clause indicates that Paul has somehow lapsed into a sub-Christian attitude, contra Preisker, *Das Ethos des Urchristentums*, 184.

91. If the unbelieving spouse consents to live with the believer, the believer should not divorce (1 Cor. 7:12–14). "But if the unbelieving partner desires to separate, let it be so. . . . For God has called you to peace" (1 Cor. 7:15).

92. For the church as "the beachhead of the coming reign of God," see, e.g., Beker, *Paul*, 303–327.

93. See Rom. 14:17, 19; 2 Cor. 13:11; 1 Thess. 5:13; Col. 3:15; Eph. 4:2–3.

94. Lev. 19:18a, LXX: *kai ouk ekdikatai sou hē cheir*, "your own hand shall not avenge for itself." The LXX translation clarifies Lev. 19:18a by using the Hebrew idiom of "saving/avenging with one's own hand," i.e., avenging by self-help, perhaps to exclude other forms of vindication from the prohibition. For this idiom, see 1 Sam. 25:26, 31, 33; Judg. 7:2; Deut. 8:17; CD 9:8–10. Philo (*Spec. Leg.* 3.91, 96; 4.7–10) and Josephus use the term *autocheir*.

95. E.g., Dunn, *Romans 9–16*, 749; see also previous note.

96. The forensic meaning of *ekdikein* is extant esp. in the papyri; see G. Schrenk, "*ekdikēsis*," *TDNT*, 2:444.

97. In addition, judicial vindication, particularly through the Roman courts, is not the meaning of the deferment to wrath in v. 19bc; contra F. Leenhardt, *The Epistle to the Romans* (London: Lutterworth Press, 1961), 319. The absolute use of *orgē* has a theological and eschatological focus in Paul; see p. 197 and n. 142 below.

98. *Echein krima*, 1 Cor. 6:7; *krinesthai*, 6:1, 6. It is not crucial to the present study whether the issue is monetary fraud, the traditional interpretation, or sexual defrauding; see esp. P. Richardson, "Judgment in Sexual Matters in 1 Cor. 6:1–11," *NovT* 25 (1983): 37–58.

99. See esp. 1 Cor. 6:7–8; E. Dinkler, "Zum Problem der Ethik bei Paulus: Rechtsnahme und Rechtsverzicht (1 Kor 6, 1–11)," *ZTK* 49 (1952): 174–175. Philemon 17–19 confirms this noncategorical preference. Paul assumes that Philemon as a slave owner can legitimately pursue his legal right for compensation, either for the loss of work incurred through his slave's defection or for some unknown injury. But Paul also implies that Philemon should give up this right to compensation; he recommends that the loss be "charged to his account" and that Philemon is himself indebted to Paul.

100. In many situations of popular and organized hostility, in which Christians were socially alienated, they would probably not be able to pursue damages.

101. Cf. *apistoi*, 1 Cor. 6:6; cf. 6:4.

102. See pp. 177–180.

103. For the general consensus regarding the interpretation taken here of the situation implied in 2 Cor. 2:1–11 and 7:8–11, see Furnish, *II Corinthians*, 153–168.

104. See p. 201.

105. Michel, *Römer*, 279.

106. Cf. Rom. 6:13: "yield . . . your members as weapons of righteousness" (*parastēsate . . . ta melē hymōn hopla dikaiosynēs*).

107. Cf. Eph. 6:10–16; here the weapons include "the equipment of the gospel of peace." On these texts and on the imagery of weapons and divine warfare in Paul, see Thomas Yoder Neufeld, "God and Saints at War: The Transformation and Democratization of the Divine Warrior in Isaiah 59, Wisdom of Solomon 5, 1 Thessalonians 5, and Ephesians 6" (diss., Harvard Divinity School, 1989). He notes that Paul deletes the imagery of the "cloak and mantle of vengeance" from Isa. 59:17–18 in his use of this passage in reference to the Christians' weapons of warfare and argues that the divine warrior motif is democratized and pacified—vengeance comes through the agency of God and the elect participate with the "warfare of love."

108. Cf. Paul's reflections on suffering in 2 Cor. 4:1–6:10: we do not lose heart (*ouk egkakoumen*, 4:1, 16; cf. Gal. 6:9; 1 Thess. 3:13); we are of good courage (*tharroumen*, 5:6, 8). Cf. also the call to be steadfast in tribulation: 1 Thess. 1:3; 3:3–5; Phil. 1:27–30.

109. E.g., Käsemann, *Romans*, 349; Cranfield, *Romans*, 2:650; Wilckens, *Römer*, 27; and Schlier, *Römerbrief*, 384.

110. Thus Rom. 12:21a is roughly synonymous with the exhortation to *hypomonē* ("endurance") in tribulation in 12:12; *hypomonē* captures both the nuances of steadfastness in faith and of nonretaliatory endurance; see F. Hauck, "*hypomenō*," *TDNT*, 4:586–588.

111. Cf. the parallel in *T. Benj.* 4:2–3, where the good which conquers evil is especially the merciful behavior of the good man. This action, which is also defined as "love" (4:3b–4), results in the abuser's repentance and reconciliation. The conflict assumed in this text, however, is neighborly, not that with persecutors of the community. See further Zerbe, *Non-Retaliation*, 193–196, 213–214, 326.

112. Cf. the use of *nikan* in Thucydides, *History* 4.19.1–4 (ca. 400 B.C.E.). The Lacedaemonians, in the peace mission to Athens seeking the release of trapped soldiers, appeal to the Athenians that to conquer foes by generosity (*aretē autōn nikan*), including clemency (*to epieikes*) toward captives, and not military dominance is what leads to a lasting reconciliation between foes. See L. Pearson, "Popular Ethics in the World of Thucydides," *Classical Philology* 52 (1957): 234–235. Cf. Diodorus Siculus's (*History* 12.19–27, esp. 27.2, ca. 60–30 B.C.E.) version of Nicolaus's

speech to the men of Syracuse; they should be lenient to the captives taken from Athens and so "conquer" (*nikan*) the Athenians with philanthropy and kindness. In contrast to these examples, however, which represent the model of clemency on the part of the powerful to achieve victory and reconciliation, Paul's exhortation expresses victory through good on the part of the abused underdogs; cf. 2 Cor. 12:8–10.

113. See, e.g., Klassen, "Coals of Fire," 347; and Cranfield, *Romans*, 2:650.

114. For a recent summary of these four arguments, see Dunn, *Romans 9–16*, 750–751.

115. E.g., Dodd, *Romans*, 200; Barrett, *Romans*, 242–243; Klassen, "Coals of Fire," 340, 346–347; Furnish, *Love Command*, 108; Ortkemper, *Leben aus dem Glauben*, 122–123; Wilckens, *Römer*, 3:26; Travis, *Judgment*, 41; and Synofzig, *Vergeltungsaussagen*, 48–49.

116. E.g., Dodd, *Romans*, 200–201; Klassen, "Coals of Fire," 345–347; and Dunn, *Romans 9–16*, 750.

117. E.g., 1QS 10:17–20; *Joseph and Aseneth* 22–28; 1 Peter 3:9–12, 16; 4:1–4, 17–19; the Q level of the Jesus tradition, where the call to love enemies is countered by proclamations of judgment upon the enemies of the community; see Zerbe, *Non-Retaliation*, 80–115, 128–171, 224–275.

118. See Piper, *"Love Your Enemies,"* 119: the notion of the failure to heed the proclamation as exacerbating guilt already appears in Jesus (Matt. 11:20–22 par.; cf. Matt. 18:23–25). See also Zerbe, *Non-Retaliation*, 224–275.

119. See Strack and Billerbeck, *Kommentar*, 3:301–302. In this interpretation the enemy signifies the evil impulse, and the bread, water, and fire signify the Torah. "Heaping coals of fire" is interpreted in terms of metallurgy and refers to the disciplinary or educative effect of the Torah. See, e.g., *'Abot de Rabbi Nathan* 16: "R. Simeon B. Eleazar says: Let me tell thee by way of parable to what this [the evil impulse] may be compared. The evil impulse is like iron which one holds in a flame. So long as it is in the flame one can make of it any implement he pleases. So too the evil impulse: its only remedy is in the words of the Torah, for they are like fire, as it is said, *If thine enemy be hungry . . . ; for thou wilt heap coals of fire upon his head, and the Lord will reward thee* (Prov. 25:21f.)—read not *will reward thee* (*yesallem lak*) but *will put him at peace with thee* (*yaslimennu lak*)" (Goldin's trans.). The alternative hiphil reading of *šlm* probably is based on Prov. 16:7; cf. *Gen. Rab.* 54:1, which associates Prov. 25:21–22 with 16:7.

This interpretation is appealed to by, e.g., Klassen, "Coals of Fire," 344; Ortkemper, *Leben aus dem Glauben*, 123; Furnish, *Love Command*, 108; Wilckens, *Römer*, 3:26; and Cranfield, *Romans*, 2:649.

120. Klassen, "Coals of Fire," 349 n. 3; and Cranfield, *Romans*, 2:649.

121. The text could be read either as a pael נְשַׁלְּמֵיהּ לָךְ, "and he will reward you," or as a hafel נַשְׁלְמֵיהּ לָךְ, "he will surrender him to you," or "he will make him to be at peace with you." See Strack and Billerbeck, *Kommentar*, 3:302.

122. For references, see Zerbe, *Non-Retaliation*, 331–332.

123. E.g., *b. Meg.* 15b, attributed to R. Eleazar, pupil of Johanan b. Zakkai.

124. Thus the alternative reading in the rabbinic interpretation is probably better read as "he will surrender him to you" than as "he will make him to be at peace with you."

125. See esp. S. Morenz, "Feurige Kohlen auf dem Haupt," *TLZ* 78 (1953): 187–192. For the text, see F. L. Griffith, *Stories of the High Priests of Memphis* (Oxford: Clarendon Press, 1900), 32: "I will cause him to bring this book hither, a forked stick in his hand and a censer of fire upon his head."

126. Ortkemper, *Leben aus dem Glauben*, 121; Cranfield, *Romans*, 2:650; and Wilckens, *Römer*, 3:26.

127. Käsemann, *Romans*, 349; and Michel, *Römer*, 279, who thinks that this may be the background, though not likely understood by the Romans readers.

128. Klassen, "Coals of Fire," 343–344, 347, 349; idem, *Love of Enemies*, 36, 120.

129. E.g., Ortkemper, *Leben aus dem Glauben*, 121; Klassen, "Coals of Fire," 344–349.

130. For carrying ashes on one's head to symbolize public humiliation, cf. 2 Sam. 13:19; to effect and/or to symbolize punishment, cf. Assyrian laws which require a prostitute to have bitumen poured on her head if she has veiled her head contrary to the law, see F. Lang, *"soreuō," TDNT*, 7:1095.

131. Such a reading would yield a meaning similar to the notion in 1 Peter 3:16—if one maintains a good conscience in suffering, one's opponents will be put to shame (*kataischynthōsin*).

132. E.g., Klassen, "Coals of Fire," 350; Ortkemper, *Leben aus dem Glauben*, 119–120; Synofzig, *Vergeltungsaussagen*, 48–49; and Travis, *Judgment*, 41.

133. E.g., Piper, *"Love Your Enemies,"* 30, 115–116. The deletion of Prov. 25:22b can also be explained as *(a)* an attempt to avoid a redundancy, since *antapodōsō* appears already in Rom. 12:19c, or *(b)* as an attempt to maintain the parallelism of vs. 19–20.

134. For these first three arguments, see also Piper, *"Love Your Enemies,"* 115.

135. See Spicq, *Agape*, 2:208; and Zerbe, *Non-Retaliation*, 335–336. Cf. also 4 Ezra 16:53 (Christian, ca. 250 C.E.), where Prov. 25:22 is interpreted as eschatological vengeance: "Let no sinner say that he has not sinned; for God will burn coals of fire on the head of him who says, 'I have not sinned before God and his glory'" (Metzger in *OTP*). This reference, however, cannot properly be taken as evidence for Paul's interpretation and belongs with the patristic interpretation of Prov. 25:22 and Rom. 12:20.

136. For the language of proclaiming blood upon someone's head as an expression of culpability for retribution, cf. Josh. 2:19; 2 Sam. 1:16; 1

Kings 2:37; Ezek. 33:4; Joel 3:4, 7; Acts 18:6. For the expression of returning evil upon someone's head, cf. Judg. 9:57; 1 Sam. 25:39; 1 Kings 2:44; 2 Chron. 6:23; Ezra 9:6; Esth. 9:25; Ps. 7:16; Obadiah 15; Ezek. 9:10; 16:43; 17:19; 22:31. For the combination, cf. 1 Kings 2:32–33; Jer. 23:19; 30:23; cf. *Ahikar Arm.* 48. On the other hand, for proclaiming blessing upon someone's head, cf. Prov. 10:6; 11:26; Isa. 35:10.

137. M. J. Dahood ("Two Pauline Quotations from the Old Testament," *CBQ* 17 [1955]: 19–24) admits that retribution is the meaning of the image in biblical usage but reinterprets the Hebrew of Prov. 25:22 to read "*removing* coals of fire *from*" the head because of the harshness of the text as it literally reads.

138. Cf. Lang, "*pyr*," TDNT, 6:944. See also the close connection among *pyr* and *antapodidonai* and *ekdikēsis* in 2 Thess. 1:4–10.

139. The regular use of "fire" as a symbol for eschatological judgment in prophetic and apocalyptic writings would also support this interpretation. See, e.g., Amos 1:4, 7, 10, 12, 14; 2:2, 5; Rev. 14:10–11; 19:20; 20:10; 21:8; *1 Enoch* 91:9; 100:9; 4 Ezra 7:35; 1QS 2:2; 4:13; 1QH 17:13.

140. Piper, "*Love Your Enemies*," 115; cf. Stendahl, "Non-Retaliation," 345.

141. BAGD, s.v. "*topon*," 2.c. Cf. LSJ: "leave room for the wrath (of God), that is, let God punish." See also E. J. Goodspeed, *Problems of New Testament Translation* (Chicago: University of Chicago Press, 1945), 152–154; F. Zyro, "Röm 12,19: *dote topon tē orgē*," *TSK* 18 (1945): 887–892; E. R. Smothers, "Give Place to Wrath," *CBQ* 6 (1944): 205–215.

142. E.g., Schlier, *Römerbrief*, 382. An eschatological focus of *orgē* is evident in Rom. 2:5, 8; 5:9; 1 Thess. 1:10; 2:16; 5:9; cf. Col. 3:6; the absolute use of *orgē* to denote God's wrath is evident in these references (exc. Col. 3:6) and in Rom. 3:5; 4:15; 9:22; 13:4, 5.

143. See, e.g., Dunn, *Romans 9–16*, 749. See esp. Rom. 1:18–32; 13:4–5. There is no basis, however, for Leenhardt's suggestion (*Romans*, 319) that Paul expressed here hope that the civic powers and courts would intervene (cf. Rom. 13:4).

144. The text of the citation agrees with Heb. 10:30 and targumic traditions, against the MT and LXX, probably depending either on current textual traditions varying from the LXX or on a group of testimonia. See Ortkemper, *Leben aus dem Glauben*, 110–111.

145. Cf. Rom. 14:11; 1 Cor. 14:21; 2 Cor. 6:16–18; see Schlier, *Römerbrief*, 382.

146. This is suggested by the larger context of Philippians, esp. Phil. 1:27–30. But the entire unit of Phil. 4:4–7 is probably directed to this situation as well; see, e.g., R. Martin, *Philippians* (Greenwood, S.C.; Attic Press, 1976), 154–156.

147. See, e.g., Martin, *Philippians*, 155; G. Barth, *Die Brief an die Philipper* (Zurich: Theologischer Verlag, 1982), 73; and Stendahl, "Non-Retaliation," 352. Paul refers to the Greek virtue of *epieikeia* to explicate nonretaliation; here it has a meaning similar to the notion of *anechesthai*

(1 Cor. 4:12) or *hypomenein* in suffering. On this usage of *epieikeia*, see Wisd. Sol. 2:19. For the Greek uses of this term, see Herbert Preisker, *TDNT*, 2:588–590; Albrecht Dihle, *Die goldene Regel: Eine Einführung in die Geschichte der antiken und frühchristlichen Vulgärethik* (Göttingen: Vandenhoeck & Ruprecht, 1962), 46–47. In this tradition, *to epieikes* as opposed to what is just (*to dikaion*) refers to the clemency or leniency that does not insist on the letter of the law.

148. Translation follows the RSV, except for *autois* in v. 28, which is better translated as a dative of respect or of disadvantage ("for them") than as an indirect object ("to them").

149. See, e.g., Martin, *Philippians*, 84; F. W. Beare, *A Commentary on the Epistle to the Philippians* (New York: Harper & Brothers, 1959), 67–68: the double token "imposes on [the persecutors] the unwelcome conviction that they are storing up tribulation and anguish for themselves against the day of judgment."

150. Most likely Phil. 3:18–19 is referring to former, misguided Christians. For discussion, see Martin, *Philippians*, 22–36; and Barth, *Philipper*, 69–71.

151. For *apōleia*, compare Rom. 9:22; Phil. 1:28; 2 Thess. 2:3; compare *apollymenoi* of non-Christians in general, 1 Cor. 1:18, 19; 2 Cor. 2:15; 4:3; 2 Thess. 2:10. Second Thessalonians 1:4–10 expresses ideas similar to Phil. 1:27–30 and illustrates how the themes of judgment upon persecutors were taken up by later Pauline tradition. Persecution and/or steadfastness are a token or proof (*endeigma*) of God's righteous judgment which entails the persecutors' punishment and the sufferers' reward: "Therefore we ourselves boast of you in the churches of God for your steadfastness and faith in all your persecutions and in the afflictions which you are enduring. This is evidence (*endeigma*) of the righteous judgment of God, . . . since indeed God deems it just to repay with affliction those who afflict you (*eiper dikaion para theō antapodounai tois thlibousin hymas thlipsin*), and to grant rest with us to you who are afflicted" (2 Thess. 1:4–7a, RSV). Differences between this text and similar texts in Paul are (1) the further description of eschatological judgment (2 Thess. 1:7–9), (2) the more explicit *lex talionis—thlipsis anti thlipsin* (2 Thess. 1:6), and (3) the explication of God as causing a deluding influence on the persecutors (2 Thess. 2:9–11; but compare the "hardening" in Romans 9:18; 11:7–10.)

152. For options and arguments, see, for example, Cranfield, *Romans*, 1:138–139. If this is part of Paul's debate with Judaism (see Beker, *Paul*, 52–93) and Paul is describing the typical Jew, the Jews' impenitence is not only their lack of fidelity to the covenant (Romans 2:17–29) but also their continued hostility to the gospel and Christ (compare Rom. 3:3; 10:16; 11:7–10, 22–23, 28a). For the moment, the nonremnant portion of Israel is on the road to destruction (Romans 11:7–10—*antapodoma*).

153. Both texts also depend on Deuteronomy 32; see Stendahl, "Non-Retaliation," 344. For Rom. 2:5, cf. Deut. 32:34 LXX: "Behold, are not

these things [the corruption of enemies] stored up with me, and sealed up in my treasuries" (ouk idou tauta synēktai par' emoi, kai esphragistai en tois thēsaurois mou); for Rom. 12:19, cf. Deut. 32:35; also Deut. 32:23: "I will gather up evil things against them [the disobedient]" (synaxō eis autous kaka).

154. For bibliography and recent discussion, see Robert Jewett, The Thessalonian Correspondence (Philadelphia: Fortress Press, 1986), 36–42.

155. On the apocalyptic background of the notion of a fixed number of sins to be committed in order to bring in judgment, cf. I. Howard Marshall, 1 and 2 Thessalonians (Grand Rapids: Wm. B. Eerdmans Publishing Co., 1983), 80; and W. Marxsen, Der erste Brief an die Thessalonicher (Zurich: Theologischer Verlag, 1979), 50.

156. This clause has been interpreted (1) in a fully eschatological sense, with ephthasen meaning "has drawn near," "has arrived" (cf. Matt. 12:28; Luke 11:20; cf. Rev. 6:17), (2) as referring to past judgment, e.g., the destruction of Jerusalem, on the assumption of inauthenticity, (3) as signifying a past event, e.g., the expulsion of the Jews from Rome, pointing to the coming judgment, or (4) as a current sentence of judgment with an eschatological limitation, taking eis telos as "until the end" (cf. Romans 11). The first interpretation seems to suit v. 16b and the mood of the entire passage best; but it should be noted that this phrase is directed especially against persecutors, not "all Israel"; see, for example, W. D. Davies, "Paul and the People of Israel," New Testament Studies 24 (1977/1978): 6–9.

157. This is probably also a key intention behind 1 Thess. 2:16. See also Col. 3:24–25: deferment to the final judgment is the rationale for slaves to submit even to unjust abuse from masters. Cf. 1 Peter 2: 18–20.

158. It should be observed, however, that judgment is not necessarily the last word upon persecutors. Eschatological wrath against persecutors entails the condition of continued impenitence and hostility.

159. Cf. 1 Corinthians 5:3–5; cf. 2 Corinthians 10:5–6. Thus, mediation through judicial procedure is one of the options in the case of internal conflict, 1 Corinthians 6:1–8. See, for example, M. Delcor, "The Courts of the Church of Corinth and the Courts of Qumran," in Paul and Qumran (ed. J. Murphy O'Connor; Chicago: Priory Press, 1968), 69–84.

160. E.g., Dinkler, "Zum Problem der Ethik," 170–171. That kosmos here refers especially to the non-Christian world or the present age is indicated by (1) the consistent usage of kosmos with this meaning in 1 Corinthians, including the immediate context (1 Corinthians 1:20, 21, 27, 28; 2:12; 3:19, 22; 4:9, 13; 5:10), (2) the immediate context of referring to "unjust judges," and (3) the overwhelming usage of kosmos in this sense in all of Paul's writings. On God judging the "world," cf. Romans 3:6, 19.

161. Dinkler, "Zum Problem der Ethik," 170–171. See Wisd. Sol. 3:7–

8; 5:1; 12:22; *1 Enoch* 1:9; 38:1; Dan. 7:9, 22; *Jubilees* 23:30; 24:29; Matt. 19:28; Luke 22:30; Rev. 20:4. On the judgment of the angels, see, e.g., *1 Enoch* 90:24.

162. The tension between 1 Cor. 5:12–13 (judgment of outsiders deferred to God) and 6:2–3 (judgment of outsiders by Christians) is to be understood eschatologically. See, e.g., C. K. Barrett, *The First Epistle to the Corinthians* (New York: Harper & Row, 1968), 136.

163. For persecution as the context of the notion of the elect judging outsiders, see esp. Wisd. Sol. 3:7–8; *1 Enoch* 1:9; 1QS 10:17–25; Rev. 20:4.

164. On this tension in 1 Peter and Q, see Zerbe, *Non-Retaliation*, 262–265, 384–388.

165. Cf. the explicit references to "words of the Lord" in 1 Cor. 7:10–11, on divorce, cf. Mark 10:11–12 and par.; 1 Cor. 9:14, on the apostles' financial support, cf. Luke 10:7 and par.; 1 Cor. 11:23–26, on the Lord's Supper, cf. Mark 14:22 and par.; 1 Cor. 14:37, on the practice of prophets, no par.; 1 Thess. 4:15, on the order of the resurrection of the dead, no par.; cf. also 1 Cor. 7:12, 25, on Paul's lack of the word from the Lord on the matters of mixed marriages and of the unmarried.

166. For the arguments for this interpretation, see Zerbe, *Non-Retaliation*, 313–316.

167. 2 Cor. 1:5; Phil. 3:10–11; Rom. 8:17; 2 Cor. 4:10–12; Gal. 6:17; cf. Col. 1:24; cf. 1 Peter 4:13; 5:1.

168. Gal. 2:19–20; 6:15; cf. 3:27; Rom. 6:1–11; cf. Col. 2:11–14; 3:3.

169. The participation in the entirety of Christ's passion, both suffering and death, is apparent especially in Phil. 3:10–11. It is beyond the scope of the present discussion to attempt to identify the precise nature of this participation and union. See, e.g., C. M. Proudfoot, "Imitation or Realistic Participation—A Study of Paul's Concept of 'Suffering with Christ,' " *Int* 17 (1963): 140–160.

170. Gal. 6:17; 2 Cor. 4:7–11; 1 Cor. 15:30–32. Paul's and Christian suffering is also on Christ's behalf: Phil. 1:27–28; 2 Cor. 4:11; 12:10. See Wolfgang Schrage, "Leid, Kreuz und Eschaton: Die Peristasenkataloge als Merkmale paulinischer theologia crucis und Eschatologie," *EvT* 34 (1974): 141–175.

171. 2 Cor. 4:12. Cf. Phil. 2:17; Eph. 3:1, 13.

172. 2 Cor. 4:17. Cf. Rom. 5:2–4; 8:17–18; Phil. 3:10–11; on the necessity of suffering, cf. 1 Thess. 3:4.

173. Esp. Phil. 2:5. In terms of the effect of the passion, cf. Rom. 15:7; Col. 3:13. For an overview of the theme of *imitatio Christi* in Paul, see Furnish, *Theology*, 218–223.

174. The context of 1 Thessalonians indicates that it is not only joy in tribulation that is being imitated but also steadfastness, love, and faith (1 Thess. 1:2–3; 2:14; 3:1–8).

175. The notion that weakness, hardships, and persecutions on Christ's behalf are the occasion for the demonstration of Christ's grace and power (2 Cor. 12:8–10) also has a christological precedent and grounding: "For

he was crucified in weakness, but lives by the power of God" (2 Cor. 13:4a). On Paul's cruciform life, see Beker, *Paul*, 299–302.

176. On the christological grounding of Paul's ethics, see, e.g., Furnish, *Theology*, 112–181; and Beker, *Paul*, 255–302.

10

"Give to Caesar What Belongs to Caesar and to God What Belongs to God": A Theological Response of the Early Christian Church to Its Social and Political Environment

Luise Schottroff

From the perspective of the theme of effectual history to be treated here, Rom. 13:1–7 is a most important and difficult text. It is not an isolated position within the New Testament. Its declaration of loyalty toward the power of the state has many relevant parallels, not only in 1 Peter 2:13–17; Titus 3:1; 1 Tim. 2:1–2 and in the three versions of the tax coin discussion (Mark 12:13–17 pars.). The four passion accounts of the Gospels also contain, at least, indications of the renunciation of resistance against the power of the state. On the contrary, no one will doubt that the Christianity of New Testament times (and beyond that) had to live through conflicts with society and the power of the state, and these were not merely marginal phenomena but necessary consequences of the Christian faith and life. Belief in a Jew as Son of God, as Messiah, crucified by the Romans, is in itself a fact of resistance in a world dominated by the Romans by means of crucifixions, among other things. The behavior of the early Christian churches in what appears as both refusal of resistance and practice of resistance, a seeming paradox, will be presented in detail in the following study of Romans 12 and 13. I

Translated by Gerhard Reimer, professor of German, Goshen College, from Luise Schottroff, *Befreiungserfahrungen: Studien zur Sozialgeschichte des Neuen Testaments* (Munich: Chr. Kaiser Verlag, 1990), 184–216 (ch. 10). Used by permission.

choose Romans 12 and 13 as the point of departure because the understanding of this Pauline text has become so difficult in the history of interpretation; thus every thesis on this subject has to stand the test in relation to this text. It is important when one is interpreting this text, as it is generally when dealing with the topic of the relationship of Christians toward the state in the New Testament, that one understands the theological ideas of the texts in their relationship to the praxis of the Christian life. Romans 13:1–7 should not be isolated either from its literary context in the Letter to the Romans or from its context of the practical behavior of the early Christian churches. We shall pursue, therefore, in the first section the question of the "life context" of Rom. 13:1–7.

The Life Context of Romans 13:1–7

Romans 13:1 is the sequel to 12:21

It is widely accepted today that Rom. 13:1–7 originates from Paul and is connected to its context by repetition in vocabulary (between 13:4 and 12:19 and/or between 13:7 and 13:8). Additionally, it is often accepted that there is a logical connection in content between 13:1–7 and 12:1–21 insofar as Paul here deals with certain areas of Christian behavior in sequence. Thus J. Friedrich, W. Pöhlmann, and P. Stuhlmacher[1] talk about 12:21 as well as 13:1–7 being the "missionary witness," on the one hand, by testimony to peace and love (12:21) and, on the other hand, a missionary testimony in daily political life. A further step, however, needs to be taken to determine the context of the content more clearly. Romans 12:14–21 presupposes that Christians will come into dangerous conflicts with persons who are not Christians: enmity (12:20), persecution (12:14), and evil directed at Christians (12:17, 19) are mentioned; these are situations that call for divine retribution. If the sequel, then, discusses the behavior vis-à-vis powers of the state, it is clear that this discussion about obedience toward the state occurs against the background of already present as well as anticipated conflicts of Christians with the society and the power of the state. The assumptions of 12:14–21 and 13:1–7 are identical. The content of 13:1, therefore, also connects to the content of 12:21: the good, which overcomes evil, is here equivalent to subordination to the power of the state. This interpretation is affirmed by later Christian tradition, in which loyalty to the state is interpreted as one possibility (among others) for overcoming evil. This connection is established in 1 Peter 2:12. A good work (1 Peter 2:12; reference here is probably to

Matt. 5:16) or *agathopoiein* (to do good; 1 Peter 2:15) is, among other good deeds, loyal subordination to those in power, by means of which the slandering of Christians is to be brought to an end and the slanderers themselves, in the final analysis, are to be brought to glorify God (1 Peter 2:15, 12). A similar connection of ideas is found in Titus 2–3 (Titus 2:5, 8; 3:1, 8) and can also be demonstrated from the martyr accounts and the apologetic writings of the second century. One example from many:[2] Theophilus (bishop of Antioch, in his Letter to Autolycus 3.14f., written shortly after 180 C.E.) wards off the accusations of sexual promiscuity and the eating of human flesh among other things by pointing to the commandment to love one's enemy and Rom. 13:1–7:

> Consider whether people who have received such teaching would practice undifferentiated and illegal sexual relations or even do that which is most godless, eat human flesh, considering that it is forbidden to us even to observe the contests of the gladiators, lest we become participants and accomplices in acts of killing.[3]

The accusation of *flagitia*/shameful acts, referred to here, already played an important role in the trials of Christians appearing before the Roman authorities, as the letter of Pliny the Younger to Trajan (10.96) from the year 110 or 112 demonstrates. This reference to loyalty to the state in the cited text of Theophilus as well as by Paul is an attempt to overcome evil with good. The loyalty of Christians toward the state is already grounded in the experiences of persecution, whose connection to the measures taken by the state are assumed. In content, Rom. 13:1–7 and 12:14–21 thus belong together. Romans 12 and 13 are not a loosely connected series of different individual opinions,[4] and Rom. 13:1–7 is not an "independent bloc" or a "foreign body" in the Pauline corpus.[5]

The "life context" of Romans 13:1–7 is the preparation of the Christian community for a situation of persecution

This thesis already follows from the preceding, from the context established by Paul in the Letter to the Romans. Moreover, this thesis can additionally be brought to life by the accounts of Christian martyrs in the second century. In the reports of these trials, which more or less correspond to actual fact, it is frequently mentioned that the accused Christians made a declaration of loyalty in the sense of Rom. 13:1–7, and in spite of this they were executed.

The accounts of the martyrs among the Christians of Scilli (180 C.E.) report that the Christian Speratus tells the proconsul of North Africa: "We have never done evil to anyone and have in no manner worked for the cause of injustice: we have never cursed, we have rather been thankful when we were mistreated; therefore we give honor to Caesar." The Christian woman Donata also declares her loyalty: "Honor Caesar as Caesar, but fear God!"[6] Romans 13:1–7 is already cited by Polycarp (who probably died in 156 C.E.[7]) in the *Martyrdom of Polycarp* 10, when appearing before the proconsul: "We have been taught to show appropriate honor to the principalities and powers (*archai kai exousiai*) ordained of God, if that does not compromise us." Romans 13:1–7 was "a requisite for the martyr apology."[8] The forensic situation of the persecuted Christians becomes the hour of trial for the commandment to love one's enemy, for the renunciation of vengeance, and for loyalty to the state. Apollonius (at the time of Caesar Commodus, 180–192 C.E.) says the following to the governor Perennis:

> He [Jesus] taught us to tame our anger, to moderate our desires, to bridle our cravings, to banish sadness, to be peaceable, to increase in love, to lay aside vanity, not to permit ourselves to be carried away with vengeance toward those who offend us, to despise death on the basis of a legal sentence, not because one has done wrong, but by bearing it patiently, additionally to obey the laws of Caesar and to honor him; however, to worship and adore God alone, the only immortal one.[9]

This statement sketches a teaching of Jesus that is not found in the same way in the New Testament but that has a parallel, however, in Rom. 12:14–21; 13:1–7, above all, with regard to renunciation of vengeance, the readiness to bear injustice and render loyalty to Caesar. It would be too superficial to explain this context simply as a fact lodged in the history of tradition. It has its basis (and therefore remains constant for a long period) in the fact that the requirement and/or the declaration of loyalty belongs together with persecution.

One could object to this thesis on the basis that at the time of Paul there was no persecution of Christians yet, for one still encounters this contention. It is true indeed that there was no persecution of "Christians" at his time, in the sense that the *nomen ipsum* already was considered punishable. Christians are being persecuted, however, on the basis of local conflicts between Christians and those who are not Christians, which leads to suspicions and denunciations. The portrayal of this situation in Acts therefore could be true to fact. The letters of Paul also reveal that Paul had experience with persecution from the Roman authorities, as especially 2 Cor. 11:25 and Rom. 8:35[10] demonstrate.

To date, the exegetical discussions on Rom. 13:1–7 have been more concerned with a "historical situation" than with a "life context." In other words, a concrete reason has been sought after, not a typical recurring life situation, which has to be the goal of inquiry for the determination of the life context in the sense of form criticism. As for the historical location—I will mention relevant theses—(Zealotism or) enthusiasm among the Christians of Rome has been considered, on the one hand (thus O. Michel; E. Käsemann),[11] and, on the other hand, a concrete emergency of the population of the city of Rome at the time of the writing of the letter to Romans, which had been caused by the ever widening extortionist taxation practices.[12] Aside from the fact that there is no indication of an anti-enthusiastic front in the text, both attempts at determining a historical location do not satisfactorily explain why Paul so emphatically and with such great theological emphasis demands loyalty. He would thus have aimed much beyond his goal. Such a relativization of Rom. 13:1–7 by means of a concrete reason would remain in tension with a text that has such basic formulation. The determination of a life context in the sense of form criticism is undertaken when the paraenesis of the community is considered as the setting for Romans 12–13.[13] Of course, the relationship of the contents of the individual admonitions, which—as we attempted to demonstrate—must be added to this.

If that is the case, however, we do not only have a Christian teacher talking about Christian behavior in a general way. Rather, he is describing and recommending behavior that has its home in the typical recurring situation which is fundamentally a part of being Christian. The determination of a life context in the sense of form criticism (e.g., "church teaching") has to follow a life context in the sense of social history, which inquires into the social location of the community (see pp. 229–230).

Romans 13:1–7 belongs to the context of the politics of religion of the Roman Caesar, which already has pre-Roman roots

The Roman Caesars generally pursued a policy of integration toward the local religions of the subjugated population. That meant, above all, that an attempt was made to combine in a peaceful manner elements of the Roman religion with the foreign religion. Thus the recognition of the state by the subjugated population was effected religiously, while at the same time they were able to practice their religion without disturbance, as long as they tolerated this integration. These unions, however, had potential for conflict. Thus if, for example, Jews were accused of disloyalty (even if this was not true) by a non-Jewish population, they had to submit to a test of loyalty. These loyalty tests, however, demanded confessions, which could not be combined with the monotheism of Jewish religion, and thus they got into the paradoxical situation, in spite of affirmations of loyalty, of being considered enemies of the state. The conflicts between Christians and the state arose according to the same pattern. There are several well-known examples of this imperial religious policy. First, I mention a pre-Roman example. King Nebuchadnezzar had a golden statue erected, to which all his subjects were now required to pray. Only as a result of denunciation the Jews, who are entrusted with the governing of the province of Babylon, are brought into the difficult situation of resisting this royal decree publicly: we serve no other gods (Dan. 3:18). They are thrown into the fiery furnace and wonderfully saved. Thereupon the king decrees the recognition of the God of the Jews and implicitly withdraws the earlier decree to pray to the golden statue, now considered overdrawn. The story of Daniel in the lions' den also describes the formation of a religious coalition between the sovereign and the subjugated Jews. Here also the conflict arises because of denunciation. These legends narrated about Nebuchadnezzar and Darius make their point in the book of Daniel as a result of the then current conflicts between religion and political loyalty under Antiochus IV Epiphanes, during whose time the book of Daniel came into existence.

A measure taken by Augustus was definitive for the Roman religious policy toward the Jews. It introduced a daily offering in the temple for Caesar. Later on, the prayers of the Christians for Caesar are connected to this institution.[14] Here, too, conflicts were not excluded; above all, the persecution of the Jews in Alexandria at the time of Gaius/Caligula also led to conflicts between Caesar and the Jews. The demands of Caligula to erect an idol with his own facial traits in the temple was a test of loyalty with which the Jews could not comply.[15] The investigation of Christians carried out by Pliny also belongs to this chain of loyalty tests. He demanded that they call on the gods, make offerings in front of idols and Caesar's insignia, and curse Christ.[16] Whenever it came to conflicts as a result of denunciation or for other reasons, the situation was hopeless for Jews as well as for Christians despite their loyalty affirmations, because the state would then set higher *religious* demands as evidence of loyalty, which ran contrary to monotheism. The confession *"Christianus sum"* was of itself sufficient evidence of nonloyalty, not because the *Christianus* was a member of an outlawed organization, but because it did not pay recognition to the religious demands of the Roman state. The catchword *"religio licita"* used by Tertullian[17] characterizes these religious policies very aptly. Indeed, one ought not to overlook their potential for conflict for Jews (and Christians) but also for the religions of other subjugated peoples. Like the tax coin discussion and the later Christian prayers for Caesar, Rom. 13:1–7 is the Christian contribution to this religious policy, which makes its appearance in the temple in the wake of the Jewish offering to Caesar. In the case of conflict, nevertheless, Rom. 13:1–7 was insufficient in the eyes of the Roman authorities, because at that point a positive recognition of the Roman gods was demanded. If one considers the context of the Roman policy of religion, Rom. 13:1–7 loses its apparently singular character and becomes a link in the long chain of declarations of loyalty of the members of subjugated peoples toward Rome. This context confirms the thesis presented above as the life context of Rom. 13:1–7. Paul, the Jew, was inevitably acquainted with the Roman policy of religion. He must have known the offerings to Caesar and the conflicts under Caligula as well as the story of his people, as it is described in the book of Daniel.

Sociohistorical considerations
concerning the life context of Romans 13:1–7:
Christ's passion is the example of the path
connected with Romans 13:1–7

There is a difference between a recognized teacher of philosophy in Rome, who propounds philosophically grounded theories concerning the essence of the state, which, as their goal, demand loyalty toward the existing state, and a Jew who believes in Christ and who writes a text for his fellow believers, such as Rom. 13:1–7. For Paul as well as for the whole Jewish nation, there was no institution for cooperation in making political decisions, not even by way of economic power. The tradition of "political" action by the downtrodden was martyrdom, putting one's own life at risk. Jesus and many of his followers, including Paul, acted in this tradition.

Up to this point I have sought to determine the life setting of the text through form criticism. Now I shall attempt to widen the question concerning the life context to the sociohistorical dimension, that is, we have to recognize that the Christian congregations of this time consisted of economically, politically, and socially weak individuals (1 Cor. 1:26–31), although with regard to our question it may remain irrelevant whether a few wealthy, powerful, and educated individuals were among them. For all of them, the path of Christ in his suffering was representative. Those who believed in Christ had to reckon with the consequences if they got into the mills of the Roman authorities, which was probable—the reasons for this I will discuss below. Therefore it is methodologically legitimate to read the passion accounts of the Gospels as though they were actually the typical path for a Christian, with Christ as the example. With his own body Jesus acted in a political manner. He declared his loyalty to Caesar and, according to the Gospels, already with clear consciousness that this declaration of loyalty would not be adequate to prevent him from being handed over into the hands of sinners (Mark 14:41). The sequence of announcements of his suffering, tax coin discussions, and passion has historical likelihood and reflects a typical situation for the imitation of Jesus. Martyrdom was already the means of politics for the powerless based on a lengthy Jewish tradition. To regard the death of Christ as a misunderstanding of the Romans, who were poorly informed and who thus considered Jesus a political rebel, fails to recognize the reality of the subjugated nations in the Roman Empire.[18] Rebellion offered no positive prospects and had to remain a purely suicidal declamation. The struggle for the life of people had a different outlook and was rightly viewed as resistance by the Romans.

The Children of God in the Face of Violence and Injustice

From the very beginning, Christians have been attacked, maligned, mistreated, stoned, and killed by the non-Christian population as well as by Jewish and Roman authorities. The facts discussed in the preceding chapter need not be developed any further, since we are now concerned with describing the peculiar behavior of Christians in these situations where violence and injustice are experienced. This conduct has its roots in the behavioral tradition of the Jewish nation, in their conception of the God of Jews and Christians, and is connected to the hope for the future, to an eschatology that is determinative for this behavior. We will clarify this with two examples:

1. The Gospel of Matthew with its representation of the teachings of Jesus for this situation and his representation of Christ's own experiences during the passion.

2. Romans 12–13, the Pauline parallel to these texts.

Do not resist evil and love your enemies: Matthew 5:38–48 and Matthew 26:47–56

God's command (*errethē*, Matt. 5:38) of legally ordained and just retribution (the *lex talionis,* Ex. 21:24f. and similar references) is interpreted for the contemporary situation in the Sermon on the Mount:[19] *mē antistēnai tō ponērō,* "do not resist evil." Within the context of 5:38 this formulation means refusal of retribution, that is, the behavior that is mentioned twice, in Rom. 12:17 and in 12:19: never paying back evil for evil to anyone and not to avenge oneself. A positive alternative (*alla* in Matt. 5:39b) is then added to this refusal to retaliate. Retribution is then replaced by the behavior described in Matt. 5:39–41. Three everyday experiences of violence and injustice are mentioned:

1. The impoverished debtor has his last possession seized in court, his *chitōn*/undershirt. According to Ex. 22:25ff. and Deut. 24:13, the creditor cannot seize his *himation*/outer garment.

2. The little man is conscripted (by the military, the administration, or also by estate owners) for transport service (*aggareuein,* to compel to render compulsory service[20]).

3. People have their faces beaten up. Above all, the slap on the cheek has led to a widespread misinterpretation of these three examples as pure symbols of all possible or imaginable experiences of insult or injustice, to which one must respond with a refusal to resist and with a posture of love, and an unlimited affirmation of one's neighbor according to the teachings of the Sermon on the Mount.[21] This interpretation is possible only if one divests the aforementioned situations of any reference to reality and accepts them as purely symbolic and if one considers the doubling of injustice (turning the other cheek, etc.) as a purely rhetorical turn, which is supposed to express "unlimited" love or "complete" renunciation of retaliation. Rather, one should regard the conduct concretely; injustice is doubled. The creditor violates God's command when he takes the coat. The aggressor is challenged to strike twice. Doubling the compulsory service means a grave injustice. This behavior in the face of experiencing injustice must be brought into relationship with shaking the dust of a hostile city off the feet of the messenger of God (Matt. 10:14 pars.[22]) or with heaping live coals on the head of an enemy (Rom. 12:20; Prov. 25:21f.; also see below). In all these cases it is, in my opinion, a matter of an action of prophetic judgment which expresses the idea that God's judgment is going to catch up with you. This action must not be confused with a curse that intends to hurt the enemy and that damages effectively. And, precisely, it is not an act of personal vengeance. Prophetic judgment

can be expressed in deeds as well as in words. The intention is always the completely unmellowed announcement of the judgment of God, of the retribution of God, which those who have committed an injustice have drawn upon their heads. One must not underestimate the public character of this or the understanding that those who knew the Bible (Amos, Isaiah especially) have for this. Roman soldiers possibly might not have remained untouched by the contents of this message.

Matthew 5:38–41 thus commands the refusal to retaliate as well as prophetic judgment of violent persons. For Matt. 5:42, I cannot tell whether—as Luke says (in the context of 6:30)—an experience of injustice is meant or whether, as in Romans 12, behavior in response to experiences of injustice are connected with commandments of friendliness toward outsiders and fellow Christians. In the sixth antithesis, then, the commandment of love toward one's enemies is added, which is unequivocally intended to describe the behavior toward persecutors. As imitators of God, Christians are supposed to confront the enemies of God with his mercies. The persecutors have precisely declined to accept the message of the Gospels and are persecuting the messengers of Christ, who now confront them with this message. The gift of love and prayer is the gift of the mercy and love of God and of the wholeness of God (5:48), who desires that the whole creation lives, including the evil and the unrighteous. Loving one's enemy in all of this certainly does not mean permitting the enemy to continue undisturbed in his injustice. Loving one's enemy is the attempt to change the violent person into a child of God through a confrontation with the love of God. That is, love of one's enemy can be concretely presented as the prophetic proclamation of the approaching sovereignty of God.

Thus Matt. 5:38–48 results in a coherent ensemble on behavior of refusal to pay retribution, expecting prophetic judgment, and the inclination of God's love toward the enemy. This apparent paradoxical juxtaposition of enacting prophetic judgment and proclaiming the sovereignty of God does not only determine the message of Jesus here, according to the Gospels. Nor should one suspend this paradox by not taking prophetic judgment seriously. Only when it is taken seriously does it become a call to conversion.

Matthew 5:38–48 does not address directly a confrontation with the power of the state, yet it corresponds to the intent of the text to take the instructions as an example that can be applied to comparable situations (which does not mean that they are to be taken symbolically). When we consider Matt. 5:38–48 in the total context of the Gospel of Matthew, then Matt. 26:47–57 must be recognized as a practical commentary on Matt. 5:38–48. This text, together with the tax coin discourse, permits us to understand the behavior of Jesus toward the power of the state. Matthew considers the power of the state for the local and supraregional Jewish administration as well as the Roman military and the Roman administration as unjust power. He is clearly opposed to the Roman imperialism with the consciousness of one belonging to a subjugated nation (see Matt. 20:25, *katakyrieuein*; to put under a yoke; to misuse power: 17:25f.; 22:20). According to Matthew, Pilate, against his better knowledge and because of political calculations, kills an innocent person (27:24) who could not defend himself against the accusation that he had said he was the King of the Jews because he was, after all, the King of the Jews (27:11–14). Jesus demands loyalty toward Caesar, especially in the matter of payment of taxes (22:21), and he does not resist being taken captive. He accepts the injustice that has been done to him as God's will. While Jesus was taken captive by the police of the high priests (26:47–54), one of the disciples cuts off the ear of one of the slaves of the high priests. Jesus forbids this resistance, which in this situation has strictly demonstrative value. He basically does not want to defend himself with military means, which, after all, is imaginable as a miracle of God. God could send him more than twelve legions of angels. The decisive element in this scene is a judgment word of Jesus,[23] which only Matthew refers to. In front of this gathered police troop, armed with sticks and short swords (*machaira*), Jesus says to the violent disciple, "All who take the sword shall perish by the sword" (26:52). The future *apolountai* does not indicate a fateful necessity but God's retribution. God's judgment will violently destroy those who have taken the sword into their hands. God's punishment is already upon those who intend to and prepare to employ violence, including the troop taking a person captive as well as the individual, for example, the disciple, who is prevented from using violence because he is powerless but who could still try to employ it at least in a small way. Because of this scene, as well as because of the passion account, Matt. 5:38–48 is applicable when one is faced with the unjust power of those in a position of power; the just power of sovereigns is unknown in the Gospel of Matthew. While the disciple of Jesus is supposed to decline retribution, he publicly announces the retribution of God against those who exercise their power unjustly. Additionally, one could interpret Matt. 26:64 as the proclamation of the coming sovereignty of God in the sense of behavior guided by love for the enemy. Jesus confronts the high priest with his hope and with the action of God unto salvation.

Provide room for God's wrath:
Romans 12:14-21

If one compares the image of the teachings and practice of Jesus vis-à-vis unjust power as found in the Gospel of Matthew with the teaching of Paul in Romans 12–13, one notices complete agreement on the one hand but also differences. The main difference is that the power of those who are in positions of power is not described as an unjust power and that the question of military defense is not reflected upon. It is only through tax resistance that Paul concretely explains the question of resistance against the power of the state (Rom. 13:6f.), whereas Matthew discusses tax resistance as well as defense with military means (even though not as an actual possibility).[24] Another difference is the fact that Paul does not distinguish in such an explicit manner between behavior toward those within the church and behavior toward those outside the church and toward the persecutors, as is done in the Sermon on the Mount. Here, however, we want to concern ourselves only with the behavior toward the persecutor and toward the state. As in the Sermon on the Mount, blessings for the persecutor, refusal to seek vengeance, and prophetic judgment are related to each other and are connected also with the refusal to resist the state and thus be subordinate to the power of the state. Romans 12:14–21 has frequently been devalued vis-à-vis Matt. 5:38–48 because of an unwillingness to forgive Paul for referring to the retaliation of God. Above all, the demand to heap coals of fire upon the head of the enemy (Rom. 12:20) has demonstrated itself as a *crux interpretum*. In my opinion, the difficulty arises when one excludes the possibility of an inner participation on the part of the Christian by expecting the anger of God toward the enemies of the gospel, because it is considered inherent to being Christian never to feel hatred, anger, and fury. Yet the Sermon on the Mount as well as Paul in this case presents the behavior of Christians on the level of actions. The level of feelings and motivation has, in my opinion, only come into the foreground as a result of contemporary questioning, so that because of this pre-understanding our access to this whole tradition of loving one's enemy has become difficult. In my opinion, it should not be questioned that it is possible for human beings to feel anger that is just and justifiable in the eyes of Jesus. Acts of loving the enemy are not an expression of repressed hatred but entirely that of a productive anger, as should be amply clear from the above. In my opinion, therefore, it is necessary in the first place to read Rom. 12:14–21 on the level of practical conduct, of actions or behavior, and only then to deliberate which feelings thereby play a role in the process. The refusal to seek retribution is described by Paul as follows:

"Do not curse." (12:14)
"Repay no one evil for evil." (12:17)
"Never avenge yourselves." (12:19)
"Do not be overcome by evil." (12:21)

Indeed, cursing might often have been the only realistic recourse for retribution of evil for the oppressed. Luke 9:54 (cf. 2 Kings 1:10, 12) shows how this might have looked in reality. Because the Samaritan villages did not accept Jesus on the way to Jerusalem, James and John, the disciples, want to punish them and they ask Jesus for permission: "Do you want us to call fire from heaven to consume them?" They would have used words—that is, a curse (or in any event magical words)—to send lightning on the houses of the hostile Samaritan villages if Jesus would have permitted it. Paul declines this kind of behavior, as portrayed in Luke's Gospel, as well as other forms of a behavior that seek retribution, that attempt to respond to evil with evil, to violence with violence. This spiral of injustice must be broken. It is not up to the Christian to exercise retribution of injustice, but up to God:

"Leave it to the wrath of God." (12:19)
"Vengeance is mine." (12:19)
"If your enemy is hungry, feed him, . . . for by so doing you will heap burning coals upon his head." (12:20)

As in Matt. 5:39b, so in Rom. 12:19, *alla* indicates that God's just judgment takes the place of individual retribution. The refusal to seek vengeance does not mean that injustice has won out. Rather, the refusal to seek vengeance is indissolubly connected to the assurance that God's judgment is just. This expectation of God's judgment also finds expression on the level of behavior and action: An enemy who is hungry and thirsty must receive food and drink and thus be given over to the wrath of God. In Prov. 25:21f., cited here by Paul, the enemy is assumed to be subordinated in a military battle. This situation in the context of early Christianity could only have been intended to serve as an example for actions that would have helped the enemy, not harmed him. One action corresponding to this early Christian situation could have been that of sharing food and drink with poor neighbors of the community who were among those who hated and persecuted the Christians. According to Paul's opinion, an action of this kind makes visible the coming judgment of God. Because of the apparent contradiction of Rom. 12:20, the image of fiery coals on the head has been understood as a sign of repentance and as an instrument for the Christian to confront the enemy with Christ and thus, possibly, bring him to repentance.[25] Yet there is no mention of the enemy repenting here, only of the action of the Christian who heaps the fiery coals on the enemy's head. Matthew 10:15 and the frequent expectation of fire as the wrathful judgment of God[26] make it amply clear that compassion toward the enemy must be understood as a visible proclamation of the wrath of God. I shall attempt to elucidate the meaning of this example with the help of Acts 19:23–40. The Christians of Ephesus consider those who earn their wages from the silversmith Demetrius to be their enemies. With their cries of "great is Artemis of the Ephesians" they want to make it impossible for Paul and his fellow Christians to proclaim the gospel and they want to lynch the Christians, even though it does not go to that extent in this case. Paul would not have asked the Christians in Ephesus, according to Rom. 12:14–21, to have kind feelings toward these incited people but to realize that God is a righteous judge and that he is full of mercy. They would have had to give bread to those who were hungry to make it amply clear with this action that those who do wrong will not escape God's judgment. The proximity of announcing judgment and extending the love of God here simultaneously become one deed. But basically Rom. 12:20 is not different from Matt. 5:38–48.

This "gift" to the enemy, motivated by the love of God, is clarified by Paul additionally as follows:

"Bless those who persecute you." (12:14)
"If possible, so far as it depends upon you, live peaceably with all." (12:18)
"Overcome evil with good." (12:21)

Concrete actions of this kind of conduct are deeds of mercy toward enemies in need and—as shown above—loyal conduct toward the state, above all in payment of taxes. The blessing could be the proclamation of the gospel (see above with ref. to Matt. 5:44). Additionally, Paul makes it clear that Christians must accept the conflicts resulting from their message and their life and that they should not already set the stage with anticipation themselves. Paul does not assume that these conflicts are avoidable.

This behavioral ensemble consisting of refusal to pay retribution, expecting prophetic judgment, and loving the enemy has its reason or its goal in the justice of God or in the sovereignty of God. Everybody, including the enemy, is implicated in God's acts of compassion and anger. He is Lord of the world and will lead human history to its goal. Their faith in the risen Christ endows Christians, as Paul would say it, with the capability to live according to the will of God, to act as children (sons) of the God who permits the rain to fall on the just and on the unjust, as the Gospel of Matthew expresses it. This hope for the eschatological peace of God for the whole world corresponds to the conduct, in terms of New Testament Christianity, whose refusal to offer resistance vis-à-vis the power of the state is accompanied by a highly resistant attitude or behavior toward those who exercise wrong. The comprehensibility of this conduct probably depends on the particularity of one's understanding of God. The acrimony of uncurtailed prophetic judgment, which makes the actual situation very clear, should not be glossed over by this conduct.

"There Is No Authority Except from God"— "Give Unto Caesar What Is Caesar's"

Unjust power is also the servant of God

In Rom. 13:1–7, Paul does not talk about the essence of the state but about the actual power of the state and its relationship to God and its subjects. This power of the government is described as follows:

"the authorities which are in power," *exousiai hyperechousai*
"there is no authority which is not (ordained) of God," *ou gar estin exousia ei mē hypo theou*
"the authorities that exist have been instituted by God," *hai de ousai hypo theou tetagmenai eisin*
"those in power," *hoi archontes*
"power," *hē exousia*

In Rom. 13:6, the authority in power is explained with a concrete example of *exousia*: the tax collectors, who are "in God's service." Angels or demonic powers[27] are not intended, although it is not insignificant that the same word, *archontes* (1 Cor. 2:8), as well as *archē kai exousia* (see esp. 1 Cor. 15:24; Rom. 8:38f.), is used to refer both to demonic powers and to those in power.

Paul as well as all his contemporaries considered the world a place filled with powers, a place in which there was no neutral spot. The authority of those in power is one of the concrete dimensions of the experience of power, but the presence of demonic powers is even more powerful and a daily reality. Paul clearly understands the experience of death in the everyday world as a sign of the far-reaching domain of the power of death, of *hamartia*/sin and the demons. Thus, also, the encounter with the power of the government can become a sign of demonic power (and at this point the words acquire a double meaning): the execution of Jesus by those in a position of power permits one to recognize the handwriting of demonic powers[28] and that in the end Christ will destroy "every *archē* and every *dynamis*" (1 Cor. 15:24). Thus one hears the two words together, that along with the demonic powers every power that God does not exercise himself, including the power of those of this world, will also come to an end. The relationship of the power of "worldly" authorities to the demonic powers is also evidenced by the proximity of Rom. 8:35 and Rom. 8:38f. The dangers resulting from the worldly authority of people over other people reveal themselves as the inferno[29] which God's creatures have made of his creation. Käsemann's formulation of the Christian faith as a change in authority is, in my opinion, in complete agreement with Pauline thought. As a result of the endowment with the power unto life, Christ encounters the pneuma. The Spirit of God and of Christ is a power that makes the believers capable of action.

Thus, even though Rom. 13:1–7 refers to those in authority, to those actually in a ruling position, the word *exousia* or *archontes* already indicates that this *exousia* does not exist by itself in this world. With the three parallel sentences, which explain each other, Paul shows that he considers it important to clarify the fact that he is here referring to those actually in authority (*hai de ousai*) and that he is referring to these without exception (*ou gar estin . . . ei mē*), that is, to those who exercise their authority, to those who are on "top" and who have subjects under them (*hyperechousai*). Without exception the actual authorities have been ordained of God and are servants of God. In doing so, Paul does not differentiate between exercising just and unjust authority. In my opinion he is merging the two in his comprehensive statement, so that, in order to explain Rom. 13:1–7 in agreement with this, one must say that even unjust authority is God's servant for good and God's tool.

The radicality and singularity of Rom. 13:1–7 become clear if one compares this text with a philosophical explanation from antiquity of the power of the state, about different constitutional forms and their quality. A philosopher who is a loyal supporter of the government will naturally differentiate between good and bad constitutions. Dio Chrysostom, for example, lists three lawful constitutional forms (the rule of a single individual, an aristocracy, a democracy), three unlawful ones (a tyranny, an oligarchy, the rule of a group of people incited by demagogues), and the degeneration thereof.[30] In detail he then describes the authority of a good king, with the implicit goal, of course, to show his emperor—Trajan—to be such a good king (or as one who is on the right path). He considers the ruler to be loved of the gods, for they are the rulers of the ruler—but only of the good ruler, not, as Paul says, of everyone who holds authority for the state. It is evident, in my opinion, that in Rom. 13:1–7 Paul sees unjust authority as a servant of God also.[31] After all, he is a citizen of a nation that had had numerous bad experiences with rulers in positions of authority in the century preceding the Letter to the Romans. Paul probably experienced the conflict with Gaius/Caligula (41 c.e.) in some form or other. The book of Daniel (ch. 7) does not explicitly say that the four animals received their authority from God, but from the context it is clear (pursuant to 2:21—as well as in the whole book of Daniel) that God ordains the kingdoms of the world and that, according to his plans, he terminates and limits them. The desecration of the temple by Antiochus IV Epiphanes (167–164 b.c.e.; Dan. 8:11) is also God's act: "and great power was given unto him"—by God (8:12).[32] Daniel, indeed, does not say explicitly, as does Paul, that *every* authority is ordained of God, but this idea is consistent with the representation of history in which all of history is based on God's plan. There has been objection to connecting the book of Daniel with Rom. 13:1 on the basis that the direction of the book of Daniel differs from that of the Pauline text. "They [Dan. 2:21 and similar texts] want to warn those rulers who are not aware of the divine origin of their authority and, therefore, behave irresponsibly."[33] Yet, in spite of their differing intent, the same idea of God and a comparable religiopolitical context lie at the base of both texts.

The radicality of Rom. 13:1 becomes additionally clear when we consider that Paul himself has had the experience of being punished unjustly, in his opinion, by the Roman authorities and that he has to fear that other Christians and he himself will have to continue to live with this danger. Attempts to explain Rom. 13:1 by saying that this Pauline statement is a consequence of the brief good years at the beginning of the rule of Nero, or to generally try to point out that at the time of the Letter to the Romans there was still no persecution of Christians,[34] avoid the acrimony of the Pauline conception; this is not all it says, that the government *precisely of that time* was ordained of God.

Romans 13:1 is not a theoretical statement about the "essence" of the "state" but a theological statement about *the acts of God* in respect to an actual given relationship to political power or violence. One's idea of God will determine one's understanding. God has ordained those actually in positions of power, and for this reason one has to be subordinate to them. In doing so, neither the injustice of those in positions of power is legitimized nor their political rule idealized. It is a matter of the relationship between the Christian and his contemporary political rulership, even if it is unjust. The faithful must not be afraid of it. Walking uprightly as one who recognizes God as the true Lord of history, the faithful confidently go about *their own* affairs. That obedience to Caesar is obedience to an unjust rulership, according to Mark 12:17a pars., results from the respective Gospel context (see above, perhaps in comparison with Mark 10:42–45 pars.).

The power of those in authority will soon end

According to apocalyptic thought and its idea of God, the exercising of power of those actually in authority is a limited (frequently a hypertrophic, cynical, short-termed) occurrence. God has ordained the authorities and he deposes them again. He brings history to a good ending: with his sovereignty there will be no hurt by anything anymore, nor to anything. Paul and the Gospels share this apocalyptic thinking. Neither war, famine, persecution of Christians, the crucifixion of Christ, the stubbornness of the children of Israel—none of these dreadful incidents comes about contrary to the will of God, but they are his will, already predicted in the Bible and predicted through Jesus: they have to be (*dei*); see Mark 13 pars. or the passion predictions. Classifying this terror as part of the history of God's acts does not legitimize misery and does not relegate the passive sufferer to a future filled with terror. This kind of thinking becomes clear only when the viewpoint of the observer, his presence and his interpretation, is understood.[35] The observer has experienced war, but it is clear to him that God will hear his anguished question about the outcome. "When, O God, will you grant us the life you have promised?"—is the basic question as it relates to apocalyptic thinking; and from this question proceeds the response: "You can see that, which happens at this point, was already foretold; you can comfort yourself in the fact that it is in God's effective hands. And God desires life and salvation for all people (or also: for the nation—in most Jewish apocalypses)."

The fact that Paul mentions that the day is at hand in Rom. 13:11f. is the clear and necessary continuation of the idea from 13:1ff. and 13:8ff. I completely fail to understand how the Christian and/or eschatological elements could have been missed in Rom. 13:1–7, or how this has been considered an incorrect association.

Even if one (inappropriately) isolates Rom. 13:1–7 from the context, this is impossible. Wherever Paul uses the word "God,"[36] it is immediately clear to him and his fellow Christians that this is the God who broke the power of sin through Christ's resurrection, that this is the God who desires life for his creation, who will quickly bring all this spooky terror to an end: "The night is far gone, the day is at hand" (Rom. 13:12).

Paul demands an unconditional subordination to authorities in power, since resistance to Satan and resistance to the rulership are not identical for him

According to Paul, all people (*pasa psychē*), thus including Christians, shall be subordinate to (*hypotassesthai*) the rulership; they shall not resist it (not *antitassesthai* and/or *anthistanai*) in any way; they shall "do good" (to *agathon poiein*; cf. *agathon ergon*); they shall pay all their tributes (*phoros* and *telos*) and honor Caesar (*timē*). They shall not fear Caesar, for only the evildoer need fear those in authority (Rom. 13:3). Even though the command "respect to whom respect is due" in v. 7 (after v. 3) would have demanded the respect/fear of the Lord more unequivocally for the ancient hearer or reader than for the modern interpreter,[37] this simply suggests the limits of loyalty. A basic problem in dealing with Rom. 13:1–7 is the fact that in these verses themselves Paul does not specify limits to this command for loyalty. Again and again he emphasizes the duties toward those in authority even to the point that he indicates that the (moral) demands of the state are in agreement with conscience (v. 5), that is, they agree with the Christian idea of the will of God (12:2 and 13:8–10). It is possible to enumerate the contents of that which pertains to doing what is right in Romans 12f. from the history of early Christianity: Christians commit neither adultery, nor theft, nor homicide (see Rom. 13:9), and so forth (cf. Letter of Pliny 10.96).

Why does Paul demand unrestricted loyalty and why does he forbid basic resistance toward those in authority? In Rom. 12:2 he has already specified a boundary which, practiced by Christians—including his own practices—will lead to conflicts with those in authority: "Do not be conformed to this world." Thus it must not be questioned that Paul would have submitted to a *religious* test of loyalty, that is, the demands of Rom. 13:1–7 have a *practical* limit for him. Later on, Christians of the first and second centuries more clearly formulated the limits along with a statement of loyalty[38] than did Paul: for example, "Fear God. Honor the emperor" (1 Peter

2:17); honor (is to be rendered to authorities and powers) according to merit, if that does not hurt us, that is, if that does not hurt us in God's judgment (Polycarp of Smyrna, n. 7 above). The martyrs of Scilli (n. 6 above) pronounce the boundary very distinctly: "I recognize no rulership of this world" (*imperium huius seculi*). Origen limits Rom. 13:1–7, among other citations, by Acts 5:29.[39] The fact that Paul does not specifically name the limit can only mean that it was self-evident to him, precisely because Rom. 13:1–7 was not an isolated statement for him, as well as the fact that he was able to fulfill and demand the loyalty as described in Rom. 13:1–7 without a problem. Refusal to pay taxes, resistance against those in authority, and evil deeds (in the sense mentioned above) are for him not points of conflict with the state. Without any problem he can fulfill the command of Rom. 13:2 not to resist (*Widerstandsverbot*) as well as the command of Rom. 12:2 to resist (*Widerstandsgebot*). To clarify the concept, I have used the word "resistance" in both cases, which Paul, in fact, does not use, although post-Pauline texts do: resistance against Satan is demanded, which, in content, coincides with Rom. 12:2, and the same word (*anthistēmi*) is used here that Paul uses to forbid resistance against the state. The very close proximity of the command not to offer resistance (Rom. 12:2) and the command to offer resistance (Rom. 13:2) make it clear that this forbidden resistance against those in authority includes only specific actions, with which the Christian can comply without any problem. The word "resist" in Rom. 13:2 must have a very concrete meaning, not a general meaning (including all thinkable reasons for and forms of resistance). Paul considers it necessary not to refuse to pay taxes, not to conduct a revolution in a military fashion, not to break the laws of the state, which he considers moral (thus one can concretize from the history of the early church, especially according to Matt. 26:47–53). Resistance against Satan, which embraced the total formation of Christian life, was not categorized by Paul as resistance against one in a position of authority, even though the Roman authorities felt that the Christian life was a disturbance of their political order (consider the crucifixion of Jesus).

The real reason for conflicts between Christians and society and/or between Christians and the governmental authority was not that Christians might have desired conflict with those in power or that they might even have desired conflict with the Roman gods. These conflicts were conflicts *resulting* from the central reason for the tension between the Christian community and society and/or the state. The role of objectors to loyalty and rebel rousers was forced upon them. The root of the problem was their resistance against Satan and sin as the true rulers of this world, the resistance that had shaped Christian practice through and through.

"Give Unto God What Is God's": Resisting Satan

The command to resist

The command to resist was widespread in early Christian tradition, of which Rom. 12:2 (*mē syschēmatizesthe . . .*) is a part: Eph. 6:10–13:

> Finally, be strong in the Lord and in the strength of his power. Put on the whole armor of God, so that you may be able to stand against the wiles of the devil. For our struggle is not against enemies of blood and flesh, but against the rulers, against the authorities, against the cosmic powers of this present darkness, against the spiritual forces of evil in the heavenly places. Therefore take up the whole armor of God, so that you may be able to withstand on that evil day, and having done everything, to stand firm.

[Schottroff uses a German translation by H. Schlier: we have simply used the NRSV—Trans. and Ed.] The present as well as the near future is understood as the time of the struggle of the end times, of the final affliction of the "evil days":

> The enemy is not this one or everyone, neither is it I myself, or flesh and blood. In this battle, of course, flesh and blood can be used as a pretense, cf. 2:3. But the conflict is more profound. This is a conflict with untold tirelessly attacking opponents which are elusive to the grasp, which have no real name, only a collective name; from the very beginning also they are superior to the human being and, as a matter of fact, because of their superior position, through their position of existence "in the heavens," superior also because of the nontransparency of their position."[40]

I have used the representation of the mythology of Eph. 6:10–13 by H. Schlier at this point, because it elucidates the existential relationship between the mythology of Satan and the demons of the text. For Paul, too, the summons "Do not be conformed to this world" (Rom. 12:2) is a summons to a final comprehensive battle. "This age" of Rom. 12:2 is likewise an apocalyptic idea, which, for Paul, contains a mythology and an existential meaning comparable to the content of Eph. 6:10–13.[41] The Christians of New Testament times understood their whole existence, their bodies, their hearts, their future, as an existence of resistance in a terrible struggle against a Hydra, against "the god of this world (age)" (2 Cor. 4:4). For them, the power of sin cannot be expressed by summing up its concrete phenomena; its collective and anonymous power demands a myth-ological explanation.[42] The word "resistance" (*anthistēnai*) is em-ployed with emphasis in this connection; see in addition to Eph. 6:10–13: 1 Peter 5:9; James 4:7f.; *Barn.* 4:9; *Herm. Man.* 12:5. In content, the temptation stories of the Gospels must also be men-tioned in this connection.

Wherever the word "resistance" is used—it may refer to very different situations—the idea of a confrontation between two oppos-ing powers is addressed. Whoever offers resistance to those in au-thority or in power (Rom. 13:2) confronts them with a power, and whoever offers resistance to Satan confronts him with the *dynamis* of God, with which believers are endowed. All conflict situations are situations in which powers oppose one another. During an ex-amination by an authority the opponents of Christians try to defeat the Christians, to confront with another power the Christians' power, which comes from the Holy Spirit. But Christians are con-vinced: no one can withstand the power of the Spirit of God (Luke 21:15; Acts 6:10; cf. also with the comparable situations of Acts 18:6 with *antitassō*: Acts 13:8, 1 Tim. 3:8ff.; 4:15). With this com-manded and forbidden resistance, there is always in both the idea that *the strongest one will win*, James 5:6: The wealthy have con-demned and murdered the just (poor) unjustly. The poor one cannot defend himself (*ouk antitassetai hymin*). In connection with Rom. 13:2, Sir. 4:27 (Hebrew text) is frequently cited as parallel in con-tent (in my opinion unjustly): "Do not resist those in authority," which, according to the context, is intended as a wise rule for the small man. The small man always gets the short end of the deal.[43]

In the struggle against Satan the believer will be able to resist, to stand, because God, whose power is greater than that of all other powers, stands at his side. An extended metaphor from the military realm is used for resisting Satan, as in Eph. 6:10, and also in Paul (see Rom. 13:12).[44] This *"militarized" language* does not mean that one now participates in the war of people against people, albeit with different means; rather, it means that Christian resistance comes from an endowment with power: with the Spirit of God, which is *dynamis,* with the armor of God, where the swift feet of the mes-senger of peace take the place of the soldiers' boots (Eph. 6:15). The idea is not to express militarization but opposition. The resist-ance of Christians against Satan is not the resistance of the power-less. God's power is on their side. The trial of Christians is only one example in which the act of resisting Satan is evident (this is especially clear in 1 Peter 5:9). All of everyday life is formed by this resistance; when Paul wants to express this inclusive aspect of faith existence as resistance he says *sōma*; present your bodies to God (Rom. 12:1) or "yield yourselves to God as [those] who have been brought from death to life" (Rom. 6:13).

Unfortunately there is no exegetical tradition that treats the practice of early Christianity's resistance, as denoted with this command to resist. In order to have a methodologically clear basis here I shall try to avoid presenting an illustration or an idea I have composed myself of randomly chosen individual aspects; rather, I shall seek to illustrate the practice of resistance in everyday life that proceeds from the texts that have been treated so far, from Mark 12:17 in the context of the Gospels and Romans 12–13.

The practice of resistance: *"Give unto God what is God's"*

The refusal to adapt to this age (world) is the "service of God in the everyday life of this world,"[45] according to Rom. 12:1–2. The service of God is resistance against Satan. In the following section the practice of resistance will be illustrated and commented on; we will use the Markan context of Mark 12:17b, with the Markan command of service to God, and the Pauline context of Rom. 12:1–2 (and 13:1–7) in the paraenesis of Romans 12–13. (One could also select other larger contexts, for example, the antitheses of the Sermon on the Mount, describing the inclusive character of life lived according to God's will as interpreted by Jesus.)

Apodote . . . kai ta theou theō; give to God what belongs to God (Mark 12:17) characterizes the inclusive claim of God on the whole person and the whole world, which is not limited by anything. The universal eschatological perspective of the lordship of God is especially clear in Mark 4:32 pars. and Mark 13:27 par. Mark 12:28–34, for example, shows that the whole person is meant. According to the meaning of the Gospels, there is not one area subordinate to the lordship of Caesar and another subordinate to the lordship of God. Rather, it is the will of God that loyalty is offered to Caesar. The first half of Mark 12:17 pars. is *just one* (tiny) aspect of the second half: the inclusive claim of God. Mark 12:17b says nothing that is different from Rom. 12:1–2.

What does this "service of God in the everyday life of the world," which is demanded here, look like? First of all, let us begin with the account itself, with the behavior of Jesus in the described situation.

He responds neither tactically nor ironically[46] to a political catch question, but courageously. The Pharisees and the Herodians have clearly understood how he behaves: you do not pay any attention to the position of a person (Mark 12:14), that is, you do not retreat when confronted with power. In the context of the Gospel of Mark this courage is accompanied by great fear. For both Jesus as well as Christians, in the context of the Gospels, it clearly states how much fear people will have to endure, who live according to the will of God (see Mark 15:34 and 14:50). The courageous response of Jesus in the situation of the discussion about the tax coin has as its background the passion announcements of his suffering (8:31; 9:31; 10:32–34). In the sense of the text it is precisely his response that makes him vulnerable. In the eyes of Pilate, however, his loyalty is not adequate to prevent his execution. In Mark 12:17 Jesus speaks as the Son of God, as the just one, who is on his way to the cross (see in this connection pp. 229–230 above). Jesus' way to the cross lies in the tradition of a fundamental Jewish act of resistance against an unjust rulership: it is *the martyrdom of the just one,* the visible public suffering and death of innocent ones because of injustice. The readiness for martyrdom in early Christianity should not be understood as an expression of a desire to suffer in an attempt to flee this world but rather as an expression of resistance against Satan, which turns into resistance against unjust practice of authority in a conflict situation. Under the political situation of the Roman Empire one's own body, one's own existence, was simply the only way to become "political." The fact that Paul sees in this tradition of martyrdom the way for himself and for his fellow Christians proceeds from the illustration, already given above, of the life context of Rom. 13:1–7. Courage and fear are discussed in Rom. 13:4. Those who have not committed any evil deeds (see above) need not fear the police sword of the Roman authorities; they can thus stand fearlessly before the rulers when they, for example, are tried or beaten. In another place (2 Cor. 1:3–11) Paul has said that this fearlessness results from fear that has been overcome and that this courage requires the support of the community.

According to Mark 12:17b and Rom. 12:1–2, this service of God (or otherwise: resistance against Satan), of which the consequence can be martyrdom, embraces all areas of everyday life, according to Paul as well as according to Mark.

Life in the community (church) is the first great change in everyday life that comes about through faith. The primary social bond is no longer the family but that of the brothers and sisters who live according to the will of God (Mark 3:31–35). Even though Christians could continue in their family relationships—for example, married couples or whole "households" became Christians—the *ekklēsia*, the *sōma Christou*, the body of Christ was for them their primary social relationship, to which the rights of family ties took second place. It led to divorces, to conflicts between parents and children, between slaves and their Christian or non-Christian owners. The community considered these conflicts their own concerns. The Letter to Philemon is a documentation of such a conflict resolution, in which case it was significant that the whole community, besides Paul, was involved (Philemon; cf. Col. 3:22ff.). Within the communities, which generally were probably not large, the Christians lived in a life community that included all of everyday life, and this community was also responsible for the financial care of the individual matters of the community. In this respect also, the communities of Christ were connected to the Jewish traditions, namely, the inclusive synagogal *caring for the poor* (see Rom. 12:8c). In addition to this, *sharing* was practiced, and along with this, economic loss of possessions was accepted. The sale of fields in Jerusalem (Acts 2:45; 4:36f; 5:1) for the benefit of the community meant an additional step in the direction of impoverishment—just as it did for a family that sells its fields in order to be able to buy food. Romans 12 addresses the economic unity of the community, especially in 12:13 and 12:8: "Where the saints are in need, share with them" (based on Wilcken's German translation); "Those who give [to the community] should do so without setting conditions."

For a Markan comparison, see Mark 10:29f., where it also becomes clear that a comprehensive economic sharing in the community is meant. The economic tie within the community also played a role between communities, for example, through hospitality but also through economic support of the poor in Jerusalem by communities in other provinces that were less poor. The collection in Jerusalem had *isotēs*/equality (2 Cor. 8:14) as its goal, that is, it was intended to amount to more than alms. For the practice of resistance it was important for the inner-communal organization to get along without a hierarchy, although in this matter there were many inner-communal conflicts. Different functions were not intended to establish relationships of rulership. We are members (in the body of Christ) in the relationship with one another (Rom. 12:5; cf. 1 Cor. 12:3ff.; Mark 10:42–45 pars.). The emotional unity of the members of the community plays an important role in Romans 12 (e.g., *agapē*, *philadelphia*, 12:9f.) as well as the intensity of the relation-

ships (*philostorgoi,* 12:10: "loving fervently/brotherly affection")
and submission to a life of faith (e.g., "*Hate* what is evil, *hold* fast
to what is good" [12:9]).

The difference between life within the community and societal re-
ality is, however, the focal point that results in the practice of
resistance, and from this also proceed the conflicts with the non-
Christian population and the state authorities. In the cities, even the
purchasing of meat at the market was a problem of conscience, since
at that time all meat was slaughtered in a cultic manner. Paul tries
to minimize this problem (1 Cor. 10:25), but as the letter of Pliny to
Trajan shows, half the province had been changed because of the
temple and meat boycott of the rapidly spreading Christian communities. The conflict with the silversmith of Ephesus, who sees his
production of devotional artifacts dedicated to Artemis endangered,
is comparable to this (Acts 19:23ff.). The difference between societal reality and the very different form of the *vita christiana* is expressed especially clearly in the *virtue and vice catalogs.* In spite of
their traditionalism, they are formulated in topical terms; that is, it
is valuable to analyze them for the inquiry at hand: "not in reveling
and drunkenness, not in debauchery and licentiousness, not in quar-
reling and jealousy" (Rom. 13:13). This is the prescribed behavior
for the faithful.

This is not the voice of worn-out sermonizing on morality but the
difference between the life of the Christian and that of society, a
difference that carried a high cost for the Christians, because the
feasts that were declined had an important function in societal life.
Festivals and celebrations, on the whole, played a dominant role in
the public life of society:

> They [the Caesars] filled free time and arranged events in both the
> religious and secular realms: in the forum, in the theater, in the sta-
> dium, in the amphitheater and in the form of contests on the aquatic
> course. With ever new entertainment they kept the population in sus-
> pense. Even when their coffers shrank, they continued to think up
> ever new forms of entertainment. Never in history has any nation
> celebrated so many festivals.

Thus writes J. Carcopino[47] about imperial Rome. Presumably already at the time of Paul, Christians did not frequent these festivities
and, by not doing so, they disturbed a political instrument of the
imperial rulership. Likewise the refusal to participate in dueling
competitions was an act of resistance that bore consequences (Rom.
13:13; cf. the catalog of vices in Rom. 1:29–31, which describes
the destruction of relationships in society in an impressive manner).

In Mark, see the catalog of vices (Mark 7:21f.[48]) that especially emphasizes the importance of relating to one another without oppressing some or giving excessive advantages to others. Many aspects of the acts of resistance of the early Christians have become strange because of societal changes and the change of the role of the cultic in everyday life (e.g., refraining from meat offered to idols or the condemning of homosexuality), yet the consistency of their resistance is still clear. We will only mention here also the distancing of the Christians from striving for economic gain (*pleonexia*), as well as the change in the role of women, the importance of sexual asceticism, and the importance of the spiritual life of the community (prophesying, prayer, speaking in tongues, etc.). For soldiers at this time in early Christianity, being a Christian might not have been the basic reason for refusing to be a soldier but rather the conflict because of the prohibitions not to participate in killing, nor in festivals and other cultic customs.

There are two points of orientation that give rise to this constellation of daily life practices that must be emphasized here: the eschatological orientation and the orientation that is determined by the needs and the reality of those individuals who occupy the bottom rung of society: "Do not be haughty, but associate with the lowly" (Rom. 12:16).

In line with this is the fact that the word *diakonia*, which describes the role in society of one who is at the lowest level of a hierarchy[49] and has to do the lowliest jobs, was also used by early Christians to describe their own identity in their relationship to other people (Rom. 12:7; cf. esp. Mark 10:42–45 pars.). Whether or not *tapeinois* in Rom. 12:16 is interpreted as neuter or masculine, the resultant meaning is that everyone in the community has to share in the existence of the lowliest (whether he performs the lowliest work or exercises practical solidarity with the lowly). This orientation with regard to the poor, the sick, and the children as the primary representatives of the people of God is clear in the writings of Paul (not only in the Gospels); see 1 Cor. 1:28. If one considers that Roman society oriented itself in all of its politics and economy to the interests of the wealthy (*plousioi*), the explosive power of the Christian faith becomes clear. The more the communities spread, the more the state was affected. Pliny the Younger, the governor, understands the Christians to be a radical disturbance in Roman society.[50] The spreading of faith in Jesus Christ was not the result of an organizational goal but the result of God's claim on the whole world, on all people. Christians understood the brutality of social reality to be the consequence of the dominion of sin and death (or the dominion of Satan), as the consequence of God's wrath. They offered resistance against the rulership of Satan and sin, not by fighting against the epiphenomena of the wrath of God (the respective authorities in power), but rather by a life controlled by the love of God, which enables one to love: they tried to overcome evil with good in the knowledge of the nearness of God. Their goal was resistance against Satan, the ruler of this world. Inasmuch as the secular rulers felt that this struggle was a political disturbance of their rulership, this resistance against Satan frequently enough took on a form, in spite of intended loyalty, that the state considered resistance against the authority of the state.

Summary

In New Testament times Christians jointly shaped their life as a service to God in the everyday world, as resistance against Satan. They treated money, women and children, and relationships with authority differently than did society around them. This behavior was due to the unrestricted claim of God on the whole person and on the whole world, in other words, because of their idea of God and because of eschatology. The consequence of this way of life, which resisted the realities of society, were conflicts with the population, which then usually ended up as conflicts with the authorities, including Roman authorities. Ever since Jesus' journey to Jerusalem, there have been persecutions of Christians (even though the word "Christian" is an anachronism for those early times).

The relationship of the Christians to the actual authorities in power is determined by an unrestricted loyalty, which, however, in case of conflict, was inadequate for the Roman authorities. If, then, the authorities demanded an additional extended declaration of loyalty and if they demanded giving up resistance against Satan, then the confrontation with the authorities turned into the moment of the actual test of this resistance, the moment of persecution for the sake of Jesus and the gospel. It is considered highly self-evident that the authorities in power are unjust and that they oppress the people. But unjust rulership is also God's servant. Its power, however, is borrowed and limited, and it will end before long.

In their confrontation with unjust power, Christians practiced a peculiar behavior: refusal to pay retribution, prophetic announcements of God's judgment against the enemy, and loving the enemy. Neither their declaration of loyalty vis-à-vis the state nor loving the enemy should be understood as the tactic of a minority[51] interested in spreading itself. Taking the unrestricted claims of God on the whole person and on the whole world does not lead to tactic but rather to resistance in everyday life on earth that is oriented toward greed and power. The goal of this resistance is the royal sovereignty of God.

Notes

1. Johannes Friedrich, Wolfgang Pöhlmann, and Peter Stuhlmacher, "Zur historischen Situation und Intention von Röm 13, 1–7," *ZTK* 73 (1976): 131–166, ref. to p. 161. It is stated somewhat differently by Ulrich Wilckens, *Der Brief an die Römer* (EKK; Zurich: Benziger Verlag, 1982), 3:31: ". . . Attitude Toward the Environment (12:14–21). Since this is aimed at behavior toward the enemies, ending up with a final summarizing admonition in 12:21, the thought then turns toward the aspect of the protection of that which is good, and in this connection also toward the authority of the state."

2. See in addition the material on the role of Rom. 13:1–7 in connection with the trials against Christ, n. 8 below.

3. Translation by J. Leitl and A. DiPauli, in *Frühchristliche Apologeten und Märtyrerakten,* vol. 2; *Bibliothek der Kirchenväter* (Munich: J. Kösel, 1913), 14:90.

4. Especially Martin Dibelius, *From Tradition to Gospel* (trans. B. Woolf; New York: Charles Scribner's Sons, n.d.), 238f., with whom many agree; see, e.g., Hans Conzelmann and A. Lindemann, *Interpreting the New Testament: An Introduction to the Principles and Methods of New Testament Exegesis* (trans. S. Schatzmann; Peabody, Maine: Hendrickson Publishers, 1988), 102: "In the exegesis of such epistolary material attention must also be paid to the fact that the individual verses must be interpreted separately and each one for itself." In my opinion this is an inappropriate guideline.

5. As Ernst Käsemann says, *Commentary on Romans* (trans. G. W. Bromiley; Grand Rapids: Wm. B. Eerdmans Publishing Co., 1980), 352.

6. Acta Scilitanorum 2 and 9; German trans.: A. Wlosok, *Rom und die Christen* (Stuttgart: Ernst Klett Verlag, 1970), 43f.; and G. Rauschen, in *Frühchristliche Apologeten und Märtyrerakten,* vol. 2; *Bibliothek der Kirchenväter,* 14:29–31 (= 317–319).

7. For the dating of Polycarp's death, see K. Bihlmeyer and W. Schneemelcher, *Die Apostolischen Väter I* (2nd ed.; Tübingen: J. C. B. Mohr [Paul Siebeck], 1956), xlii. This is the German translation of *Bibliothek der Kirchenväter,* 14:297–308, ref. to 302.

8. Thus Schelkle appropriately states in his work, K. H. Schelkle, "Staat und Kirche in der patristischen Auslegung von Röm 13, 1–7," *ZNW* 44 (1952/1953): 223–226, ref. to 227. The opposite viewpoint is maintained by W. Bauer, "Jedermann sei untertan der Obrigkeit," in *Aufsätze und kleine Schriften* (ed. G. Strecker; Tübingen: J. C. B. Mohr [Paul Sie-

beck], 1967), 263–284, ref. to 266: "It is, therefore, little wonder that the numerous martyr stories and legends almost totally bypass Rom 13." His explicitly incorrect thesis depends on his basic understanding of Rom. 13:1–7: he can only imagine that the martyr situations and Rom. 13:1–7 are essentially incompatible. He has limited himself, therefore, to a very narrow selection of material. In addition to the material collected by Schelkle, see also K. Aland, "Das Verhältnis von Kirche und Staat in der Frühzeit," *ANRW*, II.23.1 (Berlin: Walter de Gruyter, 1979), 60–246, ref. to 227–229, and in the same volume, W. Schäfke, "Frühchristlicher Widerstand," 460–723, ref. to 557f.

9. Sec. 37; trans. G. Rauschen, in *Bibliothek der Kirchenväter*, 14:319–328, ref. to 325f.

10. 2 Cor. 11:25, *errabdisthēn* = *verberatio*, a form of flogging probably carried out by "city magistrates"; see *rhabdizō* in BAGD, 733. For a discussion of this, see Theodor Mommsen, "Die Rechtsverhältnisse des Apostels Paulus," *ZNW* 2 (1901): 89 n. 1; Hans Windisch, *Der zweite Korintherbrief* (new printing of 1924 ed.; MeyerK 6; Göttingen: Vandenhoeck & Ruprecht, 1970) on text; see also Acts 16:22f.

11. Otto Michel, *Der Brief an die Römer* (MeyerK 4; 12th ed.; Göttingen: Vandenhoeck & Ruprecht, 1963), 317: "The concrete point of the Pauline admonition points to a historical occasion which might have as its basis the Jewish disturbances or a pneumatic arrogance." Also, "Paul is obviously involved in a completely one-sided struggle against the danger of enthusiasm" (Käsemann, *Romans*, 357).

12. And in the year 58 C.E. it was lightened by Nero, according to Tacitus, *Annals* 13.50f.; likewise Friedrich, Pöhlmann, and Stuhlmacher, "Zur historischen Situation," 157f.

13. See Dibelius, *From Tradition to Gospel*.

14. Concerning Roman religious policies toward the Jews and their relationship to Christian prayers for the emperor, see Emil Schürer, *A History of the Jewish People in the Age of Jesus Christ* (3 vols.; trans. J. Macpherson; Edinburgh: T. & T. Clark, 1973), 2:311–313; E. Mary Smallwood, *The Jews Under Roman Rule from Pompey to Diocletian* (Leiden: E. J. Brill, 1976), 148; and Martin Dibelius (Hans Conzelmann), *The Pastoral Epistles* (Hermeneia; trans. F. Buttolph and A. Yarbro, ed. H. Koester; Philadelphia: Fortress Press, 1972), excursus on 1 Tim. 2:2, 37–38.

15. The author comes to this conclusion in M. Stern, "The Province of Judaea," in *The Jewish People in the First Century* (Philadelphia: Fortress Press, 1974), 1:356 based on Philo, *Legatio* 203; Josephus, *Ant.* 18.261; *J.W.* 2.185; and Tacitus, *Hist.* 5.9.2.

16. Pliny the Younger, 10.96; Wlosok (*Rom und die Christen*, 30) does not recognize the continuity of this required practice of a loyalty test (already pre-Roman, see Daniel) for the Jews.

17. Tertullian, *Apologeticum* 21.1.

18. Thus Rudolf Bultmann, "Das Verhältnis der urchristlichen Christusbotschaft zum historischen Jesus," in *Exegetica: Aufsätze zur Erforschung*

des Neuen Testaments (Tübingen: J. C. B. Mohr [Paul Siebeck], 1967), 453.

19. In my opinion the so-called "antitheses" of the Sermon on the Mount are interpretations of the word of God in the Torah for the present, not antitheses, unrealistic ideals, or radicalizations.

20. Concerning *aggareuein,* see Mark 15:21 and the information in BAGD 6; for an interpretation of Matt. 5:39–41, see also Luise Schottroff, *Der Sieg des Lebens: Biblische Traditionen einer Friedenspraxis* (Munich: Chr. Kaiser Verlag, 1982), 38–41.

21. H. Braun, *Jesus: Der Mann aus Nazareth und seine Zeit* (Stuttgart: Kreuz Verlag, 1969), 124f. For an interpretation of the command to love the enemy, see also Luise Schottroff, "Nonviolence and the Love of One's Enemies," in Luise Schottroff, Reginald H. Fuller, Christoph Burchard, and M. Jack Suggs, *Essays on the Love Commandment* (Philadelphia: Fortress Press, 1978), 9–39; and Gerd Theissen, "Gewaltverzicht und Feindesliebe," in idem, ed., *Studien zur Soziologie des Urchristentums* (WUNT 19; Tübingen: J. C. B. Mohr [Paul Siebeck], 1979), 160–97. See also Klassen, n. 25 below.

22. See also Luise Schottroff and Wolfgang Stegemann, *Jesus and the Hope of the Poor* (trans. Matthew J. O'Connell; Maryknoll, N.Y.: Orbis Books, 1986), 49–51.

23. See also Luise Schottroff, "Das geschundene Volk und die Arbeit in der Ernte Gottes," in *Mitarbeiter der Schöpfung* (ed. L. and W. Schottroff; Studien zu Bibel and Arbeitswelt; Munich: Chr. Kaiser, 1983).

24. John 18:36 indicates that earlier realizable possibilities of defense were declined: that Jesus would have commanded his servants to prevent his being captured.

25. This is the thesis of William Klassen, "Coals of Fire: Sign of Repentance or Revenge?" *NTS* 9 (1963): 337–350, ref. to 349. In my opinion, this thesis in this basic essay on loving one's enemy has been stated as the result of an inappropriate negative evaluation of prophetic announcement of God's judgment. For rather it is actions dominated by prophetic announcement of God's judgment that would lead to repentance. The interpretation of fiery coals on the head as a sign of repentance (in agreement with S. Morenz, *TLZ* 78 [1953]: 187–192) cannot be maintained. Concerning the material for the counterthesis, see n. 26.

26. With regard to this, see especially Krister Stendahl, "Hate, Non-Retaliation and Love. IQS x, 17–20 and Romans 12:19–21," *HTR* 55 (1962): 343–355. Stendahl, in my opinion, however, interprets Rom. 12:21 and Matt. 5:44 in an inappropriate negative sense and disregards Rom. 12:14; F. Lang, *"pyr,"* *TDNT,* 6:945. The difficulty of interpreting the fiery coals as God's judgment from the standpoint of the material is clearly expressed, e.g., by C. E. B. Cranfield, *A Critical and Exegetical Commentary on the Epistle to the Romans* (2 vols.; 6th ed.; Edinburgh: T. & T. Clark, 1975–1979), 2:649; or Wilckens (*Römer,* 3:26): it is considered impossible that announcement of judgment is supposed to have a positive meaning for the enemy.

27. The important essay by G. Dehn ("Engel und Obrigkeit: Ein Beitrag zum Verständnis von Römer 13, 1–7," in *Theologische Aufsätze: Karl Barth zum 50 Geburtstag* [Munich: Chr. Kaiser Verlag, 1936], 90–109), which is still basic for an understanding of Rom. 13:1–7, is frequently disregarded much too easily because of its thesis that in Rom. 13:1 "divine and secular powers are considered to be connected" (p. 105), "that God's angelic authorities stand behind the government" (p. 105). In contrast, one has to argue that Paul is likely thinking only of those in worldly positions of power at this point and not also of angels standing behind them. But that still is no justification for not considering Dehn's insight. He considers the connection between Rom. 13:1–7 and apocalyptic thinking and holds that therefore Rom. 13:1–7 must receive serious *theological* consideration (p. 100): "The overwhelming positiveness of Paul . . . is, thus, comprehensible," if the government, after all, is *apo theou* (p. 105). It is not Satan who rules this world, but God (p. 106). "In a world carried by the power of the angels of God, the community can exist without hatred and fear." But the government can become demonic. "The same government which is basically of God, may, in concreto, become the enemy of God and his community" (p. 108). For categorization of Dehn's essay from the aspect of research and church history, see Ernst Käsemann, "Römer 13, 1–7 in unserer Generation," *ZTK* 56 (1959): 316–376, ref. on 351–361 (cf. also Käsemann, *Romans,* 352–354), who, in my opinion, underestimates the importance of the apocalyptic explanation of Dehn [Dehn is not mentioned by Käsemann in the English translation—Ed.]; for additional information concerning the history of research, see V. Riekkinen, *Römer 13: Aufzeichnung und Weiterführung der exegetischen Diskussion* (Helsinki: Suomalainen Tiedeakatemia, 1980), 135ff.

A. Strobel ("Zum Verständnis von Rm 13," *ZNW* 47 [1956]: 67–93) has clearly shown "that Rm 13:1–7 is filled with concepts and ideas which demonstrate that this section was written by someone who had some knowledge of Roman administrative and civil law" (p. 90); *exousia* in Luke 12:11 and/or the plural *archai kai exousia* in Rom. 13:1 corresponds to the profane idea of *imperium* (especially of the magistrate) and/or *potestas* (e.g., of the lower authorities). It is impossible to understand, however, how using the terms customary in public by the Roman state for state institutions then legitimizes Rom. 13:1 as a "factual profane text" (p. 90). Rather, as Strobel (p. 91) then says himself, theological statements are made about this profane government. In my opinion, one can especially criticize Strobel with the argument that Paul does not write "in the spirit of antique ideals of good, upright citizens" and that also the Roman public's "profane" ideas of the state were not all that profane. The Roman state always articulated its power position in religious terms.

John 19:10, incidentally, offers a good definition of the *imperium* of the magistrate: "Do you not know that I have the power (*exousia*) to release you, and power to crucify you?"

28. To take 1 Cor. 2:8 with alternative meaning, that Paul meant exe-

cution either by the Romans or by the demonic powers, is also, in my opinion, inappropriate.

29. Käsemann (*Romans*, 251) interprets the close proximity of Rom. 8:35 and 8:38f. to each other in a very striking manner: "The situations in the list in v. 35 are now replaced by the world-rulers which cause them, so that chaos is changed into an inferno."

30. Dio Chrysostom (from Prusa in Bithynia, ca. 40–120 B.C.E.), 3: 45–50.

31. Käsemann (*Romans*, 356): "Every sentence can apply also in a police state, and it simply should not be overlooked that the apostle is in fact writing under a dictatorship." Käsemann, however, sees the reason for Paul's positive statements against this background of his fear of anarchy (see also n. 11 above); Käsemann does not pay attention to the apocalyptic background of Rom. 13:1 either (see n. 27 above).

32. With regard to this, see E. Janssen, *Das Gottesvolk und seine Geschichte* (Neukirchen-Vluyn: Neukirchener Verlag, 1971), 53. Regardless of the problem of the possibly contradictory translation of these verses, the following thesis, in my opinion, is appropriate for the whole of the book of Daniel: "that the one believing in apocalyptic here sees God's guiding hand, wherein the Greek empire was merely an executor of this divine will." O. Plöger (*Das Buch Daniel* [Gütersloh: Gütersloher Verlagshaus Gerd Mohn, 1965], 125) sees it somewhat differently, when he refers to "an advancing dualistic world view" at work. Revelation 13:5 opposes Plöger's assumption, where, in like manner, God has given power to the animal from the abyss. In reality there is no basic difference between Rom. 13:1–7 and Revelation 13.

33. Martin Dibelius, "Rom und die Christen im ersten Jahrhundert," *Botschaft und Geschichte: Gesammelte Aufsätze* (ed. G. Bornkamm; Tübingen: J. C. B. Mohr [Paul Siebeck], 1956), 2:182. The citation refers to Dan. 2:21, 37; Wisd. Sol. 6:3; and other scriptures; R. Bergmeier, *Loyalität als Gegenstand paulinischer Paraklese*, e.g., agrees with Dibelius. A religiohistorical investigation of Rom. 13:1ff. and Josephus, *J.W.* 2:140 in *Theokratia* (Leiden: E. J. Brill, 1970), 1:51–63, ref. to 53. Bergmeier wants to show that Paul has grounded his loyalty theologically in Rom. 13:1. Thus God is understood as the one "who acts *presently* in this world, perhaps one could say: as . . . ruler of the world" (p. 56), a Judeo-Hellenic view, which Paul has accepted. By excluding the apocalyptic aspects of this idea, the thesis of Bergmeier remains theologically implausible: as though anyone—even in antiquity—could speak about those in positions of power without stating an opinion on "despotism," as Bergmeier thinks possible (see p. 60 n. 2).

34. This interpretation is rarely defended anymore; see, e.g., Conzelmann and Lindemann, *Interpreting the New Testament*, 368.

35. See, with reference to this, Luise Schottroff, "Die Gegenwart in der Apokalyptik der synoptischen Evangelien," in *Befreiungserfahrungen*, 73ff.

36. W. Schrage (*Die Christen und der Staat nach dem Neuen Testament* [Gütersloh: Gütersloher Verlagshaus Gerd Mohn, 1971], 54) emphasizes the "eschatological reservation" while, appropriately, referring to the Pauline context. The counterthesis is represented, e.g., by G. Delling, *Röm 13,1–7* (Berlin: Evangelische Verlagsanstalt, 1962), 65f.

37. For the reason behind the interpretation of "fear" in Rom. 13:7 as the fear of God, see also Schrage, *Die Christen*, 61 n. 132; Cranfield, *Romans*, esp. 2:59f.; stated somewhat differently H. Balz, *TDNT*, 9:214.

38. With emphasis and appropriately stated by Schrage, *Die Christen*, esp. 59f.

39. Origen, *Kommentar zum Römerbrief*, on text; Rom. 13:2 is not valid for *potestates* who persecute the believers. For these, Acts 5:29 is valid. For material on the limits of loyalty expected of Christians, see also Schelkle, "Staat und Kirche," 232f.; and Schäfke, "Frühchristlicher Widerstand," 558.

40. Heinrich Schlier, *Der Brief an die Epheser* (4th ed.; Düsseldorf: Patmos Verlag, 1963), 291.

41. Heinrich Schlier (*Der Römerbrief* [Freiburg: Herder, 1977]) gives brief, clearly arranged information on the Pauline ideas.

42. See also Luise Schottroff, "Die Schreckensherrschaft der Sünde und die Befreiung durch Christus nach dem Römerbrief des Paulus," in *Befreiungserfahrungen*, 57ff.

43. For additional material on such rules of judicious conduct toward those in power, see Schottroff, "Nonviolence," 17ff.

44. In this regard, see esp. Schlier, *Epheser*, 289ff.

45. The title of Käsemann's representation of Romans 12, though the English translation is "Worship in Everyday Life: A Note on Romans 12," in *New Testament Questions of Today* (trans. W. J. Montague; Philadelphia: Fortress Press, 1969), 188–195.

46. Erich Klostermann, in *Das Markusevangelium* (4th ed.; Tübingen: J. C. B. Mohr [Paul Siebeck], 1950), 125, e.g., interprets Mark 12:17 ("Unangreifbarkeit") as tactic. H. Braun (*Spätjüdisch-häretischer und frühchristlicher Radikalismus* [Tübingen: J. C. B. Mohr (Paul Siebeck), 1957], 2:83 n. 2) interprets it as an expression of indifference. Additional interpretations in this direction are compiled by G. Petzke, "Der historische Jesus in der sozial-ethischen Diskussion," in *Jesus Christus in Historie und Theologie* (FS H. Conzelmann; ed. G. Strecker; Tübingen: J. C. B. Mohr [Paul Siebeck], 1975), 223–235, ref. 226; and Schrage, *Die Christen*, 33 n. 61.

47. J. Carcopino, *Rom: Leben und Kultur in der Kaiserzeit* (Stuttgart: Verlag Philipp Reclam, 1977), 280f.

48. The catalog of vices in Mark 7:21f. is an interpretation of the Decalogue, the emphasis of which becomes clear upon comparing Rom. 13:8–14 with Mark 10:19, 21: cunning, jealousy, and arrogance are especially important to him.

49. In this context, see Luise Schottroff, "Maria Magdalena und die Frauen am Grabe Jesu," in *Befreiungserfahrungen*, 134ff.

50. Pliny the Younger, *Letters* 10.96.

51. Thus, e.g., R. Heiligenthal ("Strategien konformer Ethik im Neuen Testament am Beispiel von Röm 13, 1–7," *NTS* 29 [1983]: 55–61) picks up the incorrect thesis again (see n. 8 above).

11

Nonretaliation
and the Haustafeln
in 1 Peter

Mary H. Schertz

Two factors motivate the research of this essay. First is the continuing and painful irony that some of the most beautifully phrased statements of peace in the New Testament appear in the same document in which some of the most oppressive statements of class and gender-based domination appear. The same first letter of Peter that urges its readers to "seek peace and pursue it" (1 Peter 3:11) also exhorts slaves to submit to their masters (2:18) and wives to submit to their husbands (3:1). Adding to the disjunctiveness is the fact that these statements have been used, respectively, as foundational for contemporary views of nonresistance/pacifism and gender-based hierarchy, views that seem to be grounded in opposing assumptions about the values of the established social order. The arguments that use these texts, however, do not generally recognize that the rhetoric of peace and the rhetoric of oppression occur not only in the same document but also in the same literary unit within the epistle. While scholars have different opinions about how 1 Peter is structured as a whole, most agree that 2:11–3:12 constitutes a recognizable unit of thought and expression within the larger unit of 2:11–4:11.[1] One cannot escape the observation that the injunction about peace in 3:9 and the injunctions to slaves (2:18–19) and wives (3:1) coexist in the same thought unit of the text. Lack of scholarly interest in this reality raises the question of whether the coexistence of the peace and subordination injunctions does not threaten the respective prescriptions derived from them. Perhaps that threat is the reason scholars have intuitively or consciously avoided regarding the injunctions in relation to each other, which, by virtue of their presence in a common context, is the way in which they would deserve to be regarded.

While avoidance of this problem is possibly one solution, it is not the most helpful solution. A better one might be a study that assumes, as its methodological basis, that the injunctions ought to be considered in the light of each other because they share a common context in a designated literary unit. Accordingly, the purpose of this essay is to look carefully at 1 Peter 2:11–3:12 to see what point is being made by juxtaposing the rhetoric of peace and the rhetoric of oppression. A literary study of this passage discloses that the instructions to slaves and wives in 1 Peter are integrally related, by means of an artful interweaving of poetry and prose, with the theme of "not paying back in kind" as a response to evil in the world. Following the analysis of 2:11–3:12, we look at how the passage fits into its immediate textual context in 2:11–4:11 as well as at the pattern of 1 Peter as a whole. We propose a literary separation of the traditional three pairings (slave/master, wife/husband, youth/elder) of the Haustafeln, so that the author intentionally reserves the youth/elder relation for a different rhetorical context; he treats this pair quite differently from the former two pairs. The reason for this separation is the author's emphasis that the basis for the first two injunctions is his sense of an appropriate response to a violent world, while the basis for the last injunction is his sense of an appropriate response to a loving Christian community. Finally, after summarizing the exegetical conclusions of the study, we consider how 1 Peter may be appropriated for the contemporary church from the standpoint of a "critical hermeneutic of liberation."[2]

A second motivation for this study arises from the scant attention given to the literary structure of 1 Peter, though scholars have shown a great deal more interest in the doctrinal concerns of the letter[3] and, more recently, in the social location and cultural history of the recipients of the letter.[4] Such interest as has been taken in the literary aspects of the letter has been exercised as a concern for the overall structure of 1 Peter rather than an in-depth consideration of passages within the overall structure.[5] These studies may be characterized according to their method. Oscar Brooks studies the letter by means of a form-critical analysis for which the impetus arises from speculation about its "setting in life." William Dalton studies the letter from a more self-consciously literary perspective by applying certain formal criteria to the text. Charles Talbert poses a question about the conceptual "plan" or progression of the letter and applies some basic assumptions of ethical inquiry to the text in order to answer his question.

Oscar S. Brooks's 1974 study takes its cue from the tradition that sees 1 Peter as a baptismal tract and tries to show how the clause "baptism now saves" in 3:21 is the key to "how the literary design of the book is held together."[6] Thus, after exegeting the key phrase, Brooks examines the parts of the letter that precede and follow that phrase in order to see how they relate to the theme of baptism. He contends that the introductory material in 1:3–12 is a baptismal hymn that "reviews for his readers the essential place of Christ in the gospel."[7] In this view, 1:13–2:10 seeks, by way of the exodus model, to remind the baptismal candidates of the obligation to be holy and obedient laid upon them by their new relationship to God.[8] First Peter 2:11–3:12 is then an instructional elaboration of these obligations,[9] and 3:13–17 is a generalization that "a convert must maintain his faithfulness and integrity at all costs."[10] Next comes the explicitly baptismal section that, according to Brooks, provides the climax of the entire letter.[11] Brooks treats the rest of the letter summarily, saying merely that the author continues his concern for proper behavior and offers a final word or two of admonition.[12]

Several years before Brooks's effort to describe the internal integrity of the letter, William J. Dalton was inspired by some of the same concerns to try to determine how the various parts of the letter fit together. Whereas Brooks used primarily theological criteria to establish the connections, Dalton attempted a more rigorous and ambitious formal analysis. He looked for such literary devices as inclusions, link words, thematic announcements, repetition of key words, and various types of symmetry.[13] On the basis of this work, Dalton suggests that concepts of Christian vocation organize the letter. Thus 1:3–2:10 has to do with "The Dignity of the Christian Vocation and Its Responsibilities." First Peter 2:11–3:12 is labeled "Obligations of the Christian Life." Finally, 3:13–5:11 has to do with "The Christian and Persecution."[14]

More recently, Charles Talbert has contributed to the effort to discern the plan of 1 Peter with an analysis that uses "certain conceptual and content criteria."[15] Claiming that the formal criteria employed by Dalton are "legitimate but deficient," he attempts to distinguish conceptually between the grounds and the warrants of the ethical discussion in 1 Peter. He contends that 1:3–2:10 reflects the author's view of the grounds for Christian existence, or conversion—described with a variety of metaphors, such as new birth, election, tasting, and ransoming. The longer section, 2:11–5:11, has to do with the norms of the behavior required by conversion and the warrants, or motivating reasons, for the norms.[16]

All three of these studies are efforts to grasp the central thrust of the letter. Each of these is insightful and, from a literary perspective, far superior to a great deal of the scholarship on 1 Peter, because each respects the internal integrity of the epistle as a whole and tries to read it on the terms established by the letter itself. Each of these efforts, therefore, is worthy of attention and inspires gratitude. None of these studies, however, looks carefully enough at some of the smaller units within the text from a literary perspective, a deficiency occasioning need for further testing and verification of these proposals regarding the larger purpose of the letter.

In respect to methodological concerns, while the notion of reading the New Testament texts as literary documents is now generally accepted within the discipline, there is no general agreement as to the kinds of competencies, both theoretical and practical, that reading such a text in such a way entails. The method of this study is to examine the stylistics of the work (word repetition and play, literary stress, grammatical and structural emphases, arrangement of content, etc.) with a view to its rhetorical impact on the reader. Thus major attention is given to how rhetorical features of the text function, a consideration that involves some regard of selected features of Greek rhetoric.

Underlying this approach is a fundamental assumption that the arrangement of the final form of 1 Peter has meaning. Assuming a meaningful arrangement means rejecting the notion that the epistle is a mishmash, hodgepodge conglomeration of somewhat related material that could have been arranged much better. In choosing the first assumption over the second, I am not so much making a case for the first, although I think it is true. Rather, I am asking what can be learned by assuming that the parts of the text function as an intentional, persuasive whole. It seems only fair to give the text as it stands a chance.

Analysis of the Literary Units
of 1 Peter

For the sake of both convenience and illumination, we must first make some beginning efforts to separate the text under examination into some rudimentary divisions of thought. In this essay, I am accepting the common notion that 1 Peter 1:3–2:10 constitutes a section that not only establishes a relationship between the author and the readers but also orients the reader to the letter as a whole and lays some important grounds for the ethical arguments that follow. This section establishes the identity of the readers as the "holy nation" chosen by God and also establishes the God whom the readers serve as the God in continuity with the God of Israel known via the LXX and the God manifested in Jesus Christ.

Beyond that commonly accepted demarcation of the beginning section, however, there is ample room for debate. I am suggesting that 2:11–4:11 and 4:12–5:11 are two sections that are constructed in parallel fashion. In some important respects, these passages are mirror images of each other. I am also suggesting that the reason these sections are so constructed is that the first has to do with relations between the community of believers and the "world," while the second section has to do with the relations between the members of the believing community itself. While the argument about the content of the two sections must await more careful analysis of the internal arrangement of each, let us examine at this point the more formal observations that lead to this conclusion.

The first thing to notice is that both sections begin not only with a direct address to the readers but with the same form of the address. In 2:11 the readers are addressed as ἀγαπητοί ("Beloved"). In 4:12 the readers are again addressed as ἀγαπητοί ("Beloved"). Not only do the two sections begin in the same manner, they also end similarly: 4:11 closes with ᾧ ἐστιν ἡ δόξα καὶ τὸ κράτος εἰς τοὺς αἰῶνας τῶν αἰώνων, ἀμήν ("To him belong glory and dominion for ever and ever. Amen"); similarly, 5:11 closes with αὐτῷ τὸ κράτος εἰς τοὺς αἰῶνας, ἀμήν ("To him be the dominion for ever and ever. Amen"). Thus both of the sections begin with the intimate and affectionate direct address and end with a doxology couched in similar, though not identical, language. While these similarities and resonances mark the text visually for the modern reader, the oral symmetry with its opportunities for expressive presentation may have been even more obviously marked for the first-century hearer of the text.[17]

In addition to the symmetry in the beginnings and endings of the sections, there is a remarkable repetition of vocabulary in the beginning paragraphs of each section. While space does not permit an exhaustive survey, we might note the repetition of such key phrases as "wrongdoing" in 2:12, 14 and 4:15; "doing right" in 2:14, 15 and 4:19; "the will of God" in 2:15 and 4:19; and others. Related to this repetition of phrases is a repetition of key concepts or ideas which, though not couched in exactly identical words, are strongly resonant. In that category, we might note that eschatology is invoked in each section with "the day of visitation" in 2:12 and the "judgment" which begins with the household of God in 4:17. Also in that category, we might note the wordplay that hinges on the usage of the word ἀνθρωπίνῃ κτίσει ("human creation") in 2:13 and the word πιστῷ κτίστῃ ("faithful creator") in 4:19. While caution should be taken to avoid pushing the point too hard, the similarity in the word choice could well reflect a point the author wants to make. This point might be paraphrased something like this: The human creations, to which the Christians are to be subject, are, in turn, themselves subject to the Creator, to whom the Christians entrust themselves.

Finally, there is the most striking similarity of the two sections. The central part of each section contains the familiar form of ethical injunctions known as the household codes: in 2:11–4:11 there are injunctions to the slaves (2:18–20) and to the wives and husbands (3:1–7); in 4:12–5:11 there are injunctions to the elders and the youth (5:1–5). These observations lead us to conclude that the two sections are parallel or coexist in some kind of correlation. Each begins with an identical direct address, contains opening paragraphs that deal with similar vocabulary and concepts, continues with paraenetic injunctions, and closes with a doxology composed of almost identical language. These similarities demonstrate the author's careful planning and raise the question of what is meant by these arranged correspondences.

Having dealt with the larger units of the material, we must also look more closely at 2:11–4:11 in order to determine whether subsections emerge. Here I make three brief comments; further testing of these divisions will occur in the exegesis of the material. First, the rhetorical question in 3:13 suggests that the author is moving to a new mood and beginning a new kind of argumentation at that point. Second, a division at this point is confirmed by looking at the way 3:11 ends the previous material with a resounding LXX quotation. According to Dalton, this stylistic device is a common unit marker for the author of this epistle: "The great authority of the Old Testament in the mind of the New Testament writer makes it highly suitable to end off an argument or development of thought with a biblical citation. In this way the thought comes to a sort of impressive climax."[18] Third, the balance with which the section from 2:11–3:12 is constructed argues for its integrity as a literary unit. That balance, however, will become evident only as we move into the more detailed analysis of the text.

Exegesis of 1 Peter 2:11–3:12

Seeing the artistry with which the two parallel sections have been constructed should serve as a warning not to take the work of this writer too lightly. His careful design leads us to ask about the significance of his locating of the injunctions to slaves and wives in one literary unit and the injunctions to youth in another unit. To answer that question we will need to look more closely at the section containing the problematic injunctions.

An understanding of 2:11–3:12 depends upon an understanding of a ring composition or chiasm. This literary device is a construction in which the first line or element of the composition is similar to the last line or element, the second element similar to the second from the end, the third similar to the third from the end, and so forth. The innermost element may or may not have a counterpart. This construction, common in both the Hebrew Bible and the New Testament, is a device used for emphasis. While there is no hard-and-fast rule as to whether the chiasm is drawing attention to the innermost element(s) or the outermost elements, the individual chiasm usually indicates the emphasis clearly. The content of the chiasm will indicate whether the attention of the reader is being drawn inward to the core of the piece or outward to the frame. For instance, a reference to the divine in either the outermost or the innermost elements will often indicate the location of the point that the form of the construction is underlining.

To complicate matters further, the passage with which we are working here has two kinds of chiasms operating synchronically. One is an organizational, or structural, chiasm. The other is an artistic, or poetic, chiasm. As we shall see, these two types of patterns work together, reinforcing each other and the point that is being made.

We can discern the organizational, or structural, chiasm by looking at the various sections of the composition in terms of the content. In 2:13–17 there is a *general* injunction to everyone in the community to be subject to human institutions. Then, in 2:18–20 there is a *specific* injunction to servants to be subject to their masters. In 2:21–25 there is a christological hymn, which centers the chiasm. Then the repetition begins. In 3:1–7 there are the *specific* injunctions to wives to be subject to their husbands and to husbands to bestow honor lest their prayers be hindered. Then in 3:8–12 there is again a *general* injunction to all not to return evil for evil, a generalization that supplies the rationale for the whole series of injunctions that precedes it. The chiasm therefore is based on the symmetry developed by juxtaposing a general injunction, a specific injunction, the hymn, a specific injunction, and a general injunction.[19]

We can discern the artistic, or poetic, chiasm by looking at the christological hymn that forms the center of the organizational chiasm. As we will find in the closer exegesis of the passage, this hymn, which is set up as a poem in the Nestle-Aland Greek text, is composed of a remarkably regular and symmetrical pattern of lines that form a chiasm. This form draws the reader's attention to the central point of the hymn in 2:23 and clarifies that the specific Christology of the hymn, as well as of 1 Peter generally, addresses nonretaliation.

Taking a panoramic view for the moment, we might speculate that (1) the chiastic form of the hymn draws our attention inward to the model of the nonretaliatory Christ; and that (2) the chiastic structure of the surrounding material suggests that slaves and wives are particular models of this Christ type and therefore serve as examples to the community. Further, we might posit that the text is setting up the relationships in something of the following pattern:

human institution	master	tormentors	husbands	evil
community	slaves	Christ	wives	good

Obviously we need to be careful at this point not to oversimplify the text. The equations are not simple correspondences. Rather, the relationships in the equations are being treated as in some senses analogous. The subordination of Christ to his tormentors is the model for slaves and wives in relation to their non-Christian "superiors." These slaves and wives are, in turn, models for the community in the larger questions of the Christians' relations to the structures of human order and to the cosmic struggle of good and evil.

Keeping this larger sketch of the design of the passage in mind, we are now in a position to test the thesis through closer and more systematic attention to the various developments within the passage.

General injunction (1 Peter 2:11–17)

As we have already noticed in the preliminary determination of the boundaries of the passage, in 2:11 the implied author[20] changes the tone of his address to the reader. The term of endearment in the vocative voice, ἀγαπητοί ("Beloved"), and the use of a persuasive verb in the first person singular, παρακαλῶ ("I beseech"), indicate that the author is appealing to the readers' emotions, or pathos, in a new way.[21] The pathetic appeal is also heightened by the fact that the author expresses the opposition between the ψυχή ("soul") and the desires of the flesh with a military term, στρατεύονται, meaning "to wage war,"[22] which emphasizes and heightens the conflict.

All these rhetorical devices may indeed indicate that the author expects subsequent statements to require an added appeal, a conclusion that seems likely in the light of the general difficulty of the enthymemes that follow the appeal. An enthymeme is simply a statement accompanied by a supporting reason. A logical syllogism is the argumentative structure that underlies this rhetorical device, although the entire structure of the logical syllogism is rarely explicit.[23]

In the first of these enthymemes (2:12), the author enjoins the readers to sustain good behavior among the Gentiles (statement) so that those who observe this good behavior will praise God in the day of visitation (supporting reason). The second enthymeme (2:13–15) enjoins the readers to submit to every human creation (statement) because God wills that such good deeds might silence human stupidity (supporting reason). Inserted between the statement and the supporting reason of this latter injunction is a secondary kind of support in the form of a prepositional phrase that adds that the purpose of these human creations—whether kings or governors—is to punish the evildoers and praise the doers of good (κακοποιῶν/ ἀγαθοποιῶν). Thus, in carefully parallel language, the readers are introduced to what will prove to be a major theme of the passage, evil doing and good doing.[24]

Through these two enthymemes, the author not only introduces topics that will occupy the rest of the unit but makes a couple of points about these themes. First, speaking evil and doing evil are linked. Although the lack of repetitive vocabulary and the distance between the words disallow a chiastic designation, there is a kind of "turn" on the categories of "speaking" and "doing" in these verses. The anticipated charge (2:12) is that some others will speak against the believers by calling them evildoers. In this case, the proper response is not, however, a verbal denial or defense but a positive action—doing good—which, according to God's will, should silence the evil speaking (2:15). Therefore one might at least question whether the point is being made that speaking and doing are similar ethical categories and whether proper behavior toward speaking or doing evil is not responding in kind.

The second point is based primarily on the fact that the phrase "the will of God" receives greater grammatical emphasis as ὅτι, or causal, phrase than the prepositional phrase which describes the function of human powers. The point is that while human "ordering" as such is deemed good and is to be obeyed because it contains (punishes and praises) human behavior, the will of God is the higher claim.

A third point has to do with the ironic tension created between the author's assertion, on the one hand, that the purpose of the emperor and governors is to contain evil and reward good and the author's acknowledgment, on the other hand, that this purpose is not being realized—wrongdoing is rampant and the Christians are not exactly being overwhelmed with praise. If, as suggested, doing good/right is connected with submission, then one might argue maximally that some of the "foolish people" belong to the ruling class or minimally that the rulers are ineffective against the kind of evil represented by "the ignorance of foolish people."

Finally, the author is not only heightening the emotional impact of the ensuing argument by referring to the conflict between *souls* and *desires* but, in the repetition of the word ψυχή ("soul"), logically tying the argument to two previous points: that the soul's salvation is the end of faith (1:9) and that the soul is to be sanctified by obedience (1:22). While noting these previous references to ψυχή, we might also observe that the word appears in two other places within the unit—after the first christological hymn (2:25) and then, climactically, in 4:19.

Specific injunction (1 Peter 2:18–20)

In the next section, 2:18–20, the author makes explicit the connection between the concept of submission as an act of not repaying in kind and the concept of doing good by suffering. This connection is implied in the first section, but it is reemphasized and made explicit here. The point is then reinforced by the judicious placement of the christological hymn that restates the same in a formally satisfying, artistic, and liturgical manner. Hence 2:18–20 particularizes the general injunction of 2:13 to submit to every human creation. Servants are to be obedient to masters—not only to those who are good and moderate but even to the "crooked" ones (2:18). Using the pattern of the enthymeme once more, the author provides a supporting statement that is indicated by γάρ ("for"). The reason slaves are to obey crooked masters is that "credit in the eyes of God" is gained by bearing those specific sorrows dealt unjustly (2:19).

The author is herein establishing Christian behavior as not repaying in kind, as behavior that transcends human orders and human concepts of justice. In that sense, the document supports the established human order and might therefore be judged politically conservative. But, because the document deals with such anomalies as the unjust master by appealing to a higher, divine order, the document might be seen in another sense to be ultimately subversive or politically radical.

Given the same assumption that human orders are instituted for a good purpose—punishment of evil and praise of good—and given the same evidence that those who fill those positions of power in the human orders are sometimes evil or ineffective against evil, one has several options. One might deny the evil and insist that those in power define what is good. One might call for obedience to the powerful good ones because they are good and for expedient behavior toward the powerful crooked ones because they are powerful. One might call for obedience toward the good and for disobedience toward the evil. The Petrine ethic is, however, very different from all these options with respect to both the motive and the behavior invited in this injunction. The behavior instructed is obedience. The motive invited is not the inherent goodness of the system. Indeed, there is recognition that the system is unjust when the persons in possession of power within the system are unjust or when they are ineffective against injustice. Rather, the motive invited is the acquisition of credit in the eyes of God. In this way, the human creations are not only relativized but in some senses rendered irrelevant.

This point is, as has already been noted, immediately reinforced as the author interjects the first christological hymn.

The christological hymn (1 Peter 2:21–25)

First Peter 2:21–24 is a unified work arranged as a ring composition and makes its statement on the basis of that form. Because ring composition, or chiasm—the term some critics prefer—is not a form familiar to twentieth-century readers, a visual presentation may prove helpful. Therefore the hymn in the format used by the Nestle-Aland 26th edition is shown here:

21	a	8	εἰς τοῦτο γὰρ ἐκλήθητε,
	b		ὅτι καὶ Χριστὸς ἔπαθεν ὑπὲρ ὑμῶν
	c		ὑμῖν ὑπολιμπάνων ὑπογραμμὸν
	d		ἵνα ἐπακολουθήσητε τοῖς ἴχνεσιν αὐτοῦ,

22	a		ὃς ἁμαρτίαν οὐκ ἐποίησεν
	b	(14)	οὐδὲ εὑρέθη δόλος ἐν τῷ στόματι αὐτοῦ,
23	a	12	ὃς λοιδορούμενος οὐκ ἀντελοιδόρει,
	b	6	πάσχων οὐκ ἠπείλει,
	c	12	παρεδίδου δὲ τῷ κρίνοντι δικαίως·
24	a	(14)	ὃς τὰς ἁμαρτίας ἡμῶν αὐτὸς ἀνήνεγκεν
	b		ἐν τῷ σώματι αὐτοῦ ἐπὶ τὸ ξύλον,
	c		ἵνα ταῖς ἁμαρτίαις ἀπογενόμενοι
	d		τῇ δικαιοσύνῃ ζήσωμεν,
	e	8	οὗ τῷ μώλωπι ἰάθητε.

In this poetic form we first note the relative regularity in the length of the lines. Lines 21a and 24e, which begin and end the hymn, both have eight syllables. Notice also that the syllabic pattern at the center of the piece is very tight. An unusually short line, one with only six syllables, is framed by two lines of twelve syllables which are in turn framed by two lines of fourteen syllables. While the syllabication of the material between the extremities and the center is not so controlled, the hymn nevertheless tends toward the kind of symmetry characteristic of chiasm.

In addition to the syllabic regularity, there are some striking resonances in both the syntax and the semantics of the poem. The last phrase of the first line is an aorist passive, ἐκλήθητε ("you have been called"), while the last phrase of the last line is another aorist passive, ἰάθητε ("you have been healed"). While rhyme may well have less significance in an inflected language than in one that is relatively uninflected, such as English, we should at least note that these two lines do rhyme. Another observation is that the fourth line and the third line from the end resemble each other. Line 21d is a ἵνα clause, "in order that you might follow in his steps," while line 24c is another ἵνα clause, "in order that we might die to sin." The similarity of phraseology and the relative symmetry of the placement of the two expressions raise the question of whether the two ideas are not being equated in the vernacular of 1 Peter. We might posit that both clauses state responses desired of the believers— "that you might follow in his footprints" and "that having died to sin we might live for justice." This arrangement suggests that the two lines serve to explain each other. In other words, the terms of the hymn suggest that following in the footprints of the Christ involves dying to sin and, conversely, that dying to sin involves actually walking in the way of Christ.

Another pair of phrases to be compared are the second line, 21b, "that Christ also suffered [var.: died] for us," and the second line from the end, 24d, "that we might live." These two phrases form a semantic balance—he suffered or, as the variant supplies, he *died* (21b), that we might *live* (24d).

Having dealt with the outermost components of the chiastic hymn, let us turn our attention to the center and, in this case, the major concern of the poet. We might begin by looking at lines 22b and 24b. The phrases are, respectively, "nor was there guile found in his mouth" and "in his body on the tree." While both these phrases function primarily within their respective sentences, their visual and aural symmetry (ἐν τῷ στόματι αὐτοῦ / ἐν τῷ σώματι αὐτοῦ) also serves to mark the chiastic intent of the piece by framing the crucial point of the hymn.

Finally, it is that crucial point at the very center to which our attention is gradually being drawn. We observe that the center consists of the three ὅς clauses and that the two outside clauses of this unit of three exhibit symmetry in the use of ἁμαρτίαν (22a) and ἁμαρτίας (24a). These observations lead me to believe that the central point of the hymn is contained in verse 23, where, as we have already noted, the syllabication is most tightly controlled in a pattern of 12/6/12. These three lines ("who being cursed did not return a curse / suffering [πάσχων] did not threaten / but yielded to the one who judges justly [δικαίως]") refer, in this particular prose context, back to the last usage of πάσχων ("suffering") in 2:19. There it was used in connection with the behavior of slaves in relationship to their masters. That this is, in fact, the intention of the argument is strengthened by the fact that the δικαίως ("justly") of 23c resonates with the ἀδίκως ("unjustly") of 19c. Thus the injunction to slaves to submit to unjust masters and thereby to "do good" is rooted in the example of Christ who did not return a curse for a curse or a threat for suffering. These nonretaliatory actions, in the case of Christ as in the case of slaves, are rendered meaningful by the appeal to a higher order. This appeal, this act of yielding present injustice to the one who judges justly, is an act accomplished precisely by not returning in kind. In this sense, submission to every human creation is an act performed by those who are free with respect to these human institutions because they are, as θεοῦ δοῦλοι ("slaves of God," 16c), slaves of a higher order.

Verse 25, something of an anomaly by any standard, is no less so for the rhetorical critic. While it is a quotation, while it is poetic, while it is related to the last line of the christological hymn in both theme and source (Isa. 53:5–6), the differences in rhythm and style between 2:21–24 and 2:25 make the supposition that v. 25 is a part of the hymn questionable. In fact, v. 25 plays a rhetorical role that

is rather different from that of vs. 21–24. Whereas the ring composition of 2:21–24 defines the central point of the hymn and, consequently, the content of "doing good" in 2:20, 2:25 functions as an
inclusio with 2:11 by repeating the word ψυχαί ("souls"). The word
used in the context of a warning in 2:11, "Keep yourselves free from
the fleshly desires ready to wage war against the *soul*," is now used
in the context of consolation or comfort in 2:25. "You have now
turned to the shepherd and guardian of your *souls*." The path from
insecurity to security is, in the odd logic of this passage, precisely
by way of the precarious trail forged by the Christ who did not
return a curse for a curse.

In this way, v. 25 serves as a motivational appeal for the difficult
model of the nonretaliatory Christ presented in vs. 21–24. It is not
surprising that the addition of v. 25 renders the total construction of
2:21–25 in a form that has an argumentative impact similar to that
of an enthymeme. Verses 21–24 provide the basic statement, the
declaration of the model. Verse 25, introduced with the familiar
signifier γάρ ("for") and thematically interwoven with the last part
of the hymn in a sophisticated fashion, provides the motivational
support required by the difficulty of the model.

Specific injunction (1 Peter 3:1–7)

In this fourth section of the argument, the author develops the
second specific appropriation of the general injunction to submit to
every human creation with an injunction to the wives. The injunction itself is directed to the wives of non-Christian husbands, as the
parallelism of the supporting reasons of this enthymeme with the
supporting reasons of the general enthymeme in 2:12 clearly indicates. In 2:12 the believers are enjoined to have good behavior
among the Gentiles so that when this behavior is observed, the Gentiles might glorify God. Then in the following verse good behavior
is defined as submitting to every human creation so that this "doing
good" might, according to the will of God, silence human stupidity.
In 3:1–2 the wives are enjoined to submit to their husbands so that,
observing this good behavior, the husbands who are disobedient to
the word might be won. Even the qualifier, "without a word," which
describes how the husbands are to be won, resonates with 2:15 if
we recall that the evil speaking in that introductory passage was to
be silenced not with a word of defense but with doing good or, in
the terms of the epistle, submitting to the human order precisely
because one really belongs to the divine order.

Thus the parallelism between the general injunction with which the section begins and this specific injunction functions in two ways. First, it reinforces the unitary nature of these pericopes. Second, in the establishment of a similar goal (missional impact) for the solicited behavior, it reinforces the central concern of the entire unit as a concern for the believers' relationships with "outsiders" or nonbelievers.

The parallelism between the injunction to the slaves and the one to wives also reinforces this point along another line of argument. In both cases the author acknowledges that following the difficult model of the nonretaliatory Christ involves a significant loss of status for these "subordinate" social groups. The slaves are not given any hope that their masters will be won by their behavior. Perhaps the author thinks that hope is unrealistic. The slaves are, however, assured that the relinquishment of status implied in their submission to physical abuse will be rewarded by status (or approval) in the eyes of God and, presumably, in the Christian community. In a similar fashion the wives' relinquishment of status, symbolized by "outward" adornment, will be replaced with value "in God's sight" (3: 3–4). Thus, in both cases, there is a rejection of status as it is defined by those "outside" the people of God and a redefinition of the status of persons from God's point of view.

The examples of the holy women and Sarah (3:5–6) add emphasis to the author's persuasive point. While wifely submission is assumed in both cases, the emphasis is not on submission. In both cases the emphasis is on the "adornment." Thus the holy women, hoping in God, adorned themselves with their value in God's sight. Then, in the light of that understanding of their own real status, they submitted to their husbands. Sarah was also submissive, but her legacy is not just her submission. More important, Sarah's legacy is the fearlessness of knowing her true value in God's eyes. Notice how the submission of the holy women, Sarah and the wives addressed by the letter, is surrounded, framed, and contained by hope, adornment, and fearlessness. Thus wives, like slaves, acquiesce to the reality of their low status while "adorning" themselves in the knowledge of their equal status in a greater reality.

This greater reality is then concretized in the injunction to the husbands (3:7) who, since they are directly addressed by the author, are the Christian husbands to whom the author has access. The status afforded by God to persons in "inferior" classes is to be actually or concretely granted to these persons by those within the Christian community who have the wherewithal to grant it. Therefore husbands, who benefit from the stronger social, economic, and political status afforded them by their society, are to grant their wives, who have a weaker position, the honor, or status, that they lack in the society. In other words, within the Christian community, wives are to possess in concrete reality the status they possess as joint heirs in that greater reality.

Finally, the injunction to the husbands is weighted with the statement that the consequences of not granting that honor are significant. If the husbands do not put the new and greater reality into actual practice, their prayers will be hindered. They will, in other words, have broken their relationship with God. The spiritual vitality of the husbands is directly dependent on their doing justice in the marital relationship.

General injunction (1 Peter 3:8–12)

The final pericope of this section both closes the section with appropriate eloquence and restates the major point of the author's argument by offering the most explicit expression of the theme, not repaying in kind, of the entire rhetorical unit. Verse 8 serves two functions. In the first place, it provides a smooth and satisfying transition from v. 7. If v. 7 enforces via injunction the new reality wherein people are valued as God values them, then v. 8 offers an injunction that generalizes the notion of the new reality for the entire community. It is not just the husbands, but everyone, who must relinquish worldly privilege and bestow honor—that all might be empowered with the "unity of spirit." In the second place, v. 8 provides an introduction to the rest of the section. This image of the new reality provides the grounds and motivation of the central point the author is trying to make in the larger unit about how the community of believers should relate to the outside world.

It is to this concern that the author returns in v. 9 as he enjoins the believers not to return evil for evil or a curse for a curse. Employing once again the form of the enthymeme, the author follows the injunction with a reason that supports the injunction. The believers have been called (ἐκλήθητε) to this (εἰς τοῦτο) [stance of not repaying in kind] in order that they might inherit a blessing (3:8–9). The language of this supporting reason is a powerful reiteration of the first line of the first christological hymn. That repetition is, in fact, one reason we can, with confidence, posit a "stance of not repaying in kind" as the antecedent for both usages of εἰς τοῦτο ("for this"). The immediate antecedent for the εἰς τοῦτο in 3:8–9 is indubitably the double injunction to be like-minded, sympathetic, loving, and so forth, and not to return evil for evil. As we have already observed, the center of the christological hymn in 2:21–24 is the example of the Christ who did not return a curse for a curse. Thus we may assume that that to which the Christians are being called is precisely the practice of not repaying in kind.

Having made the point about the Christian's call, the author again chooses to complete the section with recourse to the poetic mood by introducing a psalm. As with the hymn in 2:21–24, the form is not only the key to the meaning of the psalm itself but, more pertinently, to its meaning within this particular context. The psalm as presented in the Nestle-Aland text appears thus:

10 ὁ γὰρ θέλων ζωὴν ἀγαπᾶν
   καὶ ἰδεῖν ἡμέρας ἀγαθὰς
   παυσάτω τὴν γλῶσσαν ἀπὸ κακοῦᵃ
   καὶ χείλη τοῦ μὴ λαλῆσαι δόλον,ᵇ
11 ἐκκλινάτω δὲ ἀπὸ κακοῦᵃ καὶ ποιησάτω ἀγαθόν,ᵇ
   ζητησάτω εἰρήνηνᶜ καὶ διωξάτω αὐτήν·ᶜ
12 ὅτι ὀφθαλμοὶ κυρίου ἐπὶ δικαίους
   καὶ ὦτα αὐτοῦ εἰς δέησιν αὐτῶν,
   πρόσωπον δὲ κυρίου ἐπὶ ποιοῦντας κακά.

This psalm progresses in three parts. The first two lines, containing nine syllables each, provide an appeal that not only serves to make the paraenetic section that follows more palatable but also, in its prose context, serves as a transition from and explanation of the εὐλογίαν ("blessing") promised in 3:9 to those who practice not repaying in kind. Those who live according to the divine reality shall "love life and see good days" precisely because their reality is not defined by those powers toward which they are called to live in a nonretaliatory fashion.

The second part of the psalm consists of the next four lines. This part is rhymed in an a,b/a,b/c,c scheme, as the double lines and small letters on the figure indicate. More important, the part contains five third-person singular aorist imperatives. The first two are negative, παυσάτω (let him/her stop) and ἐκκλινάτω (let him/her turn away). The last two are positive ζητησάτω (let him/her seek) and διωξάτω (let him/her pursue). The third imperative, the very familiar ποιησάτω (let him/her do good), is positioned as the central imperative between the two negative ones and the two positive ones. This imperative is also in the fifth (middle) line of the nine-line psalm. Thus we might posit that the central point of the psalm is "doing good." This doing of good is defined on the one hand by stopping the tongue and lips from evil, which recalls the epistle's concern with speaking evil, and on the other hand by seeking and pursuing peace.

The third part of the psalm concludes the section with a word of comfort not unlike that of 2:25. However unjust the readers' experience might be, they are to know that "the eye of the Lord is upon the just ones / and his ear bent to their supplications / but the face of the Lord is turned against the evildoer" (3:12).

In this fashion, the section of 2:11–3:12 ends with the same kinds of strong contrasts with which it began. In other words, those who maintain good conduct among the Gentiles, those who follow the model of the nonretaliatory Christ and the models of the slaves and wives by not returning evil for evil can rest assured that God is on their side.

1 Peter 2:11–3:12 in Its Larger Literary Contexts

At this point, two tasks remain to be accomplished before we move to the implications of this study of 1 Peter 2:11–3:12. The first is to look briefly at the material in 3:12–4:11 as the remainder of the larger literary unit encompassing 2:11–4:11. The second is to look briefly at 4:12–5:11 because this unit contains the third of the traditional three pairs of the household codes and, as has been stated, is formally parallel to 2:11–4:11 in some ways. While our regard of these texts will not be as detailed a study as that of 2:11–3:12, we will note major thematic comparisons and contrasts.

1 Peter 3:13–4:11

The beginning of the new material, a subsection of 2:11–4:11, is marked with a rhetorical question in 3:13 and ends with the reverberating doxology in 4:11. Within that larger section, there is a subdivision between 3:13–22 and 4:1–11. This division is less defined but nevertheless fairly clear since 3:22 ends with the cosmic statement of Jesus' present exalted location and 4:1 begins with the transitional "since therefore." We will examine each of these subsections in turn.

In 3:12–22 the author inserts a poetic interlude between two prose subsections. The section serves two primary purposes. On one level it functions as a transition between the preceding material and 4:1–11 as the author moves from well-developed considerations of specific, concrete issues to a more general consideration of a variety of issues. On another level the passage serves a purpose all its own. The author first takes up the problem posed by the discontinuity between the triumphant statement in 3:12 and the suffering experienced by the Christians which calls for nonretaliatory responses. Then, second, he brings the problem to resolution in 3:22.

That the passage serves as a transition is attested by the fact that the vocabulary is strikingly repetitive of 2:11–17, the passage that introduces that large section. This section begins with the author's rhetorical question, "Who will harm you if you are zealous for the good?" The question is then answered by arguing that even if one should suffer for justice, one is blessed. Moreover, because one participates in the realm of God's justice, a realm that transcends human justice and thereby redefines justice, there really is nothing to fear (3:13–14).

Having established the support for this new nonretaliatory behavior in the ultimacy of the higher claim, the author then proceeds to explain that not repaying in kind is not passivity but a purposeful zeal (3:13) to be employed in specific circumstances. Another part of sanctifying or reverencing Christ is being ready to make a verbal defense (ἀπολογίαν) to anyone who should make a case against this new reality which is their hope (3:15). We might notice at this point that active defense is an appropriate response not when one's behavior or reputation is being attacked but when one's hope is questioned. This defense is to be both verbal and done in the spirit of the previous injunctions to nonretaliatory behavior—with gentleness and reverence (3:16). The supporting reasons that follow are of the pattern familiar to us by this time. First, the author provides the practical, or strategic, reason that those who observe this good behavior, or nonretaliation, will be put to shame (3:16). Second, the author notes that it is better to suffer while doing good (not returning evil for evil) than for doing evil (returning evil for evil), because the former is approved in the eyes of God (3:17).

Having thus summarized the development of the themes that have to do with nonretaliation to this point, the author employs the poetic mood for the third time. The hymn appears thus in the Nestle-Aland text:

> 18 ὅτι καὶ Χριστὸς ἅπαξ περὶ ἁμαρτιῶν ἔπαθεν,
> δίκαιος ὑπὲρ ἀδίκων,
> ἵνα ὑμᾶς προσαγάγῃ τῷ θεῷ
> θανατωθεὶς μὲν σαρκὶ
> ζωοποιηθεὶς δὲ πνεύματι·

There are several pertinent items to notice in this hymn, which is the shortest of the three found in the larger unit of 2:11–4:11. The first is that it resonates with the first hymn through the use of the verb ἔπαθεν ("suffered") in relation to Christ and in the emphasis on the injustice of his suffering. The second is that the hymn "turns" on the reader. Until now, the emphasis has been placed on the reactions of those "outsiders" who observe the good behavior of the "insiders" and are thereby brought to the point of either glorifying God (2:12) or being put to shame (3:16). In doing good, the reader, as an "insider," has been aligned both with Christ, who modeled this type of behavior, and with God, who is pleased by this type of behavior. Now, suddenly, in the third line of this hymn, the perspective shifts. Because Christ suffered, the readers are reminded that Christ's nonretaliatory behavior—suffering unjustly, not returning a curse for a curse—is that which has brought *them* near to God. In other words, in the terms of the epistle, the readers, who were once outsiders themselves, once *not* aligned with God, have been "put to shame" and are now able to "glorify God" precisely because Christ chose to suffer unjustly. The readers themselves thus become their own best testimony to the missionary effectiveness of this nonretaliatory behavior to which they are being summoned. This effectiveness is then celebrated in the last two lines of the hymn as the terms death/flesh are juxtaposed with life/spirit. In the terms of this epistle the transformation from death to life involves a transformation from enmity to brotherhood and sisterhood expressed as the expected outcome of the solicited, nonretaliatory behavior and as experienced in the lives of those brought near to God through Christ.

At this point, the author intensifies this "turn" from evil to good by casting it in cosmic colors. These four verses of 3:19–22 are difficult for modern readers by any standards, and this difficulty renders humility an appropriate attitude on the part of any interpreter. I would like to suggest, however, that these four verses form a chiasm that expresses the author's point on another level. Although this chiasm is of a somewhat different nature than those previously examined, we have observed the delight this author takes in balanced construction, and it should not surprise us to find it here. We might reconstruct the chiasm in the following paraphrastic fashion:

A = 19–20a. In the spirit in which he was resurrected (an understanding drawn from the preceding hymn by means of the relative pronoun) Christ went and preached to the captive spirits. These spirits are identified as the ones who were disobedient in the days of Noah. (Presumably the author is referring to the Nephilim of Gen. 6:1–6 which precipitated the flood).

B = 20b   Noah persevered against these spirits, built the ark in obedience to God, and a few (eight) were saved.

B' = 21   The believers have their own salvific "ark," the communal bonds of baptism which, as the author explains, is not a cleansing but an appeal in good conscience to that greater reality concretized in the resurrection of Jesus.

A' = 22   Finally, the image is emphatically concluded with the author's statement that Jesus is at the right hand of God with all these (formerly disobedient) angels, authorities, and powers subject to him.

While the complex imagery of this small section may never be completely available to the reader with a modern worldview, the chiastic correspondences would suggest that the author is adding another, cosmic level to the point he has made previously from a social or moral standpoint (good behavior will shame one's opponents) and from a personal standpoint (you were brought to God by the nonretaliatory Christ). In other words, the resistance the believers offer to evil by bonding in baptism and not repaying in kind is grounded in a hope that is, in turn, grounded in a cosmic reality. The nonretaliatory Christ, vindicated by God, won over the imprisoned spirits. Therefore the nonretaliatory readers, vindicated by God, will win over their opponents.

In 4:1–11 the theme of nonretaliation functions somewhat more loosely as the author moves from a consideration of specific issues and problems that call for nonretaliatory responses and turns to a broader consideration of other ethical matters. These matters fall into two groups. In 4:3–6 the author enjoins the readers to avoid carousing, drunkenness, idolatries, and so forth, while in 4:7–11 the concern is how the members of the household of faith should treat one another and how, within that household, gifts are to be used for God's glory.

However digressive from the theme of nonretaliation these topics may appear to be, we should nevertheless note that these subject areas are placed in the framework of the ethic that has governed the text up to this point. In 4:1–2 the author formulates the transition into this section and makes the connection clear. *Since* Christ suffered in the flesh, the readers ought also to "arm" themselves with the same intention—that is, to suffer unjustly rather than to return evil in kind. We might note also that ὁπλίσασθε as a military term meaning in the passive[25] "to arm, prepare for battle" brings to mind the military terminology used in 2:11, στρατεύσονται, to describe the fleshly desires ready to "wage war" against the soul. Thus the readers cannot escape the knowledge that until this point "fleshly desires" have primarily meant returning evil in kind. It is in this sense of fleshly desires that the author makes the statement that the one who suffers in the flesh (rather than yielding to the human desire to return evil in kind) stops the self from sinning. In that sense, the meaning of πέπαυται ἁμαρτίας ("cease from sin") is both straightforward and relatively literal. In both 2:15 and 3:17 the phrase τὸ θέλημα τοῦ θεοῦ ("the will of God") was aligned with "doing good" which, in the terms of the epistle, means not returning evil in kind. Here in 4:2 the same phrase, "the will of God," is posed in opposition to "fleshly desires." This shift strengthens the case that the prohibitions against the fulfillment of fleshly desires—including carousing and drunkenness—are viewed as a part of the nonretaliatory ethic. In 4:4 it is implied that this connection between not participating in pagan pleasures and customs and the theme of not repaying in kind may be due in part to the fact that Christian nonparticipation has resulted in the kind of reviling for which nonretaliation was deemed a proper response. At any rate, the author assures the readers that those who speak against them will have to "render an account to the one ready to judge the living and the dead" (4:5), which serves as a reminder that sometime, somewhere, God's justice will reign.

Meanwhile the believers must live their lives in situations that are less than just. While I do not wish to force the theme of nonretaliation toward unwarranted service in the interpretation of this passage, perhaps the injunctions concerning the way the believers relate to one another (4:7–11) might be viewed as urging them to create samples of that divine justice, that superior reality to which they truly belong. In that sense, love, hospitality, and the employment of gifts are urged upon the community in the same way that the husbands are urged to bestow honor on their wives. While the world imposes one reality upon the readers, they are to create another reality among themselves.

How 1 Peter 2:11–4:11 fits with 1 Peter 4:12–5:11

At this juncture we need to examine how the two sections of 2:11–4:11 and 4:12–5:11 fit together. As noted previously, the two sections share a formally parallel construction evidenced in identical introductory greetings, a great deal of shared vocabulary, nearly identical doxologies at their conclusions, and, of course, the shared content of the household codes. Despite these striking, formal commonalities, however, there are marked differences in the two passages. These differences can be noted in each of the three subsections that comprise the unit.

As has been said, 4:12–19 serves as the introductory paragraph of the larger section in which it appears. As such, it shares a great deal of vocabulary with 2:11–17, which also serves as the introduc-

tion to the unit in which it is found. The important difference between these respective introductory paragraphs is that the strong
"you-they" polarity that dominates 2:11–17 is almost entirely absent
from 4:12–19. In 2:11–17 it is very clear who the opponents are—
evil-speaking, ignorant, foolish Gentiles. In 4:12–19, however, the
opponent is a depersonalized "fiery ordeal." The focus has shifted
from a concern for the relationships between the believers and the
nonbelievers to a concentration upon the believers themselves. The
believers are to rejoice in suffering, they will be glad when Christ's
future glory is revealed, they are blessed in revilement because the
spirit of glory and of God rests upon them, and so forth. The opponent is still present, but, in comparison with 2:11–17, that opponent is greatly reduced. The active verbs attributed to the opponents
in 2:11–17, "they speak against you," have been abandoned in favor
of the passive "you are reproached" in 4:14. In short, while suffering is still very much the subject of discussion, it is lifted from its
context in the human relations between the believers and the world
and imprinted with christological and eschatological significance. In
2:11–4:11, the goal of Christian suffering is primarily missional. In
4:12–19 the goal of suffering is to be proven worthy in the judgment
which is beginning with the household of God and, consequently, to
share in Christ's glory when it is revealed. The phrase τοῦ οἴκου
τοῦ θεοῦ ("the household of God") emphasizes that the focal interest of this section is the believers as the concrete manifestation of
God's new reality. Eventually, in vs. 17 and 18, those "who do not
obey the gospel of God" become objects of pity and compassion
rather than opponents. Thus, as the community itself becomes
the focus of interest, and as that concern receives overlays of cosmo-
logical and eschatological significance, the opponents fade in
importance.

It is in the context of this intense concern for the believers themselves that the injunctions to the elders and the youth are set forth in
5:1–5. Thus, while the injunctions to the slaves and wives were
given in the context of the relationships between Christians and non-
Christians, the context for these injunctions is the Christian community itself. This new context, the household of God, is the
concretization of the reality foreshadowed by the injunction to the
husbands in 3:7 and the vision of operative love and the employment
of gifts in 4:7–11.

Other differences between 2:11–4:11 and 4:12–5:11 support this
conclusion. First, while in the previous two pairings of the household code the subordinate member of the pair was addressed first,

here the elders are addressed first. While previously the subordinate members were not only addressed first but given the most space and attention, the elders receive the space and attention in this section. Second, in 5:1 the author addresses the elders as one of them and, specifically, as a co-witness of the sufferings of Christ. The implication is that a qualification for leadership, rather than for followership as in 2:11–4:11, is patterning oneself after the model of the nonretaliatory Christ as embodied by the slaves and the wives. Third, this implied leadership qualification is made explicit in 5:3 as the elders are specifically conjoined not to "lord it over" the youth but to be examples to the flock. Thus, while following the suffering Christ model becomes a qualification for leadership in the new community of believers, the model for carrying out this leadership assignment is Christ as shepherd. Most telling, the exhortation to the elders is like the exhortation to the husbands in that the benefits of privilege (shameful gain and dominance) are to be relinquished. Whereas the suffering of the believing community in relation to the outside world is cast in the image of the suffering Christ, life within the community is guided by the image of the sanctuary, the sheepfold. Fourth, while the youth are conjoined to submit to the elders, this command is not justified by an appeal to a nonretaliatory Christology. In fact, whereas in the cases of the slaves and wives of non-Christian husbands, elaborate motivations were supplied, neither a model nor any motivation at all is provided for the youth. None is needed. Obeying those more experienced in the faith makes sense to the author of 1 Peter, but it is not couched either in the language of nonretaliation or in the language of missionary appeal. The absence of these motivations and models for the youth is a substantial point. This absence can be explained only by an understanding that the context of the injunction is the church. The success of the church as a created sanctuary where there is a new basis for relationships nullifies the need to motivate the "youth."

In the final verses of 1 Peter 5, this image of the sanctuary is expanded in a way that draws both 2:11–4:11 and 4:12–5:11 together in a resounding conclusion. In 5:6–11 it is apparent that the sanctuary, with its new ethic and new relations, is grounded in a theological understanding of God's love and trustworthiness that frees the believers to create this new reality in concrete terms. As the image of the roaring lion that paces just outside the sanctuary indicates, however, this sanctuary is carved out, apart from but in the midst of the evil that the believers are experiencing in their relations beyond their communities. This surrounding reality is to be soberly watched and resisted by those inside the fold. Thus the epistle draws to its close—somewhere in the tension between the two realities, the tension expressed so graphically and powerfully in the image of the lion and the sanctuary, a tension resolved only by a vigorous and vibrant faith that the one reality is stronger than the other, that God will guide this "ark" through the storm too. For finally, it is with a resounding statement of that faith that the author concludes as he states unequivocally that the God of all grace will restore, establish, and strengthen the believers all over the world.

Conclusions

In this essay we have proposed a way of reading 1 Peter that assumes the meaningfulness of the arrangement of the material. Confronted with what seemed on the surface to be a rather strange mixture of the traditional household codes and advice about various social relations with scriptural quotations, theological statements, and christological hymns, we have suggested that the christological hymn in 2:21–24 actually provides the hermeneutical and organizational key to 2:11–3:12, the section in which the commands to the slaves, wives, and husbands are given. Further, we have suggested that the entire section of 2:11–4:11 is focused by a concern for how the communities of God function in relation to the world outside these communities. That focus has two prongs. On the one hand, there is the concern for the Christians' ill-treatment at the hands of such persons as evil speakers, revilers, unjust masters, and terrorizing husbands. As a response to this evil, whether the origin of the evil is located in the structures themselves or in the failure of these structures to contain evil, the author summons the readers to a stance of nonretaliation according to the model of the suffering Christ. On the other hand, there is the concern to bring these people into the fold. One of the motivations offered for the nonretaliatory ethic is the hope that such actions will draw people to God.

We have also looked briefly at 4:12–5:11, a portion of the text that is formally parallel to 2:11–4:11. We have suggested that the focus of this portion of the text, in which the commands to the elders and the youth are given, is the communities of believers themselves. These different literary contexts draw attention to the fact that the commands to the elders and the youth are shaped quite differently from the earlier ones. The address is different, the appeal is different, and the model is different.

These rather marked and significant differences raise some interesting hermeneutical issues. Here I identify some of these issues and discuss them briefly. Since the point of entry into the discussion was the perceived incongruity between the rhetoric of peace and the rhetoric of oppression, this discussion will take place within the framework of a liberation perspective. I offer the following points for dialogue and discussion.

1. As a result of this particular reading of the text, I conclude that, according to 1 Peter, the authority exercised within the body of believers should be based only on such universally human qualities as maturity in the faith. This maturity is focused by a commitment to not returning evil for evil and expressed by the ability to lead without domineering over others. Such distinctions as gender, race, and class are irrelevant within the community of faith. Further, when power based on such irrelevant criteria is allowed to exist within communities of faith or when persons of weaker social positions in the world are not empowered by the community of faith, these communities suffer the consequences of being cut off from God. Their prayers are hindered.

2. Sometimes the question has been raised as to whether an appropriate application of this reading of the text might be to counsel twentieth-century wives of non-Christian husbands to submit to them even when they are abusive in order to "bring them to Christ." Pertinent points from the text are *(a)* the continuity the text establishes between slavery and wifely submission; and *(b)* the missionary focus of the appeal for submission. Unless we are willing to acknowledge that when we counsel wifely submission we are also advocating all the other kinds of exploitation we have come to associate with slavery, and unless we are willing to consider soberly whether or not exploitive attitudes and actions draw people to Christ in our modern world, we can hardly counsel wifely submission and be true to the spirit of this epistle.

3. Finally, does the document stand as a genuine document of peace and justice? It seems clear that from the point of view of the text, both slavery and patriarchy are institutions that are beyond the control of the community. Further, it seems clear that the text offers no clear critique of either these institutions or the institution of government itself. All such "orders" are taken for granted as the given social reality.[26] Even though these institutions are not critiqued, however, the text recognizes that evil exists within them. While the government is the only one of these orders dignified with a statement of its purpose, there is ironic acknowledgment that it is not fulfilling that purpose. This situation exists either because there are

governors who do not understand their purpose or because these governors are ineffective in executing this purpose. In either case, the result is "foolishness" with which the Christians must contend. By contrast, slavery and patriarchy are not explicitly sanctioned and the specific cases of comment are cases of unjust masters and terrorizing husbands. The mention of bad masters and non-Christian husbands seems to indicate that slavery and patriarchy are not institutions with divine sanction but belong to those "human institutions" which are problematic for the community. Given these social realities, the author is saying, the community has a somewhat limited range of possible reactions. The option the author is encouraging is that of nonretaliation. Nonretaliation does not stand alone, of course. Two positive claims provide foundational support for this stance. The slaves know they have God's approval; the wives "adorn" themselves with their value in the eyes of God. Also, the slaves and wives belong to communities in which this real status is concretized, where they experience equality in a day-to-day way. Because the text both takes such "human institutions" as slavery and patriarchy for granted and urges the creation of concrete groups of human beings that operate apart from these systems, it is neither appropriate to claim the text as uniformly liberative nor to castigate it as a tool of the status quo. The text stands somewhere in the middle as an honest attempt to deal with certain social realities in as theologically meaningful a way as possible. In that effort, the principles of nonretaliation and the issues of alternative ways of being in the world come into focus. For these reasons alone, what has been posed as a real answer to real problems in a particular space and time seems worthy of our attention.

Taking those considerations into account, we might finally think about positive appropriations of this text in the modern church. While the letter does not really address the question of how to address the evils about which we can do something, since that is not the social situation of the addressees, it seems to me that the letter does have something to say about those situations in which we are relatively powerless. While modern Christians are, as a matter of course, active in the arenas of social injustice, there are always those components of injustice about which one can realistically do little. To be determined not to repay in kind, to adorn oneself and others by claiming our value in God's eyes, and to create sanctuaries, "arks," and "households" where those values are realized in daily life are not, it seems to me, insignificant strategies. They might even be evidences of the God of justice at work in the ambiguity of human history.

Notes

1. As representative of this consensus that 1 Peter 2:11–3:12 is a unit we may cite two contemporary authors with quite different views of 1 Peter. Despite their differences in many respects, David Balch and John Elliott agree on this issue. See David L. Balch, *Let Wives Be Submissive: The Domestic Code in 1 Peter* (SBLMS 26; Chico, Calif.: Scholars Press, 1981), 129; and John H. Elliott, *A Home for the Homeless: A Sociological Exegesis of 1 Peter, Its Situation and Strategy* (Philadelphia: Fortress Press, 1981), 234–235. For someone who disagrees slightly with the consensus, see Charles H. Talbert, "Once Again: The Plan of 1 Peter," in *Perspectives on First Peter* (ed. Charles H. Talbert; Special Studies No. 9; Macon, Ga.: Mercer University Press, 1986), 149–151. Talbert, however, still sees the 2:11–3:12 as part of the same larger unit 2:11–5:11.

2. Elisabeth Schüssler Fiorenza, *In Memory of Her: A Feminist Theological Reconstruction of Christian Origins* (New York: Crossroad, 1983), 26.

3. The studies that elucidate the epistle theologically and doctrinally are too numerous to mention. The list would include the majority of commentaries as well as many very fine monographs and articles. An important recent contribution to this effort is Earl Richard, "The Functional Christology of First Peter," in Talbert, *Perspectives on First Peter,* pp. 121–140.

4. Balch, *Wives,* and Elliott, *Home,* are examples of these interests.

5. David W. Kendall's article, "The Literary and Theological Function of 1 Peter 1:3–12" (Talbert, *Perspectives on First Peter,* 103–120), represents an exception to this observation and may be a harbinger of more studies of this nature.

6. Oscar S. Brooks, "1 Peter 3:21—The Clue to the Literary Structure of the Epistle," *NovT* 16 (1974): 290–291.

7. Ibid., 296.

8. Ibid., 296–297.

9. Ibid., 300.

10. Ibid., 301.

11. Ibid., 304.

12. Ibid., 305.

13. William Joseph Dalton, *Christ's Proclamation to the Spirits* (AnBib 23; Rome: Pontifical Biblical Institute, 1965), 75–76.

14. Ibid., 83.

15. Talbert, "Once Again," 142.

16. Ibid., 142–143.

17. It is my contention that the aurality of New Testament texts has seldom been sufficiently appreciated. By noting this aural quality, I am not suggesting that the text existed as an "oral text" before appearing in its written state. More simply, I am suggesting that in an age when literacy was not taken for granted, a writer would have been more sensitive to how a text sounds than a modern writer would be. By raising this question of

aurality in relation to the phenomena of direct address and "doxologies," I am also not necessarily designating a liturgical "setting in Life." While the materials may have been used in worship, the point that the symmetry of address and doxology suggests both visual and oral demarcation of literary units does not depend on a consideration of its actual usage in the early church.

18. Dalton, *Christ's Proclamation,* 76.

19. Talbert ("Once Again," 149–150) points out this relationship between the general and the specific injunctions.

20. For the purpose of this essay, "author" means, and will always mean, the implied author, and "reader" means, and will always mean, the implied reader.

21. "According to Aristotle (1.2.1356a) there are . . . three and only three modes of artistic proof: ethos, pathos, and logos. These categories are found in the speech of all cultures and they inhere respectively in speaker, audience, and discourse. Pathos . . . may be defined as the emotional reactions the hearers undergo as the orator 'plays upon their feelings'" (George A. Kennedy, *New Testament Interpretation Through Rhetorical Criticism* [Chapel Hill, N.C.: University of North Carolina Press, 1984], 15).

22. Barclay M. Newman, *A Concise Greek-English Dictionary of the New Testament* (London: United Bible Societies, 1971), 167.

23. Kennedy, *New Testament Interpretation,* 16.

24. This case can be argued on grammatical grounds. Because, as Kennedy says, γάρ or ὅτι is "commonly the indication of an enthymeme" (Kennedy, *New Testament Interpretation,* 16), we can assume that the primary supporting reason is the ὅτι clause (2:15), while the prepositional phrase εἰς ἐκδίκησιν κακοποιῶν ἔπαινον δὲ ἀγαθοποιῶν (2:14) provides a secondary and more incidental kind of support.

25. *A Lexicon Abridged from Liddell and Scott's Greek-English Lexicon* (Oxford: Clarendon Press, 1982), 493.

26. An analogy might be drawn to our modern exchange economy. Though it is far from clear that an exchange economy (as opposed to a gift economy or some as yet undreamed system) is just and there are many evidences of its abuse, most modern Christians simply accept the system of exchange as a given social reality. Furthermore, even Christians who question this system continue to interact with the wider world on the basis of it. There are very few other options.

12

Apocalyptic Sectarianism and Love Commands: The Johannine Epistles and Revelation

Pheme Perkins

Apocalyptic Dualism and the Language of Love

The New Testament injunction to love one's enemies includes those who persecute the community (cf. Matt. 5:44; 1 Cor. 4:12–13; 1 Peter 3:9). Several warrants are given for this response. It reflects God's own perfection (Matt. 5:48).[1] Anything less is merely playing by human standards (Matt. 5:46–47). It shows that the apostle preacher imitates the suffering and weakness of the Lord. He or she does not seek the power or acclaim of the human audience (1 Cor. 4:8–13). It may lessen the hostility of outsiders when they see that Christians have done nothing to deserve the treatment they receive. A loving response may even lead to the conversion of those who persecuted the community (1 Peter 3:14–16).[2] Each of these motives can also be found in non-Christian sources, which recommend "love of enemies" for the person who is truly wise.[3] What is unusual about the Christian case is the insistence that "love of enemies" should be the policy of the whole community, since it was central to both the teaching and the life of its founder.[4] "Love of enemies" is not merely an option for the pious to show that they are above anger and enmity. It is to be the community's response when it is persecuted.[5] Consequently, the enemies to be loved are hostile to God's word as embodied in the gospel.

However, the active hostility to righteousness and to God's word was often explained in Jewish and Christian circles as evidence that the community was living "at the end of the age." In a world dominated by evil powers, whose activities express demonic hostility to God (e.g., 1 Peter 5:8–9),[6] only the elect few will remain faithful and experience the salvation that follows upon the judgment (Mark 13:9–23).

The biblical commentaries and community rules from Qumran provide evidence of a sectarian Jewish movement that sought to preserve its integrity, holiness, and righteousness through the evils of the last days in which most of the people are being led away from God's rule. Humanity is divided between children of light and children of darkness. The community separated itself as much as possible from outsiders. It maintained a high degree of solidarity, mutual charity, and love among its members, whose behavior was constantly evaluated. Its founder had been persecuted by religious authorities from Jerusalem.

The introduction to the community rule describes entry of new members into the sect. They must turn to God with wholehearted devotion and reject everything and everyone who is opposed to God:

> that they may seek God with a whole heart and soul, and do what is good and right before Him as He commanded by the hand of Moses and his servants, the prophets . . . that they may *love all the sons of light,* each according to his lot in God's design, and *hate all the sons of darkness,* each according to his guilt in God's vengeance. (1QS 1:3–9)[7]

The parallel between this passage and the antithesis used by Matthew to introduce the "love of enemies" command (Matt. 5:44) has frequently been noted. The Essene is not commanded to hate the enemy because he or she is hostile to the sect. Rather, love and hatred correspond to God's redemptive activity. Those destined for salvation, "children of light," are loved. Those destined for condemnation are hated.[8]

The Essene writings raise an important question about the command to love one's enemies. Since "love" is not a subjective emotion or attitude but positive activity in relationship to "the enemy," how can it be exercised toward those who are active enemies of God's Law? "Hate" in the Essene code did not imply hostile actions against such persons. Members of the sect were commanded not to argue or dispute with the "sons of darkness." Sectarian withdrawal from association with evil was the action that would follow from the command to "hate."

Apocalyptic symbolism that equates the ruling powers or the oppressors with mythological images of the satanic enemy of God or the "angel of darkness" conveys the urgency of disassociation. The question of separation from the larger world arose in early Christian circles. It is evident in 2 Cor. 6:14–7:1, which many commentators think comes from a pre-Pauline tradition.[9] New Gentile converts were not separated from their former associates by the boundaries of the Jewish law. They had to maintain a distance from the behavior typical of their former life (cf. 1 Peter 4:3–5). Paul uses this tradition to urge the Corinthians to reject the false apostles who have invaded the church. Though the Pauline tradition continues to advocate love of enemies,[10] the pressures of external persecution and internal division appear to be more severe in the Johannine epistles and Revelation. "Love" requires adherence to a smaller group within the larger Christian community. The opposition is painted in the satanic terms characteristic of apocalyptic writings.

Love and Hatred
in the Johannine Epistles

Neither the Gospel of John nor the Johannine epistles repeats Jesus' teaching on love of enemies. The epistles make it evident that sectarian conflict has torn apart Christian communities that lay claim to the Johannine heritage.[11] The dualistic language of this tradition paints "the world" as a place of darkness which is in Satan's power (1 John 5:19). Consequently, Christians are exhorted not to love the world or what belongs to it (1 John 2:15–17). Separation from "the world" is part of the Johannine heritage. A second element in the ethical tradition inherited by the author of the epistles is the soteriological motivation of the love command. Love of fellow Christians is grounded in the exemplary death of Christ (1 John 3:16).[12] Love requires material assistance to needy Christians (1 John 3:17). It is associated with the separation between the community and the world, a place of hatred and death (1 John 3:14–15). Since persons "born of God" are the objects of love, it is evident that the Johannine epistles have severely restricted the sense in which "neighbor" is understood. The love command refers only to persons within the church (e.g., 1 John 2:9–11; 4:20–21).[13]

The exhortation directed toward members of the church treats the failure of love as "hatred" and evidence that such persons lack eternal life.[14] Such Christians are as much children of the "evil one" as Cain was (1 John 3:12–13). When the community itself was ruptured by schism,[15] the language of communal paraenesis becomes the rhetoric of apocalyptic condemnation. The false teaching of the secessionists is equated with the false prophets who would lead the people astray at the end time (e.g., 1 John 4:1–4). Christians are told to shun such persons. They are not to receive any hospitality. Indeed, the believer will not even greet them, since even that would mean sharing in their evil work (2 John 10–11).

The dualism of light and darkness, of children of God and children of Satan, of the spirit of truth and the spirit of falsehood recalls the apocalyptic sectarianism of the Essene communities. Some scholars have attempted to ameliorate the restrictive form of the love command in the Johannine epistles by noting that the epistles do not explicitly command believers to "hate" the children of darkness.[16] Hate language refers to the community's experience of the world (1 John 3:13) or to the Christian who does not love fellow Christians (1 John 2:9, 11). The secessionists are accused of not keeping God's commandments, just as they fail to believe the truth of Jesus' coming in the flesh (1 John 2:3–5; 3:22–23).[17] Their departure from the Johannine fellowship is evidence that they "hate" the children of light. Though the author may not speak of "hating" dissident Christians, once they have been identified as the agents of the lawlessness of the last days (1 John 2:18, 22; 4:1–5), they can hardly be the object of love. The explicit command to shun such persons (2 John 5, 10–11) is not an example of the love that Christians are to show fellow believers.[18]

Though the love command is the centerpiece of the community's exhortation (e.g., 1 John 2:7–11), the Johannine epistles show that its scope has been severely limited. The dualistic paraenesis that distinguished believers from "the world" already led to a sectarian focus on love as the relationship between believers, not between believers and outsiders. With the subsequent schism, the same rhetoric was applied to Christians who had broken fellowship with the author and his addressees. Love and hatred are determined by a shared doctrine and practice (1 John 3:23). This principle raises a problem for the student of Christian ethics. However severe the damage done the community by the secessionists, should the particularist, conventicle ethic of the Johannine epistles be accepted as sufficient Christian practice?[19] Or should it be subject to the same critique that the "love of enemies" tradition provides for other restrictive definitions of love?

Sectarian Isolation in Revelation

External persecution and internal division fuel the apocalyptic visions in Revelation. The addressees are summoned to acknowledge

Christ's sovereignty over the world by acknowledging that their existence as a "kingdom of priests" flows from God's love demonstrated on the cross (Rev. 1:5b–6).[20] A sectarian sense of "love" similar to that observed in the Johannine epistles appears to be familiar in the churches of Asia Minor. The church at Ephesus is chided for abandoning the love it had had at first and exhorted to repent and do the works that it once had (Rev. 2:4–5). However, the same church is commended for hating the heretical sect of the Nicolaitans just as the Lord does (2:6). Deterioration of brotherly love among Christians was probably exacerbated by increased external pressure to conform to some elements of the prevailing imperial cult. The "hated" Nicolaitans may have proposed a practical accommodation with the paganism of the city.[21] In Pergamum, another center of the imperial cult in the province of Asia,[22] we find that the Nicolaitans are tolerated. There the church is chided for following false prophets who lead the people to eating food sacrificed to idols and practicing immorality (Rev. 2:14–15). The accusation "idol worship and immorality" need not imply a particularly virulent libertinism. It rescinds the apostolic decree of Acts 15:29, which guarantees that the Gentile churches have not compromised with paganism. Even token participation in civic honors to the emperor might bring such charges against the church. This church had experienced the public execution of a martyr, Antipas. Though governing officials may not have sought to exterminate all Christians, when accused before them as Antipas had been, Christians were probably required to give evidence of civic loyalty by some token veneration of the emperor. Refusal meant exile, as in the case of John the prophet, or death.[23]

An inverted companion piece to the Ephesus exhortation occurs in the letter to Thyatira. The community is praised for its works, "love and faith and service and endurance" (Rev. 2:19), but condemned for tolerating a Christian prophet and her followers, who are likewise condemned for eating idol food and immorality (Rev. 2:20–23). Ethnic diversity and religious syncretism appear to have been particularly striking in this city.[24] Metallurgy in the city appears to have been a source of wealth and to have been organized in local trade guilds. The religious requirements of these guilds would demand some accommodation with paganism. The syncretism typical of the other cults in the city might have seemed a reasonable condition for Christians to avoid persecution or exclusion from the economic life of the city.[25]

In this instance, the author suggests that the followers of the false prophet constitute a well-defined group within the community.[26] Perhaps there was some connection between the woman prophet, her followers, and a particular trade.[27] Acts 16:14–15 refers to a prominent convert in Philippi, Lydia, who provided hospitality for Paul and his followers. She dealt in the purple cloth that was produced in her native Thyatira. Through her association with Judaism as a "god-fearer," she was probably led to reject "idol-meat and immorality" before her conversion to Christianity.[28] But in the case of this prophet the Jewish matrix for separation from conventional acknowledgment of the gods may not have been an option. Elisabeth Schüssler Fiorenza has suggested that the hostility to Roman power and its symbols evident in the rest of Revelation may have become urgent because Christians were less and less able to align themselves with Judaism.[29] In any event, John announces the impending condemnation of God. The prophet and her followers will suffer a hideous death. If the trade relationships are behind the impulse to follow the false teaching, then her followers' repenting and rejecting Jezebel carries severe economic consequences. Similar consequences are implied later in the visions of the beast. Christians must avoid "buying and selling" in order to stay clear of the mark of the beast (Rev. 13:16–17). Thus, Revelation advocates socioeconomic isolation from the life of the cities in Asia Minor.[30]

Revelation does not envisage any position of compromise, such as the "honor" Christians are told to accord the emperor in the Pauline tradition (e.g., Rom. 13:1–7; 1 Tim. 2:2–3). Satan stands behind the idolatrous power of the empire.[31] The apocalyptic rhetoric of the book deprives the symbols of imperial Rome so familiar to those who lived in these cities of their power. The righteous in heaven (e.g., Rev. 14:1–5) who follow the Lamb in spotless purity are the antitype of the forces that gather around the beast on earth.[32] Clearly, survival in a world where significant participation in the larger culture is impossible will require communal solidarity. "Faith and endurance" are required for the leading of such a life with its constant danger of persecution.[33]

In some instances, the forces of evil will still extract the price of martyrdom. The 144,000 follow the Lamb even to the cross (Rev. 14:4). The author appears to have thought that the male, virgin martyrs hasten the end of the present world, ruled by the beast.[34] But the passive suffering of God's elect nowhere suggests that they are to love those who follow the beast. The horrible end that the seer envisages for such persons (e.g., Rev. 14:9–11) should suffice to keep the Christian from rejecting or conveniently ignoring the author's teaching about the kingdoms of the world. Separation from the socioeconomic life of the ancient city is the only way that the believer can remain untainted (Rev. 18:4–5) and not share the fate that awaits the rest of humankind.[35]

Those who concentrate on the judgment leveled against all who are not part of God's elect have often spoken of Revelation as a book of resentment, the have-nots lusting for the power that is denied them. However, more recent commentators insist that Revelation is really a work about justice. The alleged Pax Romana has disappeared only to be replaced by anarchy and internal violence (Rev. 6:3–4).[36] The sacrifice of the Lamb was made on behalf of all (Revelation 4–5). The powers of this world prefer the demonic parody of God's rule to the peace that comes from following the Lord. Despite all apparent evidence that it might be better for Christians to assimilate to the standards of the surrounding culture, doing so only brings condemnation and judgment. Apocalyptic visions remind the reader of God's sovereignty, which will finally prevail even over the present evil world (Rev. 20:1–6; 21:24–26).[37]

It is possible that those who advocated accommodation did so by appealing to the example of the apostle Paul.[38] Revelation casts all its visions in the form of the archaic "combat myth" in which the forces of divine order must defeat the chaos dragon.[39] The dragon is not merely untamed chaos but an active rebel against God's order and the elect who represent it. "Love" cannot be commended in this instance. However, it is possible that the depiction of God's judgment against the forces of evil as well as of the reward awaiting the faithful who endure does lessen the hostility that the readers felt, living in such a precarious world.[40] The mythic vision of combat and divine victory over evil provided a structure within which their suffering endurance contributes to God's plan.

Conclusion

The Johannine epistles and Revelation both contain traditional paraenesis about love of neighbor. In both cases, that love is extended only to fellow Christians, not to outsiders. In both instances, the Christian community itself has been divided. For 1 and 2 John that division resulted from conflicting claims about the humanity of Christ and the saving power of the cross. The theological disputes over the truth of a common tradition embodied in the Fourth Gospel had led dissidents to withdraw from fellowship with the churches to which the elder writes the letters. However, as 2 John indicates, the separation between the two groups did not end all communication between them. The author forbids those in his communion to give hospitality to the secessionists or even to greet them. Their teaching represents the outbreak of false prophecy which tradition expected at the end of the age. Although he never uses the term "hatred," such behavior would clearly be considered hatred by his readers.

Revelation also commends churches for hating those whose teaching is perceived to lead others astray. Unlike in the epistles, however, these false prophets are imaged as the wicked of Hebrew scriptures, Balaam and Jezebel. The mythic embodiment of evil lies outside the Christian community in the political authorities of imperial Rome and their civic minions on the local level. It is they who seek to destroy the children of the divine mother, just as in the myths of divine offspring from ancient Near Eastern and classical sources. Yet, ironically, Roman coinage portrayed imperial identification with the infant Apollo and his mother being rescued from the dragon, Python.[41] Revelation 12–13 taught John's readers that they were the children of the divine mother. Revelation 19:11–21 pictures Christ as the divine warrior doing battle for his people.[42]

Once the persecution suffered by the community is felt in mythic terms, the accommodations to civic or guild practices advocated by other Christian prophets are impossible. There can be no Christian compromise with the satanic enemy of God. Those Christians who attempt to make such compromises will share the fate of the wicked. The letters do not spell out how "hatred" of such persons was demonstrated. Refusal to associate with them as in the case of 2 John may have been the anticipated response. Though Christians cannot be said to "love" either those Christians who follow such teaching or the external persecutors whose activities have led to the crisis, they do not participate in punishing them. The martyrs in heaven cry out to God for the end-time victory. The seer announces God's punishment of Jezebel and her followers as a near event, prior to the end-time visions.

The only active contribution that Christians make to God's victory is in their patient endurance and suffering. Since its price may include socioeconomic withdrawal from the life of the cities, love among the elect expressed as solidarity and mutual support must have played a more prominent role than the sparse references in Revelation itself might suggest. Once the specific setting of Revelation is appreciated, we recognize that it contains a powerful expression of the gospel for Christians in a sociopolitical situation marked by violence and persecution. If "love of enemy" means compromising the gospel witness, then it cannot be Christ's word to that church. If "love of neighbor," that is, associations with the non-Christian neighbor, also exposes individuals to the danger of being denounced and persecuted, then some form of social withdrawal may be the only policy. Revelation does not advocate rushing into martyrdom or punitive exile. Some, like the seer, may have that testimony thrust upon them. For the rest, love as communal solidarity, patient endurance, and refusal to compromise with the powers of evil are the key to survival. In all things, the Lamb will reign victorious.

Notes

1. Or God's "mercy" (Luke 6:36). Probably, the earlier version of the saying. It corresponds to the beatitude in Matt. 5:7 (so Robert A. Guelich, *The Sermon on the Mount: A Foundation for Understanding* [Waco, Tex.: Word Books, 1982], 233).

2. John H. Elliott, *A Home for the Homeless: A Sociological Exegesis of 1 Peter, Its Situation and Strategy* (Philadelphia: Fortress Press, 1981), 78–84.

3. See Pheme Perkins, *Love Commands in the New Testament* (New York: Paulist Press, 1982), 28–40.

4. See Pheme Perkins, *Jesus as Teacher* (New York: Cambridge University Press, 1990), 98–102.

5. Guelich (*Sermon,* 228) notes that the persecution envisaged in Matthew is religious persecution (Matt. 5:11). There is no distinction between personal enemies and those hostile to Christianity as such.

6. Elliott, *Home for the Homeless,* 81.

7. Géza Vermès, *The Dead Sea Scrolls in English* (2nd ed.; Baltimore: Penguin Books, 1975), 72.

8. Cf. Guelich, *Sermon,* 226.

9. In defense of Paul's use of this material even though he does not demand that Christians isolate themselves from all contacts with nonbelievers (e.g., 1 Cor. 5:9–10), see Victor Paul Furnish, *II Corinthians* (AB 32A; Garden City, N.Y.: Doubleday & Co., 1984), 375–383.

10. Perkins, *Love Commands,* 89–103.

11. Cf. Raymond E. Brown, *The Epistles of John* (AB 30; Garden City, N.Y.: Doubleday & Co., 1982), 42–55, 69–86.

12. Cf. Wolfgang Schrage, *The Ethics of the New Testament* (Philadelphia: Fortress Press, 1988), 307.

13. Cf. Brown, *Epistles,* 269–271; and Schrage, *Ethics of the New Testament,* 316.

14. Cf. Pheme Perkins, "The Johannine Epistles," *New Jerome Biblical Commentary* (ed. R. Brown, J. Fitzmyer, and R. Murphy; Englewood Cliffs, N.J.: Prentice Hall, 1990), 991.

15. Cf. the references to those who have "gone out" (1 John 2:19; 4:1; 2 John 7).

16. So Schrage, *Ethics of the New Testament,* 318; and Brown, *Epistles,* 272.

17. Brown, *Epistles,* 84.

18. Ibid., 85.

19. Schrage, *Ethics of the New Testament,* 317. Schrage notes that the use of the love command to refer to love of fellow Christians in the Gospel of John is not identical with the epistles. In the Gospel, external persecution requires that the community reinforce its internal cohesion. That unity is expressed in terms of the love abiding within the community. Solidarity in times of persecution should not be confused with sectarian isolation.

20. Schrage, *Ethics of the New Testament,* 331–333; the same theme without the reference to Christ's love reappears in the hymnic passage in Rev. 5:9–10. Though the communal image of "priests" appears in these passages, there is no place for a priesthood in the eschatological future envisaged by Revelation. When the kingdom is realized, there will be no temple and no need for mediation, since the lamb will dwell with the people; cf. Pierre Prigent, *L'apocalypse de Saint Jean* (Paris: Delachaux et Niestlé, 1981), 103.

21. Cf. Colin J. Hemer, *The Letters to the Seven Churches of Asia in Their Local Setting* (JSNTS 11; Sheffield: JSOT Press, 1986), 35–41, 51f.

22. "Satan's throne" is probably a reference to the temple dedicated to the imperial cult (Tacitus, *Annals* 4.37.3; cf. Heinrich Kraft, *Die Offenbarung des Johannes* [HNT 16a; Tübingen: J. C. B. Mohr (Paul Siebeck), 1974], 63).

23. Cf. Adela Yarbro Collins, *Crisis and Catharsis: The Power of the Apocalypse* (Philadelphia: Westminster Press, 1984), 101–104.

24. Hemer, *Letters,* 107–111.

25. Ibid., 121–123.

26. Cf. Kraft, *Offenbarung,* 69–70.

27. Hemer, *Letters,* 121–123.

28. *Pace* Hemer (*Letters,* 121), who thinks that Lydia may have been subject to such pressures through guild membership.

29. Elisabeth Schüssler Fiorenza, *The Book of Revelation: Justice and Judgment* (Philadelphia: Fortress Press, 1985), 1993–1995.

30. Collins, *Crisis,* 123–127.

31. Schüssler Fiorenza, *Revelation,* 195–196.

32. Ibid., 186–189.

33. Collins, *Crisis,* 126–130.

34. Ibid.

35. Ibid., 172–229.

36. Eugene Boring, *Revelation* (Louisville: John Knox Press, 1989), 118–122.

37. Ibid., 36–42, 118.

38. Collins, *Crisis,* 131.

39. Boring, *Revelation,* 155–157; and Collins, *Crisis,* 148f.

40. Collins, *Crisis,* 156–157.

41. Boring, *Revelation,* 151f.

42. Collins, *Crisis,* 130.

13

Love for One Another
and Love for Enemies
in the Gospel
of John

David Rensberger

Jerome, in a well-known passage of his *Commentary on Galatians* (6.10), relates that the apostle John in old age said nothing to his followers except, "My little children, love one another." For most readers, the Fourth Gospel as the gospel of love remains relatively unproblematic. The words of the "new commandment" in John 13:34 and 15:12—"Love one another as I have loved you"— if not easy to carry out, at least seem easy to understand.

Contemporary New Testament scholarship has changed this situation rather drastically. It has seen a rediscovery of the origins of the Fourth Gospel and its related epistles and so also a rediscovery of the Johannine problematic. A more exact understanding of John's historical context has been accompanied by a renewed awareness of the difficulties to be encountered in this most remarkable of the New Testament Gospels.

With regard specifically to the love commandment in John, Raymond Collins has identified several areas that need consideration. These include the literary relationship of the love commandment texts to their setting in John, and perhaps to 1 John as well; the commandment's "newness" and indeed the fact of its being a commandment; and the theological significance both of its designation of love as for "one another" and of its connection to Jesus' own love for his disciples.[1] Though this list may not exhaust the possibilities, these are in fact the items that recur repeatedly in commentaries and special studies. We will touch on most of them, but our primary concerns in this essay will be the commandment's literary context and the relationship between loving one another and loving one's enemies.

The Love Commandment
in the Gospel of John

It can be a bit surprising to realize that some scholars regard a theme long considered central to the Gospel of John as a secondary addition to it. The question is an important one, since the historical context or *Sitz im Leben* of the love commandment in John has a significant bearing on how we understand both its primary force and its specific nuances. Knowing at what stage of the Johannine community's history any text was written helps in determining the precise sense of particular concepts and events in the text. Our improving grasp of the history of the community, and of how the texts relate to that history, makes this all the more true.[2] When the Gospel of John was first written, the Christian community behind it was enduring a painful separation from the Jewish synagogue environment in which many of its members had evidently been nurtured. At a later time, the community was torn by internal christological and ethical conflicts, and it was at this point that 1 John was written and, according to a number of scholars, the Gospel was further edited. Clearly, the meaning of the love commandment in John could vary considerably depending on the period at which it entered the Gospel. Before we can seek to understand it in relationship to the love of enemies, then, we must first determine the stage of the Johannine community's history within which it received its peculiarly Johannine form.

The love commandment in John appears in two sections of what are commonly known as the farewell discourses, John 13:31–38 and 15:9–17. It has been clear to most scholars for some time that these discourses as they now stand are composite, and it is generally accepted that the Gospel originally ran directly from 14:31 to 18:1, while the intervening chs. 15–17 were added by a subsequent redactor or redactors. This may have been done, in part at least, by the original author of the Gospel; part of it may also be the work of later members of the same community or "school."[3] Since one instance of the love commandment falls within this redactional material, the question of its *Sitz im Leben* becomes involved with that of the supplementary farewell discourses in general and their relationship, both literary and historical, to the original discourse in chs. 13–14 and to 1 John.

As an approach to this issue, we shall consider two recent attempts to situate the Johannine love commandment at a point in the history of the Johannine community later than the original writing of the Fourth Gospel. Of course, neither the positions of the scholars in question nor an evaluation of them can be set forth in full in this context. The reader must consult the studies themselves for details of their argumentation; the assessment of them given below will of necessity be only a sketch, not a complete demonstration.

Fernando F. Segovia has found significant differences between the way love relationships are understood in the Gospel of John and their understanding in the first epistle. In 1 John the Christians' love for one another is the main emphasis, and according to Segovia this love involves the keeping of ethical commandments and accepting God's love shown in Jesus' death.[4] But Segovia also finds in John 15:9–17 a combination of elements that aligns this passage with the first epistle, not the rest of the Gospel. These elements include a focus on "abiding" (parallel to the concern for right belief in 15:1–8); an interest in right ethics; an inner-church conflict; and a concern for mutual love based on Jesus' love in his sacrificial death.[5] The similar giving of the love commandment in 13:34–35 must then come from the same redactional and historical context.[6] Segovia concludes that John 13:34–35 and 15:1–17 were added to the original text of the farewell discourses by a redactor who shared the same historical situation and theological outlook as the author of 1 John, in contrast to the earlier conflict with the synagogue authorities that shaped the Gospel.[7]

Whereas Segovia concentrated on passages in which "love" occurs, Urban C. von Wahlde focuses on the term "commandment" in the Johannine Gospel and epistles. He concludes that there are in fact two commandments of Jesus in the Gospel: to keep Jesus' word (John 14:23) and to love one another (15:12).[8] In 1 John, where commandments are more prominent (though they are always commandments of God, not of Jesus), von Wahlde again finds two: to believe in Jesus and to love one another (1 John 3:23).[9] By examining literary and theological inconsistencies, von Wahlde seeks to show that all the references to commandments in the Gospel of John, including the love commandment passages in 13:34–35 and 15:9–17, are found within secondary additions to the Gospel and have theological connections to 1 John. He concludes that all these passages are the work of a redactor in the same historical circumstances and sharing essentially the same theological stance as the author of 1 John.[10]

By concentrating on issues of linguistic nuance and the interpretation of individual phrases and sentences, Segovia and von Wahlde construct an impressive argument for the secondary interpolation of the love commandment texts into the Fourth Gospel. However, there are other questions concerning the relationship between John and 1 John within the history of the Johannine community and its tradition that must also be addressed. For instance, Segovia assumes that the early controversy with the synagogue authorities did not involve "inner-church" conflicts.[11] Yet John severely criticizes Christians who wish to remain within the synagogue framework and therefore refuse to confess Jesus as Messiah openly (John 9:22; 12:42–43).[12] Note in particular John 8:31–59, which begins with a call to Jewish believers to "abide" in Jesus' word, then progresses through an acrimonious debate until they are ready to stone him.[13] Precisely this sort of inner-Christian conflict could form the background for the call in John 15:1–8 to "abide" in Jesus.[14]

Thus the possibility is also established that redactional materials such as John 15:1–8 can be dated to the period of the synagogue conflict, as Segovia himself has demonstrated quite convincingly with regard to John 15:18–16:4a, which speaks of the disciples' hatred and persecution by the world, that is, the synagogue authorities.[15] If both this passage and 15:1–8 could have originated during that conflict, then we must ask whether 15:9–17, including the love commandment, might do the same. By the time 15:18–16:4a was added to the farewell discourse, the struggle with the synagogue authorities had evidently escalated to the point where martyrdom had come to seem a real possibility, if it was not indeed an already accomplished fact (16:2). The reference to imitating Jesus' laying down of his life for his friends in 15:12–13 makes good sense precisely within this framework.[16] In such circumstances, members of a close-knit group like the Johannine community would find the demand for mutual solidarity, that is, for mutual love, more imperative than ever.[17] Thus the juxtaposition of 15:9–17 with 15:18–16:4a, the disciples' love with the world's hatred,[18] can be seen as both natural and deliberate within the framework of intensified opposition from the synagogue authorities.

If the love commandment in John 15:12, 17 may be set in the same general period as the first edition of the Gospel, then what about 13:34–35? It must be admitted that literary arguments to the effect that these verses interrupt the flow within John 13:31–38 have considerable merit,[19] though for that very reason one might well ask why an interpolator would not have put them before 13:32 or after 13:38. Theological arguments for their being an interpolation are less convincing. Certainly the passage does not provide a basis for differentiating among disciples on the basis of behavior.[20] Quite the opposite: it emphasizes the unified front that the disciples must present *before the world,* a significant difference from 1 John, which is concerned with distinguishing between true and false Christians *within the community.* In this respect it is closer to the theme of the disciples' witness to the world found in 15:27, and especially in 17:20–23, where the reference to the community's attestation of Jesus' divine origin before the world relates to the conflict with the synagogue, not the internecine dispute in 1 John. The community's testimony consists of its oneness, a oneness created by its hierarchical communion with God through Jesus (not directly with God, as in 1 John),[21] and surely related to its members' love for one another as Jesus loved them.

We may conclude from these considerations that the love commandment passages in John 13 and John 15 are at home both theologically and socially in the context of the Johannine community's conflict with the synagogue authorities. The community's mutual love served as part of its testimony to the divinity of Jesus and also as an essential factor in the group's survival against the hatred it perceived itself as experiencing as a consequence of that testimony.

There is one further problem to which Segovia and von Wahlde give too little consideration, namely, the origin of the love commandment in John if it was not part of the original Gospel. It has been cogently suggested that much of John's material derives ultimately from a tradition independent of the Synoptics that existed before the Fourth Gospel was given its present character, whether as a written gospel[22] or as oral tradition.[23] Segovia holds that the term "love" gives little information about this pre-Gospel stage, and that the love commandment was originally completely lacking in the Fourth Gospel.[24] But love for other people was surely a significant element in the tradition about Jesus, appearing in both Mark and Q. This raises the question of how something found in Jesus tradition elsewhere could have entered secondarily into the farewell discourses at the time of 1 John without connection to Johannine Jesus tradition. In 1 John the love commandment is always a commandment of God;[25] in this hypothetical process, it would have to be transformed into a commandment of Jesus. Moreover, on this hypothesis the love commandment would be only one of a number of non-Johannine elements in 1 John. But those elements are by and large parallel to Pauline and other traditions, not to Jesus traditions. Given these considerations, and since John 15:18–16:4a makes use of items from Jesus tradition paralleled in the Synoptics,[26] it seems more likely that the love commandment came that way also than that it was an innovation at the time of 1 John.

Indeed, von Wahlde sees just that as the process: the redactor of the Gospel at the time of 1 John added the love commandment, like all the commandment material, using community tradition that had been left out of the original Fourth Gospel.[27] But we have just noted that this material is conceived in 1 John as commandments of God rather than of Jesus and that the community at the time of 1 John seems to have been drawing new material from sources other than its own Jesus traditions. It must also be asked how it happened that precisely love for one another was seen as *the* ethical commandment that the opponents of 1 John were violating. How is it that 1 John can be so insistent on this, if love was not *already* a significant factor in the Johannine tradition? And if mutual love was of such significance to Johannine Christians, why would it have been left out of the original Gospel?

We cannot enter further into the relationship between the Johannine epistles and the Fourth Gospel here. Even if the love commandment in John is entirely redactional, it probably entered the Gospel before the time of 1 John, during the synagogue conflict and perhaps not much later than the original composition of the Gospel, as increasing persecution increased the need for communal solidarity.[28] But it may also be that only the occurrences in 15:9–17 are redactional, expanding on 13:34–35 when the persecution increased.

Despite their abstractness, these questions of literary and tradition history, of "original" and "redactional," have some theological and hermeneutical interest of their own. Johannine studies in many respects are still deeply indebted to Rudolf Bultmann and his disciples. Bultmann saw the fundamental issues of theology in terms of being (authentic existence) rather than doing (authentic action) and the indicative of God's act accepted in faith as always prior to and motivating the imperative of ethical action, though the two remain dialectically unified.[29] Subsequent exegetes have therefore tended to be suspicious of any contamination of indicative by imperative, since the latter must always be secondary. Bultmann himself passed rather severe judgment on the Christian literature of the first and early second centuries on the basis of its fidelity to Paul's paradoxical dialectic of indicative and imperative.[30] His heirs, then, may naturally be predisposed toward exegetical and tradition-historical reconstructions that see ethical issues as secondary developments within the Johannine tradition. This predisposition is, of course, justified to some extent by the Johannine epistles' later date and undeniably greater interest in ethics. Yet one cannot help suspecting that the decision to regard some materials in John 13 and 14 as redactional is partly based on the judgment that they add love to faith as a mark of discipleship[31] or make Jesus' promises conditional on the keeping of commandments.[32]

José Porfirio Miranda, however, in his provocative work on the Johannine writings done from an existentialist and liberationist stance, has pushed us to see the questions of being and doing as inseparable, so that authentic existence is neither apart from nor prior to authentic action, and divine being consists precisely in ethical imperative.[33] Bultmann himself claimed that the apparent temporal succession of indicative and imperative is illusory: "The Word is only properly heard when the believer loves *in that he is a believer.*"[34] But could we not also say that the Word is heard properly when one *believes in that one is a lover?* If the two are really a unity without succession, then is it only possible to say that faith gives birth to love, without also saying that love gives birth to faith? It may be that the decision to love and the decision of faith are so inseparable that one simply cannot be distinguished from the other. Our motion of love acting for the good of the other in need may be the same motion as our motion of faith in response to the Word of God. Augustine remarks in commenting on John 15:12 that where there is love of neighbor there must be love of God also, for no one can love without believing: "nemo diligit, qui non credit" (*In Joh. ev.* 83.3).

Such a reconception of fundamental issues, to which liberation theologians are summoning us as inexorably as dialectical theology summoned exegetes of an earlier generation, may open new exegetical perspectives as well. If imperative and indicative are even less separable than we had thought, then it may seem reasonable that a commandment to love one another should appear, on the selfsame literary level, alongside the glorification of Jesus and his claim that to know him is to know God also. If we are prepared to envision faith and love truly as one, then we may also be prepared to expect that a call to love should be issued in the same historical context as the call to believe that Jesus is in God and God is in him. If this is so, then even if literary incongruity should show that the love commandment passages in John 13 and 15 are interpolations into their context, there is no theological incongruity to suggest that they derive from any other time than that in which the Johannine community was struggling most passionately to define the nature and the meaning of its faith in Jesus.

Loving One Another
and Loving One's Enemies

We have already begun to see some reasons why the love commandment is formulated in John specifically as "Love one another." Now we must go on to explore these more fully.

It is noteworthy that John calls this love commandment a "new" commandment. A number of scholars have observed that the commandment is new, not because nothing like it had ever been given before, but because of its connection with the new, eschatological age inaugurated by the mission of Jesus the Messiah and Son of God.[35] Indeed, a commandment of mutual love can already be found in Lev. 19:18: "You shall love your neighbor as yourself." "Love one another," in fact, resembles Lev. 19:18 (and so Mark 12:31) more than it does "Love your enemies." For there is general agreement that "one another" in John 13:34–35; 15:12, 17 refers to other members of the Johannine Christian community, not to humanity in general.[36]

This restriction is often felt to be troubling and to require explanation in comparison with other, broader conceptions of love in the New Testament. Sometimes the similarity to Leviticus is stressed, since Leviticus also is concerned with relations among the people of God. Raymond Collins suggests that the limitation in John derives from its similar focus on the members of a covenant community. He also points out that in the farewell discourse (testament) genre, within which the love commandment is found in John, interest always centers on relations among those being left behind, not on the world at large.[37] Thus several scholars have noted the frequent occurrence of injunctions to love one another in the *Testaments of the Twelve Patriarchs*.[38] Yet the *Testaments* do occasionally extend the scope of love to humankind in general (e.g., *T. Iss.* 7:6; *T. Zeb.* 5:1). Moreover, the Sermon on the Mount is also addressed to a Christian community but manages to call for love toward enemies outside the community (Matt. 5:44). Considerations of genre and addressees alone cannot explain the distinctive character of the Johannine commandment.

Others have suggested that the Johannine community's mission to the world allows outsiders at least potentially to come within the scope of the love commandment. According to Bultmann, the restriction to "one another" derives from the eschatological nature of the community; the world can always enter this circle by the faith to which the continued existence of the community, enabled by mutual love, calls it.[39] Victor Paul Furnish suggests similarly that, since the mission is extended to all who will receive it, the limitation of love to "one another" does not in itself exclude love for neighbors and enemies. He too insists that the term "one another" is eschatological, not narrowly ecclesiastical, in John.[40] But the latter is surely a meaningless distinction, since in John the community is an eschatological one precisely because of its exclusive claim to have accepted the Messiah sent from God in contradistinction to the "world" that has not. Potentially it is open to those who are of the world to enter the community of faith; otherwise John 3:16–17 and 20:21–23 would have no meaning. But *until* they do so (and thus cease to be "of the world" in the pejorative Johannine sense), they simply are not included in the "one another" to whom the Johannine love commandment is restricted.

J. N. Sanders already recognized that the love commandment in John is restricted because by this time "the Church had been driven in upon itself."[41] In the sense in which the term is used in contemporary sociology, the Johannine community was a sect, a group whose experience of rejection by its parent body (the synagogue, in this case) had led it into an increasing sense of isolation and alienation from the world at large. John's dualism, its sometimes baffling circularity of language, and even its presentation of a supremely exalted Jesus, rejected by and incomprehensible to the world to which he came, are all related to its sectarian character.[42] It must be emphasized that "sectarian" in this sense is a descriptive term, not a derogatory one. Some aspects of John's sectarianism may be disturbing, but others may have positive theological value.[43] It is at any rate within the framework of this sectarianism that we must understand the Johannine commandment to "love one another."

We have already seen that a call to love one another was quite understandable during the Johannine community's dispute with the synagogue. The sect, under intense pressure from outside, needed to forge its own internal bonds even more strongly. If expulsion from the synagogue was to be endured (John 9:22; 12:42; 16:2), then an alternative context of social solidarity and support had to be provided. It would no longer be possible to find validation and affirmation from the former sources; now the community's members must provide these to one another. The "hatred" from without must be balanced and opposed by love within the sect itself. When the threat of bloodshed arose, the possibility of betrayal may have come with it. In such cases, "laying down one's life for one's friends" (15:13) could have been more than just a metaphor for the ultimate kind of love.

Thus love for one another would be one of the means taken up by an oppressed minority to fend off the forces arrayed against it. We have very little evidence in John of the exact forms this love might have taken, other than the stark possibility of giving up one's life rather than betraying others to the persecution; and even that is no more than an inference from the text. Undoubtedly mutual love might take many forms in such circumstances, replacing the care that had formerly come from quarters now closed to the Johannine Christians. They may have found a variety of opportunities to provide one another with sustenance, material, emotional, and spiritual. Love given in this way would give encouragement to the community's members to maintain the messianic confession that was itself the source of their endangerment. The details, however, are simply unknown to us, and we must be wary of allowing imagination to fill them in.

How did this mutual love relate to persons outside the community? A sect is by definition a group at odds with its social environment. Relations with outsiders are on a different basis and of a different quality from relations with members of the group. This can be clearly seen in the Qumran texts that speak of mutual love. There too the sect's members are called on to love one another, sometimes in terms reminiscent of Lev. 19:18. But they are also called on to hate the "children of darkness," that is, the sect's opponents. As F. C. Fensham has shown, this love and hatred are grounded in God's love and hatred respectively for the Spirits of Truth and of Falsehood, for the members and the enemies of the sect.[44] Scholars often emphasize that such an injunction is not found in John, so that even if the Johannine love commandment does not include outsiders, it at least does not require the Johannine Christians to hate them.[45]

However, we must not overlook how far the Fourth Gospel does go in that direction. There are numerous examples in John of attitudes toward "the Jews" (meaning the synagogue authorities, but sometimes even Jewish believers whose confession of faith was evidently not up to Johannine standards) that are bitter, hostile, and even hateful. Perhaps this is to be expected in a section like John 15:18–16:4a, which deals with persecution. But it also lies beneath the surface in those characteristic passages in which "the Jews" are unable to understand Jesus and so are said to be ignorant not only of him but of God as well (e.g., 7:33–36; 8:12–27). Perhaps the most serious instance is in John 8:31–47, where Jesus declares that some Jewish believers are children not of God but of the devil. If this is not hatred, it at least comes perilously close to it.

The commandment to love one another, then, although not explicitly accompanied by an injunction to hate everyone else, still does not require love to be extended to persons outside the Johannine Christian group. There is no commandment to hate one's enemies in John, and taken in the abstract the Johannine form of the love commandment does not exclude love for them.[46] But when we consider the actual theological, social, and linguistic characteristics of the Gospel that contains this commandment, we find that in practice love for enemies is not in evidence. John does have enemies, and they are spoken of anything but lovingly. Whether these words would or could ever have carried over into action we do not know. We may agree with Furnish that Johannine mutual love is a special form of love for one's neighbor, designed to assist the community in maintaining its identity in the face of the world's hostility.[47] "Love one another" does envision the enemy and is a response to the enemy. It enables the community to stand its ground against its enemies, and to do so as disciples of Jesus the Messiah (John 13:35). But it does not imply that the community or its members loved their enemies. We cannot simply assume that the possibility of loving one's enemies remained open, or even that that of hating them was closed off, for the Johannine Christians.

The mention of John 13:35, however, brings to mind something we noted earlier, that the community's love for one another as a mark of their discipleship is linked to their unity as a demonstration to the world of Jesus' divine origin (17:20–23). Thus in Johannine thought mutual love does have a positive meaning for those outside the community. The solidarity of the group under oppression testifies not only to the strength of their conviction but also to its validity, with the aim that even those who oppress them should come to believe as well. We may wonder how effective such a testimony would be if the community's love did not reach beyond its own boundaries, for, impressive as unshakable solidarity may be, if accompanied by hostility toward the group's opponents, it may not hold much attraction for them. Indeed, according to John 15:18–16:4a, the disciples' witness to the world makes them subject to the world's hatred. Segovia points out that this hatred is parallel to that experienced by Jesus himself in John 3:20; 7:7.[48] In those passages, hatred results not simply from the world's rejection of Jesus' divine claim but from his exposure of its evil deeds. In John, Jesus reveals not only God but the world as well! Perhaps, then, we might suggest that the disciples are also hated because they reveal the world's misdeeds and that they do so precisely by their mutual love. Their actions as the community of Jesus the Messiah thus present the world with a counterculture that both confronts and attracts it. It is wholly in accord with John's ironic view of God's mission to the world and the world's response to it that precisely the alienation of the community from the world and its consequent need for a mutual love surpassing what the world can offer should be its means of drawing the world toward itself and its faith. In Bultmann's words, "It is not the effect it has on world history that legitimates the Christian faith, but its strangeness within the world; and the strangeness is the bearing of those whose love for each other is grounded in the divine love."[49]

Can we see any other indications of concern for outsiders penetrating the barriers of Johannine sectarianism? There may in fact be a number of such indications, centering on John's concept of mission.[50] Here we may focus on one item in particular, the treatment of the Samaritans in John 4. Jesus is presented there as contravening the bodily rules that served as boundary markers between Jews and Samaritans, by asking the Samaritan woman for a drink and by sending his disciples to buy food in her town (4:7–9). He is also shown abandoning Jewish claims about the precedence of Jerusalem (4:21–24), suggesting that the Johannine community had radically rethought some of its inherited norms and beliefs. In speaking of the "others" who had prepared the way for the Samaritan harvest to be carried out by his disciples (4:37–38), the Johannine Jesus may even imply that Samaritan religion is of equal value with Judaism as a starting point for faith in himself. Indeed, of the various groups in contact with Jesus in John 2–4, only the Samaritans come to true faith in him (4:42).

All of this implies a shifting of boundary lines for the Johannine community that not only excluded their former Jewish kinsfolk but also included former Samaritan enemies. Jews and Samaritans find common ground in Jesus because he brings the two competing forms of worship to an end, and reconciliation is signaled by the abandoning of such marks of division as food taboos. Jesus is acknowledged as "Savior of the world" just when his Jewish following begins to incorporate its long-standing Samaritan enemies. Thus even as John's sectarianism drew a sharp boundary between itself and its fellow Jews who now appeared as the group's opponents, it broke down other boundaries that had long been zealously guarded. Love for one another, even if it did not necessarily take in the current enemy, was not sealed off against traditional foes. Because mutual love was important both as a sign of the new eschatological era brought by Jesus and as a factor in the Johannine witness to the world, it would not stop at old established borders but readily cross them as members of once-hostile groups accepted the witness and left the world to join the believing community. However deeply involved the Gospel of John may be in prosecuting the new feud with the synagogue authorities, it shows a surprising willingness to let old feuds be healed. Those who come to profess their faith in Jesus the Messiah, whatever their origin, are subjected to no other test—except that of love for one another.

Conclusion

We have seen that the love commandment has both a distinctive form and a distinctive role to play in the Fourth Gospel. Most likely it was already present in the tradition that lay behind this Gospel, although we can say nothing about the form it took in that tradition. It was the author of the Gospel who gave it the specific formulation, "Love one another," and linked it both to the love of Jesus expressed in his passion and to the situation of the Johannine community undergoing persecution. By doing so, the Gospel writer has given the love commandment a particular force with regard not only to the community's internal relations but also to its relations with its opponents and with the world at large.

In the circumstances in which it was formulated, the commandment to love one another, though it did not forbid love for enemies, nevertheless had a share in setting limits that made such love very difficult. The people bidden to love one another were those who believed in Jesus the Messiah, in contradistinction to those who did not, particularly the synagogue authorities who threatened the believers with expulsion. Their mutual love enabled these people to withstand the assaults made on them from without and may have been a significant factor in their survival, both materially and spiritually. But we have no evidence that it encouraged them to respond with love toward their persecutors—in other words, to love their enemies. Indeed, although there is equally no evidence of hostile actions by the community, we find much in John that seems almost hateful in its attitude toward "the Jews."

On the other hand, the commandment to love one another is conceived in John as part of the community's witness to outsiders and as a continuation of Jesus' own love and possibly of his witness as well. By their unity, by their standing with one another under duress, maybe even by their willingness to die for one another, the members of the Johannine community were to demonstrate both their discipleship to Jesus and the truth of his divine origin. In this way they were to hope, perhaps, that even those who hated them would be convinced of this truth and join them in their belief.

Furthermore, this mutual love within the community seems to have extended across lines of ancient hostility, such as those between Jews and Samaritans, so that in loving one another the Johannine believers did in fact love some of those who had at one time been their enemies.

The Johannine commandment to love one another is not a commandment to love one's enemies. Indeed, in some respects it comes close to excluding such a love. Yet it provided not only sustenance against the community's enemies but a means of drawing those enemies toward the community's faith and so within the circle of mutual love itself. That at least was the hope of John's author. As with so much else, we can see only dimly the historical and social realities that existed behind and around such hopes. We know little about the extent to which the community's members succeeded in loving one another; what can be gleaned from the Johannine epistles is not very encouraging. Still less do we know how their mutual love fared in their enemies' eyes. Yet the Johannine love commandment stands as a peculiar challenge to the Christian churches in all ages, as an ideal way of life whose realization seems sometimes nearer and sometimes impossibly remote, and yet as only the beginning steps toward a love that is equally as strong, but inclusive, indeed universal, in its scope.[51]

Notes

1. Raymond F. Collins, "'A New Commandment I Give to You, That You Love One Another . . .' (John 13:34)," in *These Things Have Been Written: Studies on the Fourth Gospel* (Louvain Theological and Pastoral Monographs 2; Louvain: Peeters; Grand Rapids: Wm. B. Eerdmans Publishing Co., 1990), 217–221.

2. On the rise of the current conception of Johannine history and its overall significance, see David Rensberger, *Johannine Faith and Liberating Community* (Philadelphia: Westminster Press, 1988), 15–36. Perhaps the most influential hypothesis about this history has been that of Raymond E. Brown, *The Community of the Beloved Disciple* (New York: Paulist Press, 1979).

3. For a survey of positions on the farewell discourses and their redaction, see Fernando F. Segovia, *Love Relationships in the Johannine Tradition: Agapē/Agapan in I John and the Fourth Gospel* (SBLDS 58; Chico, Calif.: Scholars Press, 1982), 81–96. Among the commentaries, see esp. Raymond E. Brown, *The Gospel According to John* (AB 29, 29A; 2 vols.; Garden City, N.Y.: Doubleday & Co., 1966–1970), 2:581–588.

4. Segovia, *Love Relationships,* 31–79. Segovia's work is based on a

study by Jürgen Becker, "Die Abschiedsreden Jesu im Johannesevange-
lium," *ZNW* 61 (1970): 215–246.

5. Ibid., 97–121.

6. Ibid., 122–125.

7. Ibid., 197–203. See also Rudolf Schnackenburg, *The Gospel According to St John* (3 vols.; New York: Crossroad, 1982), 3:53, 89–93,
109.

8. Urban C. von Wahlde, *The Johannine Commandments: 1 John and
the Struggle for the Johannine Tradition* (Theological Inquiries; New York:
Paulist Press, 1990), 16–32.

9. Ibid., 49–70.

10. Ibid., 74–99.

11. Segovia, *Love Relationships*, 102–103, 119, 178–179, 198–199.

12. The figure of Nicodemus probably also represents such "crypto-
Christians" (Raymond Brown's term, though Brown does not apply it to
Nicodemus). See Brown, *Community,* 71–73; J. Louis Martyn, *History
and Theology in the Fourth Gospel* (2nd ed.; Nashville: Abingdon Press,
1979), 38–41, 87–88, 116–118; and Rensberger, *Johannine Faith,* 37–41,
48–49.

13. On this passage, see J. Louis Martyn, "Glimpses Into the History
of the Johannine Community," in *The Gospel of John in Christian History*
(New York: Paulist Press, 1978), 109–115.

14. Despite Segovia (*Love Relationships,* 102–103), the "true vine" in
John 15:1 suggests opposition to some other vine, not to a false conception
of Jesus, and must surely be viewed in the light of 1:9 and 6:32, which
have to do with contrasts between Jesus and an alternative, not competing
interpretations of Jesus.

15. Fernando F. Segovia, "John 15:18–16:4a: A First Addition to the
Original Farewell Discourse?" *CBQ* 45 (1983): 219–230; cf. idem, *Love
Relationships,* 127–129.

16. Segovia, having separated 15:9–17 from 15:18–16:4a, so that there
is no reference to violent persecution in the context, must take this language as purely symbolic (Segovia, *Love Relationships,* 115).

17. On the importance of mutual love as a response to outside pressure
in another early Christian context, see John H. Elliott, *A Home for the
Homeless: A Sociological Exegesis of 1 Peter, Its Situation and Strategy*
(Philadelphia: Fortress Press, 1981), 83, 145–148.

18. Cf. Schnackenburg, *Gospel,* 3:92.

19. Fernando F. Segovia, "The Structure, *Tendenz,* and *Sitz im Leben*
of John 13:31–14:31," *JBL* 104 (1985): 491–492; von Wahlde, *Commandments,* 83–84; Collins, " 'New Commandment,' " 223–224; and Schnackenburg, *Gospel,* 3:53.

20. Segovia, "Structure," 491–493.

21. This difference is part of a broad pattern of redirection of attributes
from Jesus to God that takes place in 1 John as compared with the Gospel.
Cf. von Wahlde, *Commandments,* 204–205, where, however, the persist-
ence of this pattern across redactional levels in John is not recognized.

22. Robert Tomson Fortna, *The Gospel of Signs: A Reconstruction of the Narrative Source Underlying the Fourth Gospel* (SNTSMS 11; Cambridge: Cambridge University Press, 1970); and idem, *The Fourth Gospel and Its Predecessor: From Narrative Source to Present Gospel* (Philadelphia: Fortress Press, 1988).

23. C. H. Dodd, *Historical Tradition in the Fourth Gospel* (Cambridge: Cambridge University Press, 1963); Barnabas Lindars, *Behind the Fourth Gospel* (Studies in Creative Criticism 3; London: SPCK, 1971); and Brown, *Gospel,* 1:xxxiv–xxxix.

24. Segovia, *Love Relationships,* 197–198.

25. Cf. von Wahlde, *Commandments,* 204.

26. Cf. Brown, *Gospel,* 2:693–695; Barnabas Lindars, *The Gospel of John* (NCB; Grand Rapids: Wm. B. Eerdmans Publishing Co., 1972), 493–494.

27. Von Wahlde, *Commandments,* 99.

28. Segovia envisions the addition of 15:18–16:4a taking place under just such circumstances (Segovia, "John 15:18–16:4a," 227–230). I suggest that at least 15:9–17 (and 13:34–35, if it is redactional) entered at the same time.

29. On the latter point with respect to John, see Rudolf Bultmann, *Theology of the New Testament* (2 vols; trans. Kendrick Grobel; New York: Charles Scribner's Sons, 1951), 2:79–82.

30. Ibid., 2:161–199 passim, 203–204.

31. Segovia, "Structure," 492.

32. Von Wahlde, *Commandments,* 92, 98.

33. José Porfirio Miranda, *Being and the Messiah: The Message of St. John* (Maryknoll, N.Y.: Orbis Books, 1977), e.g., pp. 36–45, 73–86, 137–148.

34. Rudolf Bultmann, *The Gospel of John* (translation ed. by G. R. Beasley-Murray; Philadelphia: Westminster Press, 1971), 547; the emphasis is Bultmann's.

35. Victor Paul Furnish, *The Love Command in the New Testament* (Nashville: Abingdon Press, 1972), 138; Collins, " 'New Commandment,' " 240–241; Bultmann, *Gospel,* 527–528; and Schnackenburg, *Gospel,* 3:54.

36. E.g., Brown, *Gospel,* 2:613; and Bultmann, *Gospel,* 528.

37. Collins, " 'New Commandment,' " 252–253.

38. E.g., *T. Iss.* 5:2; 7:6–7; *T. Zeb.* 5:1; 8:5–6; *T. Gad* 6:1, 3; 7:7; *T. Jos.* 17:1–3; cf. also the last instructions of Abraham and of Isaac in *Jub.* 20:2; 36:3–4. See F. C. Fensham, "Love in the Writings of Qumrân and John," *Neot* 6 (1972): 73; Brown, *Gospel,* 2:599, 611; and Furnish, *Love Command,* 134–135.

39. Bultmann, *Gospel,* 528–529.

40. Furnish, *Love Command,* 148.

41. J. N. Sanders and B. A. Mastin, *A Commentary on the Gospel According to St. John* (HNTC; London: Basil Black, 1968), 317.

42. On the sectarian nature of Johannine Christianity, see Rensberger,

Johannine Faith, 27–28, and the literature cited there. Note especially the pioneering work of Wayne A. Meeks, "The Man from Heaven in Johannine Sectarianism," *JBL* 91 (1972): 44–72. Though he speaks more of "revolt" than explicitly of sectarianism, Jerome H. Neyrey's *An Ideology of Revolt: John's Christology in Social-Science Perspective* (Philadelphia: Fortress Press, 1988) takes much the same view of the Johannine community at the stage of its sharpest conflict with the synagogue.

43. See Rensberger, *Johannine Faith,* 135–152.

44. Fensham, "Love," 68–70. See 1QS 1:3, 9; 3:26–4:1; CD 2:15; 6:20–21; 8:15–18; 1QH 14:10–11, 18–21.

45. Fensham, "Love," 75; Collins, " 'New Commandment,' " 253–254; and Furnish, *Love Command,* 146–147.

46. Furnish, *Love Command,* 148.

47. Ibid.

48. Segovia, "John 15:18–16:4a," 218–219.

49. Bultmann, *Gospel,* 529. Cf. Sanders, *Commentary,* 317.

50. Cf. Rensberger, *Johannine Faith,* 148–150.

51. After this essay had been completed and sent to the editor, I received Fernando Segovia's *The Farewell of the Word: The Johannine Call to Abide* (Philadelphia: Fortress Press, 1991). In this book Professor Segovia modifies some of the positions he had taken earlier. I regret that it was not possible to take these changes into account in the present essay.

BIBLIOGRAPHY

The Love of Enemy
and Nonretaliation
in the New Testament

Willard M. Swartley

Alt, Franz. *Peace Is Possible: The Politics of the Sermon on the Mount.* Translated by J. Neugroschel. New York: Schocken Books, 1985.

Archer, E. W. "Matthew v. 39." *ExpTim* 42 (1930/1931): 190–191.

Bach, Eugen. *Die Feindesliebe nach dem natürlichen und dem übernatürlichen Sittengesetz.* Kempten: J. Kösel, 1914.

Bamberger, B. J. "Fear and Love of God in the Old Testament." *HUCA* 6 (1929): 39–52.

Bauer, Walter, "Das Gebot der Feindesliebe und die alten Christen." *ZTK* 27 (1917): 37–54.

Bauman, Clarence. *The Sermon on the Mount: The Modern Quest for Its Meaning.* Macon, Ga.: Mercer University Press, 1985.

Bayer, O. "Sprachbewegung und Weltveränderung: Ein systematischer Versuch als Auslegung von Mt 5,43–48." *EvT* 35 (1975): 309–321.

Becker, Jürgen. "Feindesliebe-Nächstenliebe-Bruderliebe: Exegetische Beobachtungen als Anfrage an ein ethisches Problemfeld." *ZEE* 25 (1981): 5–18.

Berger, Klaus. *Die Gesetzesauslegung Jesu: Ihr historischer Hintergrund im Judentum und im Alten Testament; I: Markus und Parallelen.* WMANT 40. Neukirchen-Vluyn: Neukirchener Verlag, 1972.

Brinkel, Wolfgang; B. Scheffler; and M. Wächter, eds. *Christen im Streit um den Frieden.* Freiburg im Breisgau: Dreisam-Verlag, 1982.

Broer, Ingo. *Friede durch Gewaltverzicht? Vier Abhandlungen zu Friedensproblematik und Bergpredigt.* Kleine Reihe zur Bibel 25. Stuttgart: Verlag Katholisches Bibelwerk, 1984.

Bruppacher, Hans. "Was sagte Jesus in Matthäus 5:48?" *ZNW* 58 (1967): 145.

Büchsel, F. "*Apodidōmi.*" *TDNT,* 2:169.

Bultmann, Rudolf. *Das Evangelium des Johannes.* Göttingen: Vandenhoeck & Ruprecht, 1959.

Burchard, Christoph. "Das doppelte Liebesgebot in der frühen christlichen Überlieferung." In *Der Ruf Jesu und die Antwort der Gemeinde* (FS J. Jeremias zum 70. Geburtstag), edited by E. Lohse. Göttingen: Vandenhoeck & Ruprecht, 1979.

Bryant, H. E. "Matthew 5,38,39." *ExpTim* 48 (1936/1937): 236–237.

———. "Matthew 6,13 and 5,39." *ExpTim* 47 (1935/1936): 93–95.

Caird, George B. *The Revelation of St. John the Divine.* New York: Harper & Row, 1966.

Clark, Robert E. D. *Does the Bible Teach Pacifism?* England: Fellowship of Reconciliation, 1976.

Cohen, H. "Der Nächste." In *Jüdische Schriften,* vol. 1 (1924), 182–195.

Collins, Adela Yarbro. "Persecution and Vengeance in the Book of Revelation." In *Apocalypticism in the Mediterranean World and the Near East* (1979 Uppsala Colloquium on Apocalyptic). Translated by D. Hellholm. Tübingen: J. C. B. Mohr [Paul Siebeck], 1983. Pp. 729–749.

———. "The Political Perspective of the Revelation to John." *JBL* 96 (1977): 241–256.

Crossan, J. Dominic. "Jesus and Pacifism." In *No Famine in the Land* (FS J. L. McKenzie), edited by J. L. Flanagan and A. W. Robinson. Missoula, Mont.: Scholars Press, 1975. Pp. 195–208.

Dihle, Albrecht. *Die goldene Regel: Eine Einführung in die Geschichte der antiken und frühchristlichen Vulgärethik.* Göttingen: Vandenhoeck & Ruprecht, 1962.

Donahue, John R., S.J. "Who Is My Enemy? The Parable of the Good Samaritan and the Love of Enemies." In *The Love of Enemy and Non-retaliation in the New Testament,* edited by Willard M. Swartley. Pp. 137–156.

Dungan, David. "Jesus and Violence." In *Jesus, the Gospels and the Church,* edited by E. P. Sanders (FS W. R. Farmer). Macon, Ga.: Mercer University Press, 1987. Pp. 135–162.

Ferguson, John. *The Politics of Love: The New Testament and Nonviolent Revolution.* Nyack, N.Y.: Fellowship of Reconciliation, 1977.

Fiebig, Paul. "Jesu Worte über die Feindesliebe im Zusammenhang mit den wichtigsten rabbinischen Parallelen erläutert." *TSK* 91 (1918): 30–64.

Ford, Josephine M. "Reconciliation and Forgiveness in Luke's Gospel." In *Political Issues in Luke-Acts,* edited by R. J. Cassidy and P. J. Scharper. Maryknoll, N.Y.: Orbis Books, 1983. Pp. 80–98.

"Frieden und Gewaltlosigkeit." *BK* 37,2 (1982). Contributions by E. Brandenburger, I. Broer, N. Lohfink, and A. Schenker.

Fuchs, E. "Was heisst: 'Du sollst deinen Nächsten lieben wie dich selbst?'" *TBl* 11 (1932): 129–140.

Furnish, Victor Paul. *The Love Command in the New Testament*. Nashville: Abingdon Press, 1972.

Gerhardsson, Birger. "Agape and Imitation of Christ." In *Jesus, the Gospels and the Church*, edited by E. P. Sanders (FS W. R. Farmer). Macon, Ga.: Mercer University Press, 1987. Pp. 163–176.

Greeven, H., and J. Fichtner. *"Plēsion." TDNT*, 6:311–318.

Guelich, Robert A. *The Sermon on the Mount: A Foundation for Understanding*. Waco, Tex.: Word Books, 1982.

Haas, Hans. *Idee und Ideal der Feindesliebe in der ausserchristlichen Welt*. Leipzig: University of Leipzig, 1927.

Harnack, Adolf von. "Der 'Eros' in der alten christlichen Literatur." In *Kleine Schriften zur alten Kirche*. Leipzig: Zentralantiquariat, 1980. Pp. 81–94.

Hochfeld, S. "Das Gebot der Nächstenliebe." In *Die Lehren des Judentums nach den Quellen* I (1928), 328–389.

Hoffman, Paul. *Studien zur Theologie der Logienquelle*. NTAbh, n.F. 8. Münster: Verlag Aschendorff, 1972.

———. "Tradition und Situation. Zur 'Verbindlichkeit' des Gebots der Feindesliebe in der synoptischen Überlieferung und in der gegenwärtigen Friedensdiskussion." In *Ethik im Neuen Testament*, edited by K. Kertelge. QD 102. Freiburg: Herder, 1984. Pp. 50–118.

Hoffmann, Paul, and Volker Eid. *Jesus von Nazareth und eine christliche Moral: Sittliche Perspektiven der Verkündigung Jesu*. Freiburg: Herder, 1975.

Horsley, Richard A. "Ethics and Exegesis: 'Love Your Enemies' and the Doctrine of Non-Violence." *JAAR* 54 (1986): 3–31. Also in *The Love of Enemy and Nonretaliation in the New Testament*, edited by Willard M. Swartley. Pp. 72–101. See also "Response to Walter Wink," pp. 126–132.

———. *Jesus and the Spiral of Violence: Jewish Resistance in Roman Palestine*. San Francisco: Harper & Row, 1987.

———. *Sociology and the Jesus Movement*. New York: Crossroad, 1989.

Huber, Wolfgang. "Feindschaft und Feindesliebe: Notizen zum Problem des 'Feindes' in der Theologie." *ZEE* 26 (1982): 128–158.

Johnston, George. "Love in the NT." *IDB*, 3:168–178.

Kattenbusch, F. "Über die Feindesliebe im Sinne des Christentums." *TSK* 89 (1916): 1–70.

Klassen, William. "Coals of Fire: Sign of Repentance or Revenge?" *NTS* 9 (1963): 337–350.

————. *The Forgiving Community.* Philadelphia: Westminster Press, 1966.

————. "The God of Peace: New Testament Perspectives on God." In *Towards a Theology of Peace,* edited by S. Tunnicliffe. London: European Nuclear Disarmament, 1989. Pp. 121–131.

————. *Love of Enemies: The Way to Peace.* Philadelphia: Fortress Press, 1984.

————. " 'Love Your Enemies': Some Reflections on the Current Status of Research." In *The Love of Enemy and Nonretaliation in the New Testament,* edited by Willard M. Swartley. Pp. 1–31.

————. "Love Your Enemy: A Study of New Testament Teaching on Coping with an Enemy." In *Biblical Realism Confronts the Nation,* edited by Paul Peachey. Nyack, N.Y.: Fellowship Publications, 1963. Pp. 153–183.

————. "The Novel Element in the Love Commandment of Jesus." In *The New Way of Jesus,* edited by W. Klassen. Newton, Kans.: Faith and Life Press, 1980. Pp. 100–114.

————. "Peace." In *The Illustrated Dictionary and Concordance of the Bible,* edited by Geoffrey Wigoder. New York: Macmillan Publishing Co., 1986. Pp. 767–769.

————. "Vengeance in the Apocalypse of John." *CBQ* 28 (1966): 300–311.

Kuhn, Heinz-Wolfgang. "Das Liebesgebot Jesus als Tora und als Evangelium: Zur Feindesliebe und zur christlichen und jüdischen Auslegung der Bergpredigt." In *Vom Urchristentum zu Jesus,* edited by H. Frankemölle and K. Kertelge (FS Joachim Gnilka). Freiburg: Herder, 1989. Pp. 194–230.

Lapide, Pinchas. *The Sermon on the Mount: Utopia or Program for Action?* Translated by Arlene Swidler. Maryknoll, N.Y.: Orbis Books, 1986. Pp. 76–142.

————. "What Did Jesus Ask?: The Sermon on the Mount—A Jewish Reading." *ChrCent,* May 24, 1982, 139–142. Also as "Es geht um die Entfeindungsliebe: Realpolitik, wie sie die Bergpredigt eigentlich meint." *Lutherische Monatshefte* 20 (1981): 505–508.

Legasse, Simon. *"Et qui est mon prochain?" Etude sur l'objet de l'agape dans le Nouveau Testament.* Lectio Divina 136. Paris: Editions du Cerf, 1989.

Linskens, John. "A Pacifist Interpretation of Peace in the Sermon on the Mount?" In *Church and Peace* (Concilium 164), edited by Virgil Elizondo, Norbert Greinacher, and Marcus Lefebure. New York: Seabury Press, 1983. Pp. 16–25.

Linton, O. "St. Matthew 5,43." *ST* 18 (1964): 66–80.

Lohfink, Gerhard. "Der ekklesiale Sitz im Leben der Aufforderung Jesu zum Gewaltverzicht (Mt 5,39b–42/Lk 6,29f)." *TQ* 162 (1982): 236–253.

———. *Jesus and Community: The Social Dimension of Christian Faith.* Translated by J. P. Galvin. Philadelphia: Fortress Press, 1984.

———. " 'Schwerter zu Pflugscharen.' " *ThQ* (1986): 184–209.

Lohfink, Norbert. " 'Der den Kriegen einen Sabbat Bereitet.' Psalm 46— Ein Beispiel alttestamentlicher Friedenslyrik." *BK* 44 (1989): 148– 153.

Lohfink, Norbert, and Rudolf Pesch. *Weltgestaltung und Gewaltlosigkeit: Ethische Aspekte des AT und NT in ihrer Einheit und in ihrem Gegensatz.* Düsseldorf: Patmos Verlag, 1978.

Lührmann, Dieter. "Liebet eure Feinde (Lk 6,27–36/Mt 5,39–48)." *ZTK* 69 (1972): 412–438.

Luz, Ulrich."Feindesliebe und Frieden." *ThEv* 16 (1983): 3–13.

———. "Jesu Gebot der Feindesliebe und die kirchliche Verantwortung für den Frieden." In *Christen im Streit,* edited by W. Brinkel et al. Freiburg im Breisgau: Dreisam-Verlag, 1982. Pp. 21–28.

———. "Love of the Enemy and the Church's Task for Peace." *ThEv* 16 (1983): 3–13.

———. *Matthew 1–7: A Commentary.* Translated by W. C. Linss. Minneapolis: Fortress Press, 1989.

Michel, Otto. "Das Gebot der Nächstenliebe in der Verkündigung Jesu." In *Zur sozialen Entscheidung.* Tübingen: J. C. B. Mohr [Paul Siebeck], 1947. Pp. 53–101.

Minear, Paul. *Commands of Christ: Authority and Implications.* Edinburgh: St. Andrew Press, 1972.

Moffatt, James. *Love in the New Testament.* London: Hodder & Stoughton, 1929.

Molin, G. "Matthäus 5,43 und das Schrifttum von Qumran." In *Bibel und Qumran,* edited by S. Wagner. Berlin: Evangelische Haupt-Bibelgesellschaft, 1968.

Moltmann, Jürgen. "Feindesliebe." *EK* 15 (1982): 503–505.

Monselewski, W. *Der barmherzige Samaritaner.* Tübingen: J. C. B. Mohr [Paul Siebeck], 1967.

Montefiore, Hugh W. "Thou Shalt Love the Neighbour as Thyself." *NovT* 5 (1962): 157–170.

Morenz, S. "Feurige Kohlen auf dem Haupt." *TLZ* 78 (1953): 187–192.

Moulder, J. "Who Are My Enemies? An Exploration of the Semantic Background of Christ's Command." *JThSAfr* 25 (1978): 41–49.

Neugebauer, Fritz. "Die dargebotene Wange und Jesu Gebot der Feindesliebe: Erwägungen zu Lk 6,27–36; Matt 5,38–48." *TLZ* 110 (1985): 865–875.

Nissen, Andreas. *Gott und der Nächste im antiken Judentum.* WUNT 15. Tübingen: J. C. B. Mohr [Paul Siebeck], 1974.

Nygren, Anders. *Agape and Eros: A Study of the Christian Idea of Love.* Translated from the Swedish by Philip S. Watson. London: SPCK; Philadelphia, Westminster Press, 1953.

Osborn, Eric. "The Love Commandment in Second Century Christian Writings." *SeC* 1 (1981): 223–243.

Perkins, Pheme. "Apocalyptic Sectarianism and Love Commands: The Johannine Epistles and Revelation." In *The Love of Enemy and Nonretaliation in the New Testament,* edited by Willard M. Swartley. Pp. 287–296.

———. *Love Commands in the New Testament.* Ramsey, N.J.: Paulist Press, 1982.

Pesch, Rudolf. "Neues Testament—Die Überwindung der Gewalt." In *Weltgestaltung und Gewaltlosigkeit,* edited by G. Lohfink and R. Pesch. Düsseldorf: Patmos Verlag, 1978. Pp. 62–80.

Philipson, D. "Enemy, Treatment of an." *Jewish Encyclopedia,* 5:159–160.

Piper, John. "Hope as the Motivation of Love: 1 Peter 3:9–12." *NTS* 26 (1979/1980): 212–231.

———. *"Love Your Enemies": Jesus' Love Command in the Synoptic Gospels and in the Early Christian Paraenesis.* SNTSMS 38. Cambridge: Cambridge University Press, 1979.

Randlinger, Stephan. *Die Feindesliebe nach dem natürlichen und positiven Sittengesetz.* Paderborn: F. Schöningh, 1906.

Rathey, M. "Talion im NT? Zu Mt 5:38–42." *ZNW* 82 (1991): 264–267.

Ratschow, C. H. "Agape, Nächstenliebe und Bruderliebe." *ZST* 21 (1950): 160–182.

Rausch, J. "The Principle of Nonresistance and Love of Enemy in Mt. 5:38–48." *CBQ* 28 (1966): 31–41.

Rensberger, David. "Love for One Another and Love for Enemies in the Gospel of John." In *The Love of Enemy and Nonretaliation in the New Testament,* edited by Willard M. Swartley. Pp. 297–313.

———. *Johannine Faith and Liberating Community.* Philadelphia: Westminster Press, 1988.

Rese, Martin. "Das Gebot der Bruderliebe in den Johannesbriefen." *TZ* 14 (1985): 44–58.

Reuter, Hans-Richard. "Liebet eure Feinde! Zur Aufgabe einer politischen Ethik im Licht der Bergpredigt." *ZEE* 26 (1982): 159–187.

Sander, Reinhold. *Furcht und Liebe im Palästinischen Judentum.* Stuttgart: Verlag W. Kohlhammer, 1935.

Sauer, J. "Traditionsgeschichtliche Erwägungen zu den synoptischen und paulinischen Aussagen über Feindesliebe und Wiedervergeltungsverzicht." *ZNW* 76 (1985): 1–28.

Schertz, Mary H. "Nonretaliation and the Haustafeln in 1 Peter." In *The Love of Enemy and Nonretaliation in the New Testament,* edited by Willard M. Swartley. Pp. 258–286.

Schneider, Gerhard. "Die Neuheit der christlichen Nächstenliebe." *TTZ* 82 (1973): 257–275.

Schottroff, Luise. "The Dual Concept of Peace." In *The Meaning of Peace,* edited by P. Yoder and W. Swartley. SPS 2. Louisville: Westminster/ John Knox Press, 1992. Pp. 156–163. Translation by W. Sawatsky of "Der doppelte Begriff vom Frieden," in *Christen im Streit,* edited by W. Brinkel et al. Pp. 135–140.

―――. " 'Give to Caesar What Belongs to Caesar and to God What Belongs to God': A Theological Response of the Early Christian Church to Its Social and Political Environment." In *The Love of Enemy and Nonretaliation in the New Testament,* edited by Willard M. Swartley. Pp. 223–257. Translation by Gerhard Reimer of " 'Gebt dem Kaiser, was dem Kaiser gehört, und Gott, was Gott gehört.' Die theologische Antwort der urchristlichen Gemeinden auf ihre gesellschaftliche und politische Situation." In *Befreiungserfahrungen: Studien zur Sozialgeschichte des Neuen Testaments,* by Luise Schottroff. Munich: Chr. Kaiser Verlag, 1990. Pp. 184–216.

―――. "Non-Violence and the Love of One's Enemies." In *Essays on the Love Commandment,* by L. Schottroff et al. Translated by Reginald and Ilse Fuller. Philadelphia: Fortress Press, 1978. Pp. 9–39. German: "Gewaltverzicht und Feindesliebe in der urchristlichen Jesustradition. Matthäus 5, 38–48; Lukas 6, 27–36." In *Befreiungserfahrungen: Studien zur Sozialgeschichte des Neuen Testaments,* by Luise Schottroff. Munich: Chr. Kaiser Verlag, 1990. Pp. 12–35.

―――. *Der Sieg des Lebens: Biblische Traditionen einer Friedenspraxis.* Munich: Chr. Kaiser Verlag, 1982.

Schrage, Wolfgang. *The Ethics of the New Testament.* Translated by David E. Green. Philadelphia: Fortress Press, 1988.

―――. *Die konkreten Einzelgebote in der paulinischen Paränese.* Gütersloh: Gütersloher Verlagshaus Gerd Mohn, 1961.

Schrenk, G. *"Ekdikeō." TDNT,* 2:442–446.

Seitz, O. J. F. "Love Your Enemies: The Historical Setting of Matthew V.43f.; Luke VI.27f." *NTS* 16 (1969/1970): 39–54.

Smith, M. "Mt. 5.43: 'Hate Thine Enemy.' " *HTR* 45 (1952): 71–73.

Smothers, E. R. "Give Place to Wrath." *CBQ* 6 (1944): 205–215.

Soares-Prabhu, G. M. "The Synoptic Love-Commandment: The Dimensions of Love in the Teaching of Jesus." *Jeevadhara* 13 (1983): 85–103.

Spicq, C. *Agape in the New Testament.* 3 vols. Translated by M. A. McNamara and M. H. Richter. St. Louis: B. Herder Book Co., 1966.

Spiegel, E. *Gewaltverzicht: Grundlagen einer biblischen Friedenstheologie.* Kassel: Weber, Zucht & Co., 1987.

Steele, J. "Heaping Coals on the Head (Pr 25:22; Ro 12:20)." *ExpTim* 44 (1932/1933): 141.

Steinmüller, F. *Die Feindesliebe.* Regensburg, 1903.

Stendahl, Krister. "Hate, Non-Retaliation and Love. 1QS x, 17–20 and Romans 12:19–21." *HTR* 55 (1962): 343–355.

Strecker, Georg. *Die Bergpredigt: Ein exegetischer Kommentar.* Göttingen: Vandenhoeck & Ruprecht, 1984.

Sutcliffe, E. "Hatred at Qumran." *RQ* 2 (1960): 345–356.

Swartley, Willard M. "Luke's Transforming of Tradition: Eirēnē and Love of Enemy." In idem, ed., *The Love of Enemy and Nonretaliation in the New Testament,* Pp. 157–176.

————, ed. *The Love of Enemy and Nonretaliation in the New Testament.* SPS 3. Louisville: Westminster/John Knox Press, 1992.

Synofzig, E. *Die Gerichts- und Vergeltungsaussagen bei Paulus: Eine traditionsgeschichtliche Untersuchung.* Göttingen: Vandenhoeck & Ruprecht, 1977.

Tannehill, Robert C. "The 'Focal Instance' as a Form of New Testament Speech: A Study of Matthew 5:39b–42." *JR* 50 (1970): 372–385.

————. *The Sword of His Mouth: Forceful and Imaginative Language in Synoptic Sayings.* Philadelphia: Fortress Press; Missoula: Scholars Press, 1975.

Theissen, G. "Gewaltverzicht und Feindesliebe (Mt 5, 38–48/Lk 6, 27–38) und deren sozialgeschichtlicher Hintergrund." In *Studien zur Soziologie des Urchristentums.* WUNT 19. Tübingen: J. C. B. Mohr [Paul Siebeck], 1979. Pp. 160–197.

Toews, John E. "Love Your Enemy Into the Kingdom"; "Be Merciful as God Is Merciful"; and "Peacemakers from the Start." In *The Power of the Lamb,* edited by J. E. Toews and G. Nickel. Winnipeg, Man., and Hillsboro, Kans.: Kindred Press, 1986. Pp. 7–24, 45–56.

Travis, S. *Christ and the Judgment of God: Divine Retribution in the New Testament.* Basingstoke, Hants: Marshall Pickering, 1986.

van Unnik, W. C. "Die Motivierung der Feindesliebe in Lukas 6:32–35." *NovT* 8 (1966): 284–300.

Vanderhaar, G. A. *Enemies and How to Love Them.* Mystic, Conn.: Twenty-Third Publications, 1985.

Verhey, A. *The Great Reversal: Ethics and the New Testament.* Grand Rapids: Wm. B. Eerdmans Publishing Co., 1984.

Völkl, R. *Die Selbstliebe in der heiligen Schrift.* Munich: K. Zink, 1956.

Waldmann, Michael. *Die Feindesliebe in der antiken Welt und im Christenthum.* Vienna: Mayer & Co., 1902.

Weaver, Dorothy Jean. "Transforming Nonresistance: From *Lex Talionis* to 'Do Not Resist the Evil One.'" In *The Love of Enemy and Nonretaliation in the New Testament,* edited by Willard M. Swartley. Pp. 32–71.

Wink, Walter. "Neither Passivity nor Violence: Jesus' Third Way (Matt. 5:38–42 par.)." *SBL 1988 Seminar Papers.* Atlanta, 1988. Pp. 210–224. Revised in *The Love of Enemy and Nonretaliation in the New Testament,* edited by Willard M. Swartley. Pp. 102–125. See also his "Counterresponse to Richard Horsley," pp. 133–136.

Wischmeyer, Oda. "Das Gebot der Nächstenliebe bei Paulus: Eine traditionsgeschichtliche Untersuchung." *BZ* 30 (1986): 161–187.

———. *Der höchste Weg: Das 13. Kapitel des 1. Korintherbriefes.* SUNT 13. Gütersloh: Gütersloher Verlagshaus Gerd Mohn, 1981.

———. "Traditionsgeschichtliche Untersuchung der Paulinischen Aussagen über die Liebe (*Agape*)." *ZNW* 74 (1983): 222–236.

Wolbert, W. "Bergpredigt und Gewaltlosigkeit." *TP* 57 (1982): 498–525.

Yoder, John H. *The Original Revolution: Essays on Christian Pacifism.* Scottdale, Pa.: Herald Press, 1971. Pp. 34–54.

———. *The Politics of Jesus.* Grand Rapids: Wm. B. Eerdmans Publishing Co., 1972. Pp. 115–134.

Yoder Neufeld, Tom. "Review of W. Klassen, *Love of Enemies.*" *CGR* 3 (1985): 319–323.

Young, J. E. "Heaping Coals of Fire on the Head." *Expositor,* 3rd ser., 2 (1885): 158–159.

Zerbe, Gordon. *Non-Retaliation in Early Jewish and New Testament Texts: Ethical Themes in Social Contexts.* Ph.D. diss., Princeton Theological Seminary, 1991. To be published by Sheffield Academic Press in the *Journal for the Study of the Pseudepigrapha* Supplement Series.

———. "Paul's Ethic of Nonretaliation and Peace." In *The Love of Enemy and Nonretaliation in the New Testament,* edited by Willard M. Swartley. Pp. 177–222.

Zyro, F. "Röm 12,19: *dote topon tē orgē.*" *TSK* 18 (1945): 887–892.

8937